Strategic Advertising Management

Barcode in Back

Strategic Advertising Management

FOURTH EDITION

Larry Percy

Richard Rosenbaum-Elliott

Great Clarendon Street, Oxford OX2 6DP,
United Kingdom

Oxford University Press is a department of the University of Oxford.
It furthers the University's objective of excellence in research, scholarship,
and education by publishing worldwide. Oxford is a registered trade mark of
Oxford University Press in the UK and in certain other countries

First published 2001
Second edition 2005
Third edition 2009

Impression: 1

British Library Cataloguing in Publication Data
Data available

Library of Congress Control Number 2012933761

ISBN 978-0-19-960558-3

Printed by
L.E.G.O. S.p.A.–Lavis TN

Preface to the Fourth Edition

In the preface to the last edition of this book, we began by commenting upon the ongoing changes in the world of advertising and other areas of marketing communication. With the beginning of the new millennium, there was a significant downsizing in the industry, which continues today. Additionally, there has been a realignment in advertising agencies and media company functions, driven in a large part by the so-called 'new media'. Much is made of the impact of new media, but as the digital editor for the trade weekly *Advertising Age* put it in 2010: 'What makes the open web beautiful is working to undermine it.' We shall see.

The growth in new media, however, does not mean that managers must change the way in which they look at the planning and development of marketing communication. The same fundamental principles of strategic planning for advertising and other marketing communications remain the same, and the underlying principles for creative development remain the same. What has changed is that the manager now has new options for *delivering* a message. We shall be looking at this, of course, but the foundation of this book remains the same. It is to provide the understandings needed for making the decisions necessary for the development and delivery of effective communication.

As we write this, the world is beset with serious economic problems of crisis proportions. There is high unemployment, a reluctance on the part of business to invest, financial institutions are on the verge of collapse, and there are very real prospects of countries defaulting on their debt. The implications of all of this for advertising and other marketing communications are significant: consumers are spending less, and so are companies. One of the first and easiest ways for marketers to 'save' money is to cut marketing budgets, especially for advertising. This means that what monies are available must be spent wisely and efficiently. While managers are always looking for effective advertising, when budgets are cut, every execution must work that much harder. The principles and practices developed in this book will help managers to accomplish that.

As we pointed out in the preface to the last edition, most of the discussion and examples that we use in the text are consumer-oriented. This is done only as a convenience for readers who will be able to identify more closely with a snack purchase than a business-to-business purchase decision. But *all* of the principles discussed in this text apply equally to any message, regardless of the target. This means everything from consumer package goods to jet aircraft marketed to sovereign countries; rock concerts to political candidates. The only caveat is social marketing communication, which must build upon these principles, but also address social norms (which we will be covering in Chapter 13).

We wish to thank all of the people involved in helping to bring this book to print. There are so many people involved, but special thanks are due to our editors Francesca Griffin and Amanda George, and for Esther Amoda and especially Elizabeth Mamali who did all of the hard work in editing the cases. We would also like to thank John Rossiter, who helped with important comments on the social marketing communication material. And a special thanks to Kristie Hutto who again has typed all of the first author's handwritten pages (yes, he still writes everything by hand, on a yellow pad).

New to this Edition

This edition continues to build upon the earlier editions. Perhaps the most significant change is the attention throughout the book to new media. It has been integrated into the text to underscore how the principles discussed apply to both traditional and new media, as well as being given extended discussion in the media chapter, including the role of social media. The other major addition is a discussion of social marketing communication. While it must adhere to the basics of all advertising, it must also take into account the influence of significant others—the social norm mentioned above. Overall items new to this edition include:

- expanded coverage of new media throughout the text;
- a section on advertising for social marketing;
- all case studies updated and an increased number of examples, including those dealing with new and social media;
- a greater focus on ethics, which is now included in Chapter 1;
- more cases and examples of advertising on the Online Resource Centre from print, TV, and Web;
- an increased number and type of questions on the Online Resource Centre; and
- an increased number of video links on the Online Resource Centre.

Larry Percy
Richard Rosenbaum-Elliott
2011

Contents

List of Case Studies

The full versions of the case studies used in this book are available online at Warc (www.warc.com).

List of Tables

List of Figures

List of Boxes

List of Adverts

List of Plates

Plate XVI Colron — Here we have a very good example of the important ways in which the visual images used in an advert can help to facilitate learning. It is clear you are meant to be outside, observing the 'action'; the picture is large, the unique imagery encourages visual elaboration, the use of colour and white space is well proportioned, the product is shown 'in use', and the picture is seen before the words.

Plate XVII Rotari — This advert for Rotari's Talento sparkling wine provides a really good example of the viewer being included in the execution.

Plate XVIII Heal's — Consistent with the key tactic for transformational brand attitude strategies, this Heal's advert is pure emotion, eliciting a strong positive emotional association for the brand.

Plate XIX Fairy — Even though the headline in this advert comes first, the eye is still drawn initially to the picture, ensuring the desires–picture sequence for optimum processing. This advert also provides an excellent example of the correct 'anxiety-to-relief' emotional sequence necessary when dealing with negative emotion.

Plate XX Indian Ocean — Here we see a very good example of how a transformational advert shifts your emotional state from neutral or even dull to a strong positive emotional response.

How to use this Book

Key concepts

1. While the traditional cognitive inform
continues to be the most viable way o
other perspectives that can help in un
effect upon society.
2. These other perspectives may be thou
about the target audience and the lev
3. These two considerations provide the a

Key concepts

Key concepts and ideas have been outlined at the beginning of each chapter to aid your understanding of advertising and highlight essential terminology.

PIER 39

Set your
Bluetooth® phone
to discoverable

Advertising examples

A diverse selection of advertisements is included that show how commercial companies and other organizations have successfully used many of the concepts discussed in the text.

Chapter summary

In this chapter we have focused on the ways that co
edge about this can be used to develop creative s
basic processing responses of attention, learning, a
in detail how each response can be used to facilitat
tives. We explored the different levels of processin
ment, and the key role of acceptance in high-i
cognitive responses with particular attention to le
discussed the important distinction between declar
if there is any implicit processing of an advert is it u
or behaviour. We then considered the vital role o

Chapter summary

End-of-chapter summaries provide a concise overview of the core material that has been covered within the chapter, and will help you to identify the most important terms and concepts that you should take away from that section.

Questions to consider

5.1. Why is each of the five steps in the strategic
be considered in this order?

5.2. How should the roles people play in a purc
thinking about a strategic plan for a brand's adv

5.3. Why is it important to understand the diffe
awareness?

5.4. When are sales likely to be a specific objective

5.5. Why is an understanding of consumer dec
attitude strategy?

Questions to consider

You will find a series of questions at the end of each chapter which relate to the issues and advertising strategies you have encountered so far. These are a great foundation for group discussions and will help you to assess your understanding of the material you have covered in the chapter.

Case study 2 **Marmite—Please Look A Marmite Squeezy**

By 2005, the growth Marmite had enjoyed for nearly a de way to overcome the barriers to growth necessitated a ra which were met with howls of protest due to the brand's

Empirical evidence suggests getting more people into significant growth. However, winning new Marmite eater recruit children as Marmite has a very distinctive taste, ar getting smaller. After careful considerations, our back-of- option—more growth potential lay with people *already e*

Case studies

Each chapter ends with a case study which will help to contextualize the theories and techniques you have read and illustrate their strategic application in the advertising industry.

Source: APG Creative Strategy Awards 2009. © Account Pl
Edited by Elizabeth Mamali, PhD Researcher, Bath School o

Discussion questions

1. What are the awareness and attitude considerations fo
2. What are the objective and subjective characteristics o
3. Why did the 'let your mind wander' campaign work w
4. What do you think are the effects of the new positioni business men?

Case study discussion questions

A list of set questions follow the case studies which encourage you to test your knowledge and understanding of the topics covered in the chapter and prompt you to think further about current issues and the consequences of the case study scenarios.

Further reading

M. de Mooij, *Consumer Behavior and Culture: Conseq* (London: Sage Publications, 2003).
Widens the analysis from advertising to a wide range of

F. Trompenaars and P. Woolliams, *Marketing across C*
Explores cross-cultural implications for other aspects of

S. Craig and S. Douglas, *International Marketing Rese*
Gives detailed guidance on carrying out advertising rese validity.

Further reading

Here you will find a list of further reading materials where you can locate more information on specific aspects of advertising, or read further to extend your own development and understanding of specific strategies and techniques.

Notes

1. It was the emergence of cognitive science that led to a cognitive concepts as attention and consciousness we to James's position from the late 1800s. See Bryan Kolb *Human Neuropsychology*, 5th edn. (New York: Worth F of William James, *The Principles of Psychology* (New Yo
2. See D. Broadbent, *Perception and Communication* (Lor
3. A good brief explanation of this may be found in R.L. G edn (Oxford: Oxford University Press, 2004).
4. This difference in conscious versus unconscious proc

Notes

References are provided in the form of notes at the end of each chapter which will point you in the direction of other reliable sources and information on the subject so that you can expand your knowledge of specific topics and areas of interest.

Guide to the Online Resource Centre

www.oxfordtextbooks.co.uk/orc/percy_elliott4e/

Free resources available to students include:

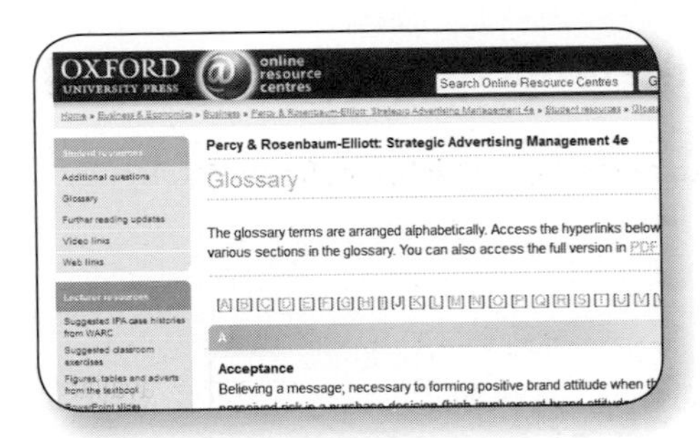

Online glossary

An interactive glossary of terms from the book is available online, allowing you to easily locate specific words and phrases from the text.

Additional questions to consider

Chapter 1 - What are Advertising and Promotion?

1. How can advertising be effective if people do not trust it?
2. There are obvious differences between advertising and promotion, but how are they similar?
3. Why do you think managers in business-to-business or industrial marketing rely less upon advertising and promotion than do marketers of consumer products?
4. What are your personal feelings about so-called 'advertorials'?
5. How does advertising 'work'?

Additional questions

The best way to reinforce your learning and understanding is through frequent revision. Additional questions are available online that provide an effective way of testing your knowledge.

Further reading updates

Sources for further reading:

- Nelson, Michelle and Hye-Jin, Paek (2008), "Nudity of female and male models in primetime TV advertising across seven countries", International Journal of Advertising, Vol. 27, Issue 5, p715-744. A paper examining TV advertising and nudity across cultures.
- Broadbent, Tim (2008), "Does advertising grow markets?", International Journal of Advertising, Vol. 27 Issue 5, p745-770. A paper examining the successful marketing campaigns to determine whether advertising increases market size.
- Okazaki, Shintaro and Mueller, Barbara (2008), "Evolution in the usage of localized appeals in Japanese and American print advertising", International Journal of Advertising, Vol. 27 Issue 5, p771-798. A paper examining the shift of local appeals in Japanese and American advertising.

Further reading updates

A list of up-to-date articles and resources specifically relevant to strategic advertising has been included online so that you can extend your knowledge of the subject area.

Web links

There are a number of recommended web sites, grouped into the sections below. They provide a resource for further information about a number of aspects of advertising, as well as specific sources for adverts and Internet advertising.

- Advertising Associations
- Adverts
- Information about Advertising
- Internet Advertising
- Marketing
- Monthly Insights Into Advertising
- Neuropsychology

Web links

Here you can click through to a list of web links. These have been categorized into sections of recommended websites and provide further information on a number of aspects of advertising, as well as specific sources for adverts and internet advertising.

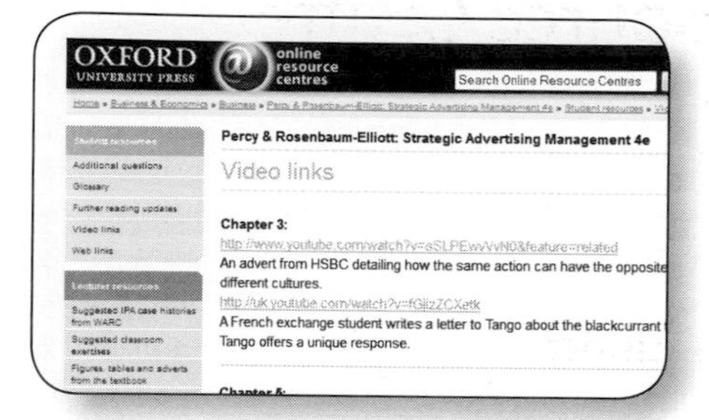

Video links

This resource contains links to suggested video clips for each chapter to help illustrate topics covered in the text.

Resources for registered adopters of the textbook include:

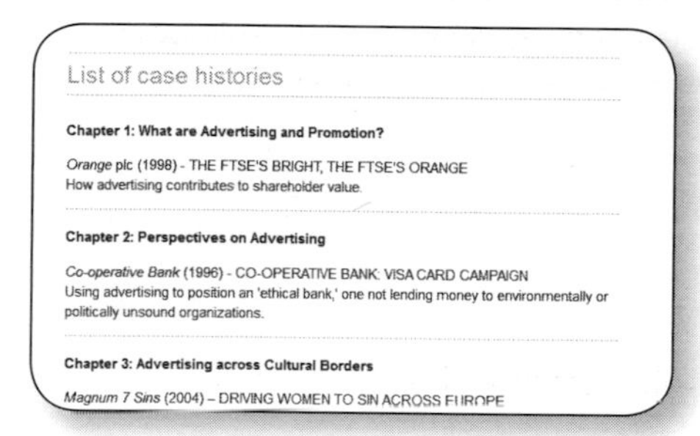

Suggested case histories from WARC

These case histories from the World Advertising Research Council offer an excellent look at a wide variety of strategic approaches to advertising problems, and are indexed in a data bank available on the web at www.warc.com.

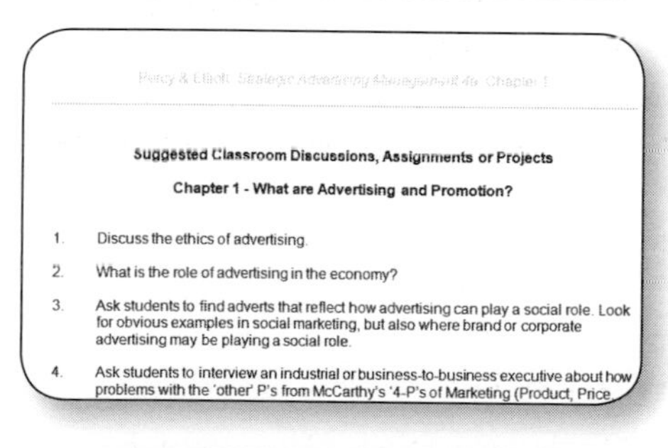

Suggested classroom exercises

This resource offers ideas for generating discussions, assignments, or projects to give to your students.

Defining Advertising

advertise - make an announcement in a place, describe or present g publicly with a view to promo sales

PowerPoint slides

Here you can click through to various sets of PowerPoint slides that accompany each chapter of the textbook. These slides can be used as a basis for lecture handouts, and also contain some of the figures, tables, and adverts from the book.

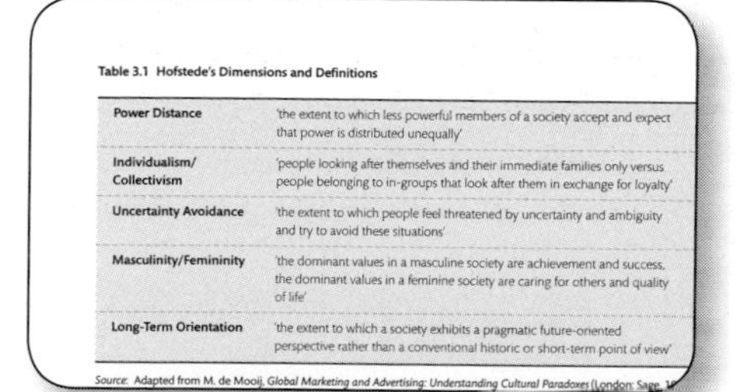

Table 3.1 Hofstede's Dimensions and Definitions

Power Distance	'the extent to which less powerful members of a society accept and expect that power is distributed unequally'
Individualism/ Collectivism	'people looking after themselves and their immediate families only versus people belonging to in-groups that look after them in exchange for loyalty'
Uncertainty Avoidance	'the extent to which people feel threatened by uncertainty and ambiguity and try to avoid these situations'
Masculinity/Femininity	'the dominant values in a masculine society are achievement and success, the dominant values in a feminine society are caring for others and quality of life'
Long-Term Orientation	'the extent to which a society exhibits a pragmatic future-oriented perspective rather than a conventional historic or short-term point of view'

Source: Adapted from M. de Mooij, Global Marketing and Advertising: Understanding Cultural Paradoxes (London: Sage,

Figures, tables, and adverts from the textbook

These have been provided for your ease of use—you can insert them into your PowerPoint slides or simply show them to students on-screen.

Part 1

Overview of Advertising and Promotion

What are Advertising and Promotion?

Key concepts

1. The basic difference between advertising and promotion is that advertising is strategically more long term, 'turning' the consumer towards the brand by creating positive brand attitude, while promotion is more short term, focusing on immediate sales.
2. Advertising 'works' when the desired communication effect is achieved, and this must *always* include creating brand awareness and a positive brand attitude.
3. Strategies for building positive brand attitude depend upon understanding the type of purchase decision and what motivates purchase behaviour, because this will dictate the creative tactics needed.
4. Advertising and promotion messages delivered in social media will be processed in the same way as in traditional media.
5. Ethics in advertising, as in life, is not an easy issue to define, and in the end, perhaps the only answer is for advertising to be truthful.
6. While there are many criticisms of advertising, if responsibly considered and presented, it will benefit the consumer and the market.

In this first chapter we will be taking a broad introductory look at just what we mean by advertising and promotion, and how they are seen in today's world. This will provide a foundation and perspective for the subject in general, before we begin to look specifically at the role advertising and promotion can and do play in support of brands, and how to manage them strategically in order positively to position and build brands.

Defining Advertising and Promotion

If we look up the word 'advertise' in the *New Shorter Oxford English Dictionary* we find the following definition: 'Make an announcement in a public place; describe or present goods publicly with a view to promoting sales.' Right after that we find advertisement defined as: 'A public announcement (formerly by the town-crier, now usually in newspapers, on posters, by television, etc.).'[1]

This is certainly what most people have in mind when they think of advertising—adverts in the newspaper or magazines and commercials on radio or TV. But this really does not begin to tell us much about what advertising actually is. In fact, we are about to spend most of this book in effect defining advertising.

A better feel for what advertising is really all about may be gained by looking back to the Latin root of the word 'advertising'. It was Daniel Starch, one of the early pioneers of advertising theory in the twentieth century, who, back in the 1920s, reminded us that the Latin root for advertising is *advertere*. This roughly translates as 'to turn towards'.[2] Returning to the *New Shorter OED*, we find that the word 'advert' is colloquial for advertisement, *and* when used as a verb means 'turn towards'. This definition is more relevant, because it implies more than simply 'an announcement in a public place'. In a very real sense, advertising is meant to turn us towards a product or service by providing information or creating a positive feeling—something that goes well beyond simply calling our attention to it. Advertising is an *indirect* way of turning a potential customer towards the advertised product or service by providing information that is designed to effect a favourable impression: what we will call a positive brand attitude. This favourable brand attitude then helps place the consumer on the path towards seeking out the product or service advertised.

If advertising is meant to encourage consumers to 'turn towards' a brand, what is the function of promotion? Returning to the *New Shorter OED*, we see that a promotion 'helps forward'. This definition is quite consistent with the Latin root of promotion, *promovere*. Roughly translated, this means 'move forward'.[3] Contrasting the Latin root of 'promotion', 'move forward', with the Latin root of 'advertising', 'turn towards', illustrates the fundamental difference between the traditional ideas of advertising and promotion. Advertising is aimed towards the long-term building of positive brand attitude by 'turning' the consumer towards the brand; promotion is aimed at the more short-term tactical goal of 'moving forward' brand sales now.

Advertising and Promotion within the Marketing Plan

It is important to realize that advertising and promotion are only one part of the marketing plan. Other key marketing considerations include product configuration (for example, making sure the product is offered in the right sizes, shapes, or colours), pricing structure, and distribution—what E. Jerome McCarthy has called the 'Four P's of Marketing' (Promotion, Product, Price, and Place).[4] We will be dealing with the idea of the marketing mix again in Chapter 7.

In fact, advertising and promotion are not the only elements in the 'promotion' or marketing communication section of the marketing plan. In addition to advertising and promotion, the promotion component of the marketing mix also includes public relations and personal selling. We will be discussing the close strategic relationship between these central concepts in Chapter 5. This is not to suggest that there is no relationship between advertising and public relations or personal selling; of course there is, especially with industrial and corporate advertisers. However, the budgets and staff involved with personal selling and public relations traditionally tend to be separate from those of advertising and promotion.

While a simple definition of public relations is that it is 'unpaid promotion', there is a lot more to it than that, and one can take whole courses in the various aspects of public relations. For our purposes, we need to remember that the position being taken in advertising must be consistent with the story being told about the campaign through public relations. The same holds true for any collateral material used in personal selling, including catalogues, brochures, and presentations used by the sales force. An added responsibility for advertising is to help pre-sell a prospect for the salesman. To do this, the selling message must be consistent with *all* other aspects of a brand's marketing communication. We shall be looking at public relations and personal selling, along with other components of the broader communication mix, in Chapter 14.

A Closer Look at Advertising

Keeping in mind how advertising fits into a company's marketing plan, and our definition of how advertising turns a potential customer towards an advertised product or service, let us look at an example to illustrate how this definition of advertising applies. Remember, we are suggesting that advertising deals indirectly with potential action on the part of someone by providing information or creating feelings that turn them towards the product or service advertised. This will be true regardless of whether we are dealing with fast-moving consumer goods (fmcgs) such as food or household cleaners, industrial manufacturer advertising of heavy equipment, corporate advertisers talking about their company, or non-profit organizations soliciting funds or reminding us to take better care of ourselves.

What do you think Kinder Bueno is trying to do with its advert (Advert 1.1)? What does it wish us to 'turn towards'? We can never really know exactly what an advertiser has in mind without actually reading their marketing plan and creative strategy. But from looking at this advert it would appear that the advertiser wants us to think about indulging ourselves, and to associate the Kinder Bueno bar with this experience. They want us to 'turn towards' the idea that the Bueno will create this pleasant experience better than any other chocolate bar. Of course, much more is *implied*. We are also asked to associate a Bueno bar with a truly satisfying, almost sensual, experience. The key to this type of advertising, as we shall learn, is an 'emotional authenticity'. With this advert we have a good example in which *we* 'feel' the pleasure and contentment of the woman receiving a massage—and that feeling is nicely linked to the brand.

The point is, this advert is not *explicitly* asking you to buy a Bueno bar now, but rather is helping to create a positive feeling and attitude for the brand. This positive brand attitude is what will lead to purchase. At the same time, the other components of the marketing mix, mediated by competitive activity in the market, will all contribute to the likelihood of someone actually purchasing a Bueno bar after seeing this advert. Advertising for a brand only plays a part, but, as we shall see through the course of this book, it is a very important, often critical, part.

How Does Advertising Work?

In a very real sense, the remainder of this book is dedicated to answering this question. But in this section we will provide a very brief introduction and overview of what is involved. Some very basic things must occur if any type of communication is to work. A person must have the opportunity to see or hear the message, must pay attention to it, must understand what is being presented, and must then act upon the message in the desired manner. This sequence is the same whether the message is from a parent, a boss, a friend, or an advertiser. In advertising we call these four steps the consumer response sequence, and it is covered in detail in Chapter 4.

Consider the Kinder Bueno advert again. What must happen for this advert to work? It ran in a women's magazine, so the first step is that potential buyers see the magazine and at least skim through it. While doing this, they must notice the advert and spend enough time with it

Advert 1.1 Advert for Kinder Bueno that illustrates a feeling of positive 'emotional authenticity' with a strong link to the brand.

Source: Kinder Bueno, 'A little bit of what you fancy', 2007 Press Campaign. Client: Ferrero; Agency: Audacity, London.

to 'get the meaning'. They must then associate a positive feeling with the brand in response to the idea of 'A little bit of what you fancy' and think to themselves, 'I'd like to try a Bueno bar.'

Realistically, of course, this is *not* likely to happen all at one go. You may glance at this advert several times without paying much attention to it. But over time, the visual imagery and short copy will begin to register and be associated with the brand. As this happens, it will help to build or reinforce a positive attitude for the brand. Then one day while shopping, you see the brand on the shelf and 'remember' the positive feelings and think 'I'll give it a try.'

If someone does pay attention to a brand's advertising, we want them to 'get' something specific. Of course, each advert will have a particular message to deliver, consistent with its creative strategy. But at a more general level, the advertising must satisfy a communication objective. All advertising and marketing communication has the ability to stimulate four communication effects: need for the category, brand awareness, brand attitude, and brand purchase intention.[5]

In a very real sense, when you pay attention to advertising, all these effects could run through your mind. While we will later devote a complete chapter to them, at this point it will be helpful to understand briefly what is meant by each of the four communication effects, because communication objectives are determined by the communication effect desired.

Category need. Before any purchase decision is made, there must be at least some interest in the product category. This is true of even the most trivial purchase. If you stop to think of it, if there were no 'reason' or need for something, why would you buy it?

Brand awareness. You must be able to identify a brand in order to purchase it. There are two types of brand awareness: recognition and recall. With recognition, at the point of purchase you recognize the brand on the shelf. With recall, you must think of the brand on your own prior to purchase.

Brand attitude. Unless a product is inexpensive or trivial, brand awareness alone will not be enough to drive you to an actual purchase. For purchase to occur, you must have a favourable attitude towards the brand, even if it is only tentative. This attitude will be some combination of what you know or learn about the brand, and any feelings you associate with it.

Brand purchase intention. Someone's mind could be full of different attitudes towards various brands. And, quite possibly, people may hold generally favourable attitudes towards several of these brands. Brand purchase intention refers to such thoughts as 'I think I'd like to try that' or 'I'll buy that', and these follow from favourable brand attitudes, perhaps encouraged by an incentive promotion. In fact, brand purchase intention is always the primary communication objective for promotion.

This discussion should provide you with a brief introduction to what we mean by communication effects. As you can see, the effects are simply a reflection of the process your mind is likely to go through prior to almost any purchase. Do you have a need? Are you aware of alternatives? What do you think about those alternatives? Will you buy one? Before you make any purchase, you will probably need to give a positive answer to each of these questions.

While each of these four communication effects can be part of the response to any advertising or promotion, they are not all required to be a specific part of the execution. Some may be implied or already understood. Those that are not become communication objectives.

The correct communication objective is critical to effective advertising and promotion. We will learn that brand awareness and brand attitude are *always* communication objectives given their importance to a brand, and that, under particular circumstances, either of the other two communication effects may also serve as a communication objective.

Let us return again to the Kinder Bueno advert. This advert assumes that a category need already exists. For this advertising to work, the reader must already eat chocolate bars. But is he or she aware of the brand? If not, the advert provides good brand name and package visibility, essential for recognition brand awareness, as we shall learn. Earlier we discussed how the advert should stimulate a positive feeling for the brand. This translates to a positive brand attitude, and could also include a positive brand purchase intention. The actual communication objective for the Kinder Bueno advert cannot be known for sure without seeing the original creative brief, but it appears to reflect the primary communication objectives of brand awareness and brand attitude. There is no attempt to 'sell' the category or to convince people to eat chocolate bars, and there is no *specific* call to purchase action. Rather, the advert does a very good job of creating an impression of a positive experience with the brand, and provides strong brand identity.

Brand Attitude Strategies

We have just pointed out that brand awareness and brand attitude are always communication objectives. Obviously, people must be aware of a brand if they are going to buy it, aware of a service if they are to avail themselves of it, aware of a company if they are going to do business with it. But the real heart of most advertising messages conveys information or communicates a feeling about the product or service being advertised. This is what comprises brand attitude.

There are four brand attitude strategies that we will be concerned with in this text, and they are covered in depth in Chapter 9. These four strategies are based upon two dimensions critical to consumer behaviour: the type of purchase decision, and the type of motivation that drives the decision.[6]

Type of purchase decision. In terms of the type of decision, we will be classifying all consumer decisions as either low involvement or high involvement.[7] When a decision is *low involvement*, it means that there is very little, if any, risk attached to the consequences of making that decision. For example, if you think you might like a new chocolate bar, trying it will no doubt be a low-involvement decision, because you will not really be risking much money. But when a decision requires a lot of information prior to deciding, and a great deal of conviction that you are making the right decision, it is *high involvement*. A good example here would be buying a car.

Type of motivation. We will be devoting a lot of time in this book to motivation. For now, in order to begin to understand brand attitude strategies, you need to know only that people do some things because of negative motivations (for example, to remove or avoid a problem) and some things because of positive motivations (for example, to make them 'feel good').

Since decisions in the marketplace are governed by type of decision and type of motivation, we know that development of brand attitude strategy in advertising must take this into account. As a result, brand attitude strategies in advertising will reflect one of the four combinations of decision type and motivation:

- low-involvement decisions driven by negative motivations;
- low-involvement decisions driven by positive motivations;
- high-involvement decisions driven by negative motivations;
- high-involvement decisions driven by positive motivations.[8]

Again, looking at the Kinder Bueno advert, what brand attitude strategy has been followed? Under most circumstances, there will probably be little risk attached to the purchase of a chocolate bar. An exception might be if you were buying a gift for someone very special and wanted a special brand such as Godiva. But in most cases, if you try a chocolate bar and do not like it, you will not have lost much. So, we can be fairly safe in assuming that this is a low-involvement decision. And the underlying motivations likely to be driving brand choice is the positive motive of sensory gratification—you want the chocolate bar you feel tastes best. This Kinder Bueno advert provides a good execution of a brand attitude strategy for a low-involvement decision driven by positive motivations.

As we shall see later, in Chapter 12, the creative tactics differ significantly for each of the four possible brand attitude strategies. If the wrong brand attitude strategy is used, the target audience will not be as likely to pay attention to the advertising or 'get' the message.

What have we learned about brand attitude strategies up to this point? We have seen that one of the jobs of advertising is to generate a communication effect, and that brand attitude is one effect that is always a communication objective. In addition, we know that, in order to create advertising that will satisfy a brand attitude communication objective, one of four fundamental brand attitude strategies must be followed. The correct brand attitude strategy will reflect the involvement in the decision by the target audience as well as the likely motivation for its choice. Once the correct brand attitude strategy is selected, the creative and media tactics required to implement that strategy will be more easily identified.

Message Appeal

Now that we have introduced the concept of brand attitude strategies, how does that relate to the appeal that should be used in creating the message? As mentioned, we shall spend a great deal of time looking specifically at creative tactics in Chapter 12, but it is also good to have a general idea about what is meant by 'persuasive appeals' in communication. Persuasion is studied by psychologists interested in attitude-change theory, and obviously what they know about persuasion informs our understanding of how advertising and other marketing communication works.

William J. McGuire, a social psychologist who taught at Yale University, is considered perhaps the foremost authority on attitude-change theory, and he has pointed out that the distinctions Aristotle made in *Rhetoric* between logos, pathos, and ethos provide a very useful way of classifying the options available for message appeals.[9] Roughly speaking, logos appeals use logical arguments, pathos appeals address our passions, and ethos appeals deal with the credibility or attractiveness of the person delivering the message.

Logos and pathos appeals correspond closely to our brand attitude strategy ideas based upon involvement and motivation. Following Aristotle, logos appeals ask the recipient of a message to draw an inference or conclusion based upon arguments presented in the message. With low-involvement decisions when the underlying motivation is negative, where a problem is to be solved or avoided, this is exactly the appeal that is necessary. When the motive is negative and the decision is high involvement, the logos requirement—accepting as true what is presented or implied—applies. When we get to Chapter 9, you will see that we call the brand attitude strategies dealing with negative motivation *informational*, because you are providing information to help to solve or avoid a problem. In essence, this means using a logos appeal.

On the other hand, a pathos appeal, as characterized by Aristotle, means a persuasive message that involves creating an appropriate *feeling* in the person receiving the message. This is exactly what we are looking for when the brand attitude strategy deals with positive motivations. We will be referring to such strategies as *transformational*, because the message appeal is meant to transform the target audience by creating an authentic emotional experience.[10]

The third message appeal suggested by Aristotle is ethos. By ethos he meant a persuasive message that relied more upon the *source* of the message than the message itself. An example in advertising would be when a popular spokesperson is used in the expectation that the target audience will be 'persuaded' to use the brand because of their endorsement (real or implied). Rosenthal made the point that ethos appeals attempt to persuade by focusing the attention of the receiver of a message on the source, while logos and pathos appeals focus on message content.[11] We consider a correct understanding of ethos to be very important when using spokespeople in advertising. This is also related to brand attitude strategy, as we shall see in our discussion of the VisCAP model of source effectiveness in Chapter 12. For example, when dealing with logical or logos appeals, *credibility* in the message source is needed, but with a pathos or emotional appeal, *attractiveness* is needed. Aristotle talked about ethos appeals in terms of tapping into someone's 'moral principles'.

A Closer Look at Promotion

When most people think about promotion, including most marketing managers, they are thinking about *sales promotion* where an incentive is usually involved. We shall be looking at this in Chapter 14. However, it is important to understand that a promotion does *not* require an incentive. All that is required is that the primary communication objective is brand purchase intention, and that the message is aimed at encouraging *immediate* action on the part of the target audience. When retailers feature a brand, or a marketer features one item from a brand's line, this will almost always be a promotion. They are featuring the brand or item in order to encourage immediate purchase.

While promotions are used tactically when there is a need to accelerate purchase or stimulate immediate trial, it is important to remember that the decision to include promotion as part of the brand's marketing communication mix is a *strategic* issue. Promotion executions must be consistent with the brand positioning in its advertising, and built upon the same key benefit. Prentice, a marketing executive in the US, talked about this years ago. He pointed out that promotions should be designed to be what he called 'consumer franchise-building', meaning that they will contribute to the brand's awareness and help to build positive brand attitude, as well as stimulate immediate action.[12] Additionally, promotions must be coordinated with the brand's advertising so that it has had an opportunity to build sufficient awareness for the brand, and at least a tentatively favourable brand attitude, *prior* to the promotion.

As we shall see in Chapter 15, when this is done successfully, the overall result for the brand will be stronger than if either promotion or advertising is used alone. Always, when promotions are considered, the manager should be thinking about how a particular promotion can be an effective part of the *whole* marketing communication effort. Simmons puts this very well when he refers to the 'two great commandments of sales promotion': it must relate directly to the objectives, and it must be compatible with the total brand proposition.[13]

Promotions are usually thought of as aimed at consumers, but in fact much more money is invested in promotion to the trade than to the consumer. There are three fundamental types of promotion: trade promotion, retail promotion, and consumer promotion.[14] We may think of a *trade promotion* as a programme of discounts or incentives to increasing distribution or merchandising collateral or incentives to help move more product; *retail promotion* as promotions offered by the retailer, and which may have originated with the brand; and *consumer promotion* as promotions offered to business-to-business customers or consumers to accelerate or reinforce the decision process.

Advertising and Promotion in Social Media

The world of 'new media' goes well beyond the Internet and mobile applications, and now encompasses what have become known as 'social media', such things as Facebook and YouTube. At the time of writing (in 2011), YouTube is only five years old, yet over *2 billion* videos a day are watched on it.[15] In 2011, some 80 per cent of companies with over 100 employees say that they are planning to include social media as part of their marketing communication.[16] Clearly, social media will play a part in marketing communication planning.

We will be taking a closer look at social media and new media generally in Chapter 10, but at this point it is important to briefly put social media in perspective with regard to advertising and promotion. From a strictly communications standpoint, which is what forms the foundation of this text, brand messages that appear in social media must follow the same 'rules' as advertising or promotion messages appearing in traditional media. As shall become clear in subsequent chapters, we are looking at what is needed to optimize the likelihood of a message being *processed*, regardless of where or how it is delivered.

How will the mind deal with information presented in social media? It will deal with the words, images, and sounds in the same way it always does, regardless of medium, with this caveat: *context*. Social media provides a very different context for a message, and this may require some attention by the manager when considering media strategy. To take but one example, with traditional media, the source of a brand's message is the advertiser. But, with social media, much of the context concerning a brand is user-generated and not under the control of the brand, including 'adverts'. This would not necessarily be a problem, except that, with today's technology, user-generated 'adverts' can look like the real thing, and easily be assumed to come from the brand. Clearly, this can be a problem.

As Bavelier and Green have pointed out, technological change does not change the fundamental abilities of the brain, and the general principles of brain organization are not likely to have changed since the advent of language many thousands of years ago.[17] So, while social media provides a new way of delivering advertising and promotion messages, they will be processed just like any other message. That means they must follow the same 'rules' for effective message processing that we will be dealing with throughout the book. Still, given its unique interactive qualities (which we shall be discussing in Chapter 10), social media can offer certain advantages in a media plan, but at the same time the manager must be alert to potential problems.

Advertising and the Consumer

There is abundant evidence in the consumer behaviour and social psychology literature that suggests that global attitudes about something will condition how specific messages related to it are received. This is a rather fancy way of saying that if you do not like coffee, you are unlikely to be persuaded to buy a particular brand. This same principle applies to marketing communication. If someone distrusts advertising generally, he or she will be less likely to trust certain advertising messages. However, this relationship is anything but simple or easily understood.

In an interesting report, Calfee and Ringold reviewed six decades of survey data dealing with consumer attitudes towards advertising.[18] What they found was a core set of beliefs about advertising that has remained relatively constant over time and across a variety of question formats. Roughly 70 per cent of consumers feel that advertising is often untruthful, seeks to persuade people to buy things they do not want, should be more strictly regulated, but nevertheless provides valuable information. In fact, despite feeling that advertising is more likely to 'seek unduly to persuade' than to 'provide useful information' (when asked to choose between the two), most people tend to feel that the benefits of advertising outweigh the deficits. As we remarked, this relationship is not easily understood.

A Question of Trust

One of the key relationships between a brand and its consumer is trust. Unfortunately, in many of today's markets, there has been a significant erosion of this critical bond. What is, or has been, the role of advertising in this erosion? One can imagine problems here at many levels. If pricing policies (for example) have led to a certain distrust of a brand, this distrust could significantly affect consumers' perceptions of the brand's advertising. At the same time, a distrust of advertising in general impedes its credibility, and this not only reduces overall marketplace efficiencies, but also acts like a cancer, attacking individual advertising messages. As Pollay and Mittal, in their analysis of consumer criticism of advertising, put it: 'High levels of distrust and cynicism put the professions of marketing and advertising in disrepute and *ultimately require greater advertising spending and creativity to accomplish the same ends*' (emphasis added).[19]

Should we expect this basic distrust of advertising to affect all advertising equally? No—and, in fact, there is some research available to help us to identify types of advertising that are more or less likely to be believed. To the extent that a consumer feels that a claim can be verified before purchase, consumer faith in that claim will be stronger than if it can be verified only after purchase ('5-year unconditional warranty', for example, versus 'tastes great'). Least credible are so-called credence claims, which ordinarily can never be verified ('best performance ever').

The alert reader will see that this could be at the heart of the seeming paradox that people often feel advertising is untruthful, yet find it a useful source of information. Some types of advertising are seen as more likely than others to be true. Following this reasoning, as we shall see when we get into this in more detail in Chapter 9, high-involvement brand attitude strategies (that is, those where there is a psychological or fiscal risk attached to the brand decision) should be seen as more credible than those for low-involvement brand attitude strategies. Again, some support for this has been found, but it is by no means something that occurs as a matter of course. Even if you are advertising a high-involvement product, credibility is far from guaranteed—and consumers are not sceptical of all low-involvement advertising. A lot of other things influence the perceived credibility of advertising in general, as we shall see.

Ippolito has talked about advertising's ability to create a bond, signalling product quality to the consumer. He goes so far as to suggest that this bond can enable advertisers to induce a useful level of credibility in their advertising simply by advertising heavily![20] The implication here is that if consumers are exposed to a message repeatedly over time, they will begin to assume that it must credibly reflect experience with the product. Consumers will reason that surely the product must be doing well since they see so much advertising for it. A rather complex notion, to be sure, but if true, this would be one way in which to induce a certain level of credibility into a brand's advertising.

In any event, there certainly are important relationships between trust and advertising credibility, and these relationships should be monitored on a continual basis. The better these relationships are understood, the greater the likelihood of maximizing credibility for one's own advertising.

Understanding Consumer Attitudes towards Advertising

Researchers have for years been surveying the public's attitudes towards advertising and have noticed no significant change in beliefs about advertising. Precisely because there is more to this than meets the eye, and its impact can significantly affect how *individual advertisers'* messages are perceived by consumers, it is important for an advertiser to have a good grasp of general consumer attitudes towards advertising. Beyond this, to the extent that someone in the business of advertising wishes truly to *understand* the business of advertising, it is critical to understand the market's perception of its 'product'. Just as it is important for an advertiser to track response to its specific advertising, it is important to track attitudes towards advertising in general.

An important question to consider here is the 'universality' of consumer beliefs about advertising. In the Pollay and Mittal article mentioned earlier, they report some preliminary findings that show significant subsets or segments within the population in terms of core beliefs about advertising.[21] As one might expect from the general findings of Calfee and Ringold that 70 per cent of consumers held consistent basic beliefs about advertising, three of the four segments Pollay and Mittal identified reflected degrees of wariness. But one segment (amounting to about a third of the population) did hold positive global attitudes. This sort of segmentation raises interesting questions. Do these segments vary in size over time? Does their make-up differ over time? Do some of the wary segments react differently to external factors such as regulation, 'false' advertising publicity, product recalls, and corporate problems, or perhaps even the vast variety of new media? Is the depth of scepticism related more to some categories or types of advertising than others? These are important issues that could be dealt with tactically in a brand's advertising, given the right information.

At the end of their article, Pollay and Mittal ask the question: *What can the industry do?* They answer: 'The industry can profit from taking the public pulse every so often, utilizing a comprehensive belief inventory.'[22] For many reasons we feel strongly that a continuous reading of consumer beliefs and attitudes is superior to 'taking the pulse every so often', because of the dynamic nature of the factors that mediate those beliefs and attitudes. But, however it is measured, it does make sense to track consumer opinion of advertising in general.

Ethics and Advertising

To begin with, it is important to understand that in talking about ethics in advertising we are not talking about what must be done legally. As Drumwright has pointed out, it is a fundamental mistake to assume that because something is legal it is ethical.[23] At root, ethics implies a code of behaviour—but *what* code of behaviour? There are written codes of behaviour throughout the world of advertising. Broadcasters, newspapers, and other media have codes of behaviour for advertisers; advertising trade groups have codes of behaviour for members; government regulators draw up codes of behaviour for advertisers. Is 'unethical behaviour' simply not following such codes of behaviour, or does the issue of ethics and ethical behaviour involve something at a much deeper level?

As Bertrand Russell has put it: 'Ethics is necessary because man's desires conflict. The primary cause of conflict is egoism: most people are more interested in their own welfare than in that of other people.'[24] And of course, advertisers are people, and are therefore likely to be more interested in their own self-interest and the success of their brand than necessarily the good of the consumer.

The real question, however, is not whether or not a manager is more interested in the brand than its customers (which is likely), but whether that leads to behaviour that is harmful to the consumer. This suggests that there are at least two issues with which we must deal: one, what would constitute unethical behaviour on the part of an advertiser; and two, even if the behaviour is unethical, if it does no harm, does it matter? Some people (as we shall see in Chapter 14) consider the use of product placement to be unethical because the *intent* is to deceive. Yet there is very little evidence that product placements work.

Dealing with these issues, of course, requires a definition of ethics. Attempts to define ethics have kept philosophers busy since before the time of Socrates. The great breakthrough by Socrates in defining ethics was the development of ethical rationalism. He argued that ethical truth was *absolute* and demonstrable, much like the truths of geometry. Plato took this and injected it into an overarching philosophical system, but his conclusions were criticized by his student Aristotle on realistic grounds. He argued that ethics are not pure science, mathematically demonstrated, as thought by Socrates and Plato. Rather they are the result of practised judgement, or *phrónêsis*. One learns the truth of how to live one's life well not by abstract reasoning, but by practical life, and by learning from experience. The Stoics and Epicureans tried to give meaning and direction to an ethical life, but without recourse to the traditional mythology of their time.[25]

What these ancient philosophers seem to have been doing was looking at ethics in terms of a study of the nature of the good life and the nature of good itself, which is what informed Christian ethics. But in the Italian Renaissance, the embrace of classical humanism was often hostile to Christian ethical teachings. Teleological ethical theory was popularized by Machiavelli, where the 'end justifies the means', and was also equally a part of Galileo's thinking. They believed that it really didn't matter what you did as long as it led to a positive outcome.[26] This set up a counter-definition to the more traditional deontological view of ethics that one must do the 'right' thing regardless of the outcome.

Philosophers that followed enlarged upon all of this thinking. Locke believed that we learn ethical ideas through our experiences, implying that ethics are wholly relative to experience. For Locke, what we call 'good' is what causes well-being; what we call 'evil' causes pain. This sounds very close to Thomas Hobbes's model of ethical thinking. As Kors has put it: 'The importance of this is dramatic. If our knowledge of ethics in the world is determined by our particular experience, then it would seem that environment determines all. Change the environment, change what causes pain and pleasure, reward and punishment in society, and you change the very thinking in ethical natures of the individuals within it.'[27]

Moving into the nineteenth century, ethics began to be understood in terms of morality. Hume argued that moral judgement is a sentiment of approval or disapproval, which is innate and not based on rational deliberation.[28] Kant's moral theory assumed a moral law within us, and this led to his 'categorical imperative': act only according to that maxim through which you can at the same time will that it should become a universal law for everyone to follow.[29] While scholars disagree about what this is, it seems to be saying that one should follow this no matter who you are or what you might otherwise desire. For example, do not say 'don't lie if you want to be trusted,' but rather say 'don't lie, period'.

In the twentieth century, Ayer, one of the leading logical positivists, argued that disputes about ultimate values are pseudo-disputes precisely because they are, in principle, unresolvable.[30] As a result, disputes about ethics are the same as arguments about aesthetics. It is a question of individual preferences. Dewey, an empiricistic rationalist, argues that there are no fixed moral ends. One's ethics guide action in pursuit of an end; they do not in themselves determine that end.[31] This leads us back to Aristotle's notion of *phrónêsis*.

The Frankfurt School in the 1930s was the first to see the role of the mass media of culture and communication in the socialization and control of contemporary societies. Its adherents argued that Hollywood films, network radio (in the days before television), advertising, magazines, and newspapers were promoting American ideology, just like Nazi Germany and Soviet Russian cultural apparatus. They were among the first to pay particular attention to advertising, packaging, and design, and the 'morality' of such influence. This was the beginning of a merger between philosophy and social science in the development of a critical theory of contemporary society.[32]

The point in looking back at how the issue of ethics has been considered over the centuries is to understand that there has not been, nor is there now, any consensus as to how ethics should be defined. This makes it rather difficult to discuss unethical behaviour in advertising. Does it simply involve intent? Or does it require a negative consequence of that intent? What if the negative consequence occurs *without* intent on the part of the advertiser: is that unethical behaviour?

We could perhaps all agree that deliberately misleading in advertising when the consequences are likely to be harmful is wrong—and most would say unethical. This would be especially true of, say, health-related products and drugs, where there are potentially serious side effects. But if the consequences are not harmful, is it unethical? From a Christian moral standpoint, the answer would be 'yes'—but then moral values are not absolute. In a Christian sense, moral merit is concerned solely with acts of will—that is, choosing rightly among available alternative courses of action, 'rightly' being defined by Christian doctrine. With other religions, and clearly among those with no religious belief, 'rightly' may be defined in widely differing ways.

Even if we look more broadly at 'community standards', such 'standards' are rarely reflected in the beliefs of everyone, and they change over time (often over short periods of time). For example, in the American Psychiatric Association's first attempt to classify mental illnesses in 1952, homosexuality was defined as a mental illness under paraphilias (the social criteria of undesirable behaviour). It was removed in 1973, and is now considered a lifestyle alternative by the American Psychiatric Association.[33]

Perhaps the best we can do is strive for the truth in advertising, allowing for a certain degree of puffery (exaggeration that is readily understood as such, for example 'fastest acting ever'). Deliberate lying would be wrong, whether considered 'unethical' or not. Additionally, if an advertiser is aware of facts that could lead to harm, whether or not it actually occurs, there is an obligation to make consumers aware of those facts. Conscious omission would be wrong, again whether considered 'unethical' or not. An exception to this can occur in social marketing where in some cases telling the whole truth could actually cause harm, an issue we will take up when talking about social marketing communication in Chapter 13.

As a footnote to this discussion, we are always taken by the fact that academics, consumer advocates, and government regulators are so very concerned that no advertising message 'deceive', even if unintentionally, when there is almost no concern over the overt lying and misleading nature of most political advertising. The consequence of misleading or 'unethical' advertising in the world of commercial speech, such as whether or not one detergent actually does clean better than another, *pales* in comparison with the potential consequences of the lies inherent in most political speech.

In the end, managers need to remember that if their advertising or other marketing activities are not truthful or are misleading, competitors will be quick to point this out, and that, over the long term, consumers are unlikely to continue buying the brand.

Criticism of Advertising

Advertising seems to be everywhere. Perhaps because of this, many people are concerned with the potential impact advertising has upon society.[34] Critics of commercial advertising raise several concerns about the impact of advertising upon society, and they are worth reviewing. As society evolved over the last half of the twentieth century, so too did the criticism of advertising. The Left especially adjusted its criticism. As Martin Davidson has pointed out, the Marxist critique, for example, now sees advertising as doubly culpable. Not only is it highly suspect in its own right as an image, but it is an image of something even *more* suspect, the commodity.[35]

Perhaps the most widely made criticism of advertising is that it makes people buy things they neither want nor need. We will examine this charge first.

Advertising Creates Unnecessary Desires

To begin with, by the time you have finished reading this book, you will be well aware that communicating with a target audience through advertising is very, very difficult. Even though people are bombarded with messages, they pay attention to very few of them. And even when they do pay attention, that does not mean they will actually learn anything from the advert, or be positively influenced by it. In fact, many studies have shown that not only do we not pay much, if any, attention to advertising, but also we do not pay much attention to the newspapers, magazines, or television shows in which the advertising runs. It is not an easy job to communicate at all with advertising. This is why advertisers go to such lengths to identify a target audience where consumers are already favourably disposed towards their product. The more philosophical question of whether advertising helps to create unnecessary wants is a much more difficult question to answer. Critics of advertising feel that, by its very nature, advertising stimulates materialism, exaggerating the requirements of a good life. But these needs are driven by other social forces well beyond advertising. A much more serious charge is that advertising creates the desire for unattainable goals. Again, we doubt that advertising alone must shoulder this charge. This is a problem with society in general. As long as contemporary movies, magazines, and television convey this image of life, some advertising is likely to reflect those images.

Advertising is Misleading

The second most generally made criticism of advertising is that it is deceptive. It seems almost an article of faith that advertising is deceptive, and this has occasioned a rather general scepticism on the part of most people towards most advertising, as we shall see. In certain cases, especially on the local level, there is no doubt that advertising can be misleading. But think for a moment about the consequences of such behaviour. If a product is misrepresented and you buy it, how likely are you ever to buy that brand again—or anything else from that company? In the long run, if advertising is deceptive, it will kill a brand.

One of the important results of advertising is the creation of brand names. Brand names bring with them almost an implied warranty of quality. Critics will argue that this image is false and that unbranded products are just as good. But are they? Is there not a social value in enhancing the benefit people perceive in a product? Research has shown that advertised brand names are felt to taste better, last longer, and so on. While advertising may have created these images, the products themselves must live up to the expectation. Davidson provides an interesting criticism here. He feels that the real problem with advertising is that it presents products in terms of values that are more important than the product itself, and that this leads to a diminution of those values.[36]

The problem with the question of deception in advertising is that it is largely a subjective one. If a claim is truly deceptive, you can be sure that the competition will be quick to let government regulatory agencies know about it. In fact, long before an advert runs, attorneys for a brand will have considered it, and the censors at the media in which it is to run will have taken a hard look at any claim the brand makes. Before a commercial is approved for showing on air or an advert is run in print media, it will require substantiation in terms of valid research for any major claim made for the brand.

In 1991, the European Union created the European Advertising Standards Alliance to provide a mechanism for dealing with false or misleading advertising. While it encourages self-regulation, the EU Misleading Advertising Directive requires member countries to institute powers to protect consumers against misleading claims.[37]

Although advertisers are permitted by law to make *obvious* exaggerations in their adverts, something called 'puffery' (for example, 'best ever', 'great taste'), any attempt to misrepresent the overall nature of a brand is unlikely. Responsible advertising will not be deceptive, for the simple reason that it is bad for business. But the grey area of misleading claims or images is more difficult to pin down. In the end, if the media let something slip by, it is unlikely that your competitors will.

Advertising Insults our Intelligence

The charge that advertising is often insulting to the reader's or viewer's intelligence is again one that is frequently heard, but hard to define. What is in bad taste for one segment of the population may not be so for another. There is no doubt that certain adverts will be found to be tasteless, insulting, or offensive to certain people—even large groups of people. If the advertising is seen as tasteless by the intended target audience, however, the advertising will be unlikely to communicate its intended message effectively. So, once again, we see that, to the extent that the charge of 'insulting to my intelligence' is true, it will tend to be counter-productive for the advertiser. It is in the advertiser's best interest to provide advertising that will be well received by its target audience. This is one of the reasons why you should test adverts before running them.

Advertising and the Economy

Another general area of advertising criticism revolves around the role advertising does or does not play in the economy. Classical economics, as a rule, provides very little comfort for advertising. But most marketers believe advertising does indeed make a positive contribution to the economy—if by no other way than pumping a great deal of money into the economy. For example, it was estimated that spending on advertising for the year 2010 was US$104 billion in Western Europe, US$106 billion in Asia-Pacific, and US$160 billion in North America.[38]

It is often argued that advertising drives up the cost of products, and that, without advertising, most things would cost less. This really is not the case. Of course, the cost of a product does include the cost of the advertising, but dropping the advertising would not necessarily drop the price of the product. Advertising helps to increase consumption, which in its turn permits certain economies of scale that help to drive *down* prices. For example, consider recent experiences with personal computers and mobile phones. Additionally, an argument can be made that price competition is enhanced by a broader awareness of price, which comes from advertising.

Chapter summary

In this chapter we have defined what we mean by advertising and promotion and introduced the key concepts related to communication effects, which will be used to organize our discussions throughout the book. We also took an initial look at social media, pointing out that messages delivered by social media will be processed by the brain in the same way as messages delivered by traditional media. The meaning of ethics in advertising was looked at in the context of the history of ethics, concluding that there is no clear-cut answer to what constitutes ethics in advertising. Finally, we discussed some of the common criticisms of advertising and the importance of consumer attitudes towards advertising and the important role played by trust.

Questions to consider

1.1 What is the major difference between advertising and promotion?

1.2 What is necessary for persuasive communication to work?

1.3 Why are brand awareness and brand attitude always communication objectives?

1.4 What is the basic difference between informational and transformational brand attitude strategies?

1.5 What problems, if any, do social media pose for advertising?

1.6 Discuss the issue of ethics in advertising.

1.7 In what ways does advertising make a positive contribution to the economy?

1.8 Do you feel that there is merit to any of the traditional criticisms of advertising?

1.9 Why is it important for an advertiser to be aware of trends in public attitude toward advertising in general?

Case study 1 Cadbury Digestives—Oh Happy Day: How Advertising Helped Biscuit Buyers to Discover a New Name in Chocolate Digestives

Cadbury is Britain's most trusted brand of chocolate. But chocolate is an indulgence. Chocolate digestives, on the other hand, are a permissible treat that we readily enjoy every day. Previous attempts to market digestives coated in Cadbury chocolate had met with little success. McVitie's sales were stagnant and its brand remained consumers' default choice. Furthermore, given the chaotic nature of the biscuit aisle, most biscuit buyers have become conditioned to operate on auto-pilot.

In order for Burton's to make a dent in Everyday Treats, we were going to have to change the way in which shoppers behave in the biscuit aisle, and that meant getting them to actively look out for the Cadbury name.

We started by looking at our target's path to purchase. Looking at our customer journey, we decided to focus exclusively on creating a campaign to generate awareness, with confidence that the desired attitudinal and behavioural changes (like, prefer, buy, and repeat) would follow. Against our awareness objective and budgetary restrictions, we concluded that television alone was the right channel.

There are two types of chocolate digestive buyer: 'the biscuit brigade' and 'chocoholics'. For the biscuit brigade, a tea break is a virtuous excuse to treat themselves to a digestive; for chocoholics, →

➜ a tea break isn't really about the biscuit—it's a guilt-free opportunity to sneak in an extra bit of chocolate into their day.

Understanding the difference between these two mindsets proved fundamental to the development of our communications strategy. The initial proposition briefed into the agency was:

> Digestives taste better covered in delicious Cadbury chocolate.
>
> *Source: Half Choc Advertising Brief (Sept 2006)*

We knew that talking about the biscuit itself would have been playing by McVitie's rules. As a challenger, we needed to take a different approach. Our strategic direction was to simplify and focus the proposition, concentrating on the news that would have the greatest impact among chocoholics: Cadbury chocolate is now available on a digestive. We needed a loud, proud, and engaging announcement of our news. And 'Thank You' is just that—a hyperbolic dramatization of the joy women experience upon discovering Cadbury Chocolate Digestives. The mood of exaltation is hit home by the music, the gospel music standard 'Oh Happy Day'.

We created a targeted media plan that would deliver optimal results among our primarily female chocoholic audience. The media buying reflected the geographic bias of biscuit buyers, with roughly twice as much investment going towards the midwest, north, and Scotland as into London and the south. The final stage in the media planning process was programme selection. We recognized that, for our audience, a digestive break is a moment to stop and savour a brief bit of down time in an otherwise hectic day.

Finally, the stature and scale afforded by television also turned out to be in important tool in helping Burton's to market the Cadbury Half Choc range to retailers, which in turn helped us to achieve our awareness objective in arguably the most important channel: the biscuit aisle.

Source: This is an edited version of a case study submitted to the IPA Effectiveness Awards. The full case study can be found at ipa.co.uk or warc.com. © Copyright Institute of Practitioners in Advertising.

Edited by Elizabeth Mamali, PhD Researcher, Bath School of Management

Discussion questions

1. Discuss the reasons why the 'Thank You' campaign worked successfully.
2. The case mentions that the advertising campaign, even though aimed at consumers, turned out to be an effective tool in marketing to retailers. What do you think are the reasons behind this success?
3. How did Cadbury make use of the 'chocoholic' segment to design its advertising campaign?
4. Suggest an alternative media strategy for the 'Thank You' campaign, taking into account the needs and habits of the target market.

Further reading

Jeff Richards and Catharine Curren, 'Oracles on "Advertising": Searching for a Definition', *Journal of Advertising*, 31/2 (2002)

Takes an in-depth look at trying to define 'advertising', looking first at a review of definitions in the literature, and then using a modified Delphi method to explore the issue.

Minette Drumwright, 'Ethics and Advertising Theory', in Shelly Rogers and Esther Thorson, *Advertising Theory* (Oxford: Routledge, 2012), forthcoming

While we take a broad, philosophical view of ethics and advertising, here it is discussed more pragmatically.

J. Xu and S. Wyer, Jr, 'Puffery in Advertisements: The Effects of Media Content, Communication Norms, and Consumer Knowledge', *Journal of Consumer Research*, 37/2 (2010), 329–343

P. Haan and C. Berkey, 'A Study of the Believability of the Forms of Puffery', *Journal of Marketing Communication*, 8/4 (2002), 243–256

We briefly mentioned the idea of puffery in advertising, but for more information, see the above.

Stephanie O'Donohue, 'Living with Ambivalence: Attitudes to Advertising in Postmodern Times', *Marketing Theory*, 1/1 (2001)

Provides a good review of research on the structure of attitudes to advertising, and then places it all within an interesting postmodern perspective.

Notes

1. *The New Shorter Oxford English Dictionary* (Oxford: Clarendon Press, 1990).
2. Daniel Starch, *Principles of Advertising* (Chicago: A.W. Shaw, 1926).
3. Daniel Starch, *Principles of Advertising* (Chicago: A.W. Shaw, 1926).
4. McCarthy introduces this idea of the so-called 'Four Ps' of the marketing mix in his original text, *Basic Marketing: A Management Approach* (Homewood, IL: Irwin, 1960).
5. The four communication effects introduced here and discussed extensively in the text were originally described by John Rossiter and Larry Percy in *Advertising and Promotion Management* (New York: McGraw-Hill, 1987).
6. This notion of type of decision, as well as the idea of motivation, is at the heart of the Rossiter–Percy grid, originally introduced in Rossiter and Percy, *Advertising and Promotion Management* (New York: McGraw-Hill, 1987), and discussed in much of the book.
7. While we talk about involvement in terms of 'risk', this is a function of the processing required, and this is reflected in traditional models of low- and high-involvement processing. Low-involvement models suggest that advertising and other forms of marketing communication cause brand awareness and a *tentative* brand attitude, but actual brand attitude is not formed until after experience with the brand. Perhaps the best example of a low-involvement model is the one advanced by A.S.C. Ehrenberg in his 'Repetitive Advertising and the Consumer', *Journal of Advertising Research*, 14 (1974), 25–34, and 'Justifying Advertising Budgets', *Admap*, 30 (1994), 11–13. Low-involvement models have been called the 'weak theory' of advertising by John Phillip Jones in 'Advertising: Strong Force or Weak Force? Two Views an Ocean Apart', *International Journal of Advertising*, 9 (1990), 233–46.

   The generally accepted model of high involvement is the so-called hierarchy-of-effects (H-O-E) model. Here marketing communication first stimulates awareness, then affects brand attitude, which leads to brand purchase. In an interesting review of tests of the H-O-E model as applied to advertising, T. Barry and D. Howard suggest that the results are 'inconclusive'. This is discussed in their paper 'A Review and Critique of the Hierarchy of Effects in Advertising', *International Journal of Advertising*, 9 (1990), 121–35. The reason why the results are inconclusive, of course, is that the model applies only where high-involvement decisions operate.
8. This follows directly from the Rossiter–Percy grid referred to in n. 6.
9. McGuire often refers to these distinctions when discussing persuasive message appeals. A good summary may be found in his seminal work on attitude change, 'The Nature of Attitude and Attitude

Change', in G. Lindsey and E. Aronson (eds), *The Handbook of Social Psychology*, iii (Reading, MA: Addison-Wesley Publishing, 1969), 136–314. Another good reference is his 'Persuasion, Persistence, and Attitude Change', in I. deSala Pool *et al.* (eds), *Handbook of Communication* (Chicago, IL: Rand McNally, 1973), 216–52.

10. Larry Percy and John Rossiter provide a review of the psychological literature associated with logos, pathos, and ethos message appeals in their *Advertising Strategy: A Communication Theory Approach* (New York: Praeger Publishers, 1980), 102–4.
11. P.I. Rosenthal, 'Concepts of Ethos and the Structure of Persuasive Speech', *Speech Memographs*, 33 (1996), 114–26.
12. See R.M. Prentice, 'How to Split your Marketing Funds between Advertising and Promotion', *Advertising Age*, (10 Jan 1977), 41–4.
13. P. Simmons, 'Sales Promotion in Marketing', in N. Hart (ed.), *The Practice of Advertising*, 4th edn (Oxford: Butterworth Heinemann, 1995), 251.
14. Simmons makes an interesting point in his discussion of sales promotion, pointing out that promotions are also directed towards employees, either for individual performance or for group performance; see P. Simmons, 'Sales Promotion in Marketing', in N. Hart (ed.), *The Practice of Advertising*, 4th edn (Oxford: Butterworth Heinemann, 1995), 251.
15. These figures were reported by YouTube in its YouTube Fact Sheet, online 10 December 2010, at http://www.youtube.com/t/factsheet
16. See D.A. Williamson, 'How much money will you spend on social-media marketing next year?', *Advertising Age* (8 Dec 2010).
17. This is discussed by Daphne Bavelier in 'Browsing and the Brain', *Nature*, 470 (2011), 37–8.
18. John E. Calfee and Debra Jones Ringold, 'The 70% Majority: Endorsing Consumer Beliefs about Advertising', *Journal of Public Policy and Marketing*, 13 (1994), 228–30.
19. Richard W. Pollay and Banwari Mittal, 'Here's the Beef: Factors, Determinants, and Segments in Consumer Criticism of Advertising', *Journal of Marketing*, 57 (1993).
20. P. Ippolito, 'Bonding and Non-Bonding Signal of Product Quality', *Journal of Business*, 63 (1990), 41–60.
21. Pollay and Mittal, 'Here's the Beef: Factors, Determinants, and Segments in Consumer Criticism of Advertising', *Journal of Marketing*, 57/3 (1993), 99–114.
22. Pollay and Mittal, 'Here's the Beef: Factors, Determinants, and Segments in Consumer Criticism of Advertising', *Journal of Marketing*, 57/3 (1993), 99–114.
23. See M.E. Drumwright's chapter 'Ethical Issues in Advertising and Sales Promotions', in N.C. Smith and J.A. Quelch (eds), *Ethics in Marketing* (Boston, MA: Irwin, 1993), 607–25.
24. Bertrand Russell, *A History of Western Philosophy* (London: The Folio Society, 2004), 747.
25. These ideas of the Greek philosophers are discussed in Bertrand Russell's *Introduction to the Problems of Philosophy* (Oxford: Oxford University Press, 1959).
26. See E. Cassiner, *The Individual and Cosmos in Renaissance Philosophy* (New York: Dover, 1963).
27. This quote is found in the transcript of a lecture given by Allan Kors in a series on Great Minds of the Western Intellectual Tradition, offered by the Teaching Company (2000), Part 4 of 7, page 47.
28. David Hume, *An Inquiry Concerning the Principles of Morals* (Indianapolis, IN: Hacket, 1987).
29. Kant's philosophy on ethics is discussed in his *Grounding for the Metaphysics of Morals* (Indianapolis, IN: Hacket, 1993).
30. See A.J. Ayer, *Language, Truth, and Logic* (New York: Dover, 1946).

31. See John Dewey, *Reconstruction in Philosophy* (New York: Holt, 1922).
32. For the definitive discussion of the Frankfurt School, see Rolf Wiggerhaus, *The Frankfurt School* (Cambridge, MA: MIT Press, 1996).
33. See the 1952 and 1973 editions of the American Psychiatric Association's *Diagnostic and Statistical Manual of Mental Disorders* (Washington, DC: American Psychiatric Association).
34. A good review of many criticisms of advertising may be found in William Leiss, Stephen Klein, and Sut Jally, *Social Communication in Advertising* (London: Routledge, 1997).
35. Martin Davidson, *The Consumerist Manifesto: Advertising in Postmodern Times* (London: Routledge, 1992), 177.
36. Martin Davidson, *The Consumerist Manifesto: Advertising in Postmodern Times* (London: Routledge, 1992), 177.
37. Matti Alderson, 'Advertising: Self-Regulation and the Law', in Norman Hart (ed.), *The Practice of Advertising* (Oxford: Butterworth Heinemann, 1995), 259–72.
38. These figures were supplied by ZenithOptimedia as reported in *Advertising Age* (20 Dec 2010), 10.

Visit the Online Resource Centre that accompanies this book for additional resources to support the text: **www.oxfordtextbooks.co.uk/orc/percy_elliott4e/**

Perspectives on Advertising

Key concepts

1. While the traditional cognitive information processing view of advertising continues to be the most viable way of thinking about advertising, there are other perspectives that can help in understanding how advertising works, and its effect upon society.
2. These other perspectives may be thought about in terms of their assumptions about the target audience and the level of explanation at which they are working.
3. These two considerations provide the axes of a 'mapping', whereby the different perspectives on advertising may be seen in terms of either passive individuals, passive social or cultural groups, active individuals, or active social or cultural groups.

For many years all areas of marketing research, and particularly advertising research, have been dominated by the cognitive information processing perspective. However, in this chapter we review a wide variety of alternative perspectives on how advertising works and its effects on society. Some of these approaches have emerged as explicit criticisms of advertising and are not concerned with advertising as a managerial practice, but some new approaches to visual imagery and meaning-based models, together with an understanding of cultural differences, hold great potential for developing more effective advertising strategies.

Audiences and Individuals

The practice of advertising has for a long time been the butt of attacks from some economists (for example, Galbraith[1]) and social and political theorists of the Frankfurt School (for example, Marcuse[2]). But recently sociology and anthropology have started to take consumption seriously as a central element in modern (or postmodern) culture, and, together with a developing interest in semiotics, advertising is now studied from a plethora of social science perspectives. To enable us to locate these differing and complex viewpoints, we can organize them along two dimensions in relation to their assumptions about the audience (active versus passive) and to the level of explanation at which they are working (individual versus cultural), and construct a map of perspectives on advertising (see Fig. 2.1). This provides us with four sectors into which we can slot most approaches to understanding advertising and society: Sector 1: Passive Individuals; Sector 2: Passive Social/Cultural Groups; Sector 3: Active Individuals; and Sector 4: Active Social/Cultural Groups.

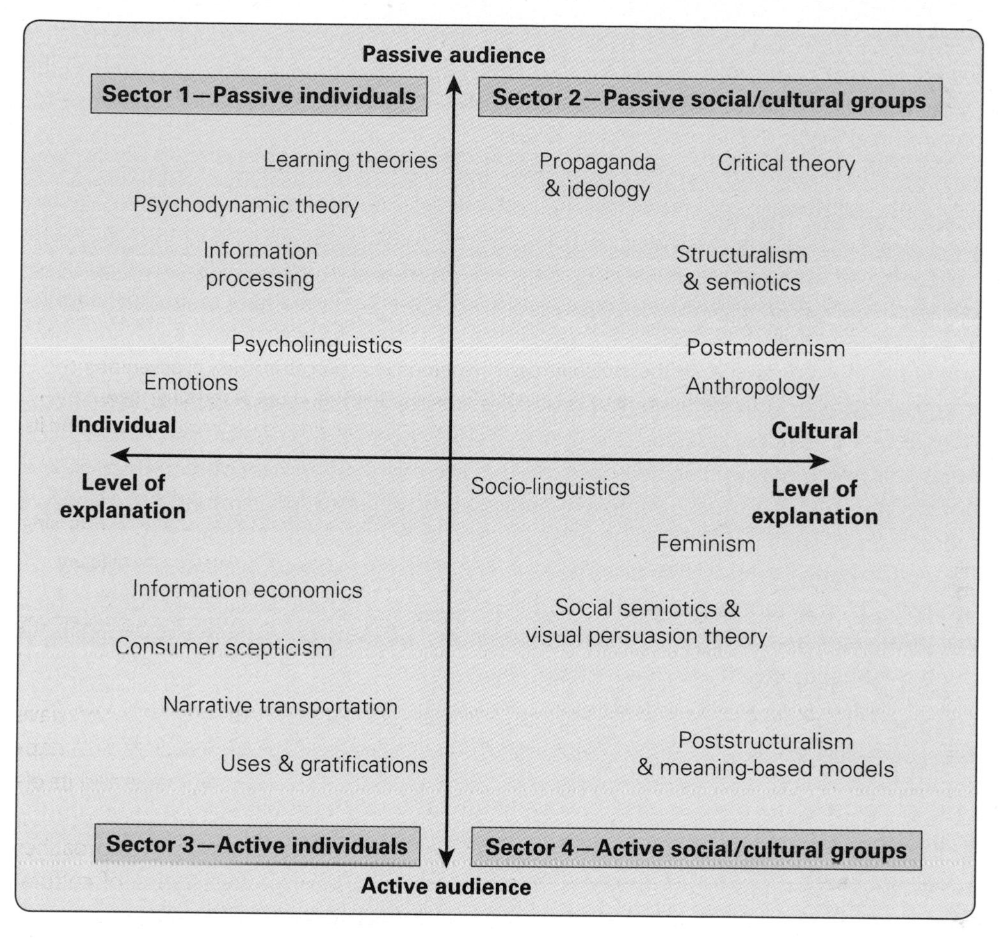

Figure 2.1 Conceptual Map of Perspectives on Advertising

Sector 1: Passive Individuals

The major theoretical approaches used by marketing academics and advertising practitioners for explaining 'how advertising works' are located in this sector.

Learning Theories and Information Processing

Learning theories such as classical or Pavlovian conditioning focus on repetition and the creation of simple associations between elements (for example, a brand name becomes associated over time with a slogan), while more sophisticated approaches to learning are concerned with how advertising messages are stored in memory. These processes of storage and retrieval are the major focus of the dominant perspective in cognitive approaches to advertising, that of information processing. The approach taken in this text is an information processing approach, which assumes that the audience can be conceived of as largely passive, and that managerial attention should be concerned with how individuals move through various stages in making a decision choice (see Chapter 7). While this model does not attempt to reflect the complex reality of communication, it is managerially useful in that it provides guidance for decision making that other perspectives do not.

Psychodynamic Theories

Psychodynamic theories of advertising have a long history in both applied marketing research and critical views of advertising effects. The theories of Freud have been most popular in this regard, although Jung's ideas of symbolism and myths have also been used (and some would say abused). In the 1950s, motivational research showed that the unconscious mind may play an important role in our responses to advertising,[3] while Vance Packard, in his notorious book *The Hidden Persuaders*, claimed that advertisers were cynically using hidden messages that were not noticeable consciously, but which had an irresistible effect on our unconscious minds via such (unproven) processes as subliminal perception.[4] We shall have more to say about this when we talk about processing messages in Chapter 11.

Freudian concepts have been fused with semiotic analysis by Judith Williamson in a sophisticated and insightful analysis of advertisements that claims to have revealed a code by which advertisers can (and do) tap into our unconscious desires and achieve their desired effects on our buying behaviour.[5] If only it were that simple!

Psycholinguistics

Psycholinguistics has been applied to advertisements by such people as Cook,[6] and Vestergaard and Schroder,[7] who take advertisements as texts that can be studied using conventional linguistic theory. This close reading of language has largely been overtaken by the sociolinguistics approach, which falls into Sector 4, and is difficult to square with the rather crucial fact that most advertising uses visual images as well as, or instead of, language.

Emotions

The relationship between advertising, rationality, and emotion is complex and the source of much heated debate. Certainly, the dominant approach to advertising has been cognitive, emphasizing rational processing, persuasion, and knowledge. However, Ehrenberg's 'weak theory' of advertising suggests that the prime effect of advertising is to reinforce emotions already connected with a brand.[8] As we discuss in Chapter 11, neuroscience and brain imaging technology is identifying the vital role of emotional responses to advertising.[9] One very interesting new finding about emotional responses is that advertising can enhance a brand's perceived trustworthiness without prior experience of the brand or overt trust claims.[10]

Sector 2: Passive Social/Cultural Groups

Many of the most negative perspectives on advertising are located in this sector, in which society is seen as being at the mercy of the power of organized capital through its vanguard weapon, which is selling the delights of consumer culture to unsuspecting dupes.

Critical Theory, Propaganda, and Ideology

An early approach was that of Raymond Williams, who posited that capitalism could function only with the help of advertising, because rational consumers would be satisfied with purely functional goods.[11] The task of advertising is to imbue products with 'magical' symbolic meaning so that we are never fully satisfied.

A seminal approach is that of the Frankfurt School, which brought a quasi-Marxist analysis to the modern phenomena of consumer society. Earlier concepts such as Gramsci's hegemony (which claimed that the masses were persuaded to accept the self-serving beliefs of the ruling classes through the power of mass communication, and thus could be used to explain why the working class would vote against its own class interest) were brought together with the concept of false needs to build a critique of the entire consumer society.[12] Marcuse describes consumers as caught within a 'happy consciousness' in which their alienation and lack of freedom are balanced with their enjoyment of consumer goods, so that they are unable to escape and achieve an authentic existence.[13] In this view, advertising's role is to maintain the hegemonic dominance of consumption as the prime source of human happiness.

Advertising has been analysed by Galbraith as a very powerful form of propaganda that uses seductive imagery to form the ways in which we think about ourselves and society.[14] This view of advertising as ideology (a communication system that supports a vested interest by making the individual believe that his or her conditions are natural, and opposition unthinkable) has been applied to advertising by Goldman, who sees its effects as inescapable.[15] However, as will be discussed in Sector 4, although advertising may be the 'super-ideology' of late capitalism, its persuasive power has to be set against the countervailing effects of polysemy (adverts can have multiple possible interpretations) and oppositional cultural practices, where subcultural groups (for example, gay rights activists) resist the intended meanings of advertisers by such means as parody and distortion.[16]

Structuralism and Semiotics

A structuralist position is taken by Williamson, who maintains that advertising operates as a structure that transforms the language of objects into that of people and vice versa, and that this translation system can be broken down into its structural elements and processes.[17] Based largely on work by Barthes,[18] her approach uses semiotics to analyse sign systems in which a sign (such as an advertisement) has two parts: the signifier and the signified. The signifier is a material object (such as a product), and the signified is an idea and/or an emotion (such as excitement). As an analytic system, semiotics has been widely used in discussions of advertising to unpack some of its communicative complexity, especially in relation to visual imagery.[19] But as more emphasis has been placed on the ability of active audiences to make their own interpretations of advertisements rather than just to accept the semiotic codes with which they are presented, semiotics has tended to be replaced by social semiotics and poststructuralism, which will be discussed in Sector 4.

Postmodernism

Writers on postmodernism have had a field day with advertising. Central to postmodern theory is the proposition that consumers no longer consume products for their material utilities, but consume the symbolic meaning of those products as portrayed in their images. Products in fact become commodity-signs.[20] 'The real consumer becomes a consumer of illusions', as Debord has put it,[21] and 'the ad-dict buys images not things', in the words of Taylor and Saarinen.[22] Based on semiotic theory, postmodernism points to the uncontrollable disconnection of signifiers and signified, the 'free-floating signifiers' in contemporary consumer culture, where any sign can stand for any aspect of a product.

Advertising is the most visible manifestation of a culture bombarded with commodity-signs, a society where reality and illusion are difficult to distinguish, a society of simulations and even hyperreality that is 'more real than the real'. The phrase 'postmodern condition' depicts a society where media images dominate and construct our consciousness, where the boundary between high culture and popular culture disappears, where style dominates substance, and where, according to Strinati, 'as a result, qualities like artistic merit, integrity, seriousness, authenticity, realism, intellectual depth and strong narratives tend to be undermined'.[23] Advertising is seen as a major form of popular culture, which people consume as signs and imagery, and adverts can be seen as cultural products in their own right, consumed independently of the product being marketed.[24] As advertising increasingly uses images and references taken from other forms of popular culture such as cinema, television, and pop music, it becomes less about telling us why we should buy a product and more about associating the product with style and image, often through a parody of advertising itself.

The complex relationship between the two symbol systems of popular culture and advertising has been explicated by Fowles, who maintains that they are the 'two grand domains of public art in these times', if only because of their ubiquity.[25] Many postmodern discussions of advertising are partly a celebration of 'mass culture' in opposition to the Frankfurt School's derision of the way in which the 'culture industries' (cinema, radio, magazines) were 'liquidating' high culture and deceiving the working class into accepting a consumer society and abandoning their heritage of great art. However, other themes in postmodernism seem to be very much informed by critical theory and are really just the Frankfurt School updated for the late-twentieth-century media environment. This dialectic continues in the cultural theories discussed in Sector 4.

Anthropology

Anthropology has drawn our attention to the fact that there may be no such thing as universal human nature, all behaviour being determined by culture,[26] and that different cultures have different communication styles. De Mooij has focused on cultural differences in relation to advertising, using Hofstede's 5-D model of culture.[27] This identifies five dimensions of culture that may affect advertising communication: power distance, individualism versus collectivism, masculinity versus femininity, uncertainty avoidance, and long-term orientation. If we then add the additional cultural dimension of high versus low context, we can start to explore the complexity of communicating with people from different cultures. De Mooij points out that all models of how advertising works are culture bound. In some cultures, advertising is assumed to be persuasive in nature; in others, it is assumed to be about building trust. The role of pictures versus words in carrying information and communicating meaning varies between cultures, as does the way in which people process information. In Chapter 6 we will discuss de Mooij's analysis of cultural differences in advertising. The overall conclusion is that, in order to maximize effectiveness, advertising must reflect local cultural assumptions and communication styles, and advertising effectiveness research must also be culture sensitive.

Sector 3: Active Individuals

In this section we look at disciplines that consider the audience for advertising as active individuals.

Information Economics

Information economics takes the view that rational consumers already know what they want, and the task of advertising is simply to inform them of availability and product specifications so as to make their search behaviour efficient.[28] However, only a minority of advertising falls into this information category. The majority of advertising does not appear to carry much information at all. Rather, it conveys implicit information about the brand or company that it is advertising.

The fundamental proposition of economic theory is that the most important information that advertising conveys is primarily of commitment to a market and that consumers are active in forming inferences about the product quality of a brand from the amount of money that is spent: 'the persuasive quality arises from the fact, not the content, of advertising', as Kay puts it.[29] This seems to assert that all advertising is equally effective and content free, and that to beat the competition you need only to spend the most money. We completely reject this perspective and maintain that there is effective advertising and ineffective advertising and that the managerial task is to know and manage the difference.

Uses and Gratifications Theory

A very different perspective that also sees the advertising audience as active individuals is uses and gratifications theory. This was the first attempt in communication theory to view the audience as active in its selection of content and messages from the media, and posits that much mass media use is goal directed. This approach has been applied to advertising by O'Donohoe, who separates the marketing-related uses (information, choice, consumption stimulation, image, vicarious consumption) from a wide range of non-marketing-related gratifications.[30] Some of these gratifications will be discussed in Sector 4 because they are social in nature, but some important individualistic 'things people do with advertising' include: entertainment, escapism, role models, reinforcement of attitudes and values, and ego enhancement.

People often consume advertising as an entertainment form in its own right without any direct relevance to purchase behaviour, and this may also apply to the use of advertising for escapism and fantasy. Advertising may provide consumers with role models or other personal aspirations. This is directly related to the way in which we may also use advertising as a raw material to help us to make sense of the world through the social construction of reality, and thus to reinforce our attitudes and our values.[31] Advertising may also help us to sustain our sense of self-worth by keeping us in touch with what is fashionable.

Narrative Transportation

A fascinating new approach to the way in which consumers may become absorbed in advertising and relate it to their lives is narrative transportation theory.[32] Narrative transportation happens when viewers of adverts become very engaged with a story, and this leads to persuasion through reduced negative cognitive responding and strong positive emotional responses.

Consumer Scepticism

Scepticism towards advertising has emerged as an important factor in advertising theory because it fundamentally changes the way in which consumers respond to advertising. They may dismiss arguments and generate more counter-arguments, or even detach themselves from interaction with advertising messages altogether.[33] The most comprehensive account of the way in which scepticism influences consumer processing of persuasive communication is the persuasion knowledge model, which points to consumers learning about advertisers' motives, strategies, and tactics.[34] This learning is amplified by mass-media discussions of consumer culture.

Sector 4: Active Social/Cultural Groups

This sector considers a number of relatively recent applications of theory to advertising. These views take a strong social orientation and assume active participation on the part of advertising's audience.

Socio-linguistics

The socio-linguistics perspective draws on speech act theory in linguistic philosophy to emphasize the social action aspects of language, and on ethnomethodology to focus on how people use language in everyday situations to make sense of their world. It has extended the study of the use of language to include contextual aspects such as relations of class, power, and gender. The fundamental assumptions of socio-linguistics and its various forms of discourse analysis are that language is a medium oriented towards action and function, and that people use language intentionally to construct accounts or versions of the social world. Evidence for this active process of construction is said to be demonstrated by variation in language. This concept of variability is central for analysis, because discourse will vary systematically depending upon the function it is being used to perform.[35] Language performs a variety of functions in the world and does not just represent it, for, as Foucault pointed out, we are only able to think within the constraints of discourse.[36] Discourse is defined here as a system of statements that constructs an object, supports institutions, reproduces power relations, and has ideological effects. In applying this to advertising, Fairclough suggests that adverts 'help' the consumer to build a relationship with products, evoking an interpretative framework that situates both consumer and product in a 'modern lifestyle'.[37] In a study of overt sexuality in advertising, Elliott and his colleagues have suggested that if consumers could classify overt sexuality within an interpretative framework of 'art', then this would function to legitimate positive interpretations by changing their category from sexual, which would be unacceptable, to art, in which the same representation could then be given approbation. This seemed to be related to the product being given very little attention in the advertisement and therefore allowing it to be transferred from the commercial to the artistic realm where moral judgement could be suspended.[38]

Myers allows more freedom to the members of the audience in the construction of their 'position as consumers', and points to the potential for multiple interpretations of advertising.[39] We will discuss the possibilities for multiple meanings—polysemy—in more detail below when we consider poststructuralism. He also points out that adverts are not consumed alone, but depend on interactions with other people in order to make socially shared meaning.

Feminism

There is a long history of feminist analysis of advertising, almost always from a critical perspective that implicates advertising in maintaining and even enhancing aspects of male subordination of women. In an early empirical study, Goffman demonstrated how many print advertisements presented woman in a subservient role to men, the men usually depicted as being above and in control of women.[40] Subsequent content analyses of female images in advertising showed a serious bias towards stereotyped sex-role portrayals of women as primarily homemakers.[41]

A particular focus for analysis has been the extent to which advertising imagery constructs women's sense of beauty, and may in fact have harmful effects on their sense of worth. Certainly, this seems to be the conclusion from a number of experiments that have shown that exposure to idealized images of women in advertising resulted in women having lower levels of satisfaction with their own attractiveness.[42] Myers suggested that women are more vulnerable to manipulation by advertising than men because their upbringing and social expectations have already been influenced towards accepting gender stereotyping.[43] However, other research has found that women are perfectly able to identify and resist unrealistic gender portrayals in advertising.[44]

Social Semiotics and Visual Persuasion Theory

The recent development of theories of social semiotics, and in particular that of the theory of visual persuasion, is an important development, because the vast majority of advertising makes potent use of visual images. Kress and van Leeuwen present an articulated theory that attempts to explain how socially meaningful images can be built into visual narrative systems.[45] In common with socio-linguistics, social semiotics assumes that language varies with social context, and also assumes that the reader of any narrative system plays an active part in its interpretation.

Messaris presented the first comprehensive theory of visual persuasion, in which he utilizes the three semiotic concepts of iconicity, indexicality, and syntactic indeterminacy, and applies them to persuasive images.[46] Iconicity relates to the fact that an image not only can represent an aspect of the real world, but also comes with a wealth of emotional associations that stem from each individual's unique experiences in addition to the shared influences of culture. These associations are communicated not just by visual content, but also by visual form. Indexicality is particularly relevant to photographs, and relates to the fact that a photographic image can serve as documentary evidence or proof of an advert's claims because of its 'authenticity'. He maintains, contrary to the claims of Kress and van Leeuwen, that there can be no precise syntax or explicit propositional system using visual images. It is precisely this relative 'deficiency' of visual syntax that gives images such persuasive power, because not only can they escape explicit interpretation by the audience and thus say what might be slightly unacceptable if fully spelt out, but they can also evade legal and moral restrictions through implicit communication. These are very important issues in relation to advertising and persuasion.

Poststructuralism

Poststructuralism is the final perspective we shall consider here, and this develops from both the uses and gratifications approach and from postmodernism. Literary analysis of texts has increasingly seen the growth of reader-response theory, which shows how a text works with the probable knowledge, expectations, or motives of the reader and leads to multiple interpretations of meaning.[47] A basic assumption here is that advertising, like other communicative texts, is subject to polysemy—that is, it is open to multiple interpretations by the audience. A number of recent studies provide empirical evidence of advertising's polysemic status.[48]

Polysemy is a potentially fatal threat to a successful advertising campaign because it can prevent the advertiser from getting the intended meanings across to the target audience. This will pose a significant limitation to a campaign's effectiveness and consequently a brand's future success in the market. In practice (rather than in theory), the interpretation made by the reader or viewer of an advert will be limited in two crucial ways. First, polysemy is limited by the text; some texts are more polysemic than others, being more or less open texts. Secondly, readers or viewers represent a polysemic limitation in that, rather than arriving at a unique, totally idiosyncratic meaning, they will subjectively interpret the text, but the end result will be a meaning that is very similar to other individuals' subjective interpretations of the same text.

These individuals form an informal social group called an 'interpretive community'.[49] Ritson and Elliott identified several interpretative communities within a group of young people, formed around readings of advertising texts, because the proximity of their social location and cultural competencies had led them to interpret the text in a similar way and with similar semantic results.[50] Indeed, several groups showed an implicit awareness of their membership in an interpretive advertising community, and used this knowledge as part of their identification with the group.

A late-twentieth-century development in advertising theory was that of meaning-based models. These see advertising not as a conduit of information, but as a resource for the construction of personal, social, and culturally situated meanings where human reality is mediated. In this view, consumers construct a variety of meanings from advertising as outcomes of a personal history and subjective interests, as expressed through their life themes and life projects. In one study, three brothers had very different interpretations of the same five magazine adverts, each one constructing interpretations that resonated with his subjective interests, goals, and ambitions.[51] Ritson and Elliott have extended the meaning-based approach from the individual's life world to social contexts, and have shown that advertising texts are often the source for a wide variety of social interactions in which advertising meanings are often changed, transferred, or solidified within the social contexts of everyday life.[52] This suggests an expansion of the concept of advertising context to include the social setting of the viewer alongside the textual setting of the advert. The impact that an advertising execution has on a particular audience and the uses to which it is put are partially dependent on the social context within which the viewer exists.

Implications for Advertising Strategy

The wide range of theoretical approaches to understanding how advertising works that we have discussed raises a number of issues for advertising management. Although the cognitive information processing approach used in this book is pragmatically the most useful for developing and managing advertising strategy, it tends to ignore the way in which people interact with advertising in their day-to-day lives. We must also remember that the audience is not usually passively absorbing our advertising messages, but is actively creating meanings that make sense to them in the context of their lives and harmonize with their own experiences. To develop really effective advertising we must pay attention to the rich social and cultural environment in which people consume products, services, and advertisements, and seek to use this knowledge to build connections between individuals, social groups, and brands. Keep this in mind as we now turn our attention to the development and management of effective advertising strategy.

Chapter summary

This chapter has reviewed a wide range of perspectives on how advertising works and on its effects on society. To help in this complex task we have introduced two dimensions that relate to assumptions about the audience (active versus passive) and to the level of explanation (individual versus cultural), and used these dimensions to construct a conceptual map. We conclude from this analysis that the cognitive information processing approach is pragmatically the most useful for advertising management, but we must also pay attention to the broader social and cultural environment.

Questions to consider

2.1 Why is it important to think about alternative perceptions of how advertising works?

2.2 In what ways do you see the different perspectives discussed in this chapter adding to our overall understanding of advertising?

2.3 Which of the specific alternative perspectives discussed in this chapter do you feel offers the most insight into how advertising works?

2.4 How can these different perspectives be used by managers in a practical way to ensure more effective advertising for their brand?

Case study 2 Marmite—Please Look After this Brand: The Launch of Marmite Squeezy

By 2005, the growth that Marmite had enjoyed for nearly a decade had essentially run out of steam. The best way in which to overcome the barriers to growth necessitated a radical change in product format, rumours of which were met with howls of protest due to the brand's status as a 'national brand'.

Empirical evidence suggests that getting more people into a brand is usually the answer to achieving significant growth. However, winning new Marmite eaters was not going to be easy. Firstly, we couldn't recruit children as Marmite has a very distinctive taste, and secondly, the pool of lapsed users was getting smaller. After careful considerations, our back-of-envelope calculations revealed another, better option—more growth potential lay with people *already eating Marmite*. Apart from its taste, another unusual Marmite property is that even die-hard fans don't eat that much of it. On average, Marmite eaters were buying just two jars per year. But there remained two intractable problems: firstly, Marmite Jars were frustratingly inconvenient, and secondly, Marmite was fiendishly difficult to spread on bread.

If we could change the product format, we were much more likely to meet our growth objectives. However, Marmite was a national institution in a quarter of UK homes and the dark glass jar was as much part of the brand as the black stuff inside. To its buyers, it was much more than just a spread. After months of careful research, a new Marmite was born: Marmite Squeezy. Identical in taste, it was slightly less thick so it could be squeezed and spread on bread—all in a squeezy, upside-down plastic container which, crucially, stayed true to the design of the iconic glass jar.

Clearly our main communication task was going to be about managing this vociferous Marmite community. We wanted to dramatize why Squeezy had been launched—its convenience and its suitability for new occasions. But we needed to do this in a particular new way—by including and engaging the Marmite community, and above all making them feel that the brand was still theirs.

Following from that, a creative idea for a campaign staged from August 2006 dramatized Squeezy convenience with a great idea to involve devotees—be creative with your Marmite! Award-winning 'Marmart' press and poster executions showcased the results of Marmite Squeezy creativity and set the context for the 'Marmart' website www.marmart.co.uk, the focal point of the online campaign.

The website ran a competition 'to find the greatest Marmartists', encouraging people to draw with Marmite Squeezy on their toast. The best entrants were displayed at the Air Gallery in London, where Linda Barker, the face of Marmart, ran workshops with artist Dermot Flynn, who created portraits of celebrities that 'divide the nation', continuing the love/hate theme. Flynn's portraits were sold on eBay and the £920 proceeds went to a charity art project.

Results revealed that, initially, increased consumption just meant that people bought Marmite more often. But, by 2007, people had begun to buy bigger jars—a sure sign that new eating habits were becoming firmly entrenched.

Source: This is an edited version of a case study submitted to the IPA Effectiveness Awards. The full case study can be found at ipa.co.uk or warc.com.

Edited by Elizabeth Mamali, PhD Researcher, Bath School of Management

Discussion questions

1. Where would you place the 'be creative with your Marmite' approach on the conceptual map of perspectives on advertising (Chapter 2) and why?
2. What are the benefits of using the Web as a channel when targeting brand communities such as the Marmite community?
3. Describe how the 'find the greatest Marmartists' competition allowed individuals to create meanings and relate to the Marmite brand.
4. Why do you think Marmite is considered a 'national brand'? Find examples of other brands that have a national icon status and identify common characteristics.

Further reading

Marketing Theory, 4/1 (2004)

Journal of Advertising, 32/1 (2003)

These special issues deal with new developments in advertising theory and consumer culture, and look at a number of subjects in the light of many of the points discussed in this chapter.

Stephen Brown, *Marketing: The Retro Revolution* (London: Sage, 2001)

Offers some very interesting insights into the entire area of retro-marketing, and takes a new perspective on looking at the influence of advertising's history on retro-advertising campaigns.

Notes

1. J.K. Galbraith, *The New Industrial Society* (Harmondsworth: Penguin, 1968).
2. H. Marcuse, *One-Dimensional Man* (London: Routledge and Kegan Paul, 1964).
3. For a review of motivational research, see P. Martineau, *Motivation in Advertising* (New York: McGraw-Hill, 1957), and E. Dichter, *The Handbook of Consumer Motivation* (New York: McGraw-Hill, 1964).
4. V. Packard, *The Hidden Persuaders* (Harmondsworth: Penguin, 1957).
5. J. Williamson, *Decoding Advertisements* (London: Marion Boyars, 1978).
6. G. Cook, *The Discourse of Advertising* (London: Routledge, 1992).
7. T. Vestergaard and K. Schroder, *The Language of Advertising* (Oxford: Basil Blackwell, 1985).
8. See J. Jones, 'Advertising: Strong Force or Weak Force? Two Views an Ocean Apart', *International Journal of Advertising*, 9/3 (1990), 233–46.
9. W. Gordon, 'What Do Consumers Do Emotionally with Advertising?', *Journal of Advertising Research*, 46/1 (2006), 2–10.
10. F. Li and P. Miniard, 'On the Potential for Advertising to Facilitate Trust in the Advertised Brand', *Journal of Advertising*, 35/4 (2006), 101–12.
11. R. Williams, 'Advertising: The Magic System', in R. Williams, *Problems in Materialism and Culture* (London: Verso, 1980), 170–95.
12. A. Gramsci, *The Prison Notebooks* (London: Lawrence and Wishart, 1971).
13. Marcuse, *One-Dimensional Man* (London: Routledge and Kegan Paul, 1964).
14. Galbraith, *The New Industrial Society* (Harmondsworth: Penguin, 1968).
15. See R. Goldman, *Reading Ads Socially* (London: Routledge, 1992).
16. See Richard Elliott and Mark Ritson, 'Poststructuralism and the Dialectics of Advertising: Discourse, Ideology, Resistance', in S. Brown and D. Turley (eds), *Consumer Research: Postcards from the Edge* (London: Routledge, 1997), 190–219.
17. J. Williamson, *Decoding Advertisements* (London: Marion Boyars, 1978).
18. See R. Barthes, *Mythologies* (St Albans: Paladin, 1973).
19. See e.g. G. Dyer, *Advertising as Communication* (London: Methuen, 1982); A. Wernick, *Promotional Culture: Advertising, Ideology, and Symbolic Expression* (London: Sage, 1991); and R. Goldman and S. Papson, *Sign Wars: The Cluttered Landscape of Advertising* (London: Guilford Press, 1996).
20. See J. Baudrillard, 'For a Critique of the Political Economy of the Sign', in M. Poster (ed.), *Jean Baudrillard: Selected Writings* (Cambridge: Polity Press, 1988).

21. G. Debord, *Society of the Spectacle* (Detroit, MI: Black and Red, 1977).
22. M. Taylor and E. Saarinen, *Imagologies: Media Philosophy* (London: Routledge, 1994).
23. D. Strinati, *An Introduction to Theories of Popular Culture* (London: Routledge, 1995), 225.
24. See M. Nava, 'Consumerism Reconsidered: Buying and Power', *Cultural Studies*, 5 (1991), 157–73.
25. J. Fowles, *Advertising and Popular Culture* (Thousand Oaks, CA: Sage Publications, 1996).
26. See C. Geertz, *The Interpretation of Cultures* (New York: Basic Books, 1973).
27. M. de Mooij, *Global Marketing and Advertising: Understanding Cultural Paradoxes* (Thousand Oaks, CA: Sage Publications, 1998).
28. See e.g. P. Nelson, 'Advertising as Information', *Journal of Political Economy*, 81 (1974), 729–54.
29. J. Kay, *Foundations of Corporate Success* (Oxford: Oxford University Press, 1993).
30. S. O'Donohoe, 'Advertising Uses and Gratifications', *European Journal of Marketing*, 28/8–9 (1994), 52–75.
31. See F. Buttle, 'What Do People Do with Advertising?', *International Journal of Advertising*, 10 (1991), 95–110.
32. J. Escalas, 'Self-Referencing and Persuasion: Narrative Transportation Versus Analytical Elaboration', *Journal of Consumer Research*, 33/1 (2007), 421–9.
33. L. Nan and R. Faber, 'Advertising Theory: Reconceptualising the Building Blocks', *Marketing Theory*, 4/1–2 (2004), 7–30.
34. M. Freistad and P. Wright, 'The Persuasion Knowledge Model: How People Cope with Persuasion Attempts', *Journal of Consumer Research*, 21/1 (1994), 1–31.
35. J. Potter and M. Wetherall, *Discourse and Social Psychology: Beyond Attitudes and Behaviour* (London: Sage Publications, 1987).
36. M. Foucault, *The Archaeology of Knowledge* (London: Tavistock, 1972).
37. N. Fairclough, *Language and Power* (London: Longman, 1989).
38. R. Elliott, A. Jones, B. Benfield, and M. Barlow, 'Overt Sexuality in Advertising: A Discourse Analysis of Gender Responses', *Journal of Consumer Policy*, 18/2 (1995), 71–92.
39. K. Myers, *Understains: The Sense and Seduction of Advertising* (London: Pandora, 1986).
40. E. Goffman, *Gender Advertisements* (London: Macmillan, 1979).
41. A number of studies have dealt with this issue, such as A. Courtney and T. Whipple, *Sex Role Stereotyping in Advertising* (Lexington, MA: Lexington Books, 1983), and S. Livingstone and G. Green, 'Television Advertisements and the Portrayal of Gender', *British Journal of Social Psychology*, 25 (1986), 149–54.
42. M. Richins, 'Social Comparison and the Idealized Images of Advertising', *Journal of Consumer Research*, 18/1 (1991), 71–91.
43. K. Myers, *Understains: The Sense and Seduction of Advertising* (London: Pandora, 1986).
44. See e.g. Elliott *et al.*, 'Overt Sexuality in Advertising: A Discourse Analysis of Gender Responses', *Journal of Consumer Policy*, 18/2 (1995), 71–92.
45. G. Kress and T. van Leeuwen, *Reading Images: The Grammar of Visual Design* (London: Routledge, 1996).
46. P. Messaris, *Visual Persuasion: The Role of Images in Advertising* (Thousand Oaks, CA: Sage Publications, 1997).
47. L. Scott, 'The Bridge from Text to Mind: Adapting Reader-Response Theory to Consumer Research', *Journal of Consumer Research*, 21 (1994), 461–80.
48. See e.g. the work of R. Elliott, S. Eccles, and M. Hodgson, 'Re-Coding Gender Representations: Women, Cleaning Products, and Advertising's "New Man" ', *International Journal of Research in Marketing*, 10 (1993), 311–24; R. Elliott and M. Ritson, 'Practicing Existential Consumption: The Lived Meaning of

Sexuality in Advertising', *Advances in Consumer Research*, 22 (1995), 740–6; and D. G. Mick and K. Buhl, 'A Meaning-Based Model of Advertising', *Journal of Consumer Research*, 19 (1992), 317–38.

49. See S. Fish, *Is there a Text in this Class? The Authority of Interpretive Communities* (Cambridge, MA: Harvard University Press, 1980).
50. M. Ritson and R. Elliott, 'The Social Uses of Advertising: An Ethnographic Study of Adolescent Advertising Audiences', *Journal of Consumer Research*, 26/3 (1999), 260–77.
51. Mick and Buhl, 'A Meaning-Based Model of Advertising', *Journal of Consumer Research*, 19 (1992), 317–38.
52. Ritson and Elliott, 'The Social Uses of Advertising: An Ethnographic Study of Adolescent Advertising Audiences', *Journal of Consumer Research*, 26/3 (1999), 260–77.

Visit the Online Resource Centre that accompanies this book for additional resources to support the text: **www.oxfordtextbooks.co.uk/orc/percy_elliott4e/**

Advertising across Cultural Borders

Key concepts

1. There is evidence that consumer behaviour across cultures is converging in some markets, but also some suggestion that it is diverging with growing affluence.
2. The basic sources of different cultural assumptions include language, ethnicity, religion, and family organization.
3. Hofstede's dimensions of culture have been found to be useful in many studies, especially the individualism/collectivism dimension.
4. The differences between high-context versus low-context communication cultures are important for advertising using symbolic visuals.
5. A gradient of cross-cultural adaptation based on level of consumer involvement and emotion, and degree of cultural differentiation can be used to aid decisions about advertising strategies across cultures.
6. Cultural value systems can be used to segment the world into three basic clusters of countries.

The key issue in advertising across cultural borders relates to the extent to which consumers are really so alike around the world that advertisers can ignore differences and standardize their advertising behind global brands. This issue is still being keenly debated, but there is evidence that there is some convergence in consumer behaviour in some markets, and that guidelines can be developed to guide advertising management decisions about when and where global advertising may be appropriate and when it may not.

Convergence or Divergence

Back in 1983 Ted Levitt started the pursuit of a 'magic bullet' that would solve all of the difficulties of marketing across cultures: he claimed that consumers around the world were converging on a single set of needs and wants, so that all marketing from now on would just be global marketing. However, as de Mooij[1] points out, this claim in the *Harvard Business Review*[2] was based on the assumption that consumers make rational decisions and that they would converge on high-quality/low-priced global products rather than higher-priced customized products. This has proved to be an accurate prediction in technological product categories, e.g. computers, cameras, MP3 players, and to some extent motor cars, where brands are produced and advertised on a global basis. However, consumer behaviour in

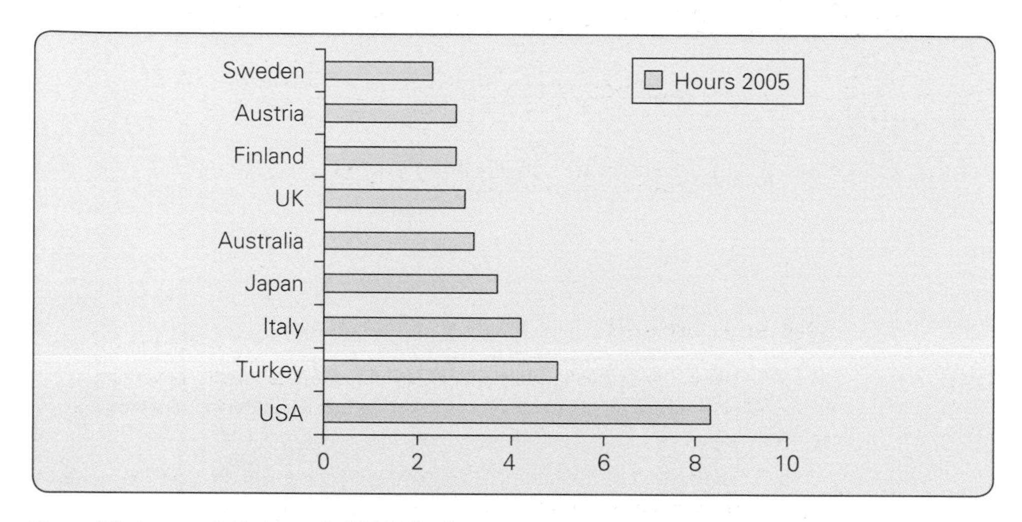

Figure 3.1 Average Daily Household TV Viewing

many areas instead of converging has diverged; just as many organizations are standardizing their marketing, so consumers are demanding localized products and services. For example, Coca-Cola's CEO, explaining his company's falling profits, said: 'We kept standardizing our practices, while local sensitivity had become essential to success.'[3] De Mooij[4] presents a convincing set of studies that demonstrate that consumer behaviour has converged in some areas, but in most areas has diverged. What seems to be happening is that, with increasing economic development, consumption of some products, such as TV sets, telephone main lines, computers, and cars, is converging in terms of levels of ownership per thousand population, but how they are actually used at the household level differs across countries. For example, see Fig. 3.1, which shows that, despite similar levels of TV ownership, the average US household watches nearly four times as much television as the Swedish household. In fact, de Mooij reaches the conclusion that 'As people become more affluent, their tastes diverge'.

But there is evidence to suggest that there is one particular global group with convergent tastes: the global teen market.[5] Sharing high involvement with music, media, sports, and communication, teens are seen as a global targetable group. However, the homogeneity of the group was contested by Moses,[6] who argued that not only are teens not alike worldwide, but they are also segmented into six value clusters that differentiate them globally and within specific countries. This large-scale study used elements of the cultural value theory of Schwartz[7] and this was also the conceptual base for another study,[8] which also identified six global segments and related these to global advertising strategy and media consumption. We will discuss this study later in the chapter. But, in order to understand the cultural dimensions of communication, we need to analyse the basic sources of culture and different cultural assumptions, the cognitive organization of cultural values, and the way in which these values are expressed in consumer behaviour. The fundamental elements of language, ethnicity, religion, and family organization structure cultural value systems that are then expressed in consumer behaviour. See Fig. 3.2.

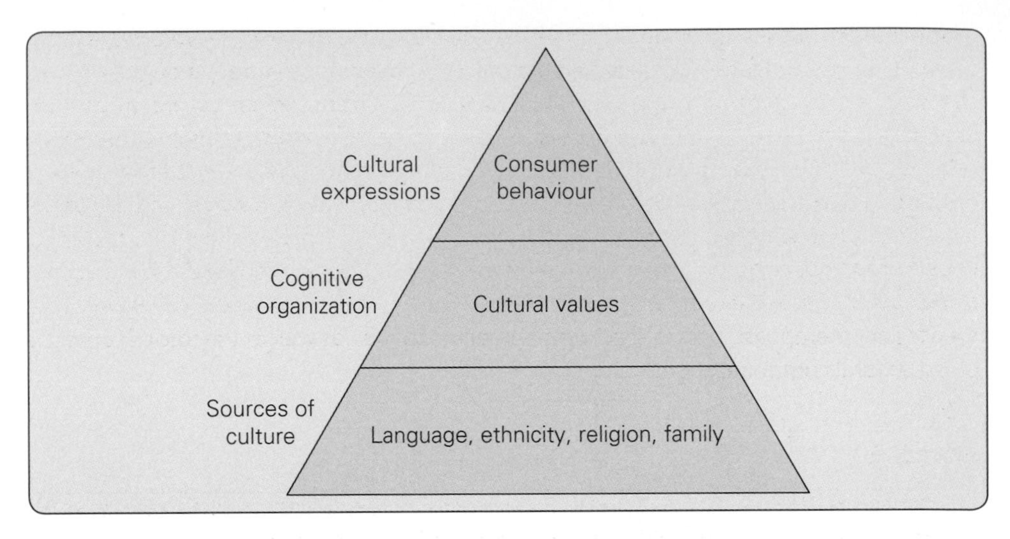

Figure 3.2 Culture, Values, and Consumer Behaviour

Basic Sources of Different Cultural Assumptions

The foundation for understanding the cultural dimensions of communication, as we see in Fig. 3.2, is built upon language, ethnicity, religion, and family. In many ways, they are interrelated, but at the heart is language. As language is acquired, it is influenced by the ethnicity, religion, and the family environment of a child; once language is formed, it influences a person's understanding of their own ethnicity, religion, and family. Each of these cultural dimension building blocks is briefly discussed below.

Language

The Sapir–Whorf hypothesis of linguistic relativity claims that language creates mental categories that organize how we perceive the world and construct reality:

> the real world is to a large extent built up on the language habits of the group. No two languages are ever sufficiently similar as to be considered as representing the same reality. We see and hear and otherwise experience very largely as we do because the language habits of our community predispose certain choices of interpretation. The worlds in which different societies live are distinct worlds, not merely the same world with different labels attached.[9]

The 'strong' claim that thought depends on language is disputed by some linguists, but not by neuroscientists, who generally believe that thought is dependent upon words. The key insight ('weak' claim) that language can influence ways of thinking has considerable empirical support.[10] The idea that the availability of words structures thought has been influential in the literature of politics and oppression: for example, in Orwell's *Nineteen Eighty-Four*, Newspeak has replaced standard English and thought is controlled by removing words so that what cannot be said cannot be done. In Elgin's *Native Tongue*, set in a future extreme patriarchal society, women develop a feminist language in secret in order to resist male oppression.

Somewhere between the linguistic and the novelistic, and of particular relevance to advertising, Lakoff and Johnson[11] analysed the power of metaphor to frame thought, demonstrating that metaphors are vital in creating meaning and thus influencing behaviour. The essence of metaphor is understanding and experiencing one kind of thing in terms of another. They use the example of the metaphor 'Argument is war' to demonstrate that this is not just linguistic usage, but also has real-world consequences on how we actually argue. Lakoff[12] has applied linguistic relativity to political analysis demonstrating that metaphor can be used to deceive and persuade. The influence of language on cultural differences will be discussed later in the chapter, in particular by reference to Watzlawick's[13] communication theory and its emphasis on analogue non-verbal modalities, as well as the role of context in cross-cultural communications.

Ethnicity

The rather broad term of ethnicity relates to a process of identification with an ethnic group and is intimately bound up with the social context in which a person grows up and matures.[14] This means that ethnicity involves a wide range of factors, being intimately concerned with the symbolic activities of language, customs, representations of the past, religious beliefs, and a sense of common origin.[15] However, ethnicity may not just be imposed and there is an implication that one of the choices inherent in a postmodern culture is a choice of which ethnic group to connect to. In fact, Bouchet[16] argues that postmodern ethnicity is a lifestyle choice, particularly for second- and third-generation immigrants. The importance of ethnicity for marketing involves the concept of ethnocentrism: 'the universal proclivity for people to view their own group as the center of the universe . . . the symbols and values of one's own ethnic or national group become objects of pride and attachment, whereas symbols of other groups may become objects of contempt.'[17] We will discuss the importance of considering levels of consumer ethnocentrism in the marketing of global brands later.

Religion

One of the most powerful influences on cultural values and consumer behaviour may be a function of religious beliefs. Taboos against beef for Hindus and pork and alcohol for Muslims obviously have a major influence on consumer behaviour in many areas of the world. Islamic beliefs against charging interest on loans create the need for specialist Islamic banking practices.

Family

The social organization of the family is closely linked with religion and varies widely around the world. In particular, the role of the extended family is pervasive in many cultures and takes many forms including the *baradari*, or joint family, which is a feature of Hinduism. The centrality of family and kinship relations is a core element in the cultural assumptions underlying collectivist cultures rather than individualistic cultures and we will explore this in detail later.

Cognitive Organization and Cultural Values

The seminal work on systematic differences in cultural values is that of Hofstede,[18] who originally identified four dimensions of culture based upon thirty years of quantitative research in seventy-two countries and in twenty languages: power distance, individualism/collectivism, uncertainty avoidance, and masculinity/femininity. This was later updated, and a fifth dimension added: long-term orientation.[19] Hofstede's definitions for these dimensions of culture are shown in Table 3.1.

In cultures characterized by power distance, organizations tend to be hierarchical and unequally accepted. Countries that score high on power distance include France and Mexico; the US is relatively low, and Denmark and Austria very low. Individualistic cultures tend to be task oriented, and verbal; more collectivist cultures are relationship oriented. Most Western cultures tend to be higher on individualism; Asian and Latin American cultures tend to be more collectivist. Uncertainty avoidance implies exactly what it says: people in some cultures are comfortable with a certain level of uncertainty; others hate it. Cultures that score high on the dimension include Germany and Japan, while low-scoring cultures include the UK and Scandinavian countries such as Sweden and Denmark. Anglo-Saxon cultures tend to score high in terms of masculinity, and Scandinavian cultures low.

The addition of the fifth dimension, long-term orientation, resulted from research into trying to find an explanation to Asian economic success. Originally labelled 'Confucian dynamism' because it included values of Confucian philosophy, it includes values of family, duty, hierarchy, and long-term perspective. Those scoring high on long-term orientation tend to have a sense of perseverance, and order relationships by status; low scorers have a focus on more short-term goals related to happiness. Most Asian countries, especially those with large Chinese populations, score high on long-term orientation, and Anglo-Saxon cultures low.

Table 3.1 Hofstede's Dimensions and Definitions

Power distance	'the extent to which less powerful members of a society accept and expect that power is distributed unequally'
Individualism/ collectivism	'people looking after themselves and their immediate families only versus people belonging to in-groups that look after them in exchange for loyalty'
Uncertainty avoidance	'the extent to which people feel threatened by uncertainty and ambiguity and try to avoid these situations'
Masculinity/femininity	'the dominant values in a masculine society are achievement and success; the dominant values in a feminine society are caring for others and quality of life'
Long-term orientation	'the extent to which a society exhibits a pragmatic future-oriented perspective rather than a conventional historic or short-term point of view'

Source: Adapted from M. de Mooij, *Global Marketing and Advertising: Understanding Cultural Paradoxes* (London: Sage, 1998).

High-Context versus Low-Context Communication Cultures

Hall[20] identified two different approaches to communication which he calls 'high context versus low context'. A high-context culture is one in which most of the information in a communication is either part of the context or internalized in the audience; very little is made explicit as part of the message, relying often on visuals and symbols. A low-context culture is characterized by explicit verbal messages carrying facts and data. Asian, Arab, and Mediterranean countries tend to be high-context cultures, and body language and non-verbal cues are essential to understanding the 'words' spoken. In low-context cultures such as Britain and the United States, the interpretation of spoken words is less dependent on non-verbal cues. In fact, serious misperceptions of meaning can occur when this is not taken into account. The important implications of this for advertising will be examined later, because there is evidence that advertising in high-context cultures makes much use of symbolic visuals.

This is very like Trompenaars'[21] distinction between neutral cultures in which feelings are not usually shown overtly, but are controlled, and affective cultures in which verbal and non-verbal displays of thought and feelings are the norm. These cultural differences in emotional expression have obvious implications for advertising.

Hall[22] makes an interesting distinction between cultures based upon assumptions about time, which he called 'monochronic versus polychronic' cultures. In monochronic cultures, time tends to be seen as limited, structured in a sequential linear fashion, whereas in polychronic cultures, time is experienced as unlimited and simultaneous.

Universal Cultural Values Systems

A theory that has gained much credence recently is that of Schwartz and Bilsky,[23] who maintain that all humans share a set of seven motivational values, which are differently combined in different cultures, and this has been validated across a number of countries. The seven values are shown in Fig. 3.3 and display some correlation with Hofstede's individualism/collectivism values.

This approach has been developed in a large-scale study by Chow and Amir[24] in thirty countries with a sample of over 25,000 people, which identified six value dimensions that form a universal structure of values. These six values and some of their typical contents are described in Table 3.2.

The weighting of the values varies markedly between countries: for example, Sweden is dominated by intimate values, whereas Saudi Arabia is dominated by devout values. This is illustrated for four countries in Fig. 3.4.

Importantly, this value structure has been used to develop a value segmentation model that has been related to global brands, which we will use to discuss implications for advertising management later in the chapter.

Cultural Differences and Values in Advertising

A number of studies have used content analysis to examine advertising executions from different cultural locations to explore the values portrayed and have compared them with elements of the theoretical value structures above. A comparison of Chinese and American TV

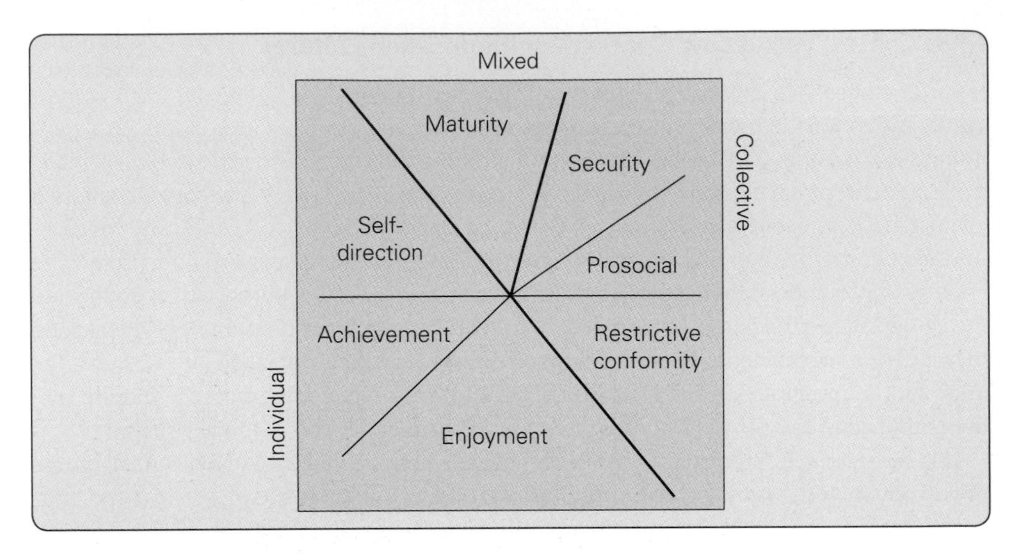

Figure 3.3 Universal Value Structure

Source: S. Schwartz and W. Bilsky, 'Toward a Theory of the Universal Content and Structure of Values: Extensions and Cross-Cultural Replications', *Journal of Personality and Social Psychology*, 58/5 (1990), 878–91.

Table 3.2 Content of Universal Value Dimensions

Striver	Fun-seeker	Creative	Devout	Intimate	Altruist
Power	Excitement	Beauty	Spirituality	Honesty	Preserving the environment
Status	Leisure	Fulfilling work	Tradition	Personal support	Justice
Ambition	Individuality	Self-esteem	Duty	Enduring love	Social responsibility
Material security	Pleasure	Freedom	Obedience	Authenticity	Equality
Public image	Live for today	Knowledge	Modesty	Friendship	Social tolerance

advertising[25] found that Chinese advertisements utilized the following cultural values more often than US advertisements: a soft-sell appeal, veneration of the elderly, group consensus, and status appeals. In contrast, the US advertisements used the following cultural values more frequently: a hard-sell appeal, individualism/independence, time orientation, and product merit. This finding of Chinese advertising being more consensual and family oriented is a common one across many studies about East Asian countries. Similar findings about traditional

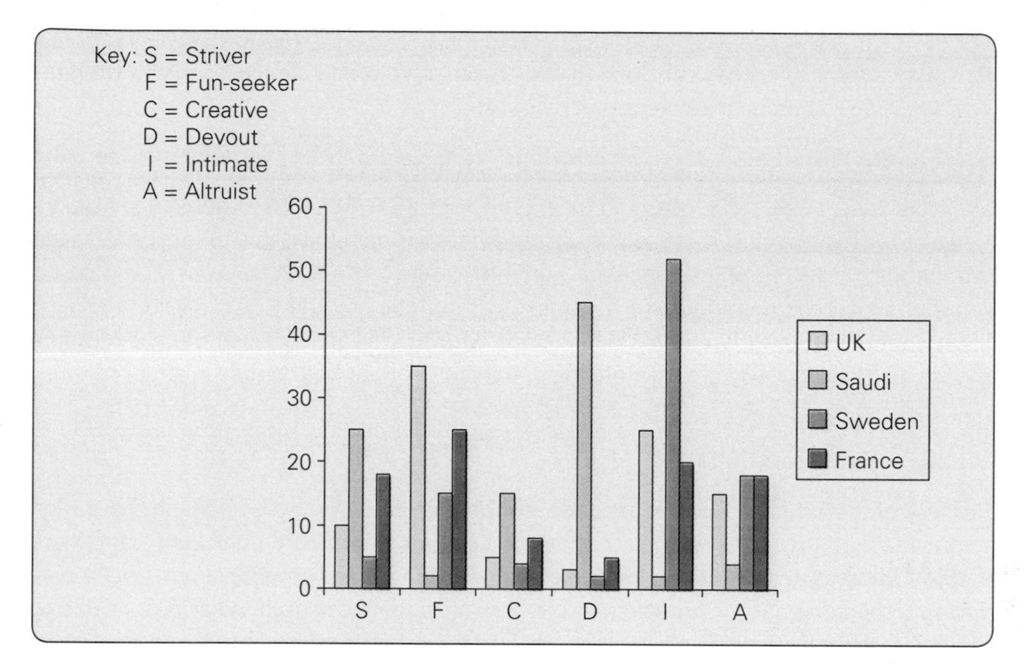

Figure 3.4 Distribution of Value Segments in Four Countries

Source: Adapted from S. Chow and S. Amir, 'The Universality of Values: Implications for Global Advertising Strategy', *Journal of Advertising Research*, September (2006), 301–14.

cultural values being expressed have also been found in comparisons between Arab and American advertising.[26] Less extreme differences have been found between the US and France and, despite a shared language, even between the US and UK.[27] However, with globalized communications, there are indications that traditional values are becoming less ubiquitous in some East Asian societies: for example, values of modernity and individualism are becoming prevalent in advertising aimed at younger, affluent Chinese people.[28]

Cultural Values and the Effectiveness of Executional Elements

Cultural values will inform how advertising is processed, and should be reflected in the way in which the message is constructed and executed. In this section we shall be looking at some executional elements that have been shown to depend upon cultural values for effectiveness.

Appeals

Matching appeals and arguments to cultural differences on the individualism/collectivism dimension demonstrates that culturally congruent appeals are most effective.[29] Collectivism and uncertainty avoidance are highly correlated, and it seems that high uncertainty avoidance leads to more positive response to loss-framed advertisements than to benefit-framed advertisements.[30] Similarly, utilitarian appeals performed better in a 'masculine' culture (US) than did 'image' appeals, but no difference was found in a 'feminine' culture (Taiwan).[31]

But even within Europe, audiences react differently to appeals[32] and to representations of female beauty.[33] So we can conclude that even across culturally similar countries we must pay attention to potential differences in responses.

The role of context (high versus low) has been found to influence audience responses to direct comparative advertising, which is more persuasive in low-context cultures.[34] But 'likeability' of executional techniques and their influence on purchase intentions varied across a range of five high-context Asian countries.[35] Another consideration is the distinction between rational-digital and emotional-analogue communication made by Watzlawick,[36] who points out that digital communication (low context) carries little emotion compared to analogue (high context). The implication is that brands wishing to emphasize emotional meaning should be especially careful to identify the dominant communication style in target cultures.

Visual Factors across Cultures

Because of the limitations of language use around the world, some global brands have tried to put an emphasis on visual rather than verbal elements in their communications, and there is some evidence that this tactic may be effective as long as the emotional portrayal is perceived to be authentic.[37] However, the role of context (high versus low) has been found to affect the response to the visual components of advertising. In high-context cultures such as Japan, Korea, and China, much more use is made of symbolic visuals and celebrity models as featured characters, while low-context cultures such as the US, UK, and Germany make more use of literal visuals.[38]

In processing colour, there appears to be both cross-cultural similarity and difference. For example, blue, green, and white are liked across cultures and share similar meanings. In contrast, black and red received high 'liking' ratings, yet their meanings were considerably different.[39] Visually complex advertising, such as television commercials, raises even more problems across cultures because the images used are not always universally interpreted in the same way, as viewers use culturally sited advertising knowledge and visual signs to interpret meaning.[40]

Learned, Cultural, and Biological Schemas

Up to this point we have been looking at general characteristics of culture and how they might affect advertising. But we can also look at the issue of advertising across cultural borders more specifically in terms of the knowledge and assumptions people will bring to bear on processing that advertising. In the execution of any advertising or promotion, it is important that the target audience immediately understands that the message is for them. It must quickly and easily 'resonate' with them, and the words and images used must be immediately understood in the way in which the advertiser intended. This will depend upon the schema used in processing the advertising, and in many cases that will be a function of culture.

In very broad terms, schemas represent categorical or general knowledge in a way that researchers in cognitive science found more useful than semantic networks. Kroeber-Riel[41] has suggested three levels of schema: learned, cultural, and biological. What this means is that in our memory we have some things we have learned that tend to be restricted to a particular group to which we belong (learned schema). Some memories are culturally determined, and are found in such things as the myths and arts of a culture (cultural schemas). These cultural and learned schemas are what is involved in the cultural values we have been talking about. But there are other things in memory that are there because we are human, and tend to rely upon deeply psychological responses that have a relatively strong impact upon behaviour *without* our conscious awareness (biological schemas).

This means that people may react to an image in terms of things they have learned to associate with a particular group or thing, their culture, or innate psycho-biological responses. Let us look at some examples of what we are talking about. If you are a real fan of a particular football team, certain associations or images linked to that team are likely to mean something very different to you than they do to others who are not fans of that team, and have not learned those same associations. We can all think of cultural stereotypes, but cultural schemas can be much more subtle. If a group of Eastern Europeans were to see a crowd of people all pushing in a mass to enter the just-opened doors of a theatre, it would seem perfectly normal. But if an English group were to observe this, they would be surprised at the seemingly unruly behaviour, because the English queue under these circumstances. There is not a 'correct' behaviour here; the response will depend upon cultural schemas.

The importance of what we have been discussing up to this point in the chapter is that cultural differences indeed imply distinct cultural schemas in place in memory. It is these common understandings that bind cultures, and provide the schemas that will be used in processing advertising messages (or any type of communication for that matter). Cultural schemas reflect genetic, as well as learned, factors. An interesting side bar here is the way in which we learn language. It is *strongly* informed by culture.

Words are made up of phonemes, which are the smallest distinguishable vocal utterances. Exposure to language as an infant establishes dedicated connections between auditory receptors and neurons in the auditory cortex, where each phoneme will have a specific site. Different languages are made up of different phonemes, and different numbers of phonemes. English has forty-three phonemes, but Hawaiian has only fifteen. This is significant because after a phoneme site is established (and this will be before the age of 1), people become functionally *deaf* to sounds not found in their native language.

Certain words in English, for example, cannot be 'heard', and so not processed, by the Japanese because certain phonemes in those English words are not found in Japanese. With hard work, it can be learned, but it is not easy. So, there are not only basic cultural differences to account for in terms of the knowledge and assumptions that make up a cultural schema, but also, for broadcast advertising, certain words may not even be 'heard' because of the phonemes involved in particular languages.

Whenever you are not certain that your target audience shares a common learned or cultural schema, or when using a multinational campaign across many cultures, the message should tap into biological schemas. This means using words and images that are associated in memory at a limbic level, universally understood because they are part of our evolutionary development as humans. These images should also tap into primary emotions, also universal across cultures.

Basically, these are reactions that in some way relate to latent survival responses. This is why almost everyone reacts to an infant with a warm, nurturing feeling, and with alarm to the high-pitched cry of a baby. Some very fascinating work by Jay Appleton[42] deals with this same idea. He has developed something he calls 'prospect and refuge theory' that suggests we respond to our environment in terms of both prospect and refuge. When humans first wandered the plains, they needed to be able to see out to the horizon (prospect). This provided a sense of opportunity, as well as ample warning of danger. Humans also needed a place to hide for security (refuge). Appleton argues that we still respond to our environment in these same ways, a response based upon biological schemas, and recent empirical studies support him.

The implication of this work is significant. When people are looking at advertising, they are *unconsciously* reacting to the visual environment depicted. If we want the target audience to feel secure, the visual image should be consistent with refuge; if the target audience is to feel a sense of opportunity, the image should be consistent with prospect. To be effective, advertising must be consistent with commonly shared learning or the cultural values of the target audience—or it must reflect a biological schema that is universally understood.

Brand Perceptions across Cultures

Just as we have seen that cultural values inform how advertising will be processed, culture will also be a factor in how brands are perceived. In this section we shall be looking at some key characteristics of brands that are culture dependent.

Credibility

The credibility of brands is a key factor in the information economics view of brand equity and this has been found to be consistently important in choice across a range of cultures.[43] However, the positive effect of brand credibility on choice is greater for consumers who rate high on collectivism (increasing perceptions of quality) or uncertainty avoidance (decreasing perceptions of risk).

Brand Personality

The basic approach is that human personality traits come to be associated with a brand and Aaker[44] demonstrated that five major factors summarized the traits that consumers attributed to a wide range of brands: sincerity, excitement, competence, sophistication, and ruggedness. Obviously, advertising is a major source of brand personality perceptions. Subsequent work has shown that personal meanings of brands vary across cultures. Indeed it has been shown that there are important boundary conditions for the generalizability of Aaker's brand personality model, because, when applied across different cultures, the five factors of brand personality have to be revised. In Japan and Spain, only three of the factors transferred from the US,[45] and similar results were found in Russia.[46]

Perceived Brand Globalness

There is some evidence that brands that have a 'global image' may gain some advantage through perceptions of prestige and product quality.[47] However, the effect is weaker for ethnocentric consumers. 'Globalness' can also be applied to positioning strategy in advertising in emerging global markets, in which it can be differentiated from local consumer culture positioning and foreign consumer culture positioning. It has been found to apply to meaningful percentages in TV advertisements across seven countries on three continents.[48]

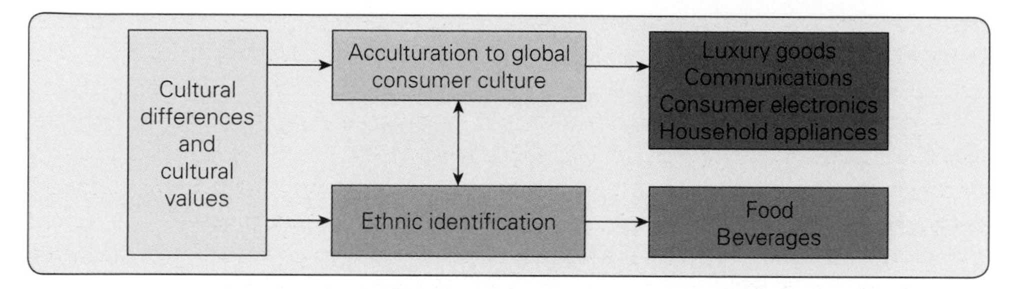

Figure 3.5 Global Consumer Culture, Ethnic Identification, and Consumer Behaviour

Source: Adapted from M. Cleveland and M. Laroche, 'Acculturation to the Global Consumer Culture: Scale Development and Research Paradigm', *Journal of Business Research*, 60 (2006), 249–59.

As globalization of marketplaces increases, the tension between global and local cultural influences impacts on brand perceptions and consumer behaviour. This tension can be expected to differentially affect product categories. For example, in food and beverages, ethnocentrism may have its strongest influence, while in luxury goods and electronics, acculturation to global consumer culture may be most powerful.[49] See Fig. 3.5.

When a brand integrates the foreign with the local to create a new culturally rooted product, this has been called 'creolization'.[50] This goes beyond the so-called 'glocal' brand, which merely adapts some parts of its marketing mix in a particular geographic region, and 'may fuse the outer elements of the foreign with the local to give birth to crossover products, images, or identities'.

Perceived Brand Localness

A brand's perceived localness creates unique values for the consumer because it enhances the brand's relevance and acceptability to the local market.[51] By retaining its own local identity and culture, it can 'out-localize' global brands by developing symbolic meanings of authenticity. Local brands across major European countries show higher levels of awareness, trust, and reliability than do international or global brands.[52]

Some Implications for Advertising Management

The major implication of the cultural factors we have discussed in this chapter is that advertising strategies can be located on a gradient of adaptation depending on the level of consumer involvement and emotional arousal in the product category, and the degree of cultural differentiation in the target marketplace. See Fig. 3.6.

We can take the basic structural components of the Rossiter–Percy grid, of level of involvement and positive or negative motivation (this is covered in detail in Chapter 9), and combine them with an evaluation of just how much cultural differentiation exists between the source culture (often US/European) and the target culture. At low levels of cultural differentiation and in product/market categories with low consumer involvement and emotional arousal, we can

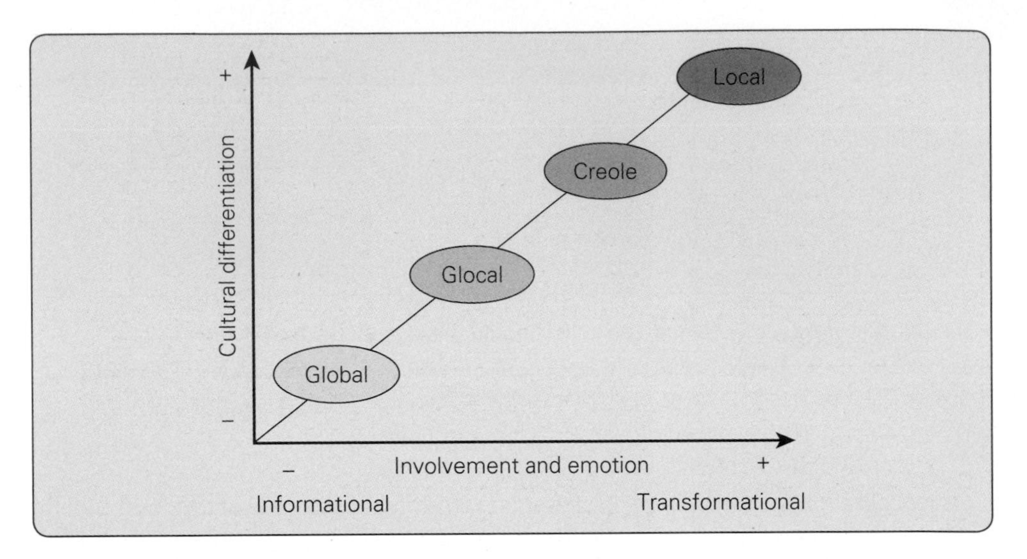

Figure 3.6 Advertising Strategies across Cultures

assume that a global campaign will be relatively effective, but as we ascend the gradient, we can maintain most of our global strategy, but may have to adapt our advertising to some local conditions and therefore our strategy should be 'glocal'. However, further up the gradient, we have the opportunity to work with consumers' culturally rooted interpretations to co-create a creolized version of a global strategy that makes full use of emotional responses (see Chapter 11). At the head of the gradient where cultural differentiation is at its peak, an essentially local brand and advertising strategy is required for optimum effectiveness.

Culture and Advertising Message Characteristics

Some general guidelines for advertising creative strategy can be drawn from cultural theory. For example, Zandpour and his colleagues[53] have linked four cultural characteristics with appeals used in advertising messages. This has been summarized in Fig. 3.7.

In highly *individualistic* cultures, advertising should be more likely to include information, and less likely to make use of psychological appeals or symbolic language and images. If what they call *uncertainty avoidance* dominates a culture, advertising appeals should be more likely to utilize arguments or imitation, and less likely to use drama, or symbolic language or images. When *power distance* is the primary cultural factor, psychological appeals will be more likely to be used, and argument and symbolic language and images less likely. Finally, when the dominant cultural factor in a market is *polychronic*, advertising is more likely to be informative and to use symbolic languages and imagery. Here advertising messages would be less likely to use argument or imitation.

Looked at another way, information is more likely to be used in advertising messages when individualism or polychronic is the dominant cultural factor; argument and imitation when uncertainty avoidance dominates; psychological appeals with power distance; and symbolic language and images when polychronic is the dominant cultural factor. In fact, this is the only

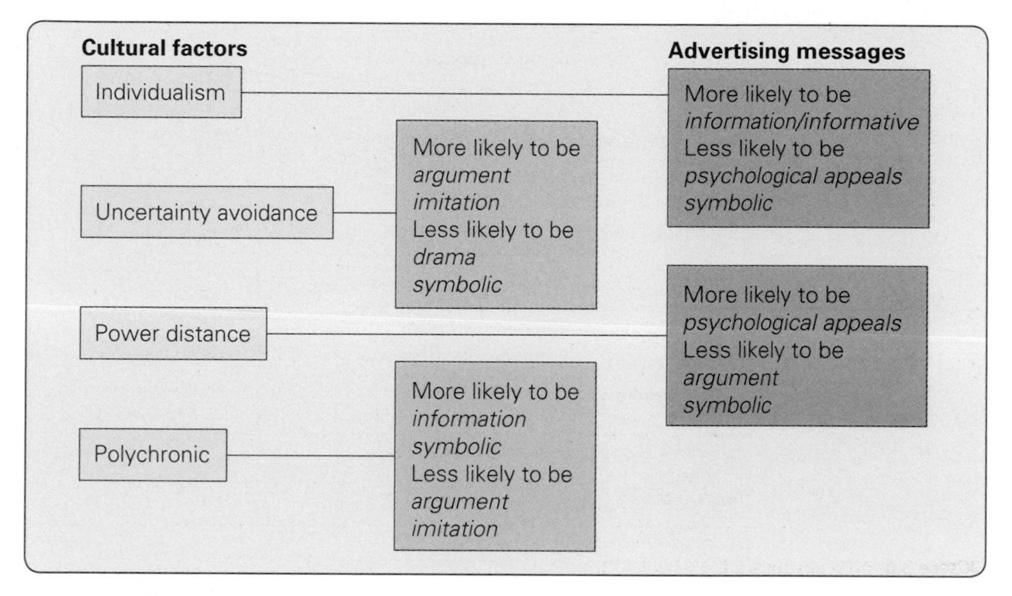

Figure 3.7 Culture and Advertising Message Characteristics

Source: Adapted from F. Zandpour *et al.*, 'Global Reach and Local Touch: Achieving Cultural Fitness in TV Advertising', *Journal of Advertising Research* (1994), 35–63.

context in which you are likely to find symbolic messages because they are unlikely with any other cultural characteristic.

Cultural Perspectives on the Self and Advertising

The role of the self has been located within the Western individualist tradition versus the Confucian collectivist tradition, and related to the consumption of luxuries, by Wong and Ahuvia,[54] and this has important implications for brand strategy and advertising for high-involvement brands in many East and South Asian countries. In particular, it suggests that while luxury brands in the West may be acquired primarily by the self and for the self, in Eastern Confucian culture, they are often acquired through gift exchange. It also suggests that the symbolic meaning of a brand in the West may be used to express self-image; in the East, it may be used to locate the individual in a social hierarchy. See Fig. 3.8.

It is clear that the same product can have very different meanings in different cultures, so that advertising for symbolic brands should be based on their cultural value and local consumption practices.

Global Value Segments and Advertising

Earlier in the chapter we discussed universal value systems and the existence of six value segments (see Table 3.2). These six segments have been mapped in relation to some global brands and two underlying dimensions emerged: self-direction versus conformity, and hedonism versus prosocial. See Fig. 3.9.

Western individualistic tradition

- Independent self
- Group & society exist to meet needs of individual
- Hierarchy is suspect
- Individuals should be judged on their own merits

Marketing implications

Western	E. Asian
Focus on the goods as	
Source of pleasure	Publicly visible
Luxuries acquired often	
By self for self	Through gift exchanges
Product choice often reflects	
Individual taste	Social norms
Symbolic goods often	
Express one's self	Locate individual in hierarchy
Brands are	
Potentially misleading indicators of quality	Important indicators of quality

E. Asian Confucian tradition

- Interdependent self
- Individual conforms to group & society
- Hierarchy is legitimate
- It is legitimate to judge individuals by their lineage

Figure 3.8 Conspicuous Consumption and Consumer Societies

Source: Adapted from N. Wong and A. Ahuvia, *Psychology and Marketing*, 15/5 (1998), 423–41. Reprinted by permission of John Wiley and Sons, Inc.

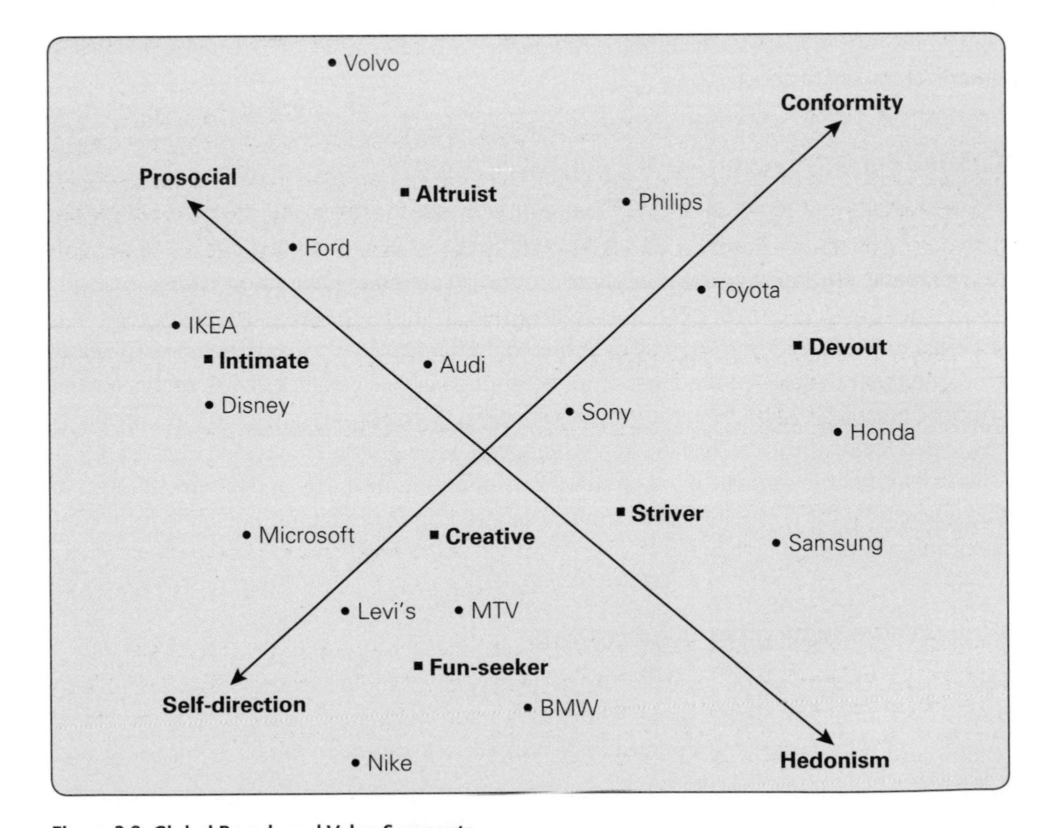

Figure 3.9 Global Brands and Value Segments

Source: Adapted from S. Chow and S. Amir, 'The Universality of Values: Implications for Global Advertising Strategy', *Journal of Advertising Research*, September (2006), 301–14.

According to Chow and Amir[55] there are perhaps only three basic clusters of countries: a modern and hedonistic cluster dominated by striver and fun-seeker ideals (US, UK, Canada, Australia, Germany); a more traditional and conformist cluster, but still high on striving (China, India, and South-East Asia); and a third cluster that tends to be more prosocial and altruistic (Sweden, Japan, Argentina). Locating a target country within these clusters can point to the dominant values and therefore appropriate advertising strategies.

Chapter summary

It should be obvious by now that cultural differences are not reducible to simple rules. The best we can provide are guidelines, which point to some key issues when thinking about advertising across cultural borders. We have suggested that global advertising may be appropriate in some limited situations, but there will always be a tension between efficiency and effectiveness. Unfortunately our state of knowledge of advertising across cultural borders is rather limited, but the best advertising is always likely to be rooted in 'truths' about consumers that are context dependent, and which draw on shared cultural understandings and common experiences. When there is any doubt, or if you know that cultural differences are likely to interfere with how a message will be processed, tapping into biological schemas can enable you to develop multinational campaigns that will avoid these problems.

Questions to consider

3.1 How might differences in ethnicity, religion, and family organization affect the marketing of financial services?

3.2 As traditionally collective societies become wealthier through globalization, might this lead to a change towards individualism? What might be the implications for advertising strategy?

3.3 Identify two creolized brands in your cultural location and consider how they have combined elements of the foreign with the local. Has this been carried through to their advertising strategies?

3.4 What are the implications for developing creative strategy in a polychronic versus a monochronic society?

3.5 What product categories are most likely to be affected by ethnocentrism? Why?

3.6 How might local brands of food and drink in your cultural location develop and communicate symbols of authenticity?

3.7 How might the advertising for a luxury brand in East Asia reflect cultural values?

Case study 3 Johnnie Walker—From Whisky Producer to Global Icon: The Story of 'Keep Walking'

In global terms, Johnnie Walker is one of the most famous and valuable brands. In 1999, however, Johnnie Walker was on red alert. In the three years since 1996, volume sales had dropped 14 per cent. The brief was twofold: to reverse the immediate fortunes of the brand in terms of sales, and to develop a future-proof, global communications strategy that would ensure sustained growth. Johnnie Walker had to be not just a whisky brand, but a global icon brand.

➜

→ Understanding Icon Brands

The world's most iconic global brands have three key things in common.

1. Fame—they are branded with a universally recognized icon that is symbolic of everything they stand for.
2. Resonance—they are founded on a set of fundamental human values.
3. Adoption—they take on meaning outside their product or service categories: they are used by people to express themselves and to signal their identification with those values.

The whisky category has always represented masculine success. We knew that to walk away from these values would have been to ignore whisky's fundamental role in consumers' lives. Global qualitative research was commissioned to understand the nature of masculine success at the dawn of the twenty-first century. We found an emerging trend: to men all around the world, success was no longer about material wealth or ostentatious displays of status; it was now an internal quality, about becoming a better man, having an unquenchable thirst for self-improvement. Progress was the insight with which Johnnie Walker would transcend market idiosyncrasies to inspire men throughout the world. In our language, the brand's key brand benefit, its statement of intent, became 'Johnnie Walker Inspires Personal Progress'.

We then needed to own this idea through a universally recognizable brand icon. The answer lay in the brand's history: the Striding Man. The Striding Man had been central to advertising that ran around the world for fifty years. Recently, however, he had been left out of communications—the brand's forgotten hero. We wanted him to be the standard behind which the revitalized brand would march. From this, the campaign idea was born, encapsulated in the powerful exhortation 'Keep Walking'.

There have been two main phases. At the first phase, central control and consistency was essential in ensuring that the idea was launched effectively. The same ads ran everywhere. At the second phase, the campaign was broadened to accommodate specific market needs and to achieve more diverse business tasks. This helped the local markets to feel a sense of ownership of the campaign.

From 2005, Formula 1 sponsorship represented significant investment for Johnnie Walker. Keep Walking enabled the brand to maximize this opportunity by linking the Striding Man with Formula 1 drivers—the Striding Men of their sport.

The Research International 'Brand Fame Rating' measures the percentage of consumers throughout the world who agree with the statement '[Brand logo] is one of the world's most famous logos'. In 2005, it showed the Johnnie Walker Striding Man to be equal to the world's most established icon brands, including Nike and Apple.

Source: This is an edited version of a case study submitted to the IPA Effectiveness Awards. The full case study can be found at ipa.co.uk or warc.com. © Copyright Institute of Practitioners in Advertising.

Edited by Elizabeth Mamali, PhD Researcher, Bath School of Management

Discussion questions

1. What would be the best way for competition to react to such an internationally successful advertising campaign?
2. Drawing upon the case, pick a brand of your choice and design a strategy to a turn it into an iconic brand.
3. Taking into account the value dimensions by Chow and Amir presented in Chapter 3, explain how the Keep Walking campaign does or does not appeal to each category.
4. Describe how the Johnnie Walker brand has achieved creolization through the Keep Walking campaign.

Further reading

M. de Mooij, *Consumer Behavior and Culture: Consequences for Global Marketing and Advertising* (London: Sage Publications, 2003)
Widens the analysis from advertising to a wide range of consumer behaviours across world markets.

F. Trompenaars and P. Woolliams, *Marketing across Cultures* (Oxford: Capstone Press, 2004)
Explores cross-cultural implications for other aspects of marketing management.

S. Craig and S. Douglas, *International Marketing Research* (Chichester: John Wiley, 2005)
Gives detailed guidance on carrying out advertising research across cultures and methods for increasing validity.

Notes

1. See M. de Mooij, 'Convergence and Divergence in Consumer Behaviour: Implications for Global Advertising', *International Journal of Advertising*, 22 (2003), 183–202.
2. See T. Levitt, 'The Globalization of Markets', *Harvard Business Review*, May–June (1983), 2–11.
3. *Financial Times*, 27 March 2000.
4. See de Mooij, 'Conveyance and Divergence in Consumer Behaviour', n.1.
5. See C. Walker, 'Genworld: The New Generation of Global Youth', *Admap*, 476 (2006), 15–19.
6. E. Moses, *The $100 Billion Allowance: Accessing the Global Teen Market* (Chichester: John Wiley, 2000).
7. S. Schwartz and W. Bilsky, 'Toward a Theory of the Universal Content and Structure of Values: Extensions and Cross-Cultural Replications', *Journal of Personality and Social Psychology*, 58/5 (1990), 878–91.
8. See S. Chow and S. Amir, 'The Universality of Values: Implications for Global Advertising Strategy', *Journal of Advertising Research*, September (2006), 301–14.
9. E. Sapir, 'The Status of Linguistics as a Science', *Language*, 5 (1929), 207–14.
10. See K. Au, 'Making Sense of Differences: Language, Culture and Social Reality', in S.H. Ng *et al.* (eds) *Language Matters: Communication, Culture and Identity* (Hong Kong: CU Press, 2004), 139–53.
11. G. Lakoff and M. Johnson, *Metaphors We Live By* (Chicago, IL: University of Chicago Press, 1980).
12. G. Lakoff, *Moral Politics* (Chicago, IL: University of Chicago Press, 1996).
13. P. Watzlawick *et al.*, *Pragmatics of Human Communication* (New York: Norton 1967).
14. See A. Epstein, *Ethos and Identity* (Chicago, IL: Aldene, 1978).
15. See J. Costa and G. Bamossy, 'Ethnicity, Nationalism and Cultural Identity', in J. Costa and G. Bamossy (eds), *Marketing in a Multicultural World* (London: Sage, 1995).
16. D. Bouchet, 'Marketing and the Redefinition of Ethnicity', in J. Costa and G. Bamossy (eds), *Marketing in a Multicultural World* (London: Sage, 1995), 68–104.
17. See T. Shimp and S. Sharma, 'Consumer Ethnocentrism: Construction and Validation of the CETSCALE', *Journal of Marketing Research*, 24 (1987), 280–9.
18. See G.H. Hofstede, *Culture's Consequences: International Differences in Work-Related Values* (Beverly Hills, CA: Sage, 1984), 32–3.
19. The updated version of Hofstede's dimensions are in his *Cultures and Organizations: Software of the Mind* (New York: McGraw-Hill, 1991), and his dimensions are fully discussed in an advertising context by Marieke de Mooij in her *Global Marketing and Advertising: Understanding Cultural Paradoxes* (London: Sage, 1998), 72–88.

20. E. Hall, *Beyond Culture* (New York: Doubleday, 1976).
21. F. Trompenaars and C. Hampden-Turner, *Riding the Waves of Culture* (Maidenhead: McGraw-Hill, 1997).
22. See Hall, *Beyond Culture*, n.20.
23. See Schwartz and Bilsky, 'Toward a Theory of the Universal Content and Structure of Values', n.7.
24. See Chow and Amir, 'The Universability of Values', n.8.
25. See C. Lin, 'Cultural Values Reflected in Chinese and American Television Advertising', *Journal of Advertising*, 30/4 (2001), 83–94.
26. See M. Kalliny and L. Gentry, 'Cultural Values Reflected in Arab and American Television Advertising', *Journal of Current Issues and Research in Advertising*, 29/1 (2007), 15–32.
27. See Z. Caillat, and B. Mueller, 'The Influence of Culture on American and British Advertising', *Journal of Advertising Research*, May/June (1996), 79–88.
28. See J. Zhang and S. Shavitt, 'Cultural Values in Advertisements to the Chinese X-Generation', *Journal of Advertising*, 32/1 (2003), 23–33.
29. See L. Teng and M. Laroche, 'Interactive Effects of Appeals, Arguments, and Competition across North American and Chinese Cultures', *Journal of International Marketing*, 14/4 (2006), 11–128.
30. See J. Readon, C. Miller, B. Foubert, I. Vida, and L. Rybina, 'Antismoking Messages for the International Teenage Segment: The Effectiveness of Message Valence and Intensity across Different Cultures', *Journal of International Marketing*, 14/3 (2006), 115–38.
31. See C. Chang, 'Cultural Masculinity/Femininity Influences on Advertising Appeals', *Journal of Advertising Research*, September (2006), 315–23.
32. See U. Orth, H. Koening, and Z. Firbasova, 'Cross-National Differences in Consumer Response to the Framing of Advertising Messages: An Exploratory Comparison from Central Europe', *European Journal of Marketing*, 41/3 (2007), 327–48.
33. See R. Bjerke and R. Polegato, 'How Well Do Advertising Images of Health and Beauty Travel across Cultures? A Self Concept Perspective', *Psychology and Marketing*, 23/10 (2006), 865–84.
34. See A. Shao, Y. Bao, and E. Gray, 'Comparative Advertising Effectiveness: A Cross-Cultural Study', *Journal of Current Issues and Research in Advertising*, 26/2 (2004), 67–80.
35. See K. Fam and R. Grohs, 'Cultural Values and Effective Executional Techniques in Advertising', *International Marketing Review*, 24/5 (2007), 519–38.
36. See Watzlawick *et al.*, *Pragmatics of Human Communication*, n.13.
37. See C. Young, 'The Visual Language of Global Advertising', *Admap* (2003), 438.
38. See D. An, 'Advertising Visuals in Global Brands' Local Websites', *International Journal of Advertising*, 26/3 (2007), 303–32.
39. See T. Madden, K. Hewett, and M. Roth, 'Managing Images in Different Cultures: A Cross National Study of Colour Meanings and Preferences', *Journal of International Marketing*, 8/4 (2000), 90–107.
40. See S. Bulmer and M. Buchanan-Oliver, 'Advertising across Cultures: Interpretations of Visually Complex Advertising', *Journal of Current Issues and Research in Advertising*, 28/1 (2006), 57–70.
41. The work of Kroeber-Riel represents perhaps the most productive research into understanding the effects of visual imagery in advertising. Unfortunately, much of his work is not available in English, including his important book on pictorial communication, *Buldkommunikation* (Munich: Vahlen, 1993). However, an introduction to his ideas on emotional elements in advertising can be found in W. Kroeber-Riel, 'Non-Verbal Measurements of Emotional Advertising Effects', in J. Olson and W.K. Sentis (eds), *Advertising and Consumer Psychology*, iii (New York: Praege, 1986).

42. See Jay Appleton, *The Symbolism of Habitat: An Interpretation of Landscape in Art* (Seattle, WA: University of Washington Press, 1990), and *The Experience of Landscape*, rev'd edn (Chichester: John Wiley and Sons, 1996).
43. See T. Edrem, J. Swait, and A. Valenzuea, 'Brands as Signals: A Cross-Country Validation Study', *Journal of Marketing*, 70 (2006), 34–49.
44. J. Aaker, 'Dimensions of Brand Personality', *Journal of Marketing Research*, 34 (1997), 347–56.
45. See J. Aaker, V. Benet-Martinez, and J. Garolera, 'Consumption Symbols as Carriers of Culture: A Study of Japanese and Spanish Brand Personality Constructs', *Journal of Personality and Social Psychology*, 81/3 (2001), 492–508.
46. See M. Supphellen and K. Grønhaug, 'Building Foreign Brand Personalities in Russia: The Moderating Effect of Consumer Ethnocentrism', *International Journal of Advertising*, 22 (2003), 203–26.
47. See J. Steenkamp, R. Batra, and D. Alden, 'How Perceived Brand Globalness Creates Brand Value', *Journal of International Business Studies*, 34 (2001), 53–65.
48. See D. Alden, J. Steenkamp, and R. Batra, 'Brand Positioning through Advertising in Asia, North America and Europe: The Role of Global Consumer Culture', *Journal of Marketing*, 63 (1999), 75–87.
49. M. Cleveland and M. Laroche, 'Acculturation to the Global Consumer Culture: Scale Development and Research Paradigm', *Journal of Business Research*, 60 (2006), 249–59.
50. See K. Hung, S. Li, and R. Belk, 'Glocal Understandings: Female Readers' Perceptions of the New Woman in Chinese Advertising', *Journal of International Business Studies*, 38 (2007), 1034–51.
51. G. Ger, 'Localizing in the Global Village: Local Firms Competing in Global Markets', *California Management Review*, 41/4 (1999), 64–83.
52. See I. Schuiling and J. Kapferer, 'Real Differences between Local and International Brands: Strategic Implications for International Marketers', *Journal of International Marketing*, 12/4 (2004), 97–112.
53. F. Zandpour *et al.*, 'Global Reach and Local Touch: Achieving Cultural Fitness in TV Advertising', *Journal of Advertising Research* (1994), 35–63.
54. N. Wong and A. Ahuvia, 'Personal Taste and Family Face: Luxury Consumption in Confucian and Western Societies', *Psychology and Marketing*, 15/5 (1998), 423–41.
55. See Chow and Amir, 'The University of Values', n.8.

Visit the Online Resource Centre that accompanies this book for additional resources to support the text: **www.oxfordtextbooks.co.uk/orc/percy_elliott4e/**

Part 2

Planning Considerations

What it Takes for Successful Advertising and Promotion

Key concepts

1. For any type of persuasive communication to work, McGuire has identified six behavioural steps an individual must complete.
2. The difficulty is that these six steps reflect compounding probabilities, which means that *all six steps* must occur for communication to be effective.
3. For advertising and promotion, these six steps may be thought about in terms of a communication response sequence with exposure to the message, processing of the message, creating the desired communication effect, and the target audience taking action.
4. Strategic planning for advertising and promotion must take the communication response sequence into account to be successful.

Now that we have begun to get some idea of what advertising and promotion are all about, it is time to turn our attention to how advertising works. The first step in learning just how advertising and promotion are meant to communicate a specific message to a particular group of consumers is to understand the various responses we must have to the message if it is to be successful.

If you were to ask most people, even most people involved with advertising, what the function of advertising is, almost everyone would say that advertising's job is to 'sell' a product. While ultimately it is true that advertising should lead to sales (or some other behavioural response, depending on the message—for example, taking cans to a recycling centre or not drinking when driving), rarely is this the *specific objective* of a single advert or advertising campaign. Nevertheless, a marketer is unlikely to spend money for long on advertising if it does not in the end lead to more sales, and eventually more profit to the company.

Our point here is that advertising in and of itself is rarely meant to have a direct effect on sales. Rather, it usually initiates a series of responses on the part of the consumer that, if successful, will *lead* to sales. With promotion, of course, sales is the immediate objective.

The Communication Response Sequence

Some time ago William J. McGuire developed a theory of attitude change, and over the years it has been applied to advertising.[1] If you stop to think of it, more often than not advertising messages deal with the maintenance or changing of attitude. In fact, as we have already mentioned, *brand attitude* is always a communication objective. This being the case, we have a great deal to learn about effective communication from attitude-change theory. According to McGuire's notion of attitude change, there are six behavioural steps through which the information contained in any persuasive message (advertising and promotion in our case) must pass—something he called an information processing paradigm. At each of these steps, if the message is to be successful, there must be a positive response. The important point here is that if we have failure at *any* of these six behavioural response steps, the communication will not be successful.

McGuire argues that, for any persuasive message to be successful, obviously, the message must first be *presented* to the target audience. Once the target audience has had the opportunity of seeing or hearing the message, the next step required is that they *pay attention* to the message. Once the target audience has paid attention to the message, it is necessary for them to *comprehend* what is in the message, correctly understanding the conclusions being urged and, to some extent, the points being offered in support of the conclusion. Now that the target audience understands the message, for the message to be successful, the target audience must *yield* to the arguments in the message. Next, assuming that we are not asking for an immediate response (for example, to pick up the phone and order the promoted product straight away), the target audience must *retain* the arguments in the message and the fact that it has yielded to them or accepted them, and intends to behave positively as a result. Finally, if the message is ultimately successful, the target audience will in fact *behave* as urged by the message.

A critical point in understanding this sort of hierarchical model (that is, one in which each step is necessary, and must occur in the order presented) is that it reflects *compounding probabilities*. Let us suppose that McGuire is correct in his assessment that six behavioural steps are required for a persuasive message to be successful. If that is the case, the probability of someone actually going out and buying a product as the result of an advertising message will be:

$$P(p) \times P(a) \times P(c) \times P(y) \times P(r) \times P(b)$$

where:
$P(p)$ = probability of being presented the message
$P(a)$ = probability of paying attention to the message
$P(c)$ = probability of comprehending the message
$P(y)$ = probability of yielding to the message
$P(r)$ = probability of retaining the intention
$P(b)$ = probability of behaving

Given a rather optimistic likelihood of 50 per cent of a target audience responding positively to each of the six behavioural steps, the overall probability of an actual purchase would be less than 2 per cent (0.50 × 0.50 × 0.50 × 0.50 × 0.50 × 0.50 = 0.0156). What this arithmetic exercise underscores is the very difficult job one is confronted with when trying to communicate effectively. Everything must work, and, even when it does, you cannot expect to see great changes in consumer behaviour as a direct result of advertising or promotion.

While McGuire's model was designed to explain how communication 'works' from a psychological standpoint, clearly it closely parallels what we know must happen if advertising and promotion are to work. For advertising and promotion to be effective, we must have exposure to the message, processing of the message, the correct communication effect, and target audience action.

Responding to Advertising and Promotion

The very first step that is necessary in order for advertising or promotion to be successful is for the prospective consumer to be *exposed* to the message. This means that it must be placed somewhere that the prospective buyer can see, read, or hear, as appropriate. The opportunity for exposure to the message takes place through media of one kind or another. Exposure alone, however, is not sufficient. The prospective buyer must next *process* (respond to) one or more elements in the advertising or promotion if it is to have an effect. Processing of the message consists of immediate responses to the various elements in the advert or promotion (the words and pictures). First must come attention, then learning—and, in some cases, as we shall see in later chapters, acceptance. Emotional responses will also be a part of processing.

The immediate responses to advertising and promotion must lead to a more permanent response; importantly, this permanent response must be associated with the brand or whatever other subject may be the object of the message, such as a company's image or a particular service. These more permanent, brand-connected responses are the *communication effects* that were introduced in Chapter 1: the two universally necessary communication effects of brand awareness and brand attitude, plus category need and brand purchase intention.

If the advertising or promotion message has been correctly processed, the resulting communication effect associated with the brand will lead to a particular response when a member of the target audience decides whether or not to take *action* as a result of the message, such as purchasing the brand. More broadly, this is called buyer behaviour, although, in an advertising context, we are generally seeking a response from a particular segment of the market that is known as the target audience. For example, if you are the manager of a company that manufactures concrete paving blocks, you might want to use advertising specifically 'targeted' to architects and builders whom you want to consider using your pavers in their designs and buildings.

Exposure corresponds to McGuire's presentation step; *processing* encompasses both the attention and comprehension steps of McGuire's model; *communication effects* encompass both the yielding and retention steps; and *target audience action* corresponds to McGuire's behaviour step (see Table 4.1).

As McGuire has remarked, these sequences are just common sense. Our extension of his work also makes good common sense in understanding advertising and promotion. If you do not see the advertising or promotion, it has no opportunity of working. If you do not process the message, there can be no effects, or if you process the message incorrectly, you do not achieve the desired effect, If the correct communication effect and response both follow, then target audience action will result. While Rossiter and Percy provide an interesting argument for referring to these four essential steps as a 'buyer response sequence',[2] we like to think of them as *communication* response steps.

Table 4.1 How the Communication Response Sequence Compares with McGuire's Information Processing Paradigm

Communication response sequence	Information processing paradigm
Exposure	Presented
Processing	Attention comprehend
Communication effects	Yield retain
Target audience action	Behave

Following through an actual example of what we mean here should help you to see why these four steps are necessary for advertising or promotion to be successful. Exposure, processing, communication effects, and target audience action are steps through which you yourself go when buying a product as a result of having seen or heard some advertising or promotion for it, even if you do not associate the behaviour with the advertising or promotion. Let us think about a campaign for, say, Nescafé coffee.

Exposure. Assuming that you watch TV even occasionally, you have probably been *exposed* to one or more commercials for Nescafé. The Nestlé Company runs a fairly heavy TV media campaign for this brand, along with print advertising and promotion.

Processing. If you were exposed to the advertising, sooner or later you probably paid attention to at least some parts of at least one of the commercials, or saw one of the print adverts. In other words, you *processed* the Nescafé advertising in some fashion, even if it was simply noting the brand name.

Communication effects. If you have learned the brand name 'Nescafé' from the advertising, and remembered what the brand's package looks like, you have responded to one of the core *communication effects*, brand awareness. If you have also formed an opinion for or against Nescafé, you have responded to the second core communication effect, brand attitude. Brand awareness plus a favourable brand attitude will largely determine whether or not you have actually tried the brand.

Target audience action. The ultimate target audience *action* for Nescafé is purchase. If you have purchased Nescafé, then the advertising has no doubt influenced you positively through the first three steps, leading to a positive behavioural response.

But, as we have already discussed, advertising is rarely responsible for purchase in and of itself. The rest of the marketing mix must contribute too: product performance, such as the coffee's taste (especially important for repeat purchase following trial of the brand); price, assuming that the price is competitive with other coffee brands; distribution, assuming that you can find the brand where you shop; and other forms of promotion, such as coupons or favourable comments from your friends. But the advertising undoubtedly has played a large part, especially if you were not previously aware of the brand.

Repetition and Response to Advertising and Promotion

Advertising in most cases must repeatedly influence this process in order to initiate trial and to maintain repeated purchases of a brand, or to encourage response to a promotion. The one exception to this repetition or 'recycling' of the four steps is direct response advertising. With direct response advertising (which is a special case of promotion because the objective is immediately to action), the target audience goes through the sequence once, then terminates with action in the form of a single purchase. However, as you might imagine, most advertising tasks require repetition. For example, you may have had a number of opportunities to be exposed to advertising for a brand before you finally paid attention and processed the message sufficiently for the communication effects (probably brand awareness and brand attitude) to work and be strong enough for you actually to try a brand for the first time.

After you have purchased a brand for the first time, the advertiser obviously wants you to purchase it again and become a regular user. This generally requires repeated exposure to the advertising. You now have direct experience with the brand, which will affect your exposure, processing, and communication effects the next time around. This is especially true of brand attitude, which is now being influenced by experience. If you liked the product, positive brand attitudes can develop or be reinforced. But if you disliked it, this negative experience would probably prevent positive processing of future messages, leading to negative communication effects such as declining brand awareness and a change to a negative brand attitude. While, in an ideal world, one could hope that, after sufficient numbers of people have formed positive brand attitudes, continued advertising would be unnecessary, this ideal is rarely reached. Not many brands can survive without advertising for any extended period. Communication effects become weaker or are interfered with by advertising and promotion for competing brands. Once this happens, the advertiser must begin again, creating new advertising that must be exposed to the target audience, then working through the full sequence.

To summarize, there are four steps in a communication response sequence that must be satisfied before advertising and promotion can be successful. First, the target audience must be *exposed* to the advertising. Next, they must *process* the information. We will deal with just how the mind processes information at some length in Chapter 11. After processing, there must be a *communication effect*. Finally, the target audience must take *action*. If any one of these steps is not influenced positively by the advertising or promotion, and reinforced over time, the advertising simply will not work. And if the advertising or promotion does not work here, it obviously cannot contribute to sales and market share, or to profit. All four steps in the sequence must be successfully accomplished if sales, market share, and profit are to increase.

Planning Overview

Careful planning is critical to the success of any venture, and understanding what processes are involved obviously leads to better plans. It is important to understand that overall advertising and promotion planning must correspond to what it takes for advertising and promotion to be successful—the four steps we have just reviewed. After a company sets profit objectives, which are based upon a certain level of sales or market share, a marketing plan lays out how marketing communication efforts will help the company to meet those objectives (*action* sought by the

Table 4.2 Planning Sequence versus Communication Response Sequence

Planning sequence		Communication response sequence
Step one	Target audience action	Step four
Step two	Communication effects	Step three
Step three	Processing	Step two
Step four	Exposure	Step one

target audience) and the marketing communication plan what the best message for the brand will be (*communication effects* needed) to maximize those marketing efforts. From the marketing communication plan, the company and its advertising agency are able to develop a positioning and creative strategy to execute that message (to ensure *processing* of the message), and finally a media strategy (to ensure *exposure* to the message) to deliver the message.

Interestingly, you will notice that, after the marketing objectives have been set, the *planning* sequence is the reverse of the sequence needed for advertising and promotion to be successful.[3] A marketer must begin by thinking of the action to be taken by the target audience. Next, they must consider the communication effects needed from the advertising or promotion to help to facilitate that action. Then they must be concerned with how the message will be processed in order to ensure those effects, and finally where to place the advertising and promotion to optimize the likelihood of reaching the target audience (see Table 4.2). Each of these planning steps is discussed next.

Step One: Objectives for Target Audience Action

Once the overall marketing objectives are set, the manager must decide where, from among all of the people in a market, the brand can expect to find the greatest likelihood of brand trial and usage. This will form the core of the target audience for advertising and promotion. This group of people, however, will not be particularly easy to identify, at least if we are looking for the best group possible. What we want are people who will respond to the advertising and promotion because they recognize something in it that connects, in their mind, the attributes of the advertised product with particular benefits that satisfy the reason or reasons why they are interested in products from that particular category in the first place.

Depending upon the actual target audience chosen, the action desired will usually be trial for the brand or repeat purchase. For non-users of the brand, the behavioural objective would quite naturally be trial. But for those who have tried the product, we would want to encourage continued or more frequent repeat purchase of the brand. This issue will be dealt with in much more detail in Chapter 6.

Step Two: Communication Effects

Advertising and promotion work only if they can stimulate a communication effect that will lead to action. The manager, in this second step of planning, must determine how to position the brand in the communication and which communication effects need to be established in the mind of the target audience in order to cause them to take action. Once the manager has determined the appropriate communication effects, they become communication *objectives* for the advertising and promotion. Those communication objectives are selected from options within the four basic communication effects already introduced: category need, brand awareness, brand attitude, and brand purchase intention. Chapter 9 will cover this subject in depth.

Returning to our Nescafé example, when the brand was first launched, the brand manager probably set a number of communication objectives for Nescafé advertising and promotion.

1. Since Nescafé was the original 'freeze-dried' version of soluble coffee (or 'instant'), the introductory advertising probably tried to stimulate interest in the soluble category as a whole, since Nescafé would benefit from an increase in primary demand for soluble coffee (category need).
2. Potential consumers of Nescafé would also need to learn the new product's name, and learn to recognize the product on the supermarket shelf (brand awareness).
3. Further, before trying Nescafé, potential new consumers would have to develop at least a tentatively favourable opinion of the brand (brand attitude), perhaps by positioning it against the belief that freeze drying improves the taste of soluble coffee.
4. Also, a definite intention to try it at the first opportunity would no doubt be a likely advertising communication objective (brand purchase intention), along with a promotion to increase the likelihood of following through on the intention.

Step Three: Processing

Once the communication objectives for a campaign have been determined, the next step in planning is to devise (if in an advertising agency) or to approve (if the advertiser) a creative strategy that will achieve the communication objectives. This involves designing specific advertising and promotions that not only meet the communication objective set in the marketing plan, but also maximize its likelihood of then being *processed* by the target audience in the intended manner to produce the desired communication effects. Since it is impossible to know beforehand if a new advert or promotion will accomplish these very important goals, that advert or promotion should be tested.

At this point it is important to understand that there are many possible ways in which to position a brand in marketing communication and to achieve a particular communication effect, something we shall be taking up in Chapter 8. Positioning will inform communication strategy, which reflects the desired communication effects. Let us return to our Nescafé example. If brand attitude was the primary communication objective, Nescafé's advertising agency may have proposed positioning the brand on the freeze-dried attribute and its taste advantage. Or the focus could have been on the same freeze-dried attribute, but its emphasis directed towards 'fresh' as a benefit. Either of these positionings (or many others) could probably have been capable of delivering the required communication objective. We would hope that the actual positioning and communication strategy that was pursued was chosen

competitors', our sales would increase at our competitors' expense without running into problems with the consumers' self-imposed limits. Consumers would still be buying the same amount, but they would be buying more of our brand. Similarly, the target audience selected will directly affect the communication strategy, because of its particular behaviour and attitudes. If the wrong communication strategy is chosen, this would not mean the target audience strategy was wrong. Advertising based upon the wrong communication strategy would be unlikely to satisfy the goals of the marketing plan, but this would not be the fault of the target audience selected. In the same way, the media strategy developed will be set based upon the target audience and communication strategy. Each step is sequential, guiding the decisions made at the next step. But a mistake made at one step does not affect the *planning* that has gone before.

So, while both the communication response sequence and the strategic planning process are hierarchical (remember, that is where one step must precede another), because of the starting point for the four-step communication response sequence, there are no alternatives to the successful execution of the desired response at each step in the sequence. On the other hand, there is room for adjustment in the planning process.

Relating Objectives and Goals to the Communication Response Sequence

In the marketing plan certain objectives will be set for the brand, and the manager must be able to relate these brand objectives to his or her advertising and promotion planning. On the face of it, there are certain obvious reasons for this. With clearly stated objectives, it is possible to coordinate advertising and promotion programmes with the plans of other company units. For example, financial planning and production plans should be matched with the advertising expectations of the brand. If we know our product sells significantly better at certain times of the year, advertising strategy will be geared to those peak selling periods. In terms of cash flow for the company, more money will be required during these periods for marketing expenses, as well as for raw materials and perhaps labour as well. Production will need to plan for greater manufacturing demands for the brand in terms of raw materials, labour, and time. With written objectives, all of the managers involved will know what the demands upon the company will be at any given time.

These written objectives are important for the advertising agency as well. If everyone working on an account—account service, creative, media, planning—knows what the advertiser's objectives are for the brand, there is less opportunity for misunderstandings between the agency and the client advertiser, or between groups within the agency. A third advantage to having written objectives is that they provide something against which both the advertiser and the agency can evaluate the brand's performance.

A distinction often made in marketing management, and an important distinction, is the difference between *objectives* and *goals*. In the broadest sense, objectives define the general ends sought by the company, while goals are objectives that have very specific definition. For example, a reasonable objective for a brand might be generally to increase share among a particular target market, while a goal would be specifically to increase share from 15 to 18 per cent in the

Table 4.4 Setting Goals and Objectives Relative to the Communication Response Sequence for Individual Adverts versus Campaigns

	Setting goals	Setting objectives
Exposure	Adverts	Campaign
Processing	Adverts	Campaign
Communication effects	Campaign	Adverts
Target audience action	Campaign	Adverts

next year. Generally speaking, most companies will have specific goals of one sort or another when they put together their marketing plan. After all, without some estimate of likely sales, not only will it be difficult to determine what money will be available for marketing expenditures, but also the company will not be able to plan effectively for things such as production schedules, raw material acquisition, and so on. If only the vague objective of increasing sales has been adopted, it should be clear that important planning decisions will be very difficult, if not impossible, to formulate.

Having said all this, we must ask ourselves if it is also important to set goals rather than objectives for advertising as well. The answer is that 'it depends'. The reason it depends is that for advertising to be effective it must successfully negotiate each of the four steps in the communication response sequence, and each step makes different demands in terms of planning. Additionally, rarely are we considering the effect of a single advertisement or commercial. We will be much more likely to be considering a campaign made up of several adverts, as well as other marketing communication. In fact, we can actually look at this question of goals versus objectives for each of the four steps we have been talking about as depending upon whether we are considering a single ad, or an entire campaign. Let us now examine whether or not goals or objectives are more appropriate for each of the steps (see Table 4.4).

Exposure. The first step is exposure and here it makes sense to set *goals* for an individual ad, but only objectives for a campaign. Why? Think about what we are attempting to do in this first step. We have been given a target audience definition and, as we plan for and buy media, we estimate that a particular advert that is a part of the plan will reach a certain percentage of the target audience. Goals for this percentage can and should be set. But over the course of the entire media planning period, many adverts will run, and run in different media and various media vehicles (for example, a specific programme or magazine). As a result, more broadly based objectives are made, such as maximizing reach or frequency. We will learn more about these important terms in Chapter 10. For now, simply put, *reach* means the percentage of the target audience likely to be exposed to a message, and *frequency* the number of times that these people will have the opportunity to be exposed.

Processing. At the second step, we again find that it is appropriate to set goals for an individual advert, and objectives for a campaign. The reason here is that while we can set goals for message processing, for example that 45 per cent of our target audience should learn the brand's primary benefit as a result of the advertising, it would be much more difficult to think of specific goals for an entire campaign. Remember, promotion and other types of marketing communication may be involved in the campaign. Instead, more broadly based objectives make sense here, such as increasing overall attention to our advertising as a whole.

Communication effects. At the third step, goals should be set for the overall campaign rather than any specific advert within the campaign. An appropriate goal for communication effects might be to raise overall favourable attitude to our brand from 4.0 to 4.5 on a five-point attitude scale (where 5 means very favourable). Communication effects are meant to result from a campaign, not from a single advert or commercial within the campaign. Objectives for a single advert might be something like helping to increase positive brand attitude.

Action. To complete the four steps, goals should be set for target audience action only at the campaign level, and not for any single advert within the campaign. For example, a goal for the campaign might be to increase usage of our brand from 50 to 56 per cent, while the objective for each advert is to contribute to this goal. However, individual goals should be set for specific promotions.

To summarize our discussion of goals and objectives as related to the communication response sequence, we have seen that objectives are set at every level of planning, but goals are set only where they make sense and can be measured. This means that goals are set for an individual advert's contribution to exposure and message processing, and for a campaign when considering communication effects and target audience action.

Chapter summary

This chapter has introduced the communication response sequence of four behavioural steps that are required for advertising to be successful: exposure, processing, communication effects, and action. We have then compared these steps with the sequential steps of strategic planning, and emphasized the importance of relating brand objectives and goals to the buyer response sequence.

Questions to consider

4.1 Why is it so important to understand McGuire's information processing paradigm?

4.2 How does the communication response sequence help the manager to better understand what is needed for effective strategic planning in communication?

4.3 What are the major benefits of sequential planning?

4.4 What is the role of the marketing plan in strategic planning for advertising and other marketing communication?

4.5 Why is it important to understand the difference between goals and objectives in strategic planning for advertising and other marketing communication?

Case study 4 De Beers—Billion-Dollar Ideas

De Beers is one of the most famous names in diamonds. Diamonds are precious because of their beauty, history, and cultural associations; however, this is also a threat because they have no functional role. Like all products without a tangible benefit, consumers can abandon them in difficult times. Furthermore, the new millennium brought unprecedented competition in the supply of rough diamonds. This created the prospect of increased supply coinciding with a possible collapse in consumer demand.

After carefully considering our options, we decided to focus on the US market. This decision brought challenges, because it was one of the most saturated markets and engagement ring sales had been flat for many years.

Facing these challenges, we developed a strategy to increase the value of the US diamond jewellery market. We decided to prioritize and focus on 'heavy owners'—women with eight or more pieces of diamond jewellery. Our aim was for them to become heavy owners *as early as possible in their lives* to increase their lifelong value to the category.

Recognizing that people need stories, dreams, and fantasies, we developed a narrative that captured the emotions and meanings a diamond can symbolize. This narrative would prove powerful as it enhanced the emotional value of diamonds—key to encouraging more sales at higher prices.

We developed and launched three ideas, called *Beacons*. These ideas were built around a narrative highlighting the three stages of love—its past, present, and future. The basis of the strategy was that we could provide women with new occasions and opportunities to acquire diamond jewellery.

To launch the idea, we used a product already in existence. Three-stone jewellery and rings had existed for years, but sold in low volume, being considered old-fashioned and, most importantly, carrying no meaning. The idea was that jewellery with three stones could tell a unique story: one stone symbolizing your past, one your present, and the final your future. Hence, a new tradition began—'Past, Present, Future'.

Meaning was brought to the existing design through an emotionally charged TV launch, alongside impactful call-to-action press. This positioned the idea around gifting, with a focus around anniversaries. Our communication objectives were to create awareness of the narrative and to create desire.

All three Beacons had high awareness. Looking at the desire created by communications, all three Beacons have achieved levels above norm. Most importantly, this desire has translated into intent, with above-norm scores for more likely to buy/acquire. In the US, 14.2 million women would most like to acquire a Past, Present, Future piece as their next diamond acquisition. Furthermore, in the six years from 2001 to 2006, Beacons sold 21.6 million pieces of diamond jewellery, *adding US$18.9 billion retail sales value* to non-bridal diamond jewellery. By 2006 alone, Beacons grew to $6.4 billion annual sales value.

Today, a diamond is still forever, and is still a perfect way in which to mark and celebrate marriage. But now, thanks to the Beacons, diamonds can allow people to express and celebrate other emotions.

Source: This is an edited version of a case study submitted to the IPA Effectiveness Awards. The full case study can be found at ipa.co.uk or warc.com. © Copyright Institute of Practitioners in Advertising.

Edited by Esther K-Amoda, Doctoral Student, Bath School of Management

Discussion questions

1. What factors contributed to the success of the De Beers Beacons campaign?
2. Applying McGuire's information processing paradigm, discuss the campaign approach.
3. Discuss the impact of the planning sequence on the campaign.
4. Identify possible objectives and goals set by De Beers in its strategic communications planning.

Further reading

S. Bellman, 'The Residual Impact of Avoided Television Advertising', *Journal of Advertising*, 39/1 (2010), 67–87

Today many television viewers find ways to avoid watching commercials, and this issue has been addressed by Steve Bellman and his colleagues in their paper. From their study, they offer constructive strategies for dealing with the problem.

Gerguly Nyilasy and Leonard Rerd, 'Agency Practitioners' Theories of how Advertising Works', *Journal of Advertising*, 38/3 (2009), 87–96

—, 'Agency Practitioner's Meta-Theories of Advertising', *International Journal of Advertising*, 28/4 (2009), 639–68

The authors discuss how advertising agency practitioners think advertising 'works' in these two articles.

Joep Cornelisseu, *Corporate Communication: A Guide to Theory and Practice* (London: Sage, 2008)

A look at communication planning within a corporate perspective; provides a good overview.

K.D. Frankenberger and R.C. Graham, 'Should Firms Increase, Decrease, or Maintain Advertising Expenditures during Recessions?', Marketing Science Institute Working Paper, April 2003

How to deal with budgets in a recession.

Leslie de Chernatony, *From Brand Vision to Brand Evaluation* (Oxford: Butterworth Heinemann, 2001)

Offers a broad perspective of how the manager can take a brand's vision and build a stronger brand, providing a broader context for the issues discussed in this chapter.

Notes

1. Perhaps the definitive work on attitude-change theory is McGuire's original essay, 'The Nature of Attitudes and Attitude Change', in G. Lindsey and E. Aronson (eds) *The Handbook of Social Psychology*, iii (Reading, MA: Addison-Wesley Publishing, 1969), 136–314. This work and others of McGuire's are reviewed in terms of their implications for advertising by L. Percy and J.R. Rossiter in *Advertising Strategy: A Communication Theory Approach* (New York: Praeger, 1980).
2. J.R. Rossiter and L. Percy, *Advertising Communication and Promotion Management*, 2nd edn (New York: McGraw-Hill, 1997).
3. This is something originally pointed out by J.R. Rossiter and L. Percy in *Advertising and Promotion Management* (New York: McGraw-Hill, 1987).

Visit the Online Resource Centre that accompanies this book for additional resources to support the text: **www.oxfordtextbooks.co.uk/orc/percy_elliott4e/**

The Strategic Planning Process

Key concepts

1. Before the manager can begin the strategic planning process, it is essential first to review the marketing plan, in general, and advertising in particular, because marketing communication must be consistent with, and support, the overall marketing plan.
2. The strategic planning process itself follows five steps: identifying the target, determining how the target behaves in the category, looking at the best way in which to position the brand in the communication, developing a communication strategy, and then setting a media strategy for how best to deliver the message to the target audience.
3. At the heart of this process is an understanding of brand awareness and brand attitude strategy.

The actual strategic planning process, as you might imagine, is much more specific than the general planning sequence we introduced in Chapter 4. While that provided a good way of relating planning overall with the communication response sequence, a good strategic plan must go further. What must we do in order to link the target audience to our marketing objectives? How do we actually decide upon the appropriate communication effects? What determines the optimum creative strategy? What do we need to know in order to deliver our message effectively?

Some have tried to argue that, in the age of new media, and especially with social media such as Twitter and Facebook, strategic communication planning no longer has a role. They are wrong. Strategic planning for marketing communication remains essential for effective communication: the development and execution of messages likely to be processed by the appropriate target audience and leading to the desired response. The strategic planning process outlined in this chapter and then discussed in detail over the next five chapters provides a framework for identifying what a manager must understand and act upon in order to accomplish this.

Regardless of how a message is delivered, it must be addressed to the appropriate target audience.

- It must be consistent with that target audience's involvement with the purchase and the motivation driving the brand decision, and one must know where in the decision process the message is most likely to have a positive impact.
- It must reflect a positioning that links the brand to the appropriate need and a key benefit that is important to the target audience, and one that they feel the brand can or does deliver (the fundamental basis for building positive brand attitude).

- The execution must be based upon this positioning, and reflect the correct brand awareness and brand attitude objective—and media selected to deliver it must be consistent with the processing requirements of these objectives.

In many ways this process is even more critical when dealing with new media, especially when new media is selected simply *because* it is new media. Many brands feel that they must include new media in their media plan so as not to 'miss out'. Regardless of why it may be included in a media plan, as for any other medium, the other steps of the strategic planning process are critical to ensure that the message reflects the appropriate positioning for the target and that the creative tactics used are those likely to optimize the likelihood the message will be processed.

The only exception to this is when a brand is looking to consumer-generated content for social media. In this case, the brand has no real control over the message, a point raised early in Chapter 1, and must hope for the best. Perhaps not the wisest thing to do, but we shall be considering this later in Chapter 13 when we talk about crowdsourcing.

In this chapter we will be considering the five specific steps a manager should take in developing a strategic plan for a brand's marketing communication. Then, in the next part of the book we will devote a chapter to each of these five areas as we explore in detail the important issues involved at each step. Before discussing these steps in more detail, we will want to consider some of the things managers should be looking for in the marketing plan.

Review the Marketing Plan First

All marketing communication must be consistent with, and in support of, the overall marketing plan. Before a manager even begins to think about specific communication issues, it is important to review the marketing plan. Once this review is completed, it is then helpful to outline briefly 'what we know' about the market and the specific marketing objectives and goals for the brand. This sort of information often has a significant bearing upon what it is that we will want to communicate to the target audience, and it provides important background information for those charged with creating the message.

There are at least five key areas which the manager will want information on *before* beginning the strategic planning process for marketing communication. Each of these five areas is discussed briefly below, and outlined in Table 5.1.

Product Description

What are you marketing? This may seem too obvious to think about, but that is precisely the point. While it may be obvious to the manager, it may not be quite so obvious to the target market. Think carefully, and write out a description of the product or service to be advertised or promoted in such a way that someone totally unfamiliar with it will understand exactly what it is. This description will then serve as background for the creative staff who will be charged with executing the brand's marketing communication.

Table 5.1 Marketing Background Issues in Strategic Planning

Key areas	Issues
Product description	What are you marketing?
Market assessment	What is your overall assessment of the market in which you compete?
Source of business	Where do you expect business to come from?
Competitive evaluation	What is your competition and how does it position itself?
Marketing objectives	What are the marketing objectives for the brand?

Market Assessment

What is your overall assessment of the market in which you compete? It is important that your source of information here is absolutely up to date. The background information in the marketing plan could be as much as a year old. Be certain that nothing has happened in the market that could possibly 'date' this information. What is needed here is information about the market that might influence the potential success of the brand. How are brands performing relative to category performance? Where does the market seem to be heading? Are there potential innovations or new entries on the horizon? This is also a good time to review any recent market research that has been conducted for the brand. It is important here to provide enough information to convey a good sense of the market, but only those things likely to have a real impact upon a brand's performance should be included.

Source of Business

Where do you expect business to come from? It is necessary here to consider potential customers as well as competitors. Do we expect to increase our share of business by attracting new customers to the category, or by attracting users of other brands (a trial action objective)? Or are we looking to increase usage by our existing customers (a repeat purchase action objective)? What is there about the purchase behaviour of potential customers that we need to know? To what extent does our brand compete with products or services *outside* its category?

Competitive Evaluation

What is the competition and how does it position itself? It is essential to have an accurate understanding of just who the competition is in the *minds of the consumers*. Does the competitive set change depending upon how the product is used? What are the creative strategies of the competition? It is a good idea to include examples of competitive marketing communication to illustrate the benefits they emphasize and their executional approach. As we shall see in Chapter 13, advertising and promotion must be unique, with their own consistent 'look and feel'. What media tactics are used by competitors? How do they employ advertising and audience attitudinal and behavioural patterns that are relevant to a brand's marketing communication and media strategies. This means knowing what the proposed target audience's category behaviour is now, or is likely to be in response to our campaign, and how their underlying brand attitudes and motivations affect choices.

Where does the Trade Fit in?

The manager must never lose sight of the fact that the trade is almost always a part of our target audience. It is easy to fall into the trap of thinking only about consumers when considering a target audience. But our strategic planning requires a *total* look at the marketing communication task, and when advertising and promotion to the trade are used, they must be integrated with advertising and promotion to the consumer. Even if the message is different (as is likely), the 'look and feel', the theme, must be consistent with the overall creative umbrella. Why this is so important will be evident when we talk about the five decision roles in the next section. It would not be unusual for the trade to be either an 'initiator' or an 'influencer' in a brand decision, especially for high-ticket consumer goods or in business-to-business marketing.

Step Two: Understand Target Audience Decision Making

Once the target audience has been selected, we must next gain an understanding of how that target audience goes about making purchase decisions in the category. This is important, because if you are to affect the purchase decision positively and increase the likelihood of your brand being selected, you must understand what is involved in the making of that decision. As we shall see in Chapter 7, quite a lot may be involved. Who is involved in making the decision? How do they go about it? Where can advertising and promotions or other marketing communication influence the process?

To begin with, those who study consumer behaviour remind us that in a decision to buy or use a product or service a number of people may be involved, and they may play different roles in that decision process. In Chapter 7 we will discuss the importance of focusing the manager's thinking on the various roles that people may play in the decision to buy and use a brand. Basically, there are five possible roles involved:

- *initiators*, who propose purchase or usage;
- *influencers*, who recommend (or discourage) purchase or usage;
- *deciders*, who make the actual choice;
- *purchasers*, who make the actual purchase;
- *users*, who use the product or service.

One person may play all five roles in the decision process, or others may be involved, playing one or more roles. It is critical to understand who is involved and what roles they are playing. When we address the members of our target audience, we are talking to them as individuals, but as *individuals in a role*.

Once we have an understanding of those involved in the decision and the roles that they play, we must then develop a model of how consumers actually make a purchase decision.

This involves determining the stages the target audience goes through in choosing, purchasing, and using a brand. Looking at consumer decision making provides a dynamic view of the process that a target audience is likely to go through in making a decision to buy or use a product or service. It provides valuable insight into the likely motives driving behaviour. Understanding *why* people do what they do is critical in establishing an appropriate brand attitude strategy (which we develop as part of Step Four in the strategic planning process), and the brand attitude strategy is at the heart of successful advertising and promotion, as it is with *any* marketing communication. Additionally, identifying the various people involved in the purchase or usage decision, along with the roles they play, helps to target messages more effectively to the appropriate audiences in their appropriate roles.

Using this consumer decision-making model, the manager is in a position to determine how best to influence the decision process positively in order to maximize the opportunity for your brand to be chosen. With this model in hand, a manager will know where in the decision process it is most important to communicate with the target audience, and the type of message that will be required.

Step Three: Determine the Best Positioning

The third step in the strategic planning process is to determine how best to position the brand. While the basic brand positioning will no doubt already be established (except for new products), the strategic planning process must address the particular *communication* positioning that will be adopted for a brand. The manager must decide whether to link the brand in the target audience's mind to the category need in which it already sees it competing, or *re*position the brand by linking it to another category need in which the brand will have a stronger competitive advantage. In such cases the repositioning rarely involves a drastic change, but rather a switch to another branch or level of the way in which the overall product category is partitioned in the mind of the target audience.

We shall spend a great deal of time in Chapter 8 discussing the importance of understanding how markets are partitioned. To give you an idea of what we mean by partitioning, think about snacks. What comes to mind? Is it a packet of crisps, say, or a chocolate bar? Clearly both are snacks, but would you position a chocolate bar against crisps? Unlikely. Chocolate bars are a different type of snack, and likely to satisfy a different category need. We might imagine the overall snack category dividing (that is, partitioning) into savoury versus sweet snacks. Sweet snacks might then be seen as splitting into baked snacks like biscuits or pastries versus confections like chocolate. Chocolate bars, then, following our example, would be in the confection category, and positioned against the category need associated with it.

But even within the chocolate bar category itself there may also be different types of bar that offer various positioning options against more specific category needs. For example, there could be 'luxury' bars to satisfy an exotic indulgence, like Inca in France; or basic chocolate bars, like those marketed by Cadbury, to satisfy a need for just chocolate; or filled bars, like Lila Parse in Germany. The issue of how the category need is defined for our brand is a critical decision in the strategic planning process.

In addition to establishing the category definition in order to identify the market where the brand or service will compete, positioning also requires us to look for a differential advantage for our brand. How will the brand be presented to the target audience? What benefit does the than others to creating these effects. As a result, the choice of communication objectives will *directly* affect the choice of which type of advertising or promotion is to be used. The communication objective will also affect the media choice, both traditional media and new media such as the Internet and text (SMS) messaging.

Brand Awareness and Brand Attitude Strategy

In the development of a communication strategy for a brand's marketing communication, getting the brand awareness and brand attitude strategy right is critical. Step Two in the strategic planning process helps the manager to determine if the purchase decision follows from recognition or recall of the brand, if there is perceived risk in making the brand choice, and whether positive or negative motives are driving behaviour in the category. It is these determinations that will inform brand awareness and brand attitude strategy.

What is the Brand Awareness Strategy?

As we briefly mentioned earlier, there are at least two types of brand awareness that the manager must consider: recognition and recall. Brand awareness strategy deals with getting this right. *Recognition* brand awareness is when someone 'sees' the brand at the point of purchase and is reminded of a need for it. *Recall* brand awareness occurs when someone has a need and must 'remember' the brand as something that will satisfy that need. There are important creative strategic and tactical issues that must be considered in relation to the type of brand awareness, as we shall see later in the book, depending upon whether recognition or recall is central to how products or services are chosen.

What is the Brand Attitude Strategy?

The answer to this question follows from an understanding of the four quadrants detailed in the Rossiter–Percy grid.[2] This concept was briefly introduced in Chapter 1, and will be covered in depth in Chapters 9 and 12. As part of their grid, Rossiter and Percy suggest that brand attitude strategy is a function of the two fundamental considerations that we introduced in Chapter 1: (1) whether there is low or high involvement with the purchase or use decision, based primarily upon the target audience's perceived risk (either in fiscal or psychological terms); (2) whether the underlying motivation that drives behaviour in the category is positive or negative. Combining these two considerations produces the four brand attitude strategy quadrants of the grid: low involvement with negative motives; low involvement with positive motives; high involvement with negative motives; and high involvement with positive motives.

Understanding these constructs is critical for identifying the appropriate brand attitude strategy, which in turn is critical for creative strategy. That is why we shall spend so much time on this issue later in the book. At this point, all we need is an initial understanding of its importance and where it fits in the strategic planning process.

The creative tactics that maximize the likelihood of an effective message are directly linked to the brand attitude strategy that follows from the appropriate quadrant defined by the Rossiter–Percy grid. These tactics differ significantly for each quadrant. Strategies associated with negative motives require *information* to help to solve or avoid a problem, while those associated with positive motives must help to *transform* the consumer—for example, by gratifying a want by meeting a need for social approval. As you might imagine, the creative message needed for brand attitude strategies associated with negative motives will be quite different from those associated with positive motives. For the informational strategies, the focus will probably be on benefits associated with the brand, while for transformational strategies, the focus will generally be centred around the emotions associated with attitudes towards the category or brand.

This will all become much clearer in Chapters 9 and 12. For now, the contrast between Adverts 5.1*a* and 5.1*b* should help to illustrate the point. The advert for Sparkford (*a*) deals with an informational strategy, and you can see the benefit emphasis is on specific claims: 'The Natural Choice', 'extensive range of pre-designed or bespoke timber products', 'worry free service' and more. The advert for Jordans Luxury Muesli (*b*) reflects a transformational strategy, and you can see that the benefit focus is more 'emotional', utilizing a strong visual that projects a very positive feeling, with the copy in the headline reinforcing the overall sense of luxury and contentment.

Creative tactics also differ as a function of involvement. Because involvement is defined in terms of risk, when there is low involvement, it is not necessary for the target audience to be really convinced before buying. If people make a mistake, they have not suffered much of a loss. On the other hand, when involvement is high, the potential buyer does not want to make a mistake. In this case the target audience must be convinced by the marketing communication before buying. Consider how much an advert would need to *convince* you that a new snack was 'great-tasting' or that a new personal computer was the 'best yet' before you would think of buying. Before buying the computer, you would certainly want to know more, but you would probably be willing to take a chance on buying the new snack based only on the feeling that it might be something you would like.

The advert for Nike's Swim brand shown in Plate II is an excellent example of what we are talking about for a low-involvement decision. The strong image presents the benefit of low resistance in the extreme—'water without resistance'. Is it really that good? Because there is little risk involved, you can try and see. The advert for Philips Bodygroom shown in Plate III offers a very good example of how to believably present a brand's primary benefit for a high-involvement decision. No words are really necessary. If the product can remove the 'fuzz' from the delicate skin of a fruit with no nicks or cuts, it should do the same for you. Comfort, effectiveness, and no cuts are all believably implied by this image, and reflect what people will be looking for in a product like this.

What we have are four potential brand attitude strategies based upon involvement and motivation: low- versus high-involvement informational strategies and low- versus high-involvement transformational strategies. The quadrant that best reflects the decision process of the target audience is what determines the brand attitude strategy.

Promotion Strategy

When creating brand purchase intention is a communication objective, the manager must decide if promotion should be part of the communication strategy for the brand. We have noted that brand purchase intention is rarely an objective for advertising. While advertising is meant to contribute to the target audience forming a positive intention to buy a brand, in most cases this follows from the positive brand attitude formed as a result of the advertising.

If brand purchase intention is an objective, the key to whether or not a promotion should be part of the overall communication strategy is whether that intention is to be acted upon

But, from the brand's perspective, there is a world of difference. Consumer promotions are initiated by the brand, not the retailer, and the brand controls the content. Even though consumers may think about promotions as 'advertising', they tend to have a pretty good idea about how often brands offer incentive promotion.[4] This is important to the brand, because it will affect consumer buying strategy for the brand in light of the perception of the brand's availability on promotion. So, even if marketing managers do not have control over retail promotions that include their brand, it is essential that they have knowledge of them and include that knowledge in their promotion strategy.

Retail Promotion

When people think of retail promotions, the first things that probably come to mind are newspaper, food, or pharmacy adverts. But, of course, almost any retailer can use promotion, and car dealers, mass merchandisers, shoe stores, and even banks frequently do so. Retail promotions are also found in local magazines, and even on local radio and television. Retailers may carry out traditional advertising as well, and we must not confuse the two. If a retailer is talking about something related to the store or image, this is *not* retail promotion.

You may be wondering why we are treating retail promotions separately from trade promotions when retailers are a major part of the trade. It is because retailers form a very specific subset of the trade, one that has direct contact with the end consumer. Other aspects of the trade, such as brokers or wholesale distributors, do not, as a rule, deal directly with consumers. As a result, the effects of promotion to non-retail trade may or may not be passed on to the consumer through retailers.

We have just pointed out that a brand may not have control over how a retailer will use a particular promotion. A very interesting study has shown that the objective for many retail promotions is not simply to attract shoppers to a store, but also to move product off the shelf, in effect reducing inventory costs.[5] This strategy may not always be consistent with the strategy behind a promotion offered to retailers. This can be a real problem for a marketer. In trying to integrate all of the elements of a brand's marketing communication, retail promotion can be a wild card. Later in Chapter 14 we will be looking at channels marketing, which is an attempt by marketers to gain better control over retail promotion, and better integration with advertising and other brand marketing communication, all an important part of the strategic planning process.

An important consideration with retail promotions is that they are independent of a brand's marketing strategy. While the brand would like to coordinate retail promotions with its own marketing and communication strategy (as we will see when we discuss channels marketing), the reality is that retail promotions are offered *independently* of the pricing policy or other trade or consumer promotions offered by the brand. Often a retailer's promotion strategy is geared more to competitive activity than to anything else. It is very important during this stage of the planning process to have as good an understanding as possible of the likely use of promotion for the brand by the retailer.

There will be occasions, of course, when the retailer and the brand will be the same. In such cases, the retailer will develop both an advertising and promotion strategy. The promotion for Really Wild Clothing Company shown in Plate IV provides a good example where the product and retailer are basically the same. The execution does a good job of delivering retailer brand awareness, and with a strong and appropriate visual image it helps to build positive attitudes not only for its clothing, but also for the image of its retail store. The visual clearly contributes to a positive emotional response, important for transformational brand attitude strategy. If this were all there was to the execution, it would be considered a good advert. But look at the copy: 'contact us at our flagship store', 'visit us at our new on-line shop', and a special offer of a Really Wild T-shirt for ordering online. Clearly these are all promotion-like messages designed to encourage immediate action, including the offer of a premium. This is what makes this a promotion.

Trade Promotion

Trade promotion takes up a significant proportion of most marketing communication budgets. Whether the promotion directly affects pricing or indirectly affects volume through merchandising material, the trade views trade promotions from the manufacturer as a way in which to move more money to its bottom line. Most trade promotions do this directly through a price-related promotion of one kind or another. These can include such things as direct price-off reductions from invoices, agreements to buy back any unsold product, and, at the retail level, slotting allowances.

Slotting fees are a fee to stock new items, and have become a cost of doing business for fmcg brands. The reasoning is that, with an ever-increasing demand to handle new products and line extensions, and given the high failure rate, the trade feels it needs help in dealing with the cash flow and overheads involved. While there is certainly some truth to this, it is estimated that as much as 70 per cent of slotting fees go directly to the bottom line and not to defraying cost. With the general trend of retailers to merge into larger chains, slotting fees are expected to be applied to products other than fmcgs.[6]

If a consumer or business-to-business marketer is offering a discount on its price to the trade, the trade has the option of retaining all or part of the discount, sending it to its bottom line. To the extent that any of the trade discount is passed on to the retailer or directly to the consumer, these trade promotions are still expected to increase volume, also leading to larger profits for the trade. This is also the reasoning behind the trade's interest in merchandising promotion. Here the brand will supply collateral material such as in-store banners, special end-aisle displays, or sales incentive premiums for target sales goals. Of course, the brand is looking for something in return: such things as better stocking and shelf positioning (for example, more package 'facings' and at a more desirable height on the shelf),[7] counter displays, and other opportunities for better exposure.

In many markets the distribution channels, especially mass retailers, have become so powerful that, even when trade promotions are given, there is no guarantee the trade will offer anything in return. It is important to remember that the brand's goals and the trade's goals are not necessarily the same. The trade profits from category sales. It does not particularly care which brands are stocked as long as it maintains or increases its margins. The marketer, of course, is vitally interested in its *brand*, whether consumer or business-to-business.

This underscores a very important point. Too often trade promotions (and retail and consumer promotions as well) are seen only as a way in which to buy share or sales in order to satisfy an immediate, short-term sales goal. True, promotion is a short-term *tactic*, but it must be seen within a larger marketing communication *strategy* for the brand. As we shall see in Chapter 15, this means integrating trade promotions with all other promotion and advertising activity.

Using Direct Marketing

In considering direct marketing as part of an integrated marketing communication programme, there are three questions the manager must ask (see Box 5.2). First, does direct marketing make any sense given the brand's communication objectives? We have just reviewed a number of strategic differences between advertising and direct marketing. Obviously, if you are addressing a mass audience, direct marketing is not likely to be as effective as other means of marketing communication. Also, given the tactical nature of direct marketing, brand purchase intention is the most appropriate communication objective. If brand attitude is the primary objective (remember it is *always* an objective, along with brand awareness, even if something else is the primary objective), direct marketing is likely to be less effective than other means of marketing communication.

If direct marketing does make sense for a brand's marketing communication programme, the next question is whether or not a good database for the target audience is available. If the brand has used direct marketing in the past, then an updated database should be available. If not, you must be able to acquire or build a target list before you can even think about developing a direct marketing programme. This suggests that even if direct marketing is not currently a part of a brand's marketing communication efforts, it will still make sense to develop a database for possible future use. The importance of a good list for direct marketing cannot be understated. Studies have shown that the quality of a list accounts for some 40 per cent of the effectiveness of a direct marketing campaign, equal to the 40 per cent attributed to the headline of the message (the remainder of the message accounts for the other 20 per cent).[11]

If direct marketing makes sense for the brand and you have a good database, the final question to ask is how you will deliver the message. There are four basic direct marketing media available: direct mail, telemarketing, mass media, and interactive media. Generally only one of these four media will be used for a particular direct marketing programme. An exception would be if various segments of the target audience were more easily reached with one medium than another (see Box 5.3).

- Does direct marketing make sense given the brand's communication objectives?
- Is there a good database available for the target audience?
- How will you deliver the message?

Box 5.2 Questions Managers Must Ask when Considering Direct Marketing

- Direct mail
- Telemarketing
- Mass media
- Interactive

Box 5.3 Four Basic Types of Direct Marketing Media

Disadvantages of Direct Marketing

There is no question that the growth of direct marketing has been fuelled by advances in technology, especially computer-driven systems and software. But there are some disadvantages that should be considered. The first is the image of some direct marketing media. Remember, consumers do not distinguish one type of marketing communication from another. Marketing managers may call a direct mail campaign a promotion, or it may be direct marketing, but the consumer is more likely to see any such mailing as 'junk mail'. The image of telemarketing is even worse. Those on the Internet are likely to see unsolicited email from a brand as an unwanted intervention by 'spammers' (indiscriminate senders of email). We have also pointed out that direct marketing can be expensive compared with other forms of marketing communication. Still, when carefully considered and planned, direct marketing can be an important and effective part of a brand's marketing communication effort.

Chapter summary

We have now introduced the five decision steps in the strategic planning process: select the target audience, understand target audience decision making, determine the best positioning, develop a communication strategy, and set the media strategy. We have explored each stage at the preliminary level and the following chapters will discuss each stage in depth. We have considered how the Rossiter–Percy grid can be used to guide brand attitude strategy and creative tactics, and the role of promotion strategy was introduced. Direct marketing was introduced, because whether or not to use direct marketing should be part of the overall strategic planning.

Questions to consider

5.1 Why is each of the five steps in the strategic planning process needed, and why must they be considered in this order?

5.2 How should the roles people play in a purchase or usage decision influence a manager's thinking about a strategic plan for a brand's advertising and other marketing communication?

5.3 Why is it important to understand the difference between recognition and recall brand awareness?

5.4 When are sales likely to be a specific objective for advertising messages?

5.5 Why is an understanding of consumer decision making critical for an effective brand attitude strategy?

5.6 How do involvement and motivation affect brand attitude strategy?

5.7 When should promotion be considered as part of the communication strategy?

5.8 What must the manager consider when matching media options with communication objectives?

5.9 How can direct marketing contribute to a brand's marketing communications?

5.10 Find an example of direct marketing that does not involve a promotion.

Part 3

Developing the Strategic Plan

Chapter 6	**Selecting the Target Audience**	Identify target audience and establish trial vs repeat purchase *target audience action objectives*
	⇩	
Chapter 7	**Understanding Target Audience Decision Making**	*Determine level of involvement* and *motivation* to guide communication strategy, and identify where media can effectively reach the target audience
	⇩	
Chapter 8	**Determining the Best Positioning**	*Link brand to category need* to guide brand awareness strategy, and *link brand to benefit* to guide brand attitude strategy
	⇩	
Chapter 9	**Developing a Communication Strategy**	Establish communication objectives and determine *recall vs recognition* brand awareness strategy, and brand attitude strategy in terms of *involvement* and *motivation*
	⇩	
Chapter 10	**Setting a Media Strategy**	Identify media options, in terms of specific *brand awareness and brand attitude* strategy

6 Selecting the Target Audience

In this and the next four chapters we will be laying the foundation for effective advertising and other marketing communication by determining what is necessary in order to implement the strategic planning process. The first thing the manager must do is select the appropriate target audience, which will be a function of the brand purchase objective laid out in the marketing plan. This, in turn, will have implications for both communication and promotion strategy, as shown in the Step 1 diagram and discussed further in Chapter 9.

Implementing the Strategic Planning Process

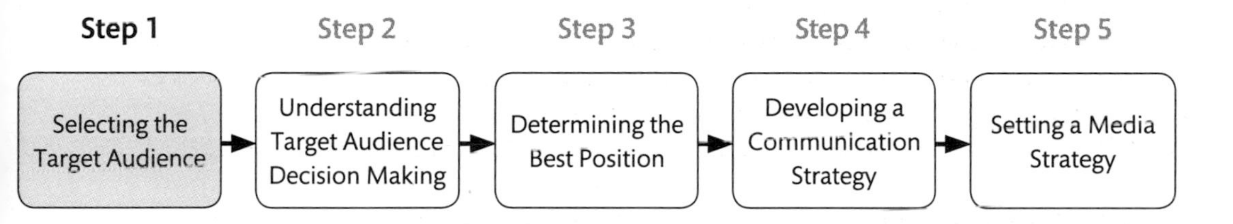

STEP 1 SELECT THE TARGET AUDIENCE			
Target audience action objective		Objective for communication strategy	Options for promotion strategy
Repeat purchase ⟶	Users	• Strengthen existing brand attitude	• Loyalty and loading devices • Premiums • Sweepstakes, games, contests
Trial ⟶	Non-users	• Generate brand awareness • Encourage a more favourable brand attitude	• Coupons • Refunds and rebates • Sampling

Key concepts

1. The most practical way of looking at target audience selection is in relation to buyer behaviour because it is easily measured, but the real key is brand loyalty.
2. Brand loyalty is a reflection of awareness, attitudes, and behaviour.
3. There are many other ways in which to describe a target audience, and these profiles are helpful in creative development, but not for selection.
4. The fundamental distinction made in marketing plans between brand users and non-users is directly related to the target audience action objectives of trial and repeat purchase.
5. Overall, attitude is the most important thing to understand about a target audience.

As we saw in Chapter 5, the first step in the strategic planning process for marketing communication (or for *any* advertising or promotion programme) is to select the appropriate target audience. The marketing, plan establishes marketing goals and defines the target market. From this target market, it is necessary to identify the specific target audience required for a particular marketing communication programme. If we are advertising, are we more interested in attracting new users, or encouraging existing users to buy or use more often? If we are running a promotion campaign, is it to reward loyal customers or to attract new users?

Selecting the appropriate target audience is not as easy as it may seem. From the examples above, a simple distinction between customers and non-customers may seem to suffice. But this is *not* enough. Much more definition is required. For example, what if someone is a customer only because he or she has not yet found something he or she likes better? Or what if someone is a customer because he or she simply would not think of using any other brand? Obviously it will be important to understand just what type of customers (and non-customers) comprise the market if the manager is to make intelligent target audience decisions.

Target Audience Groupings

There are a number of different ways in which to think about target audience groups. Gerrit Antonides and W. Fred van Raaij take a broad view of target audience groups, describing them in terms of three levels: general, domain specific, and brand specific.[1]

At the *general level*, they consider target audience groups in terms of descriptive characteristics such as standard demographics (for example, age, income, geographic location), lifestyle variables (for example, active in sports, travel), and psychographics (for example, outgoing, risk-taking).

At the *domain-specific level*, target audience groups are described in terms of those characteristics associated with a product or product category. This would include such things as category usage behaviour (for example, 'eat a lot of frozen food', 'own three cars'), attitudes towards the product category (for example, 'vitamins are a waste of money'), and how decisions are made in the category (for example, a need is aroused in the product category, a set of brands is considered, one is selected, purchased, and used).

At the *brand-specific level*, they describe target audience groupings in terms of such things as brand loyalty (will buy one brand in the category all of the time, or at least most of the time), beliefs about the brand (for example, Brand A has more cleaning power than Brand B), and brand buying intentions (for example, will buy Brand A if it is on special offer, otherwise will buy Brand B).

In effect, Antonides and van Raaij look at possible target audience groupings in terms of their overall descriptive characteristics: how they behave generally in the product category, and how they behave towards specific brands. Rossiter and Percy, on the other hand, discuss target audience groupings primarily in terms of their brand purchasing behaviours.[2] They suggest that a brand could potentially be purchased by any of five buyer groups: *brand loyals*, who regularly buy your brand in the category; *favourable brand-switchers*, who buy your brand, but also buy competitor brands; *other-brand-switchers*, who buy more than one competitor brand, but not your brand; *other-brand loyals*, who regularly buy a competitor brand; and a fifth group of *new category users*, who are entering the category for the first time or re-entering after a long time.

The idea of looking at a target audience in terms of purchasing behaviour is that it may be seen as a reflection of brand attitude. Brand loyalty is generally assumed to follow from a positive attitude toward the brand. This positive attitude, over time, leads to a certain 'immunization' to competitive advertising and promotion. This idea of positive attitudes leading to resistance to competitive marketing communication follows from McGuire's notion of inoculation theory.[3] Initial counter-arguing to a brand's message, after trial and usage, will tend to be adopted as a defence against competitive communication much in the way a small inoculation of a flu virus stimulates resistance to the flu.

In addition to brand attitude, brand awareness will also figure in purchase behaviour, and as a result, brand loyalty. This may seem obvious, because if you are not aware of a brand, you will not be looking to purchase it. But, as we shall see as we look more deeply into this below, there is more to it. As Rossiter and Percy have suggested, brand loyalty is an awareness-attitude-behaviour concept.[4]

The Antonides and van Raaij classifications of target audience groupings offer the manager a general-to-specific way of profiling potential target groups. However, this classification screen does not really help the manager to *select* an optimum target audience. In this regard the Rossiter–Percy notion of looking at brand purchase behaviour is more helpful. In fact, it makes a great deal of intuitive sense. It is a logical refinement of the basic customer versus non-customer division of the target market.

Obviously, a brand will want to retain consumers who are loyal to it and reinforce that loyalty. This is the hard core of any business. Those who buy a brand along with the occasional competitor brand, however, probably make up the bulk of any business. Here it is necessary to retain these customers and try to encourage less usage of other brands. As we shall see later in this chapter, the objective with these two groups is *repeat purchase*.

If we are looking for new customers, those who buy more than one other brand, but not ours, probably offer the best potential. Since they already buy more than one brand, it should be possible to persuade them to include our brand (either in addition to, or in place of, one of the brands they now buy). The most difficult prospect would be those who tend to be loyal to a competitor brand. But those who do not use the category will not be easy to attract as new customers either. In addition to persuading them to buy your brand, you must also persuade them to enter the category in the first place. Again, as we shall see later, the objective for these non-users of your brand is *trial*.

This division of target audience potential into repeat purchase versus trial behaviour is reflected in the five Rossiter and Percy buyer behaviour groups. A repeat purchase objective means selecting a target audience from among brand loyals and what they call favourable brand-switchers. A trial objective will mean selecting a target audience from among what they refer to as other-brand-switchers, other-brand loyals, and new category users. But beyond this obvious distinction, brand awareness and brand attitude will be playing an important role.

Those loyal to a brand should have the highest awareness and most positive attitudes toward the brand, although, as we shall see in the next section, this does not necessarily always follow. A brand's most loyal buyers will always be of critical importance to any brand, but if driving up repeat purchase is the objective, they may not be the best target for increasing business. The manager must understand their attitudes toward the brand *and the category*. Brand loyals must be more than just happy with the brand if increasing their usage is part of the strategy. They must also be amenable to using more. However, with some categories, it would make very little sense to even try to increase usage. Think about categories such as toothpaste or cold remedies. We would need to encourage brushing more, or hope for the target to have more colds.

The bulk of any brand franchise, and where to look for increasing brand usage, is among what Rossiter and Percy called favourable brand-switchers, those who buy our brand, but also buy others as well. Here, awareness should be strong, but it must be *maintained* because if the salience for the brand slips, the greater will be the likelihood that those other brands will be purchased. Understanding this group's attitude toward the brand is important in order to help the manager to assess the extent to which these switchers (or some segment of them) have the potential for increasing their purchase of the brand, and perhaps becoming brand loyals. It will also be important for the manager to understand the extent to which the group's sustaining behaviour is driven by incentive promotions.

When considering a trial strategy for increasing business, the manager must first know what the awareness and brand attitudes are among non-users. Other-brand-switchers' behaviour, those who switch among brands, but do not include our brand, argues well for considering them when looking to add new users because they already switch among several brands. But what if they are not aware of our brand, or hold neutral or even negative attitudes toward our brand, or see the brand as too expensive? Any of these awareness or attitude states would affect the potential cost of persuading them to try the brand. The manager must understand the level of awareness and brand attitude among potential triers in developing the communication strategy and its cost.

Those loyal to a competitive brand will have the least potential as new triers because of the strong positive attitude they hold for that brand. As discussed above, this will tend to 'immunize' them to our advertising and promotion. On the other hand, suppose those attitudes are not strongly held. Suppose they are not aware of our brand, and only consider the brand they are 'loyal' to as the best of the available alternatives. As we shall see in the next section, brand loyalty, as measured behaviourally without an understanding of brand attitude, will not paint the whole picture.

Those potential triers with no experience, or no recent experience, in the category—the group Rossiter and Percy described as new category users—may or may not offer potential for a brand. The key here is not so much brand awareness and attitude as it is *category* awareness and attitude. Both must be strong to consider this group as part of the target audience when trial is an objective. There are reasons why these people have not been using products in the category, and the manager must understand those reasons before deciding if these people offer any potential.

A special case of new category users might be thought of as 'evolving' category users. As one moves through life, certain events, along with the simple fact of ageing, will move you into new categories of brand behaviour. For example, a new mother will suddenly be in the market for any number of products she had no need for up until that point in her life. Managers of such brands must look to target these potential new category users *prior* to actual need, building brand awareness and an initial positive attitude toward the brand.

In earlier chapters we talked about the importance of brand awareness and brand attitude to effective marketing communication strategy. Here we have seen that it is also an important component of target audience selection. Both help to identify and define brand loyalty, especially brand attitude, *and* attitude toward the category (see Table 6.1). In the next section we take a closer look at this relationship between a person's attitudes and their loyalty to a brand.

Loyalty in Target Audience Selection

The notion of brand loyalty is closely related to brand attitude, and to brand equity. When thinking about brand loyalty, it is important to understand the *degree* of loyalty, both to our brand and to competitors. As we have been discussing it, loyalty refers to a tendency to purchase a brand based upon awareness of it and some level of preference based upon the consumer's

Table 6.1 Awareness and Attitude Considerations for Potential Target Audience Buyer Groups

Buyer group	Awareness and attitude considerations
Users	
Brand loyals	• Highest awareness • Most positive brand attitude, likely to immunize against competitive message
Favourable brand-switchers	• Awareness should be high, but must be measured • Positive brand attitude, but only moderate preference
Non-users	
Other-brand-switchers	• May or may not be aware • Attitude likely to be neutral or positive
Other-brand loyals	• May or may not be aware • Strong positive attitude for loyal brand likely will immunize against our message
New category users	• Both brand awareness and attitude less important than *category* awareness and attitude

attitude toward the brand. Being loyal to a brand does not necessarily mean buying only one brand. It means buying the brand or brands that one *prefers*.[5] Many brand loyals do prefer to buy a single brand in a category, but others may be loyal to two or three brands. This does not make them 'switchers' in the way in which we have discussed them. Brand loyals have strong preferences for the brand or brands that they buy in a category, while switchers have only moderate preferences for the brands they switch between. Again, it is a matter of attitude.

A number of models have been proposed that seek to identify 'loyal' consumers. Perhaps the most familiar is the so-called 'conversion model'.[6] This model looks at consumer attitudes towards brands in a category as well as their involvement with the category. It analyses consumer attitudes on four key dimensions: interest in competitive alternatives, overall satisfaction, category involvement, and intensity or ambivalence. On the basis of a 'black-box' analysis,[7] consumers are assigned to one of four groups based upon their 'vulnerability' to switching brands: the more vulnerable, the less loyal.

We would like to introduce our own loyalty 'model' based upon how involved a person is with the category and how satisfied he or she is with a current brand. As discussed briefly in Chapter 1, involvement is a key dimension for defining brand attitude strategy for advertising and promotion. It is also a key dimension in determining brand loyalty. How much 'risk' does a consumer see in switching brands? Obviously, for most fmcgs, there will be very little perceived risk in switching brands. But, for more durable goods and for purchases and services such as banking and healthcare, there can be a good deal of perceived risk. If the perceived risk in switching is low, people *may* be open to switching brands; if the perceived risk is high, even if people are open to the idea of switching, it may be seen as too much trouble. If consumers are very satisfied with the brand they use, they will be less likely to switch; if they are unsatisfied, they will be more open to switch.

If we combine these two dimensions of perceived risk in switching and satisfaction, we can look at the target market in terms of four loyalty-related potential target audience groupings (see Fig. 6.1). The four loyalty groupings are defined as:

- *loyal*—highly satisfied with their brand and unlikely to switch;
- *vulnerable*—satisfied with their brand, but little perceived risk in switching;

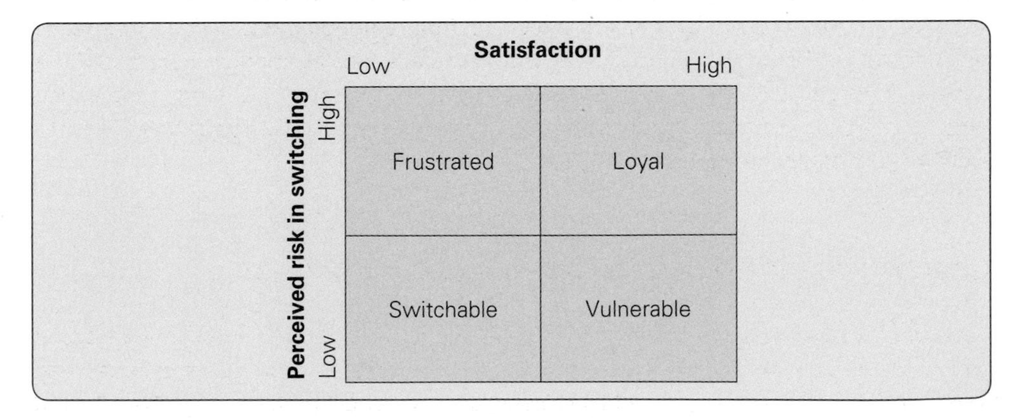

Figure 6.1 Loyalty Model Groupings

- *frustrated*—not satisfied with their brand, but feel that the risk is greater than the potential gain in switching;
- *switchable*—neither satisfied with their brand nor inhibited from switching.

This model offers more than simply looking at brand purchase behaviours, in that people who regularly buy a brand may be loyal *or* frustrated. If they are frustrated, the manager must find out why and address the problem in order to retain them as customers and build brand equity. On the other side, someone who regularly buys a competitor's brand may also be either loyal or frustrated. Those who are frustrated obviously offer more potential for trying our brand if we can overcome the perceived risk in switching. Looking at consumers who buy more than one brand in a category (for example, Rossiter and Percy's favourable brand-switchers and other-brand-switchers), we see that they can be either switchable *or* vulnerable. Those who buy our brand along with others in the category may or may not be satisfied with our brand. They may see *all* brands as merely adequate, and be open to something better. For our switchable customers, it will be necessary to build a more positive brand attitude; for our vulnerable customers, we will want to reinforce the already favourable brand attitude, strengthening brand equity to reduce the likelihood of their using other brands. Switchable competitive brand users should be open to trying our brand, given the right message. They already use more than one brand, but are not particularly happy with any of them. Our competitors' vulnerables, on the other hand, will be a tougher sell. They do use multiple brands, but are generally satisfied with them. To attract these switchers, we must convince them that they should also be using our brand.

It might help at this point to think about this idea of brand loyalty with regard to some of your own brand purchase behaviour. Think about some of the things you buy. Do you regularly use the same brand of toothpaste or shampoo? What about chocolate or snacks? If you do, how open would you be to trying other brands? For most people, they *really* like only a few brands they use, and are not likely to try others in those categories even with a substantial promotional inducement. In fact, for personal use products such as toothpaste and shampoo, about 40–50 per cent of all customers are loyal to a single brand.[8] Those are the brands that have a strong *brand equity* for those consumers. But the vast majority of brands people use are bought more out of habit than from a strong commitment to the brand.[9]

In effect, loyalty is simply a function of *attitude*. The more positive attitude is toward a brand, the more likely someone will be loyal to that brand. This reflects brand equity. As positive affect for a brand builds over time, it takes on a strong emotional association that extends well beyond just 'liking' the brand. This is what brand equity is all about.[10] Preference for a brand is internalized, going beyond any objective consideration of it. Strong brand equity leads to brand loyalty, which tends to last over time, reducing any potential vulnerability to such things as competitor promotions.

Cost Implications in Selecting a Target Audience

When the manager selects a specific target audience, it is not enough simply to look at the projected market share or revenue potential. Equally important is the *cost* of gaining these new customers (a trial objective) or of increasing usage (a repeat purchase objective).[11] If the objective is to gain new users for a brand, the cost will be greater than protecting or building on current business. The cost of attracting potential users who are not new to the category will be substantial, but going after regular users of a competitor brand will be even more expensive.

In selecting a target audience, a manager must be consistent with the marketing plan, but he or she must also approach selection with an eye on the return on investment (ROI). Except in very rare circumstances, you should consider a prospective group as a target audience only if the expected return outweighs the cost. The manager must give this matter careful attention. At a very basic level, it will cost less to maintain your business than to build on it, and to build on it than to attract new business. In selecting the target audience to satisfy the marketing objective for the brand, the manager must consider the *value* of successfully reaching the appropriate target audience group. What is the potential increase in business relative to the cost of the advertising and promotion required to secure it?

Profiling a Target Audience

Whether you are dealing with brand loyalty groupings or brand buyer groupings, it is usually helpful to have a more detailed understanding of the target audience selected. This means looking at your target audience in terms of those characteristics that Antonides and van Raaij describe as 'general-level' characteristics.[12] They consider general-level characteristics to be more or less permanent characteristics of people, and classify them as either objective or subjective. *Objective characteristics* are things such as age, education, income, and place of residence—what are known as demographics and geographics. *Subjective characteristics* are things such as lifestyle, personality, and values—what are known as psychographics. Next we shall take a closer look at these general-level characteristics.

Demographics

Demographics are perhaps the best known and most familiar of all target audience descriptions. Because they are objective characteristics, they are not only easy to identify, but also, conceptually, it is quite easy to think about them. If you market laundry soap powder, it is only natural to think in terms of women, especially women with families, as your target audience. But this does *not* describe a target *audience*. Are you really interested in all women with families? Hardly, since some are loyal to other brands, and others use liquid laundry detergents. It is certainly true that some products or services suggest a very specific demographic group as a target: toys are for families with young children, baby products for mothers with infants, retirement services for older adults, and Ferraris for people with high incomes. Advert 6.1 for Senior Railcard from National Rail offers a good example of an advert specifically targeted to a particular target market segment—in this case, those aged 60 or older. The imagery suggests travel, and the benefit is simple and clear: save money on rail travel. The benefit of saving '1/3 on most Standard and First Class rail fares throughout Britain' should be particularly attractive to this target segment.

But these are demographic characteristics that define a *target market*, not a target audience. This is a very important distinction. It may make sense to define a target market in terms

Just one trip and a Railcard could pay for itself.

(Imagine how much you could save in a year.)

60 or over? Buy a Senior Railcard for £20, and you'll save 1/3 on most Standard and First Class rail fares throughout Britain. So, if you make one journey normally costing £60, or a couple of shorter trips, you will have covered the cost of your card, just like that.

- New! Buy online at www.senior-railcard.co.uk
- Pick up a leaflet at your nearest staffed train station
- Or call 08457 48 49 50 for your local Train Company number

Advert 6.1 This advert for a Senior Railcard provides a good example of an advert targeted to a specific market segment.

Source: Advertisement supplied by the Association of Train Operating Companies.

of particular demographic characteristics, but then, *within* that demographic, we must select the target audience in terms of brand loyalty or brand buyer groupings. Once the target audience has been selected, additional demographics (or geographic or psychographic characteristics) may be looked at in order further to refine the target audience for a particular campaign. Cosmetics may be targeted at women (the target market), but, once the appropriate brand loyalty or brand buyer groupings are used to select the target audience, it would not be unusual for a particular campaign to target younger or older women—not all younger or older women, but younger or older women within the appropriate brand loyalty or brand buyer groupings.

One of the major reasons why demographics are inappropriate as primary criteria for selecting a target audience is the large amount of individual variation that can exist within a particular demographic. For example, one of the most popular misuses of demographics is with socio-economic classification. This is an attempt to group individuals in terms of their supposed 'social class', related to occupation and education or income. Antonides and van Raaij have defined social class as a 'summary of people's ranking in society with respect to profession and education'.[13] But there are potential pitfalls with such a classification.

Perhaps the most fundamental error is the assumption that all members of a particular class behave in the same way and hold the same basic attitudes about a product or service they use. This is rarely, if ever, the case. In a very interesting study conducted by Nestlé, a group of upper-middle-class shoppers, all with substantial six-figure incomes, were questioned about their use of higher-priced frozen foods. All used frozen foods, but some refused to consider the somewhat more expensive brands. When asked why, they answered that they couldn't afford to *indulge* themselves because of large, pressing expenses such as school fees or dental braces for children. When it was pointed out that the actual difference in price was very small, and in terms of the frozen food they bought would amount to no more than a euro/dollar or two per month, this simply did not matter. They could easily afford the money. But because of the 'luxury' image of these higher-priced frozen foods, this group of wealthy people felt they could not 'indulge' themselves, even though they could well afford it.

At an even more fundamental level, demographics can be misleading when used to profile a target audience. Someone with a high income may have a lot of expenses, while a retired couple with a lower income may nevertheless have significant disposable income. Age, in many ways, is less a matter of actual years than a state of mind. As Robert East has stated so well, 'demographic factors are only loosely connected to the attitudes, beliefs, and opportunities that more directly control behaviour'.[14]

Demographics can be useful, but the manager must be very careful how they are used. They should *never* be used as the primary selection criteria for a target audience, but they can often prove helpful in profiling the brand loyalty or brand buyer groupings for particular campaigns.

Geographics

It is always important to understand the geographics of your target audience. But, as we noted with demographics, this is generally a part of the *target market* descriptions. Are we looking at a multi-country marketing programme, or a programme restricted to a particular country or small group of countries, or are we dealing with a regional or local product or service? Geographics can clearly help to define the target market, but they can also be useful in better defining a target audience. Because of regional preferences or attitudes (more about this when we discuss culture below), campaigns may be targeted for particular geographic areas. If so, this becomes part of the target audience definition for that campaign. Geographics, then, can help to define a target market area, and can be used (if needed) to help to narrow down the *location* of the target audience as defined by brand loyalty or brand buyer groupings. But, just as we saw with demographics, they should *never* be used as primary selection criteria for a target audience. Do we really think that just because people live in a certain area they hold identical attitudes towards, and preferences for, particular products or brands? Of course not. Unfortunately, this is the underlying assumption of something called 'geodemographics'.

Geodemographics

By combining geographic information with demographic information, markets can be described in terms of geodemographics. One of the best-known geodemographic systems in Europe is offered by Acorn (which is an acronym of A Classification of Residential Neighbourhoods).[15] Acorn classifies residential neighbourhoods on the basis of postal codes, with certain demographics (usually income or social class) in common.

The assumption here is that people who live in a particular neighbourhood will have similar buyer behaviour patterns. While Acorn does include demographic profiles in its database, this underlying assumption is wrong. There is simply no reason to believe that people living in similar neighbourhoods are going to be loyal to the same brands, or will be more or less vulnerable or frustrated in a particular product category.

What has made geodemographic systems like Acorn (and other systems such as Mosaic and Pinpoint) so popular is that they make it very easy to target direct mail on the basis of postal codes. But the manager must ask: just what is being targeted? Once a target audience has been defined in terms of brand loyalty or brand buyer groups, *if* a correlation is found between the target audience and geodemographic classifications, fine. However, geodemographics should never be the sole, or even primary, criterion for selecting a target audience.

Psychographics

The word 'psychographics' first entered the vocabulary of advertising in the late 1950s following the introduction of a new technique for studying consumer behaviour called *motivational research*. The father of this technique was a psychologist, Ernest Dichter. The idea behind motivational research was to conduct a number of in-depth personal interviews with consumers in order to discover why they behave as they do in the market. Dichter suggested from one of his studies, for example, that men buy convertibles as a surrogate mistress, reflecting the sublimated desire of the purchaser for the lifestyle of a roué.[16] You can see why creative people in advertising loved this sort of thing.

In the twenty-first century psychographic or lifestyle variables, while still used as a subjective classification, reflect a broad assessment of non-product-related characteristics that could influence purchase- or usage-related behaviour. Psychographics give you a picture of a person's lifestyle by looking at such things as his or her general attitudes, interests, and opinions (often referred to as AIO). Some general examples of psychographics would be someone's attitude towards sports or fitness, willingness to take risks, traditional versus modern taste, concern with the environment, political opinions, concern with fashion, and innovativeness.

You can see how knowing such things about a target audience would help in better understanding them, but, as with the more objective demographic and geographic characteristics, they cannot define the target audience. The primary use of psychographic information is in helping to guide creative development of the message, and possibly in helping to select specific media vehicles that reflect a particular lifestyle.

One UK advert for a Ford Explorer (Advert 6.2) clearly reflects a 'lifestyle' dimension. It depicts a young, upscale family that enjoys spending time outdoors. But the fact that a Ford Explorer 'fits' this lifestyle does not mean that this lifestyle should define the target audience. There are many people who enjoy an outdoor lifestyle yet have no interest in a sports utility vehicle (that is, they are not in the category), or, if they are interested, may be interested in a different size (for example, the Mercedes M-Class), or have a loyalty to another brand (for example, a Land Rover). So, while lifestyle can help to target a *message*, as is well illustrated in the Ford Explorer advert, the message must be for those *within* the appropriate brand loyalty or brand buyer grouping who have that lifestyle.

Another difficulty with trying to classify people in terms of lifestyle is that it is generally not stable across product categories. At a very general level there tends to be some

Advert 6.2 An example of how an advert can reflect the lifestyle of its target audience, increasing the likelihood of its being processed.

Source: Reproduced with kind permission © Ford Motor Co.

commonality, but not at the specific level. For example, someone who has a keen interest in outdoor activities may not be interested in some specific outdoor activity.

Social Class

Back in our discussion of demographics we spent some time talking about social class. Practically speaking, it is a demographic variable, but many marketers also consider it a lifestyle variable. As Rossiter and Percy have put it, although social class is measured by *combining demographics*, it functions as a *lifestyle* variable.[17] The assumption is that people in different social classes are likely to have different lifestyles. One of the more popular European classifications of social class is provided by the Joint Industry Committee for National Readership Surveys. It classifies people into six groups: (A) Upper Middle Class, (B) Middle Class, (C1) Lower Middle Class, (C2) Skilled Working Class, (D) Working Class, and (E) those at the lowest levels of subsistence.

Even though Antonides and van Raaij feel that social class is an important determinant of consumer behaviour,[18] as we pointed out in our earlier discussion, and while there may be a certain *implied* relationship between social class and consumer behaviour, it is more likely to be at the target market, not target audience, level. We may be targeting the upper middle class or middle class for designer clothing, but, for our brand marketing communication strategy, we must understand the appropriate brand loyalty or brand buyer groupings from the social classes in order to pinpoint the target audience. As Fill has reminded us, relying upon social class can be misleading and prone to excessive generalization.[19]

Values

Another popular lifestyle measure is centred around 'values'. But again, assuming that we can find a good summary measure of someone's values, while this may be useful in profiling a target audience or in trying to explain behaviour at a general level, it has more utility in the development of creative *execution* than it does for communication strategy. There are a number of value classification systems used by advertisers, but we would recommend *extreme* caution with all of them.

Perhaps the best known such value system is VALS, introduced in the late 1970s (VALS-1) and revised in the late 1980s (VALS-2) by SRI International in the US. VALS-2 classifies people into eight groups based upon two dimensions: 'resources' (things such as education, skills, and income) and 'self-orientation'. The names of the eight resulting groups are meant to suggest the 'most important value' to that group: Strugglers, Believers, Fulfilleds, Strivers, Achievers, Makers, Experiencers, and Actualizers. Of course, rather detailed descriptions are available for each of these groups.[20]

One of the many problems with VALS has been its inability to be applied across countries—not only, say, between the US and Thailand, but also between more homogeneous-seeming countries in Europe such as Sweden and Germany. Another problem stems from the fact that a person can belong to only one group. This is always a problem with any rigid system that aims at too much generality.

Another values system is marketed by Synergy Brand Values in the UK and Europe. Its system is based upon Maslow's hierarchy of needs. It utilizes the dimensions of 'inner-directed', 'outer-directed', and 'sustenance-driven' to classify people into seven groups: Self-explorers, Experimentalists, Conspicuous Consumers, Belongers, Survivors, Social Resisters, and the Aimless. These groups vary in size from the Aimless at 6 per cent of the population to Survivors at 23 per cent.

These social value groups, however, have the same problems as those discussed above for VALS, as well as the fact that they are based upon Maslow's work. We are in agreement with the many authors cited by Landy[21] who feel that Maslow's theory is of more historical than functional value, and conclude that there is really no evidence to support the high regard in which his theory seems to be held by many marketers.

Culture

Another important lifestyle characteristic is culture, a subject covered in some detail in Chapter 3. We have chosen to consider culture as a lifestyle variable rather than a demographic or geographic variable because the idea of 'culture' is not necessarily fixed. To say that someone is from England or France or Germany is not the same thing as saying that he or she is English, French, or German. Antonides and van Raaij have defined culture as 'the entirety of societal knowledge, norms, and values', very much as they define lifestyle as 'the entire set of values, interests, opinions, and behaviour of consumers'.[22]

Culture is clearly related to how people behave, and for that reason is an important target audience profile variable. But additionally, in Europe as elsewhere in the world, how people look at or understand advertising messages is heavily influenced by their culture. In fact, as de Mooij has pointed out, the advertising 'style' of different European countries clearly reflects the cultural values of that country (see Table 6.2). There seems little doubt that culture conditions perceptions, and this influences how people respond to advertising.[23] A cultural assessment of your target audience provides a very important profile variable, and is essential for multi-country or global advertising.

Personality

Personality is definitely not something ever to consider as a primary characteristic by which to select a target audience—and personality characteristics do not help to determine a target market. So why consider personality as a profile variable? Its importance as a target audience profile variable comes from the effect that personality characteristics have on how advertising and promotion messages are *processed*. And while it is almost impossible to know the personality characteristics of a target audience, it is important for managers to be aware of how they could be influencing message processing. This is especially true of the *verbal content* of marketing communication.

Generally, when we think of personality, we are thinking about *personality traits*. These are the more or less permanent characteristics of personality that lead people to respond to life in a basically predictable fashion. In the psychological literature, of all of the possible mediators of persuasion in communication, personality traits have probably been studied more than any other. But we must also be aware of *personality states*. As we all know, in certain circumstances, we may exhibit personality traits that are not usual for us—for example, undue anxiety during times of stress.

Table 6.2 **How European Advertising Style Reflects Cultural Values**

Britain	• **Reflects a highly individualistic society** • Ads show individuals or couples (large groups are rare) • Much use of direct address • Strong focus on humour • Only European country in which class differences are recognized in advertising
Germany	• **Reflects the need for structure, directness, and facts** • Characterized by the need for structure and explicit language to avoid ambiguity
Italy	• **Reflects a collectivist culture** • Drama and theatre, with strong role differentiation reflected in depiction of males and females
Spain	• **Reflects collectivist culture, but takes into account individualistic claims** • As a result, less direct than advertising style of Northern Europe • Use of visual metaphors
France	• **Reflects a need to be different** • A propensity for the theatrical and the bizarre • Sensual and erotic style
Netherlands	• **Strongly reflects the levelling attitude induced by a feminine culture** • Softer, more entertaining advertising • Hype is not appreciated, nor are pushy presenters
Sweden	• **Reflects a very feminine culture** • Men are shown doing the work in the home • Entertainment is frequently used, often within a context of disrespect for authority

Source: Adapted from M. de Mooij, *Global Marketing and Advertising: Understanding Cultural Paradoxes* (Thousand Oaks, CA: Sage, 1998). Reprinted by permission of Sage.

Personality Traits

We mentioned that personality traits are one of the most widely studied variables affecting persuasion in communication. Interestingly, the results of all of these studies often produce quite opposite-seeming conclusions. These contradictions mean that you must be very careful when looking at personality traits and their probable effects on how a target audience will process advertising.[24] Three personality traits that particularly influence how advertising messages are processed are self-esteem, intelligence, and introversion/extroversion.

Self-esteem is perhaps the most widely studied personality trait, at least in relation to how susceptible someone might be to a persuasive message. When a message is *simple*, the higher someone's self-esteem, the less likely he or she is to be persuaded; the lower the self-esteem, the more likely. But when the message is more *complex* or specific, the higher someone's self-esteem, the *more* likely he or she is to be persuaded; the lower the self-esteem, the less likely.

Intelligence is a highly relevant personality trait for advertising, again in terms of the target audience's ability to deal with the complexity of a message. It should make intuitive sense that a more intelligent person will be better able to deal with a complex message, and this is true. Additionally, especially for high-involvement advertising, a more intelligent person should require fewer repetitions to learn the message. Remember that we are talking about the personality trait of raw intelligence here, *not* a surrogate such as education.

Something else to be considered here is that when advertising or other marketing communication is *written* in English (or the audio in radio or television is in English), people whose first language is not English should be thought of as 'less intelligent' as far as processing the message is concerned. It is not that they have lower IQs. They are simply not as competent in English as a native speaker. This means that English-language advertising running in continental Europe (or *any* other non-English-speaking country) should avoid complex messages, and the copy should be kept simple.[25]

Introversion/extroversion is one of the few personality traits that is in fact strongly correlated with actual behaviour and attitudes.[26] For example, extroverts have been shown to like novelty and change, even while being realistic and practical in their attitudes. They are adventure seeking, more likely to use tobacco, and more likely to drink coffee and alcohol. Introverts, on the other hand, value privacy and close friendships, and tend to be anxious in social situations.[27]

The population is roughly split in terms of whether introversion or extroversion is the dominant trait (with a slight edge to extroverts). Informational appeals (those addressing a negative purchase motive) should be more effective with introverts, while the more outgoing extrovert should be more responsive to appeals addressing positive motives such as social approval.[28]

Personality States

A personality state is really nothing more than a temporary activation of a personality characteristic that is not enduring for that individual. Since it actually operates like a trait when it is activated, we can think of it in much the same way. This means that it can have an important effect upon how the verbal content of communication is processed. As an example, let us look at *anxiety*, a personality characteristic that is often aroused by outside stimulation acting on a personality state. If you are planning to drive to the French Alps for a skiing holiday and, on the day you leave, the weather report forecasts heavy snow en route, this could very well raise your anxiety level. What is happening is that the anxiety state is 'warning' you to consider avoiding the storm because it is thought to be potentially threatening. This is really what anxiety is all about: a state that warns you to avoid a future situation.

How might anxiety as a personality state affect the processing of advertising? Anxiety can interfere with the likelihood that or the length of time that people pay attention to your message; even if they do pay attention, anxiety can interfere with their comprehension. If what you see or read in an advert raises your anxiety level, you simply tune it out, either actually by turning away or leaving the room, or mentally. This is something that often happens with some of the more gruesome social marketing communication against drug and alcohol abuse. But it can also occur with insurance company or car tyre advertising that depicts bad accidents, or healthcare advertising showing realistic emergency treatment. We do not want to leave the impression that anxiety is always a problem. In fact, if the message makes you anxious, but you still pay attention, you are actually *more* likely to be persuaded. The trick is to make sure that the creative execution does not go too far and raise anxiety so high that it interferes with attention. We shall return to this subject in Chapter 13 when we are dealing with social marketing communication.

While there are a few predictable situations that tend to arouse some personality states (for example, when a target audience might be tired), the manager's concern should be with the potential of the advertising itself, along with the context within which it is delivered, to arouse a personality state.

Personality and its Relationship with Advertising

Figure 6.2 provides a simplified idea of how personality traits and states can affect or be affected by advertising and other marketing communication. People's prior experiences and their attitudes will always affect how a message is processed, and we will spend a lot of time dealing with this in later chapters.

As we have seen, personality traits, because they are enduring characteristics, can influence how someone processes a message. For example, if someone whose personality reflects a high level of nurturance (a personality trait that suggests a desire to look after and care for people) sees an advertisement for a product positioned as helping you to take better care of your family, their naturally high level of nurturance should mean they will pay more attention to the advertising and there will be a greater likelihood of them responding positively to the message.

Personality states, because they are temporary, can influence message processing in two ways. If some outside event has aroused a personality characteristic, this could influence how a message is processed at that time, or the message itself could arouse that state. Continuing with our nurturance example, while someone may not naturally exhibit a high degree of nurturance, we all occasionally experience it as a state. Think about how you feel when you see a baby, or even a puppy. This is something known as an 'innate releasing mechanism'.

Suppose you have just watched a particularly heart-warming programme on television and have a warm, contented feeling. This could certainly affect how you process any advertising within the programme or immediately after. On the other hand, a particularly 'warm and

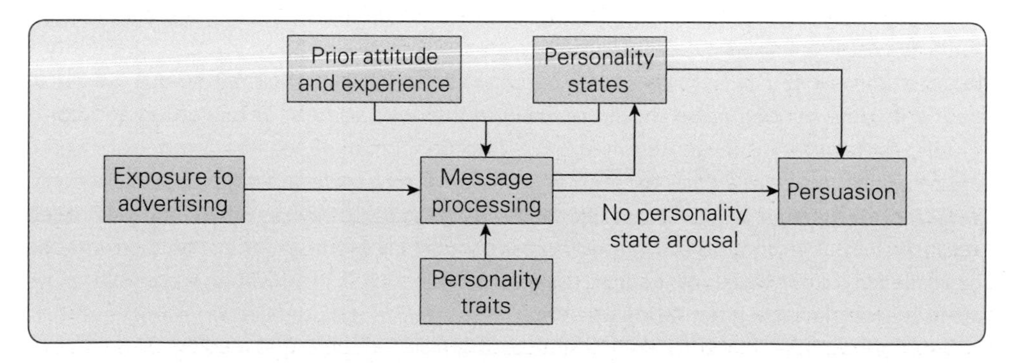

Figure 6.2 Personality and its Influence on Advertising and Persuasion

fuzzy' advertisement could itself stimulate a temporary warm feeling that could influence how you process the message. In order to account for the effects of personality in your target audience, it makes sense to test a sample of the brand loyalty or brand buyer groups selected as your target audience *if* you feel a particular personality trait might have either a positive or a negative effect upon how they process your message. Recall the examples we discussed in the section on personality traits. To address personality states, the manager must pay attention to the context in which advertising or other marketing communication is likely to be seen—for example, in a situation comedy, on a bus poster, or at a sporting event. Additionally, if a personality characteristic could potentially be aroused by the message—for example, positively by a very 'warm and fuzzy' execution or negatively by a 'frightening' message—check for these effects when pre-testing the advertising.

Segmentation

This is a good place to talk about segmentation. Segmentation is a powerful tool for understanding a market and helping to optimize targeting, but we will not spend a great deal of time discussing it in this book. Why not, if it is so important? The reason is that the primary use of segmentation is in defining a target *market*, not a target audience. As noted earlier, this is an important distinction, and one not often made.

Any good marketing or consumer behaviour text will have a chapter on market segmentation (and it should). We like Fill's definition of market segmentation as 'the division of a mass market into distinct groups which have common characteristics, needs, and similar responses to marketing action'.[29] Although this definition is in a marketing communication text, it is in a chapter on *marketing strategy*. This is where market segmentation belongs, in discussions of marketing strategy.

Having said this, segmentation does have a place in better defining a target audience. When we talked about buyer groups as perhaps the best way in which to select a target audience, we pointed out that this is because loyalty reflects the target market's *attitude* towards the category and its brands. Segmentation relevant to marketing communication must be based upon attitude. Attitudes bear directly upon communication strategy because it is attitude that determines how someone is likely to respond to a message, and how he or she behaves. It is easy to become confused because all of the target audience variables that we have just discussed can and are used as *market* segmentation variables. But, as we have continually pointed out, knowing that someone is young or old, lives in the country or the town, is outgoing, likes sports, or travels a lot is simply not good enough to identify a target audience. It may help you to understand the target audience better, but it will not define it. How segmentation should be used in the development of marketing and communication strategy is illustrated in Fig. 6.3. Traditional market segmentation looks at the entire market, using as a basis for segmentation any and all relevant variables. These could very well be demographics, geographics, or psychographics, what Rothschild has called 'enduring variables' that do not change across product categories, or they could be what he has called 'dynamic variables', such as usage or benefits.[30] It is of course also possible to use attitudes for market segmentation as well.

But once we have set our marketing strategy and selected the target market, we must then identify the target audience. Here the only correct segmentation variable is attitude.[31] We are

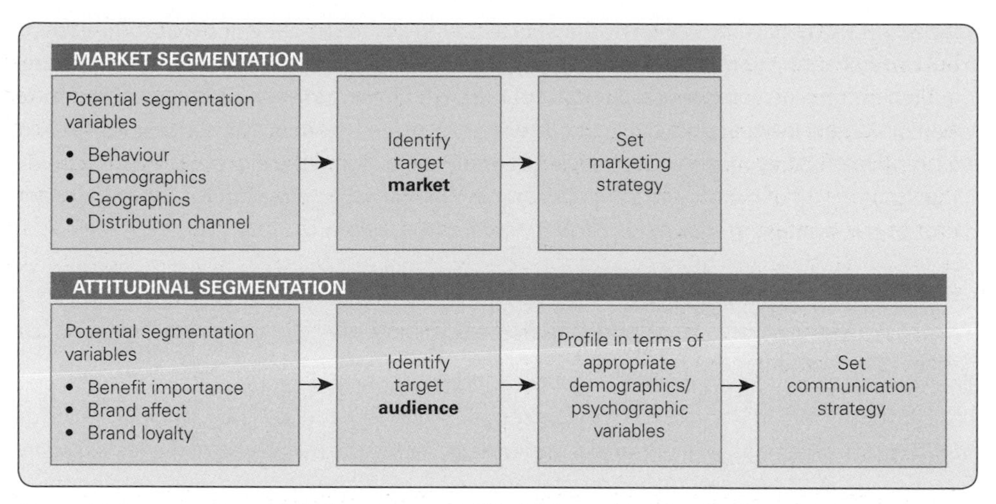

Figure 6.3 Segmentation and the Development of Marketing and Communication Strategy

looking for groups of people in the target market who hold relatively similar attitudes towards category usage and brands within the category. While more often than not target audience selection should be based upon appropriate buyer groups, it is also important to know how the target audience segments generally in terms of other relevant attitudes if we are to optimize communication strategy. The target audience 'segments' will likely have common attitudes in terms of their brand behaviour, but is what they are looking for, say, in terms of benefits the same?

This is why a communication-based attitudinal segmentation is so desirable. Without it, the manager must select the target audience only in terms of brand-buying behaviour. While it is easy to select a target audience in this way because brand purchase data is readily available (for example, from the TGI, the Target Group Index[32]), to develop the most effective communication strategy and creative executions, an understanding of our target audience's category and brand attitudes is essential. It is not enough simply to understand purchase behaviour.

The target audience, whether identified from brand loyalty or brand buyer groupings, is selected to satisfy the objectives of the marketing strategy. But to *communicate* effectively with the target audience, the manager must fully understand what fundamental attitude segments they reflect. This, along with appropriate demographic, geographic, and psychographic profile variables, enables the manager to put together an effective communication strategy, as well as help in media selection.

Target Audience and Strategy

Once the target audience has been selected and profiled, it remains to link the target audience with the marketing strategy and that with the communication strategy. Indeed, the selection of the target market and then the target audience will have followed from the marketing objectives set out in the marketing plan. What we are more concerned with are the specifics of the *behavioural* objectives associated with the target audience that should result from our marketing communication, the target audience action we talked about in the communication response sequence. The selection of the target audience will have determined whether we are looking principally at customers or non-customers (or perhaps both), and this in turn will determine whether the target audience action objective is *trial* or *repeat purchase* or use.[33] All of this should be spelled out in the marketing plan, but must now become a part of our strategic communication planning.

Target Audience Links to Marketing Strategy

The marketing objectives as detailed in the marketing plan will generally specify whether concentrating on new customers or on repeat business is to be the principal path for building or maintaining the brand. If a market is growing, the marketing manager is usually looking for new customers. In a more stable market, maintaining share or increasing business is more likely to come from current customers, or from both new and existing customers if the objective is to increase business. For example, with fmcg products, about 60 per cent of sales growth comes from attracting new customers who continue to purchase, and 40 per cent from encouraging existing customers to buy more.[34] These marketing objectives clearly help to specify the target audience at a macro level: will it be primarily customers or non-customers?

We need to keep this in mind when planning our communication strategy. If the target audience is made up primarily of customers, the action objective will be repeat purchase or use; if the target audience is primarily non-customers, the action objective will be trial. This distinction will hold regardless of whether we are talking about a consumer, business, or trade target audience. Typical examples of trial and repeat purchase objectives linked to a marketing strategy are offered below.

Consumer target audience. The types of trial behaviour sought from consumers include such things as encouraging people to try a brand if it is an fmcg, or to take the first step towards considering higher-involvement, higher-risk purchases. This could be anything from making a phone call to request information to visiting a dealer. When the action objective is repeat purchase, we may be looking for our customers to continue purchasing at the same rate (especially those loyal to the brand), to increase the number of units that they buy at a time, or to buy our product more often.

Business target audience. These same general action objectives apply to business-to-business marketing. When we are looking for new customers, the specific trial behaviours desired could include such things as enquiries about a new product, requests for a demonstration or feasibility study, or asking to see a sales rep. If we are looking to customers for repeat business, just as with consumers we may want them to maintain their current level of business, to increase the number of units they buy at a time, or to use our product more often.

Trade target audience. In addition to consumer and business markets, many companies must also market to trade—the wholesalers or retailers that carry or distribute their products. If you are looking for new trade outlets, this corresponds to a trial action objective. If you are trying to get the trade to maintain premium shelf space or display, or to move more of your brand, this corresponds to a repeat purchase action objective.

Target Audience Links to Communication Strategy

The target audience links to marketing strategy address the fundamental distinction between customers and non-customers, and relate that distinction to the behavioural objectives of trial and repeat purchase. Now we must also consider this same distinction within the context of communication strategy for both advertising and promotion. As you might suppose, the communication strategy that drives trial will be different from that driving repeat purchase. In Chapter 9 we will see that coupons, refunds and rebates, and sampling promotion techniques work best for trial, while loyalty and loading devices, sweepstakes, games and contests, and premiums work best for repeat purchase objectives.

While a target audience based only upon brand buyer groupings already accounts for the distinction between customers and non-customers, brand loyalty groups do not. Both brand users and non-users (with the exception of those not category users at present) can fall within one of the four brand loyalty groupings, and the target audience action objective will vary accordingly. This distinction is summarized in Table 6.3.

Throughout this chapter we have been underscoring the importance of *attitude* in selecting and understanding the target audience. Brand loyalty groupings, and at heart even brand buyer groupings, result from an individual's attitude towards the category and its brands. We have pointed out several times that brand attitude (along with brand awareness) is *always* a communication objective. It should be no surprise that the attitude of the target audience towards the brands in the category will be instrumental in formulating the overall communication strategy.

At a very basic level, we can see how the attitudes towards a brand that underlie the brand loyalty groupings will influence strategy. When loyals are part of a target audience, it will be essential at least to maintain their already high positive brand attitude. Frustrated and switchable consumers, because of their lower satisfaction with a brand, will require the building of a more favourable brand attitude. Vulnerables, even though they are generally satisfied with

Table 6.3 Target Audience Action Objectives and Groupings

Target audience action objectives	Brand buyer groupings	Corresponding brand loyalty groupings
Non-users	NCU	None
Trial objective	OBL	L
	OBS	F/V/S
Users	BL	L
Repeat-purchase objective	BS	F/V/S

NCU: New category users; OBL: Other-brand loyals; OBS: Other-brand-switchers; BL: Brand loyals; BS: Brand-switchers; L: Loyal; F: Frustrated; V: Vulnerable; S: Switchable

→ content, but also about what kind of readership club they were joining. At best, they saw it as an authoritative academic, but more often as a smug banker in a pinstriped suit. So we did something a little unusual in the second part of our research: we forced our reticent respondents to experience *The Economist's* actual content first hand to see what would happen. We gave them the content pages and a fluorescent marker, and asked them to highlight what they would like to read in the following twenty minutes. And so they read, for twenty minutes.

Afterwards, two-thirds left with the magazine under their arm. What had converted them and not the other third? A fundamental difference stood out. Our converts had chosen to read about subjects they knew little about, expanding upon these new areas with other elements of their personal knowledge, which explained why those topics had interested them. Our non-converts had chosen to read articles in areas they were already knowledgeable about and had felt let down by the lack of depth, because they only had one edition at their disposal.

This allowed us to distinguish the two modes of knowledge gathering that 'Generation Why' use.

- *Beachcombing*: beachcombers start with what's out there and find something worth picking up. They naturally connect what they randomly find to other pieces of knowledge to build a broader personal web of interconnected thoughts.
- *Coal-mining*: coal-miners start from their area of interest and then dig deeper. They use the information that they find to further their understanding of the area in question.

Our new audience switches between both modes, according to the context they find themselves in and their personal predisposition. Importantly, *The Economist* is particularly relevant for these readers when they are in beachcombing mode. Therefore, for 'Generation Why', we needed to position *The Economist* as:

- *broad*—it enables them to expand their web of knowledge into new areas;
- *fact-based*—it helps them to keep their web of knowledge connected with reality;
- *analytical*—it points out links and connections, making articles stickier and more connectable to existing ideas and material in their own web of knowledge.

But how could we bring this to life in our creative work?

We needed to change our briefing strategy. We decided to free everyone from words. *The Economist's* advertising heritage was entirely verbal, as were our briefs. So instead of briefing with more words, we drew a picture, a picture of 'beachcombing'. We mapped out all of the connections we had heard our seventy-one intellectually curious respondents make during our six weeks of research. The result was a map of connections, linking articles with respondents' knowledge, creating a web of interconnected ideas. With this visual stimulus, we showed the teams how our audience think in links. The best creative work we saw next was a visual metaphor for the exploratory journey of your mind wandering from one idea to the other, serendipitously jumping from one connected thought to another. We had moved from rational words in print and poster, to an emotional spectacle, placing film at the heart of our repositioning effort.

The film opens on a normal guy, in jeans and trainers. He is walking casually in a busy street. Suddenly, his attention is drawn to a red wire in front of him. This wire starts from the ground and stretches up into the air. He starts to walk on to the wire. Each step takes him higher. The crowd around him is oblivious to this young man walking on a tightrope above them, underscoring the idea that he is on a mental journey of pleasurable discovery. We enjoy the exhilaration of his movements from wire to wire. Finally, we see the words: '*The Economist.* Let your mind wander.' The rest of the campaign communicated online and below the line, delivering the behavioural and literal side of the journey, enabling readers to explore *The Economist* through one connection to another in a random fashion.

As we put pen to paper, this bold decision to go after 'Generation Why' has already revolutionized all areas of the business. Brand marketing, circulation, subscription, and digital departments have all transformed their plans to reflect the new target and positioning. The subscriptions team is conducting new research on students. The retail team is reviewing its strategy to incorporate SMS alerts and direct sales, better suited to target the new audience. Distribution channels are shifting to reflect the fact that 'Generation Why' Londoners buy magazines in supermarkets, whilst the rest of the country favours corner shops. And the most ambitious plan: delivering *Economist* content using beachcombing principles as a navigational guide. Building this *Economist* tool, as inspired by the map of connections used in creative briefing, is top of the 2010 agenda.

Source: APG Creative Strategy Awards 2009. © Account Planning Group, London www.apg.org.uk. Edited by Elizabeth Mamali, PhD Researcher, Bath School of Management.

Discussion questions

1. What are the awareness and attitude considerations for the new target audience?
2. What are the objective and subjective characteristics of 'Generation Why'?
3. Why did the 'let your mind wander' campaign work well with the new target audience?
4. What do you think are the effects of the new positioning on the older, elite target group of business men?

Further reading

Ronald Paul Hill, 'Consumer Culture and the Culture of Poverty: Implications for Marketing Theory and Practice', *Marketing Theory, 2/3* (2002), 273–93
Offers interesting insights into understanding potential target audiences, and deals with the role of marketing in the lives of the poor

Rob Lawson and Jonah Todd, 'Consumer Lifestyles: A Social Stratification Perspective', *Marketing Theory, 2/3* (2002), 295–307
Argues that lifestyle dimensions should be looked at from Weber's social stratification approach to status rather than that of psychographics.

Marteke de Mooij and Geert Hofstede, 'The Hofstede Model: Applications to Global Branding and Advertising Strategy and Research', *International Journal of Advertising*, 29/1 (2010), 85–110
More information on the Hofstede culture model and difference in global advertising.

S. Dibb and L. Simkin, *The Market Segmenter Workbook: Making it Happen* (London: Routledge, 2007)
An extended framework for segmentation.

Notes

1. Gerat Antonides and W. Fred van Raaij talk about target groups in their book *Consumer Behaviour: A European Perspective* (Chichester: John Wiley and Sons, 1998). Interestingly, the subject does not come up until quite near the end of the book in a section on market segmentation.
2. J.R. Rossiter and L. Percy, *Advertising Communication and Promotion Management* (New York: McGraw-Hill, 1997).

33. While the fundamental behavioural objectives are trial and repeat purchase or use, Rossiter and Percy, in *Advertising Communication and Promotion Management* (New York: McGraw-Hill, 1997), 63, point out that there are 'finer gradations' based upon behavioural considerations such as occurrence, rate of purchase, amount purchased, timing, and persistence.
34. See A.L. Baldinger, E. Blair, and R. Echambadi, 'Why Brands Grow', *Journal of Advertising Research*, 42/1 (2002), 7–14.

Visit the Online Resource Centre that accompanies this book for additional resources to support the text: **www.oxfordtextbooks.co.uk/orc/percy_elliott4e/**

Understanding Target Audience Decision Making

After selecting the target audience, the manager must now gain an understanding of how the target audience goes about making purchase decisions in the category. This involves establishing who is likely to participate in the decision and the roles that they play in the process, and developing a Behavioural Sequence Model (BSM) that identifies the likely stages the target audience goes through in making a purchase decision. Once constructed, the model provides important insights into positioning, communication, and media strategy.

Implementing the Strategic Planning Process

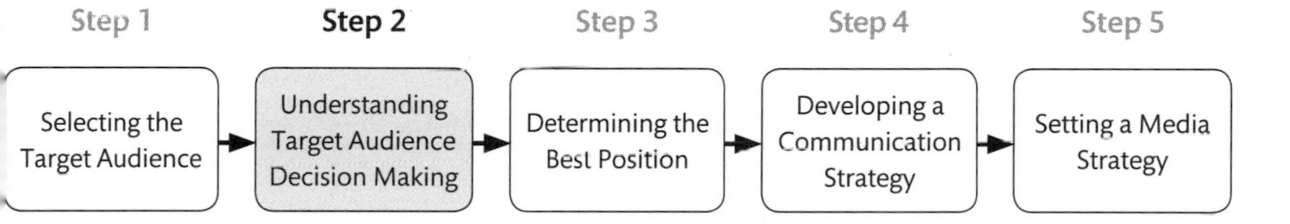

STEP 2 UNDERSTAND TARGET AUDIENCE DECISION MAKING	
Behavioural Sequence Model	
Determine decision stages, then for each stage establish: • individuals involved and roles they play • probable location • time and timing • capsule description of how it is accomplished	Completed model guides positioning, communication, and media strategy—steps 3, 4, and 5 of the strategic planning process

Key concepts

1. The key to understanding how the target audience makes purchase decisions is to develop a Behavioural Sequence Model (BSM) to determine the various stages they go through, from when a need for the product first occurs, until they have selected, purchased, and used a particular brand.
2. Then establish who is involved at each stage and the roles that they play, where each stage occurs, the timing, and how each stage in the decision process occurs. This will help guide positioning, communication, and media strategy.
3. It is important to understand not only who is participating in a purchase decision, but also the *roles* that they play in the decision process, which may be as an initiator of the process, an influencer, a decider, a purchaser, or a user.
4. A person may play all of the roles in a purchase decision or participate only in some; advertising must address people in terms of the role(s) that they play, not just as individuals.

The importance of understanding how consumers behave in a category before attempting to develop marketing and communication strategies may seem obvious to us today. Yet, oddly enough, the formal study of consumer behaviour as such is a relatively recent phenomenon. It was not until the 1960s that consumer behaviour became an academic field of study in its own right, and the first textbooks on the subject were written. From the very beginning, however, researchers and academics have noted the important link between understanding how consumers behave and creating effective marketing and communication strategies.[1]

Also from the earliest days of the study of consumer behaviour as a discipline, those working in the area have been interested in modelling how consumers behave, and have included in these models the important link between how consumers deal with information and how that influences the way in which they go about making decisions.[2] In Antonides and van Raaij's book on consumer behaviour from a European perspective,[3] the authors devote an entire chapter to the consumer decision process, and one to situation and behaviour. People who study consumer behaviour know how important it is to understand how consumers go about making decisions to buy products or utilize services, and it is *equally* important to the study of the management of advertising and other marketing communication.

It has been suggested that theories of decision-making behaviour fall into two categories: behavioural processes and cognitive processes.[4] Most people involved in the study of consumer behaviour think about decision making as a cognitive process, with a few notable exceptions, such as Gordon Foxall. The Behavioural Sequence Model (BSM) we will be discussing in depth later on in this chapter, despite using the term 'behavioural', is squarely in the tradition of cognitive notions of decision making.

Proponents of the behavioural process in decision making do not believe it is possible to even discuss what is going on in a consumer's mind, let alone to base a theory upon it. For them, we must rely upon analysis of observations or self-reports of actual behaviour. This idea is informed by Skinner's theory of operant behaviourism.[5] Foxall has advanced this idea in recent years, arguing that insight into behaviour follows from an examination of the environment surrounding the behaviour of interest, both past and present.[6]

Those who advocate a behaviourist approach to understanding consumer decision making feel that the job of marketing communication is to stimulate the correct environmental cues: for example, messages that relate a brand's benefit specifically to the positive consequence of using it or the negative consequence of not using the brand.

Those who look at consumer decision making in terms of a cognitive process look at it in terms of how the mind is processing information when making a decision.[7] Most of the early models of consumer decision making were built upon this idea, while also looking at it as a *process*. In other words, they were interested in understanding, in modelling, what went on in the consumer's mind during a series of steps or stages that are involved in reaching a decision.

The processes outlined in these models range from the rather straightforward representation offered by Howard to much more involved models. Howard identified three potential processes in consumer decision making: routinized response behaviour, limited problem solving, and extensive problem solving.[8] These have been adopted by Solomon as a 'continuum of buying decision behaviour', reflecting (as he puts it) the amount of effort that goes into the decision each time it is made.[9] More complicated models have grown out of the early Howard and Sheth model to multicomponent models such as that offered by Engel and his colleagues.[10] These are very extensive models, but basically outline a series of stages associated with some identification of need, information search and evaluation, purchase, and post-purchase evaluation.

While it is beyond the scope of this book to undertake an in-depth study of consumer decision making,[11] it is nonetheless important for the manager to have a way of looking at how people in his or her target market are likely to go about making decisions to buy or use products or services. A very practical tool that can help managers to deal with this issue is the Behavioural Sequence Model (BSM) first introduced by Rossiter and Percy in 1987.[12] The BSM is strongly rooted in previous cognitive process models of buyer behaviour, but it deals much more specifically with the decision *process*, and how that process is likely to be affected by marketing communication. In this chapter we will look at the foundation of the BSM, and at how this can be used to help to guide the development of marketing communication strategy.

Developing a Model of Target Audience Decision Making

The Behavioural Sequence Model utilizes a grid format that requires you first to identify the probable *stages* involved in making a decision, and then, for each stage in the process, to determine: *who* is involved; *where* that stage in the decision is likely to occur; *when* each stage occurs in relation to the other decision stages; and *how* that stage is likely to occur. The result is a detailed flow chart that identifies where potential members of the target market are likely to be making decisions and taking actions that lead to actual purchase and use of a product or service.

The objective of any model of consumer decision making is to provide a useful format to help managers to begin to think of where in the target audience's decision process marketing communication may be expected to influence brand choice. Once the model has been developed, it helps the manager to identify specific targeting objectives. It is surprisingly easy to

Table 7.1 Generic Consumer Decision-Making Model

	Decision Stage			
	Need arousal	Brand consideration	Purchase	Usage
Individuals involved and decision roles				
Where stage is likely to occur				
Timing of stage				
How stage is likely to occur				

construct a decision-making model like the BSM, utilizing what those involved with a brand know about their market. As the manager works through the model, if 'gaps' in the understanding of the brand are uncovered, it will be necessary to conduct whatever research is required in order to feel comfortable that the model does indeed accurately reflect how consumers are making choices in the brand's category.

While it is important that a target audience decision-making model be developed specifically for a particular product category, utilizing the decision stages most likely to be operating for that category, a generic model can be helpful in initiating the process. The generic model shown in Table 7.1 illustrates how four general decision stages are combined, with the decision roles involved at each stage, where each stage is likely to occur, the timing for each stage, and how each stage is likely to happen. Each of the components of the model will now be discussed.

Decision Stages

From as long ago as the beginnings of consumer behaviour theory, the idea of 'stages' of a consumer's decision process has been central to notions of how consumers make choices.[13] Complete models of consumer behaviour have almost always included some stepwise component dealing with the decision model, as we have mentioned earlier. While these models can often be very intimidating, they do acknowledge the necessity of understanding the consumer's decision process, and the stages in the decision, in order to understand consumer behaviour.

Perhaps the most widely known and most enduring of these general models is that originally offered by Engel and his colleagues in the 1960s. In a recent version of their model, we find a five-stage decision process component composed of: need recognition, search, alternative evaluation, purchasing, and outgoings.[14] The similarity of this to our set of decision stages in the generic model is not accidental. Some such 'flow' of thought and action is at the heart of any consumer purchase behaviour, and this is what we want to capture with a target audience decision-making model.

However, the important point to understand is that the exact words we use are not the crucial thing. What is important is that the manager begin to think about how consumers make decisions in the category, and at what points in this process advertising and other marketing communication can influence what brand is chosen. While the decision stages in the generic model are useful, and can generally be adapted to almost any product category, it is best to develop *specific* decision stages that more closely reflect how you understand decisions to be made in a brand's category. Some decisions may be quite simple, others more complicated. The decision stages for most fmcg products among brand loyals are simply need arousal—purchase—usage. For example, if you have a favourite chocolate bar that you regularly buy, when you want a chocolate bar (need arousal), you will probably seek out your favourite brand and buy it (purchase), then eat it on the spot (usage).

But if we consider a decision for something like a holiday trip, the decision stages involved would likely be much more involved. Something will get you thinking about your next holiday, and you will begin to look into various alternatives. You will evaluate the options, and decide where you would like to go. Then you will need to check on availabilities and see if you can schedule the trip. You make the arrangements, go on the trip, and hopefully enjoy yourself, then 'relive' the experience afterward with pictures and discussions with friends.

The decision stages in this holiday example are much more descriptive than those in the generic model, but they still reflect the basic generic stages. Starting to think about a holiday is need arousal; looking into and evaluating places to go is brand consideration; checking into availability and scheduling the trip is purchase; and going on the trip and 'reliving' it is usage. Modifications of the generic stages to fit specific circumstances enhances the utility of the model. The whole idea is to capture the essence of the decision process in order to facilitate marketing communication planning. Even though we are only at the first step in constructing the model (admittedly the most important), already we can see how laying out the decision stages can help to pinpoint opportunities for affecting choice outcomes with advertising and other marketing communications.

Continuing with our holiday example, if we were the marketing manager for a resort on the southern coast of France, we would want to be sure that potential guests are aware of the resort so that it comes to mind when they begin to think about a holiday and look into various alternatives. In later chapters we will discuss the importance of building this link between what we call category need (going on a holiday in this case) and brand awareness (our resort). We will want to be sure that potential guests have the information they need about our resort to evaluate it favourably. This could mean print advertising in appropriate magazines or direct mail brochures, as well as collateral material for travel agents. To facilitate the decision in our favour, perhaps we will want to offer some sort of incentive (especially at off-peak times of the year). At the resort itself, we will want to remind the guests of what a great choice they have made. The resort will, of course, need to meet the guests' expectations, but in many ways marketing communication can help to reinforce this positive experience. Once guests have returned home, follow-up direct mail and general advertising can continue to reinforce the experience, building a stronger brand attitude, and increasing intentions to return. It should now be clear that managers must do more than simply decide they want to advertise and perhaps run the odd promotion or two. Marketing communication must be considered in the light of how it is most likely to influence consumers positively as they are going through the process of making decisions. A good understanding of the decision stages is a key element in strategic marketing communication planning.

→ genuinely prompted for a response regarding the Masters programme. Online PR posts were used by the client to syndicate key press releases to targeted audiences. The online PR was more targeted to the decision maker and parents of potential students. The press releases had an editorial style and provided factual data that would aid the decision maker in their assessment of the programme value. The site link was also added to various user-generated content sites (such as Wikipedia) and was distributed to a host of free-to-list directory sites.

Source: This is an edited version of a case study submitted to the IPA Effectiveness Awards. The full case study can be found at ipa.co.uk or warc.com. © Copyright Institute of Practitioners in Advertising.

Edited by Elizabeth Mamali, PhD Researcher, Bath School of Management

Discussion questions

1. Identify the decision participants and their roles for London Business School's new MSc programme.
2. Identify the similarities between the generic consumer decision-making model and the three filtering stages of the online campaign discuss in the case. Discuss how the two could be working in parallel.
3. Discuss the possible implications of launching a new MSc programme for inexperienced graduates with regards to London Business School's traditional highly experienced, older-aged target groups.
4. Identify the reasons why a campaign based solely on the Internet was successful in achieving the set objectives.

Further reading

Gordon Foxall, 'Foundations of Consumer Behaviour Analysis', *Marketing Theory*, 1/2 (2001), 165–200

A different perspective on consumer decision making and behaviour; talks about an interpretative approach.

Jonathan Levar, Ran Kivetz, and Cecile K. Cho, 'Motivational Compatibility and Choice Conflict', *Journal of Consumer Research* , 37/3 (2010), 429–42

Explores the importance of product attribution to resolving choices between brands.

M. Laroche, 'Selected Issues in Modelling Consumer Brand Choice: The Extended Competitive Vunerability Model', in A.G. Woodside and E.M. Moore (eds) *Essays by Distinguished Marketing Scholars of the Society for Marketing Advances*, Vol 11 (American: JAI/Elsevier, 2002), 115–38

Another look at the role of benefits in brand choice.

R. Donovan and N. Henley, *Social Marketing Principles and Practice* (Melbourne, Australia: IP Communications, 2003)

We have seen how decision stages should be customized for each situation; offers useful examples of decision stages for health and safety behaviours

Notes

1. One of the first textbooks in the field of consumer behaviour was Francesco M. Nicosia, *Consumer Decision Process: Marketing and Advertising Implications* (Englewood Cliffs, NJ: Prentice Hall, 1966).
2. One of the first and most comprehensive models of consumer behaviour is found in John A. Howard and Jagdish N. Sheth, *The Theory of Buyer Behavior* (New York: John Wiley and Sons, 1969).

3. Gerrit Antonides and W. Fred van Raaij, *Consumer Behaviour: A European Perspective* (Chichester: John Wiley and Sons, 1998).
4. See D. Pickton and A. Broderick, *Integrated Marketing Communication*, 2nd edn (Harlow: Prentice Hall, 2005), 70.
5. For an introduction to behaviourism, see the father of behaviourism B. F. Skinner's *The Behaviour of Organisms* (New York: Century, 1938).
6. In the 1990s Gordon Foxall argued for a behavioural approach to understanding consumer decision making. See G.R. Foxall, *Consumer Psychology in Behavioural Perspective* (London: Routledge, 1990) and 'Situated Consumer Behaviour: A Behavioural Interpretation of Purchase and Consumption', in R. W. Belk (ed.), *Research in Consumer Behaviour* (Greenwich, CT: JAI Press, 1993), 6.
7. See H. Assael, *Consumer Behaviour and Marketing Action*, 5th edn (Cincinnati, OH: South Western College Publishing, 1995).
8. John Howard dedicated a book to exploring these three consumer decision-making processes, *Consumer Behaviour: An Application of Theory* (New York: McGraw-Hill, 1997).
9. While not referencing Howard's work, Soloman and his colleagues specifically describe his three decision-making processes (although, in the text, rewording routinized response behaviour to habitual decision making) in N. Soloman, G. Bamossy, and Søren Askegaard, *Consumer Behaviour: A European Perspective* (New York: Prentice Hall Europe, 2002), 237.
10. Now in its tenth edition, the most recent example of Engel's model may be found in R.D. Blackwell, R.W. Miniard, and J.F. Enge, *Consumer Behaviour* (Cincinnati, OH: South-Western College Publishing, 2005).
11. There are a number of recent books on consumer behaviour from many different perspectives, in addition to the Antonides and van Raaij book. Examples include Robert East, *Consumer Behaviours: Advances and Applications in Marketing* (London: Prentice Hall, 1997); Frank R. Kardes, *Consumer Behaviour and Management Decision Making* (Reading, MA: Addison-Wesley, 1999); and Solomon, Bamossy, and Askegaard, *Consumer Behaviour: A European Perspective* (New York: Prentice Hall Europe, 2002).
12. In J.R. Rossiter and L. Percy, *Advertising and Promotion Management* (New York: McGraw-Hill, 1987), and subsequently expanded in their *Advertising Communication and Promotion Management*, 2nd edn (New York: McGraw-Hill, 1997), as well as in L. Percy, *Strategies for Implementing Integrated Marketing Communication* (Lincolnwood, IL: NTC Business Press, 1997).
13. In *Consumer Behaviour: An Application of Theory* (New York: McGraw-Hill, 1997), Howard, one of the fathers of consumer behaviour theory, dealt with the idea of stages in the consumer decision process, integrating how managers, psychologists, and economists view them. This discussion marked an extension of his original work with Jag Sheth (see n. 2).
14. This model was first introduced in J.F. Engel, D.T. Kollat, and R.D. Blackwell, *Consumer Behavior* (New York: Holt, Rinehart and Winston, 1968), and is remarkably similar to the Howard and Sheth model (see n. 2). Authors of consumer behaviour textbooks continue to include this model or a close variation in their books. For example, R. East, *Consumer Behaviour: Advances and Applications in Marketing* (Hemel Hempstead: Prentice Hall, 1997), includes the most recent version of the Engel *et al.* model. While not completely immune to criticism, principally because of its cognitive nature—see especially A.S.C. Ehrenberg, *Repeat Buying: Theory and Applications*, 2nd edn (London: Charles Griffin and Co., 1988)—this general model of consumer behaviour has proved to be remarkably long-lived.

Visit the Online Resource Centre that accompanies this book for additional resources to support the text: **www.oxfordtextbooks.co.uk/orc/percy_elliott4e/**

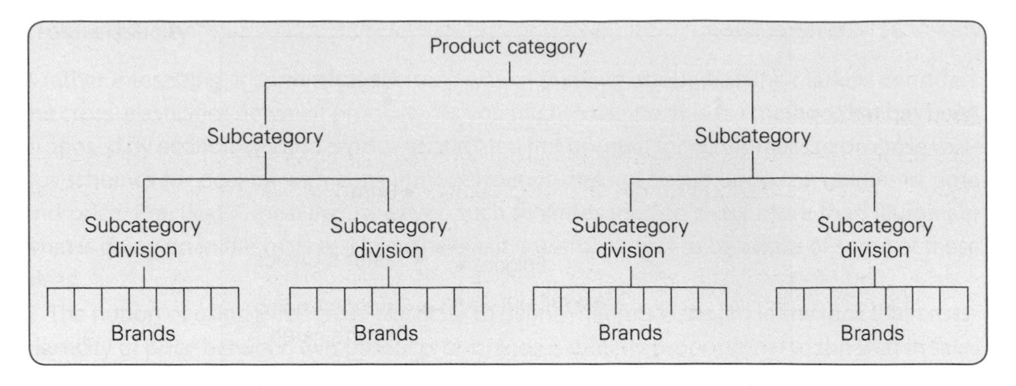

Figure 8.3 Hierarchical Partitioning of a Product Category

type or of brand. Actually, these mappings have much more value in defining the relationship among products or brands than in defining markets.

Hierarchical Market Definition

We encountered the idea of a hierarchical process in our discussion of the four-step response sequence. You will recall that we talked about the compounding problem, where what comes before determines what comes later. One way to look at how consumers define markets is to look at the order in which they consider characteristics of a product in the decisions that they make.[6] In marketing terminology this is often referred to as *partitioning* a market.

The idea of partitioning follows from classical categorization theory in psychology, which posits that all 'concepts' are organized in memory according to some hierarchy,[7] working from the more abstract down to the more specific. Even though neuropsychologists no longer feel that this is how constructs are actually established in memory, *markets* are partitioned by consumers in terms of some sort of hierarchical system, and this structure informs how brand decisions are made. In fact, when making a product or brand choice, consumers will always have 'partitioned' the category.

The thinking that underlies a hierarchical definition of a market is that an overall product category (such as beverages, deodorants, cars, and so on) can be divided and then subdivided several times into subcategories that define narrower markets, and which will tend to end when consumers make their actual choice. Several things are implied in this notion of partitioning markets about the way in which consumers behave. First of all, as we proceed down the hierarchy, we assume that consumers see different brands in the market as more and more alike, and hence that they are more substitutable. Then, assuming that consumers see brands as more and more alike, they will be increasingly more willing to switch among brands. This idea is illustrated in Fig. 8.3. You can see that advertising and other marketing communication must be able to deal with this tendency of consumers to view brands as more or less alike as they move down the partitioning hierarchy. It must correctly position the category need in relation to the appropriate decision level in the hierarchy, and work to create a unique positioning for a brand against the competition. This should become clearer soon, when we illustrate hypothetical executions of partitioning hierarchies for the drinks category.

Bases for Partitions

When consumers are asked to describe how products in a category differ, they do not make a hierarchical distinction, but tend to talk about brands and products in terms of four general characteristics:

- *type of product*—for example, in frozen foods there are full dinners versus just main dishes, main dishes versus side dishes, main meals versus breakfast, and so on;
- *end benefit*—for example, aspirin could be taken to ease pain or to help to prevent a heart attack, or you could buy an expensive Scotch because you like the taste or because you want to impress your friends;
- *usage situation*—the end benefit that you are seeking in a product may vary as a function of when or how the product is used, for example 'instant' or soluble coffee only for breakfast, but ground roast for when you have friends over;
- *brand name*—finally, the brand itself implies many things and could be a key factor in defining markets, for example we can all think of brands we consider 'quality' brands versus 'price' brands.

Notice some important things about these characteristics. They could all be used to describe the same product or brand, but the *order* in which they are used by consumers in arriving at a choice is what will determine how consumers define markets. You should be able to see how each factor, depending on which is the final arbiter of choice, will suggest different advertising strategies to deal with it.

Thinking in terms of these four characteristics, if we were to define the coffee market, we would want answers from consumers to questions like these:

- Why do you drink coffee?
- When do you drink coffee?
- What are the differences among various brands of coffee?

Answers to questions like these begin to explain how consumers see the coffee market, and help the marketing manager to define the market strategically just as consumers themselves do.

If you were the marketing manager for a coffee brand, how do you think the market structure would be defined? This is actually a more complicated question than you might imagine. If you consider simply what coffee 'is', it is something people drink. Fig. 8.4 suggests a reasonable product-based hierarchical partition of the drinks market. If this is an accurate representation (and research suggests it is), then, at the product level, coffee competes with non-alcoholic, hot drinks. But this is really much too simple, and is actually misleading.

When you ask consumers to talk about coffee, addressing questions like those above, they do talk about it in terms of product characteristics, especially ground roast versus 'instant' (i.e. soluble). But they are *much* more lively when discussing coffee in terms of end benefits and usage situations.[8] Figures 8.5*a* and 8.5*b* illustrate how we might imagine the drinks market partitioned along these lines.

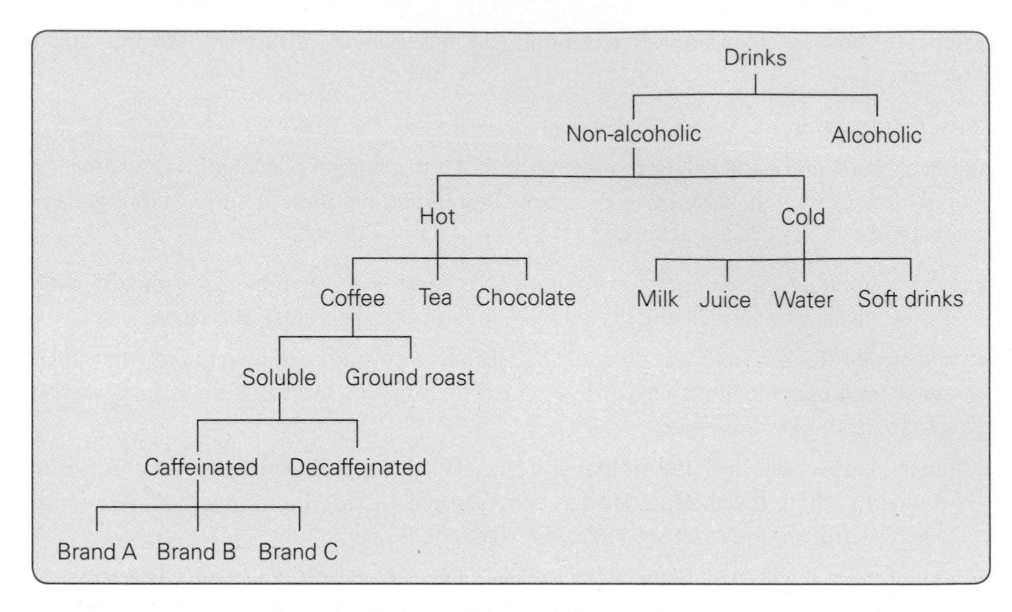

Figure 8.4 Hypothesized Hierarchical Partitioning of the Drinks Market for Coffee

Seeking a Differential Advantage

Up to this point we have looked very broadly at how various components of the marketing mix influence the overall market positioning of a brand, and how markets are defined. Now it is time to look more specifically at how a brand is to be positioned *within* the market definition. In a sense, up to now we have been dealing with the first half of the positioning definitions introduced at the start of the chapter: *identifying the market in which you compete*. This is what helps to pinpoint the *category* in which the brand competes, and frames something we have been calling category need.[9]

Category need defines why the target audience wants the product or service offered by the market. A category, at its basic level, is what people think of spontaneously when asked: 'What is this?' When asked this question, people tend to respond in such terms as 'beer', 'coffee', 'soft drink', or perhaps a brand name. They do *not* talk in terms such as 'a beverage', although they may very well describe something like this as 'something to drink'. You can see that people tend to think about categories, and as a result category needs, well down the hierarchical market definition.

For consumers, brands exist to satisfy a need, and it is this 'need' that defines the category for them. It does not matter what or how a marketer defines the category for their brand; what is important is how the consumer defines it, and that will be in terms of satisfying a particular need.[10] We will be dealing a lot more with this idea of category need in later chapters because it is an important communication effect to consider when setting marketing communication strategy.

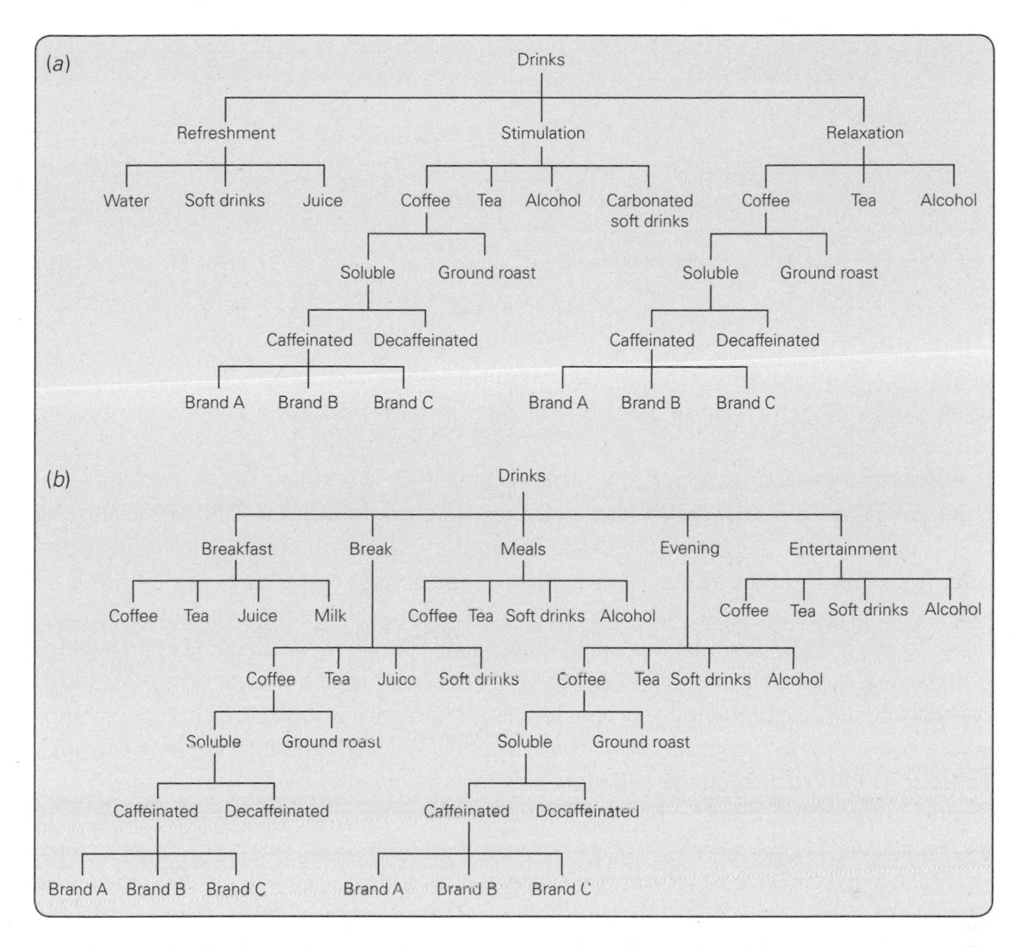

Figure 8.5 **(*a*) Hypothesized Hierarchical Partitioning of the Drinks Market Driven by End Benefit; (*b*) Hypothesized Hierarchical Partitioning of the Drinks Market Driven by Usage Situation**

What we want to do now is turn our attention to the second half of the positioning definition: *seeking a differential advantage*. This is where we must identify the optimal way of presenting our brand in advertising and other marketing communication.

Initial Positioning Decisions

Managers should always take a fresh look at the brand's positioning in the development of a marketing communication plan. Markets change, competitor positionings change, and what the consumer is looking for in the product could change. As we look more specifically now at positioning a product or service for marketing communication, there are two decisions that the manager must make: how should the brand be positioned with regard to the product category; and whether the brand's position in relation to other brands should be in terms of product users or the product itself. In order to make these

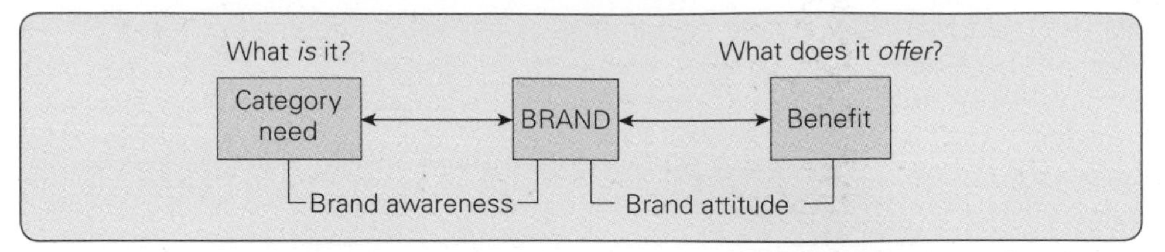

Figure 8.6 General Model of Brand Positioning

decisions, we must begin by asking two questions about the brand: what *is* it, and what does it *offer*? Together, these questions provide a framework for a general positioning model (see Fig. 8.6).

Answers to these questions are critical because they are linked to the two universal communication objectives of brand awareness and brand attitude. The answer to the question 'What is it?' connects the brand to category need, sometimes referred to as the brand's *market* position. There are two ways in which this can be done. A brand can be positioned in relation to the product category or category need either *centrally* or *differentially*. To be centrally positioned, a brand must be able to deliver on all of the main benefits of the category. In effect, it will be positioned as the *best* brand in the category. Because a centrally positioned brand more or less defines the category, it should be limited to brands with a strong market position. Often, this is the first really successful brand in a category. Think of brands such as Xerox and Hoover, which *literally* define their categories. Xerox *means* copying ('Xerox that for me please'); Hoover *means* vacuuming ('Hoover that rug, it's a mess').

This idea of centrally positioned brands reflects what some in psychology have called 'prototypes', something that helps people quickly and accurately to identify things (such as a brand).[11] In fact, one could think of a brand such as Xerox as an archetype that helped to define future copiers. In psychology, some theories define a prototype as an abstract representation in memory, others as a concrete representation.[12] Yet a third theory posits that people create an abstract idea of what the typical product in a category would be, and then associate it with a specific brand.[13]

While some people have suggested that it is possible for a 'me-too' brand to adopt a central positioning if the people can in fact *objectively* determine that, compared with the leading brand, it can equally deliver the category's primary benefit, and do it at a lower price, this is not easy to do.[14] Store brands often adopt this strategy, offering the same benefits as the category leader, but at a lower price, and almost always using the same positioning as the market leader.[15] However, it will usually only be a brand seen as a strong market leader that should be centrally positioned. And, with a centrally positioned brand, it is important that the perception of it doing the best job in delivering the primary category benefit be constantly confirmed.

In all other areas, which means for most brands, a differentiated positioning strategy is called for. We already know the answer to the question 'What does it offer?' for a centrally positioned brand. It will be the primary category benefit. But, for a differentiated positioning, we must look for another benefit the brand offers, different from the primary category benefit that helps to position the market leader centrally. Creating a distinct positioning is what helps to differentiate a brand from the estimated 10,000 brands the average adult has represented in memory.[16] Identifying the best benefit to differentiate your brand from the market leader and other competitors is what we will be taking up later in the section on selecting the appropriate benefit.

We have looked at the 'What is it?' and 'What does it offer' questions in order to help us to decide how the brand should be positioned with regard to the product category. Now the manager must consider a second decision: whether the positioning strategy should place the brand, relative to its competition, in terms of the user or of the product itself. This decision follows consideration of whether the brand should be centrally or differentially positioned because either may be implemented via a user- or a product-benefit orientation.

User-Oriented Position

While both user- and product-benefit-oriented positioning strategies (covered next) make use of brand benefits in the message, in the former the message is specifically addressing the user: the *user* is the focus, not the product. User-oriented positionings make sense when a brand is marketed to a specific segment, satisfying its particular needs. But this does not necessarily mean that a brand positioned towards the user is appropriate only for that specific target audience, only that it is positioned that way. For example, a performance wear brand advertised for the 'serious runner' or Scotch for the 'discerning drinker' would be examples of a user-oriented positioning, because a strategic decision has been made specifically to position the brand to a particular segment of the market.

Another case where a user-oriented positioning should be considered is when the underlying purchase motivation in the category is social approval. We will be dealing with this issue of motivation in more detail shortly, because benefit selection and focus should always be related to the appropriate purchase motivation. For now, we need only know that social approval is a positive motive that reflects purchase decisions made because the user is looking for social rewards through personal recognition in using the brand.

When most people in a brand's target audience are driven by social approval in their brand selection in that category, a user-oriented positioning makes sense. By focusing on the users, you are reminding them of how good *they* will feel in using—and, importantly, displaying—your brand. This is why brands of luxury cars and high fashion often employ user-oriented positionings. But you can also choose to tap into an otherwise latent social approval motive. Most people, for example, do not buy peanut butter for social approval, but Procter & Gamble has, for many years, utilized a user-oriented positioning for its Jif peanut butter brand. It focuses upon a mother's (and recently also a father's) nurturing feelings for her (his) children, positioning Jif 'for mothers who really care'.

Product-Benefit-Oriented Positioning

Addressing a specific segment or when the underlying purchase motive is social approval are the two circumstances in which the manager may *consider* using a user-oriented positioning.

Table 8.2 **Options for Positioning Brand Relative to Competitors**

User-oriented positioning	• When marketing to specific segment • When social approval is primary purchase motivation
Product-benefit-oriented positioning	• In all other cases

But this is only one option. In either case one could instead choose to use a product-benefit-oriented positioning.

While a manager must always consider whether or not a user-oriented positioning is appropriate, in the majority of cases a product-benefit-oriented positioning should be used (Table 8.2). With product-benefit-oriented positioning, the product is the hero of the positioning, and the positioning will be defined by specific benefits related to the product, not the user. In a product-benefit-oriented positioning, *product characteristics* are the message; in a user-oriented positioning, *user characteristics* are the message.

Selecting the Appropriate Benefit

Now that we have a broad understanding of where to locate the brand within the overall positioning framework of the product category and brand benefits, the manager must determine what benefit (or benefits) to emphasize in the positioning. What we want to do is select those benefits that will best distinguish our brand from competitors in a way that is important to the target audience. Ideally, these benefits will reflect the underlying motivation that drives purchase behaviour because they are at the heart of brand attitude communication strategy. What we want to do is be able to 'tap into' the purchase motivation via the benefit presented in the advert or other marketing communication. The difficult question, however, is what benefit should be emphasized in order to get the job done.

We will be looking for a benefit that is *important* to our target audience in influencing purchase, one that our target audience believes (or can be persuaded to believe) our brand can *deliver*, and one that the target audience believes (or, again, can be persuaded to believe) our brand can deliver *better* than other brands (Box 8.1).[17] This is what we are looking for, but finding it is not easy. One way is to explore the basic, underlying attitudinal structure used by the target audience in evaluating brands. Perhaps the best way of doing this is to use a multi-attribute model based upon Fishbein's notion of expectancy value.[18]

- It is *important* to the target audience.
- The brand can *deliver* it.
- It can be delivered *better* than other brands.

Box 8.1 **Considerations in Selecting Benefits for Marketing Communication**

Plate I BirdsEye

This Birds Eye advert is a very good example of a category leader using a category benefit to build overall demand for the brand through category growth.

Source: Reproduced with kind permission © Birds Eye. (See 'Implement the Five-Step Strategic Planning Process', p. 83.)

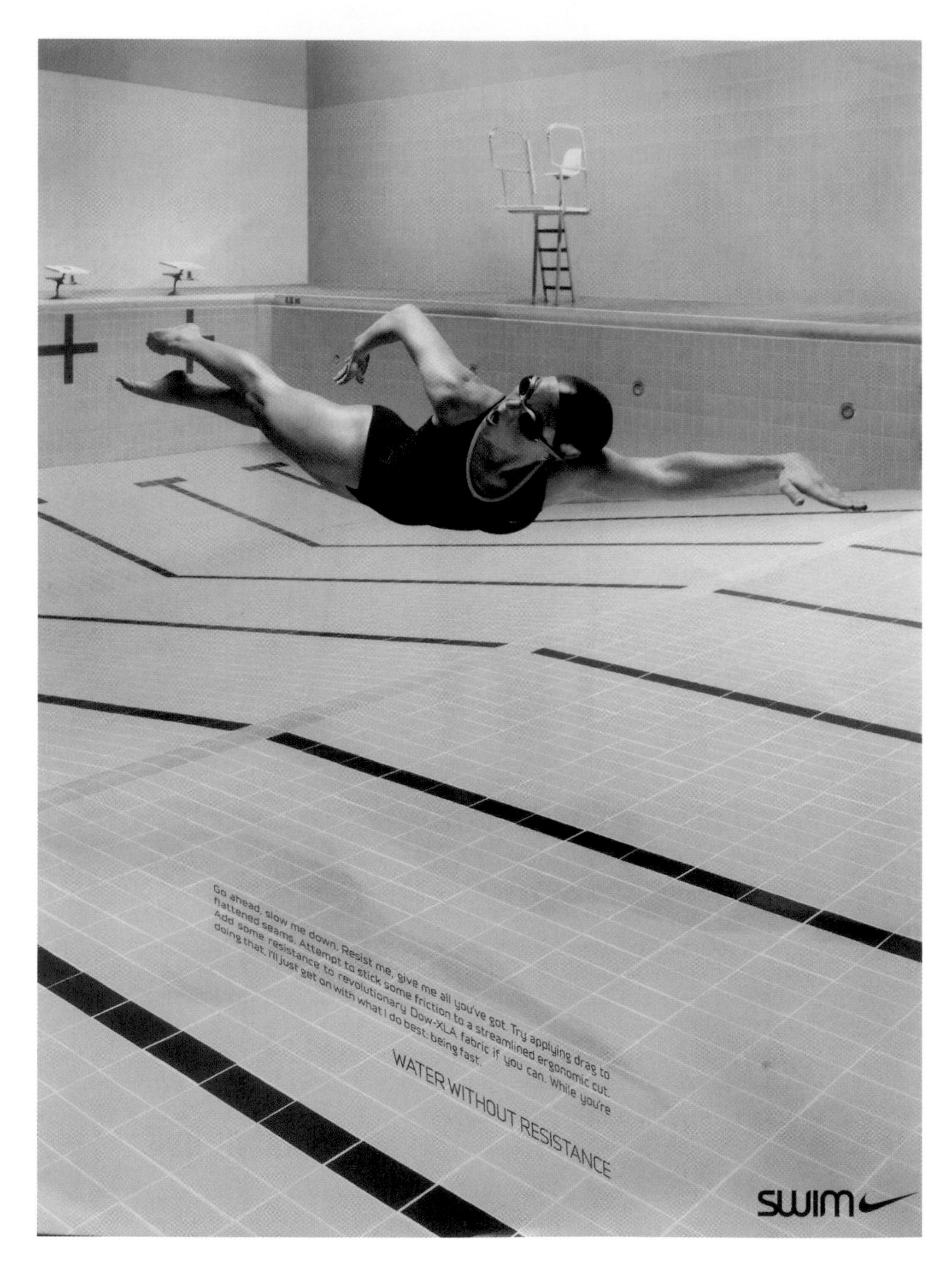

Plate II Nike

Here we see the benefit for Nike's swim brand shown in the extreme, an excellent example of the appropriate creative tactic for a low-involvement decision.

Source: Reproduced with kind permission © Nike. (See 'Implement the Five-Step Strategic Planning Process', p. 85.)

Plate III Philips Bodygroom

This advert for Philips Bodygroom provides a very good example of how to believably illustrate a primary benefit for a high-involvement decision.

Source: Philips Bodygroom advert, 2007, created by DDB. Reproduced with kind permission. (See 'Implement the Five-Step Strategic Planning Process', p. 85.)

Plate IV Really Wild Clothing

Here is a good example of where a product and retailer are basically the same, and the execution delivers strong brand awareness as well as positive images for both the store and Really Wild's clothing.

Source: Reproduced with kind permission. © Really Wild Clothing. (See 'Implement the Five-Step Strategic Planning Process', p. 88.)

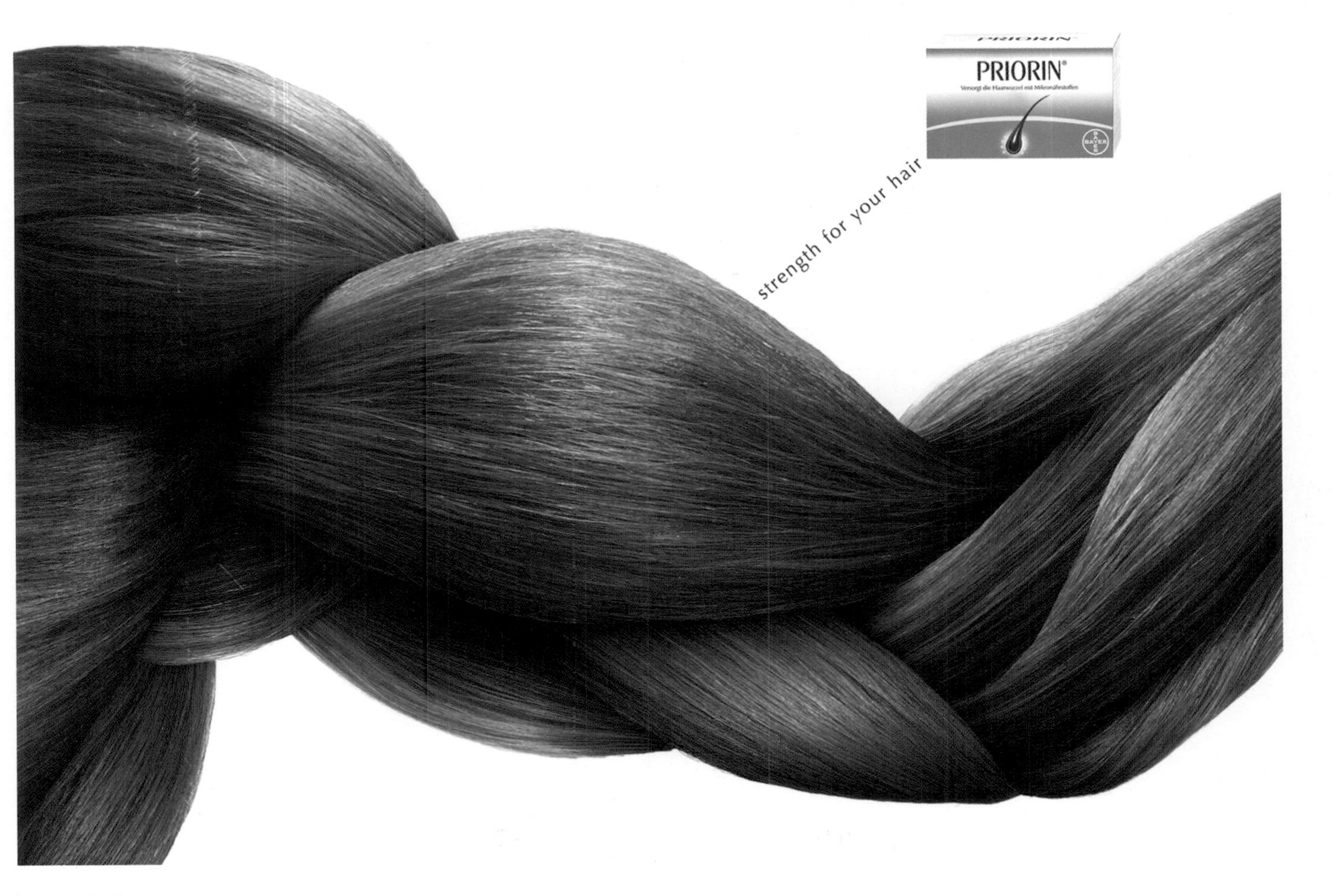

Plate V Priorin

This advert for Priorin is a great example of a low-involvement informational benefit delivered through the visual, communicating in this case 'strength for your hair'.

Source: Reproduced with kind permission. © Priorin / JWT. (See 'Importance of Involvement and Motivation', p. 187.)

The award winning Peugeot RCZ from £21,245. Now available with quad exhausts, sports grilles and side stripes as part of the exclusive Feline Pack. Be the cat that got the cream.

PEUGEOT

MOTION & EMOTION

PEUGEOT TOTAL Model shown is an RCZ Sport THP 156 Petrol manual available at £21,685 OTR plus £649.99 for the Feline quad exhaust fully fitted. Go to peugeot.co.uk for full terms and conditions. Official Fuel Consumption in mpg (l/100km) and CO_2 emissions (g/km) for the RCZ Range are: Urban 27.4 – 41.5 (10.3 – 6.8), Extra Urban 50.4 – 62.7 (5.6 – 4.5), Combined 38.6 – 53.2 (7.3 – 5.3) and CO_2 168 – 139 (g/km).

Plate VI Peugeot

This Peugeot advert, while simple in execution, nevertheless does an excellent job in creating a strong emotional association with the RCZ, helping the target to 'feel' the excitement of driving.

Source: Reproduced with kind permission © Peugeot Motor Company plc. (See 'Importance of Involvement and Motivation', p. 194.)

Plate VII Surf™

An excellent example of a low-involvement informational strategy in which the benefit is presented in a humorous and extreme way.

Source: Reproduced with kind permission © Unilever UK. Surf is a registered trademark. (See 'Importance of Involvement and Motivation', p. 194.)

Plate X Gravetye Manor

With high-involvement transformational strategies, a strong emotional response is needed from those who personally identify with the feeling elicited, and this advert for Gravetye Manor does just that, providing strong visual images that encourage those who identify with them to want to visit.

Source: © Gravetye Manor. Reproduced with kind permission. (See 'Importance of Involvement and Motivation', p. 195.)

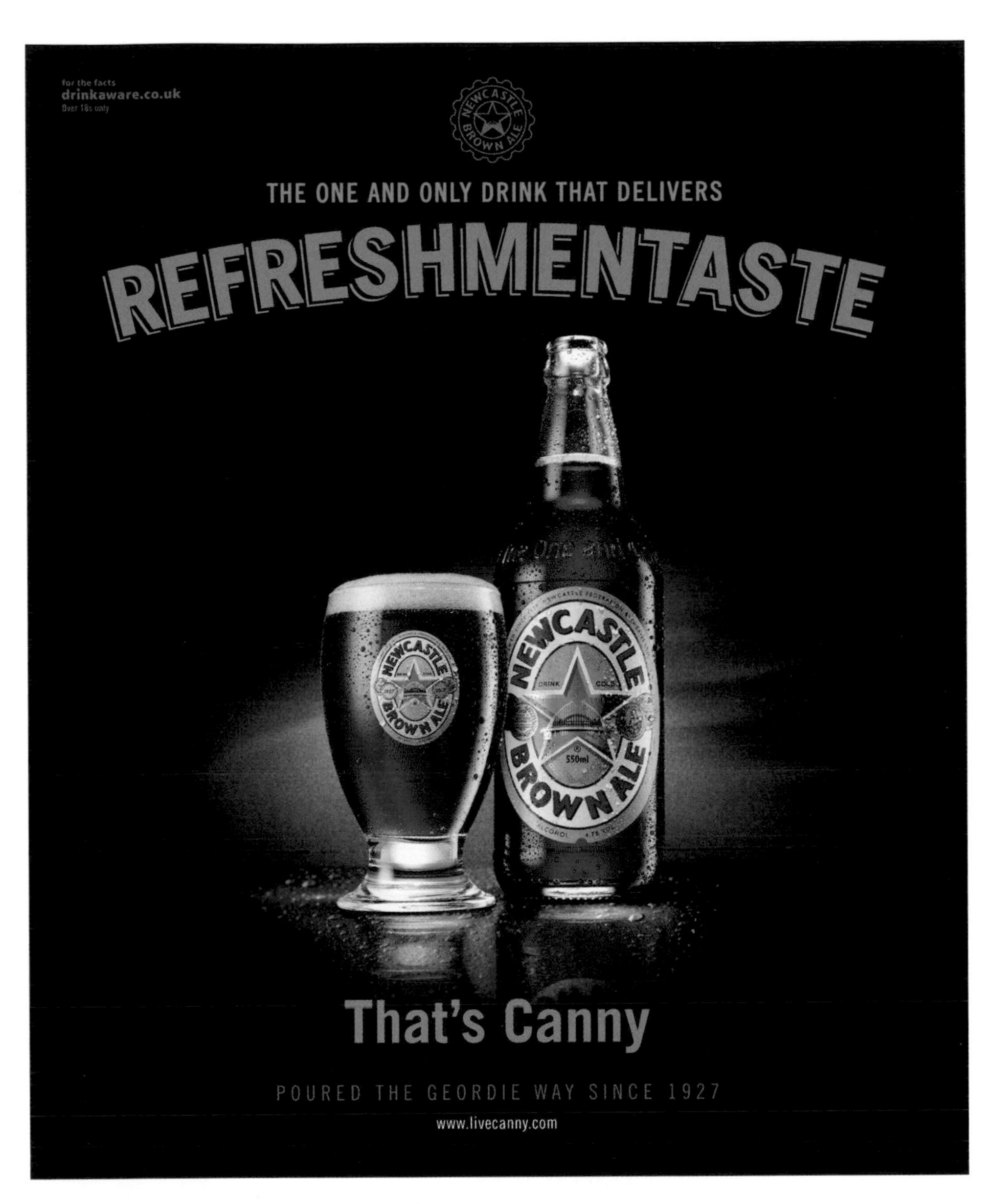

Plate XI Newcastle Brown Ale

The headline in the Newcastle Brown Ale advert provides a really good example of using something unexpected in an execution to attract and, importantly, to hold attention.

Source: Reproduced with the kind permission of Heineken UK Limited. (See 'Tactics for Attention', p. 268.)

Plate XIV Brittany Ferries

This advert for Brittany Ferries provides a good example of placing the target audience in action, encouraging them to personally identify with the benefit.

Source: Reproduced by kind permission of Brittany Ferries. (See 'Tactics for Learning', p. 274.)

Plate XV Anthisan

This advert for Anthisan is a very good example of what Maloney has called 'curious disbelief'.

Source: Reproduced with kind permission of Sanofi Aventis. (See 'Brand Awareness and Brand Attitude Creative Tactics', p. 278.)

Plate XVI Colron

Here we have a very good example of the important ways in which the visual images used in an advert can help to facilitate learning. It is clear you are meant to be outside, observing the 'action', the picture is large, the unique imagery encourages visual elaboration, the use of colour and white space is well proportioned, the product is shown 'in use', and the picture is seen before the words.

Source: Reproduced with kind permission © Ronseal Ltd. (See 'Tactics for Learning', p. 275.)

Plate XVII Rotari

This advert for Rotari's Talento sparkling wine provides a really good example of the viewer being included in the execution.

Source: © Gruppo Mezzacorona. Reproduced with kind permission. (See 'Tactics for Learning', p. 272.)

Plate XVIII Heal's

Consistent with the key tactic for transformational brand attitude strategies, this Heal's advert is pure emotion, eliciting a strong positive emotional association for the brand.

Source: Reproduced with kind permission © Heal's. (See 'Brand Awareness and Brand Attitude Creative Tactics', p. 281.)

Plate XIX Fairy

Even though the headline in this advert comes first, the eye is still drawn initially to the picture, ensuring the desires–picture sequence for optimum processing. This advert also provides an excellent example of the correct 'anxiety-to-relief' emotional sequence necessary when dealing with negative motives.

Source: Reproduced with kind permission © Procter & Gamble UK. (See 'Tactics for Learning', p. 274, and see 'Brand Attitude Creative Tactics and Emotion', p. 282.)

STUNNING OUTDOOR FURNITURE ?
PUT YOURSELF IN THE PICTURE

The UK's largest selection of contemporary and classic outdoor furniture - made exclusively in the finest teak, stainless steel, aluminium and the latest woven materials. Discover more by calling 0870 7804813 for a free catalogue or go to www.indian-ocean.co.uk

www.indian-ocean.co.uk

STORES IN LONDON, SALISBURY & CHESTER, BROADWAY, DURHAM, GLASGOW, LEATHERHEAD, NORTHAMPTON, NORWICH, SAFFRON WALDEN, WROTHAM AND YORK

AND SELFRIDGES&Co LONDON

Plate XX Indian Ocean

Here we see a very good example of how a transformational advert shifts your emotional state from neutral or even dull to a strong positive emotional response.

Source: Reproduced with kind permission © Info Associates. (See 'Brand Awareness and Brand Attitude Creative Tactics', p. 283.)

The Expectancy-Value Model of Attitude

What this model suggests is that a person's attitude towards an object (A_o) is the sum of all of the things they believe about it (b_i), weighted by how important each of those things are to them (a_i). Mathematically, this is expressed as:

$$A_o = \sum_{i=1}^{n} a_i b_i$$

where A_o = attitude towards the object
a_i = importance of belief
b_i = belief about the object

Do not be put off by the mathematical equation, because this is really not very complicated. Think about chocolate bars. Using the model, how would you determine someone's attitude towards, say, Snickers? What the model says is that a person's attitude towards something, Snickers in this case, will be the sum of its perceived characteristics and how important they are to what *motivates* that person to buy a chocolate bar.

What are some of the characteristics of chocolate bars? The obvious attributes are ingredients such as chocolate, caramel, and peanuts, but the characteristics of a chocolate bar will also include more intangible ones such as 'provides energy', 'is an inexpensive snack', and 'is an indulgence'. While there are clearly more characteristics than these, we will work with this set to see how we can learn something about people's attitudes towards Snickers.

Table 8.3 Expectancy-Value Model of Attitude for a Chocolate Bar

	Importance weight (a_i)	**Beliefs (b_i)**	**Benefit ($a_i \times b_i$)**
Chocolate	3	3	9
Caramel	1	1	1
Peanuts	1	3	3
Provides energy	0	1	0
Inexpensive snack	1	3	3
Indulgence	3	1	3
$A_o = \sum_{i=1}^{n} a_i b_i =$			19
	3 = Essential	3 = Definitely delivers	
	1 = Desirable	1 = Does OK	
	0 = Of no importance	0 = Does not deliver	

Look at Table 8.3. This hypothetical example shows: that people feel that chocolate and a sense of indulgence are essential to a chocolate bar; that caramel, peanuts, and being an inexpensive snack, while desirable, are not essential; and that it really is not important that a chocolate bar provides energy. Their perception of Snickers is that it really delivers chocolate and peanuts, and it is seen as an inexpensive snack, but it does only an OK job in providing caramel and energy, and as an indulgence. Computing an expectancy-value measure of Snickers' brand attitude, using the appropriate numbers and following the model, yields 19.

So what does '19' mean? By itself, very little. The important thing here is to look at *how* the attitude is determined. We can see that, for the chocolate bar attribute most important to people, chocolate, Snickers is seen to do a very good job delivering the benefit. It also delivers well on peanuts, but peanuts are less essential in a chocolate bar. Caramel is desirable, but not essential, in a chocolate bar, and Snickers does an OK job on this attribute.

Looking at the more benefit-oriented characteristics, Snickers is seen as definitely an inexpensive snack, which is desirable, but not essential. People believe that Snickers does an OK job in providing energy, even though that is not important. But in terms of being seen as an indulgence, which is essential for a chocolate bar (in our example), Snickers is seen only as OK.

Positioning with the Expectancy-Value Model

If the expectancy-value attitude does not mean much on its own, then why compute it? The reason is that it provides an important *relative* feel for what people's attitudes are likely to be, depending upon how they perceive a brand. This is why the model is so important for positioning.

The strength of people's attitudes towards Snickers in this example is that it is seen as having everything important in a chocolate bar, except for doing only an OK job as an indulgence. But suppose that, among chocolate lovers, the beliefs about chocolate and caramel were reversed? If that were how chocolate lovers saw Snickers, it would mean that it was seen as doing only an OK job on the two things most important to them in a chocolate bar—chocolate and being an indulgence.

In the first example, where Snickers is seen by the general population as really delivering on the chocolate attribute, the overall attitude score is 19; in this second example, where it does only an OK job on chocolate among chocolate lovers, while really delivering on caramel, the overall attitude score is only 13. If the first example were to reflect general attitudes towards Snickers in the market and the second to reflect the attitude of chocolate lovers towards Snickers, how would we need to position Snickers to attract the chocolate lover?

Looking only at the attitude scores, we know that attitudes towards Snickers in the general population are much more favourable than they are among chocolate lovers: 19 versus 13. But even more importantly, as we look at the beliefs and their weightings, we know that the reason for this less favourable attitude among chocolate lovers is their perception that Snickers is more about caramel and peanuts than it is about chocolate. This suggests that if Snickers is to attract chocolate lovers, it must be positioned more strongly against that benefit. Since we know (again in our hypothetical example) that, in a chocolate bar, chocolate is more important than caramel or peanuts, taking a strong chocolate positioning would reinforce the already held beliefs of the general population while building this perception among chocolate lovers.

Table 8.4 Comparative Expectancy-Value Model of Attitude for Two Chocolate Bars

	Importance weight (a_i)	Beliefs (b_i)	
		Snickers	Cadbury
Chocolate	3	3	3
Caramel	1	1	0
Peanuts	1	3	0
Provides energy	0	1	1
Inexpensive snack	1	3	3
Indulgence	3	1	3
$A_o = \sum_{i=1}^{n} a_i b_i =$		19	21
	3 = Essential	3 = Definitely delivers	
	1 = Desirable	1 = Does OK	
	0 = Of no importance	0 = Does not deliver	

Let us take this idea one step further and look at hypothetical beliefs about two chocolate bar brands, Snickers and Cadbury. Assume that consumer attitudes toward these brands are the results of the weighted beliefs shown in Table 8.4. These figures suggest that the overall attitudes towards Snickers and Cadbury, as measured by an expectancy-value model, are roughly equal, although the edge goes to Cadbury.

If you were the brand manager for Snickers, what would you do to position the brand more strongly against Cadbury? The two most important benefits are chocolate and indulgence. Cadbury delivers both, while Snickers lags behind on the indulgence benefit. In other words, Snickers does not deliver as well as Cadbury on this important benefit; Cadbury does it better. One way for Snickers to build a more positive brand attitude would be to position itself more as an indulgence. If it were to succeed, its overall attitude score would jump to 25, better than Cadbury at 21. Another option would be to *drive down* the importance of indulgence, while playing up the 'extra' taste of caramel and peanuts. If the importance weighting of indulgence were to drop from essential to desirable, Snickers would enjoy a slight edge in overall attitude (17 versus 15). Add to this a heightened awareness among chocolate bar buyers that Snickers really delivers on caramel, and the advantage becomes even stronger (19 versus 15).

We must remember that in these examples the numbers have been made up in order to illustrate the points, and also that there could be many other important benefits we have not considered. But the important thing to understand is that you can use an expectancy-value model to identify the importance of benefits to your target audience, the degree to which it

Table 8.5 Different Aspects of a Benefit

Attribute	An *objective* component of a product (antibacterial, no calories)
Characteristic	A *subjective* claim about a product (easy to use, tastes great)
Emotion	A *feeling* associated with the product (excitement, relief)

perceives that you and your competitors can deliver those benefits, and which benefits one brand is seen to deliver better than its competitors.

In using the model, include those benefits seen by the target audience as being important or potentially important, and have the target audience evaluate your brand and two or three key competitors. Remember that this exercise must be done for the *appropriate target audience*, not the population at large (unless, of course, that happens to be the target audience). As you work out the numbers, it will be possible to evaluate positioning options in terms of:

- reinforcing or building a uniqueness for your brand on important benefits;
- capitalizing upon competitive weaknesses on important benefits;
- emphasizing important benefits that your brand delivers better than others;
- increasing the importance of benefits that your brand delivers better than others (if not already seen as essential);
- decreasing the importance of benefits that your brand does not deliver better than others.

Benefit Focus

One final consideration in benefit positioning is how to focus on or emphasize the benefit in marketing communication. At this point we need to look more closely at what is meant by a 'benefit'. Up until now, we have been talking about benefits in a rather general way. But in order correctly to understand benefit focus we need to 'deconstruct' benefits, and look at what it is about a product or brand that someone is likely to see as a benefit.

A benefit may be experienced in different ways: an objective *attribute* of a product (antibacterial, no calories) might be seen by some as a benefit; a subjective claim or *characteristic* of a product (easy to use, tastes great) might be seen as a benefit; or an *emotion* (excitement, relief) could be experienced as a benefit. In effect, a benefit might be thought of in terms of what you *want* from a product, and you may find that in terms of what a brand *has* (attribute), what you *experience* with a brand (characteristic), or what you *feel* (emotion). This is summarized in Table 8.5. How we focus on the benefit will depend upon what aspect of the benefit is involved, and upon the motivation associated with purchase in the brand's category. This will depend upon the motivation associated with purchase in a category. As we shall discuss in Chapter 9, brand attitude communication strategy depends upon understanding the correct underlying purchase motivation. We shall defer a detailed discussion of this to then. For now, we need know only that some advertising and marketing communication strategies are based primarily on providing 'information', others on addressing 'feelings'. When the motive is negative, information in some form is provided in order to address a problem of some kind:

'how do I get my clothes looking better?', 'what is the best washer?', 'what can I take for real pain?' When the motivation is positive, messages must address the target audience's 'feelings' in some way: 'I want a car everyone will notice', 'I want to indulge myself', and so on.

The way the brand positioning in a message addresses the benefit should reflect this fundamental distinction between purchase motivations. When the motive is negative and the advertising and other marketing communication is basically providing information, the emphasis should be *directly* on the benefit. You can draw attention to the benefit by simply focusing on an attribute of the product. But, this is really effective only when dealing with an 'expert' target audience. Experts are those people who are looking only objectively at a product, evaluating its specific characteristics. They will infer the benefit from the 'data'. The attribute (or attributes) will tell them if the product is likely to solve their problem. Otherwise, when dealing with negative motivations, you want to focus on the benefit by drawing attention directly to a subjective characteristic the target audience is looking for in the product (as identified in the benefit selection process), using objective attributes to support a subjective characteristic or claim (the subjective characteristic, again having been identified in the benefit selection process), or indirectly by focusing upon a negative emotion that is dispelled by the subjective characteristic or claim associated with the brand (see Table 8.6).

Let us look at a few examples of how some advertisers have used various benefit focus reflecting negative motives (all of which are presented in Table 8.7). Kira St John's Wort uses a straight attribute focus (a), dealing with the negative motive of incomplete satisfaction: 'Kira St John's Wort tablets contain 900 micrograms of Hypericin.' Dove Summer Glow body lotion uses a direct, simple headline implying a subjective characteristic of the brand (c): 'Basking in the glow.' To support its claims of being the best facial skincare product (a subjective characteristic) Nivea Visage Beauty Boost relies upon the fact that it is the 'best facial skincare product in a poll of over 12,000 consumers' (a $\rightarrow$ c). For women who have a problem with their lipstick fading (e^-), Max Factor Lipfinity asks 'Is your lipstick still on?' and goes on to 'solve' that problem with the claim 'sexy lips 100% guaranteed all night'. Here we have a negative emotion occasioned by lipstick that doesn't last removed by the long-lasting characteristic of Lipfinity ($e^- \rightarrow$ c).

When the motive is positive and the advertising and other marketing communication is addressing the target audience's 'feelings', the emphasis should be on the *emotional consequences*

Table 8.6 Benefit Focus Options

Negative motivation	• Draw attention to an attribute or attributes (**a**) if dealing with an expert target audience • Draw attention directly to a subjective characteristic of the brand (**c**) • Use an attribute to support a subjective characteristic of the brand (**a** $\rightarrow$ **c**) • Dispel a negative emotion or problems with a subjective characteristic associated with the brand (**e^-** $\rightarrow$ **c**)
Positive motivation	• Use a subjective characteristic to draw attention to the emotional consequences of using the brand (**c** $\rightarrow$ **e^+**) • Simply deliver an emotion (**e^+**)

Questions to consider

8.1 What is meant by positioning?

8.2 How do you determine the best basis for defining a market?

8.3 In what ways can using hierarchical positioning help the manager in developing advertising?

8.4 What is the difference between a central versus a differentiated positioning, and why is it important?

8.5 What are the key questions a manager must ask when first developing a positioning strategy?

8.6 How can the expectancy-value model of attitude help in positioning a brand?

8.7 What should the manager be looking for in selecting the best benefit to focus upon in positioning a brand in advertising?

8.8 What are the important considerations needed for getting the benefit focus right in advertising and other marketing communication?

Case study 8 **Kenco—How Kenco Made it Easy to Be the Good Guy**

Kenco positions itself as a high-quality instant coffee brand because it uses the same beans as in its roast and ground. However, twenty years of single-minded communication of the 'same beans as roast and ground' message meant that Kenco's quality message had already got through. The reality was that with no significant news in the category for decades, consumers had lost interest. There was so little to choose between when it came to the leading brands that consumers were shopping on autopilot.

Because of its origins as an importer, Kenco had always held the belief that the best coffee came from caring deeply about where its beans came from. Now it was time for Kenco to modernize its dedication to provenance by setting a new ethical agenda. Consumers were showing increasing interest in brands that defined themselves as ethical, as demonstrated by the explosion in sales of Fair Trade products from increasingly diverse categories. A 2007 segmentation study identified five stages of consumer involvement in sustainability, from most to least engaged:

- Principled Pioneers (4 per cent of the population);
- Vocal Activists (4 per cent);
- Positive Choosers (31 per cent);
- Conveniently Conscious (35 per cent);
- Onlookers (26 per cent).

The most involved segments, Principled Pioneers and Vocal Activists, were already well served by specialist ethical brands. More mainstream consumers however, the Positive Choosers and Conveniently Conscious segments, which represent 66 per cent of the population, did not have a sustainable option that met their price and quality demands. At this point, the new vision was identified: to become the mainstream sustainable coffee brand.

As an instant coffee, there were two key issues above any others that had to be tackled: sourcing and packaging.

Sourcing

An insight that came from qualitative research was that many consumers were actually put off by brands speaking about sustainability issues unless they could relate to them in their own world. Clean water, education, and housing were topics that consumers could closely relate to. By choosing Kenco, they could help to improve the lives of coffee-growing communities. TV, press, and online display would focus on announcing a new partnership with the Rainforest Alliance, educating on what the Alliance means and reassuring that Kenco would always be great quality. The idea: as well as growing great coffee, Kenco was now helping to grow communities.

Packaging

The second step on Kenco's sustainability journey was a more familiar one for consumers—reducing packaging. Kenco's refill pack used 97 per cent less packaging than its jars by weight. The decision was taken to relaunch the format as 'Eco-Refill' and begin to communicate its environmental credentials. However, research revealed an important issue. Buying instant coffee in jars was a habit as old as the category itself. Consumers had no spontaneous desire for an alternative. TV and outdoor advertising would focus on raising awareness of the Eco-Refill pack and reassuring that Kenco would always be great quality. The idea: depicting a world in which coffee packaging had been reduced too far, by 100 per cent, to show that in fact Kenco Eco-Refill, with 97 per cent less packaging, was a much better alternative.

Source: This is an edited version of a case study submitted to the IPA Effectiveness Awards. The full case study can be found at ipa.co.uk or warc.com. © Copyright Institute of Practitioners in Advertising.

Edited by Elizabeth Mamali, PhD Researcher, Bath School of Management

Discussion questions

1. Why did Kenco use almost all kinds of media (TV, print, the Internet, in-store display, PR, etc.) to run the campaign?
2. What are the differences between Kenco's old and new positioning?
3. Evaluate Kenco's positioning by applying the expectancy-value model.
4. Suggest future strategies for Kenco to further enhance its positioning.

Further reading

Jean-Noël Kapferer, *[Re]Inventing the Brand* (London: Kogan Page, 2001)

A book that has significant implications for positioning; asks the question, can top brands survive the new market realities?

Stephen Brown, *Free Gift Inside!!* (Chichester: Capstone, 2003)

From a totally different perspective, argues that, in positioning brands, it is time to forget about the consumer.

John Rossiter and Larry Percy, 'The A-B-E Model of Benefit Focus', in T.J. Reynolds and J.C. Olsen (eds), *Understanding Consumer Decision Making* (Mahwah, NJ: Lawrence Erlbaum Associates, 2000), 183–214

A detailed discussion of benefit focus.

J. Hofmeyr and B. Rice, *Commitment-Led Marketing* (Chicester, England: Wiley, 2000)

An interesting way of looking at positioning to appeal to potentially available consumers

Notes

1. David Jobber, *Principles and Practice of Marketing* (New York: McGraw-Hill, 1998), 193.
2. Graham Hooley and John Saunders, *Competitive Positioning: The Key to Market Success* (London: Prentice Hall, 1993), xi.
3. Peter Doyle, *Marketing Management and Strategy* (London: Prentice Hall, 1994), 79.
4. A discussion of the marketing plan may be found in any number of marketing textbooks, and is covered in detail by W.A. Cohen in his book *The Marketing Plan*, 2nd edn (New York: John Wiley and Sons, 1998).
5. Perceptual mapping was developed in the late 1960s at Bell Laboratories in the US. One of the best books on the subject is still Paul Green and Vilhala Rao, *Applied Multidimensional Scaling: A Comparison of Approaches and Algorithms* (New York: Holt, Rinehart and Winston, 1972).
6. See J.R. Bettman, *An Information Processing Theory of Consumer Choice* (Reading, MA: Addison-Wesley, 1979).
7. See G. Franzen and M. Bouwman, *The Mental World of Brands* (Henley-on-Thames: World Advertising Research Center, 2001), 232.
8. This finding comes from research conducted by Larry Percy for a major multinational coffee company. The company was so disturbed to learn that its traditional view of the market, based upon a product definition, was wrong that it refused to complete the project.
9. In *Advertising Communication and Promotion Management* (New York: McGraw-Hill 1997), J.R. Rossiter and L. Percy discuss the first half of this definition in terms of product location—how a brand can be located within the product category with either a central or a differentiated position. Simply put, a central location requires the brand to be positioned to deliver all of those benefits associated with the category (generally a positioning for market leaders), while a differentiated location means finding a unique or differentiated positioning. Generally speaking, most brands should pursue a differentiated positioning.
10. In a pioneering study by B. Loken and J. Ward on the determinants of brand typicality, we see the basis of this idea of category need and its relationship to market definition: 'Alternative Approaches to Understanding the Determinants of Typicality', *Journal of Consumer Research*, 17/2 (1990), 111–26.
11. Franzen and Bouwman, *Mental World of Brands*, (Henley-on-Thames: World Advertising Research Center, 2001), 234.
12. These definitions are discussed in D.L. Medin and M.M. Schaffer, 'A Context Theory of Classification Learning', *Psychological Review*, 85 (1978), 207–38.
13. The dual idea of both abstraction and concreteness in developing a prototype is discussed in N. Cantor and J.F. Kihlstrom, 'Social Intelligence and Cognitive Assessment of Personality', in R.S. Wyer and T.K. Sroll (eds), *Advances in Social Cognition*, vol.ii (Hillsdale, NJ: Lawrence Erlbaum Associates, 1984).
14. For a more detailed consideration of a model that deals with this point, see Rossiter and Percy's discussion of what they call an I–D–U (Importance, Delivery, Uniqueness) model of benefit emphasis in *Advertising Communication and Promotion Management* (New York: McGraw-Hill 1997).
15. See S. Sayman, S.J. Huch, and J S. Raju, 'Positioning of Store Brands', *Marketing Science*, 21/4 (2002), 378–97.
16. While only an estimate, this figure reported in W. Gordon and S. Ford-Hutchinson, 'Brains and Brands: Re-thinking the Answers', *Admap*, January (2002), 47–50, suggests the difficulty involved in positioning a brand to 'stand out.'
17. See G.S. Carpenter and K. Nakamoto, 'Consumer Preference Formation and Pioneering Advantage', *Journal of Marketing Research*, 26/3 (1989), 285–98, for some examples.

18. While it can be argued that Harry Triandis actually developed the idea of an expectancy-value model of attitude, Martin Fishbein is generally credited with its development. See M. Fishbein and I. Ajzen, *Belief, Attitude, Intention, and Behavior: An Introduction to Theory and Research* (Reading, MA: Addison-Wesley, 1975).

Visit the Online Resource Centre that accompanies this book for additional resources to support the text: **www.oxfordtextbooks.co.uk/orc/percy_elliott4e/**

Developing a Communication Strategy

The positioning strategy has helped to establish how the manager should address the two core communication objectives of brand awareness and brand attitude. Now it is time to establish communication objectives and the specific brand awareness and brand attitude strategies that reflect what was learned about how the target audience makes decisions in the category. Depending upon how awareness is used to identify the brand for purchase, a recognition or recall brand awareness strategy will be required, and the level of involvement with the purchase decision, along with the motivation driving category behaviour, will determine the brand attitude strategy, as we see in the Step 4 figure and discuss in this chapter.

Implementing the Strategic Planning Process

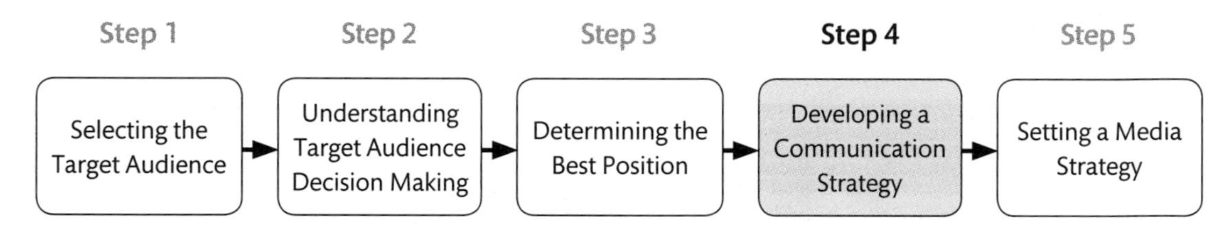

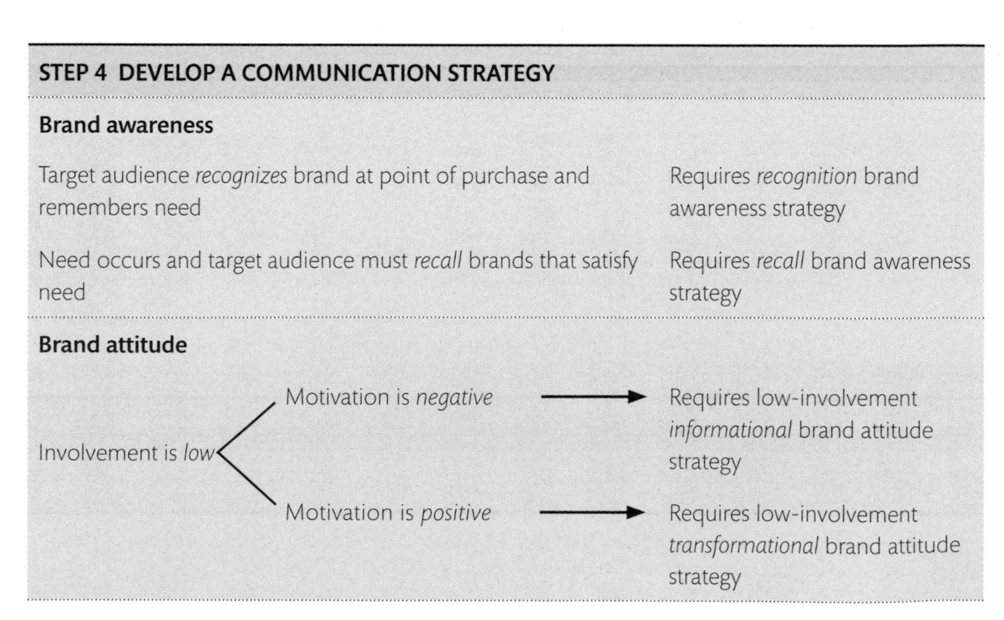

STEP 4 DEVELOP A COMMUNICATION STRATEGY

Brand awareness

Target audience *recognizes* brand at point of purchase and remembers need	Requires *recognition* brand awareness strategy
Need occurs and target audience must *recall* brands that satisfy need	Requires *recall* brand awareness strategy

Brand attitude

Involvement is *low*	Motivation is *negative* →	Requires low-involvement *informational* brand attitude strategy
	Motivation is *positive* →	Requires low-involvement *transformational* brand attitude strategy

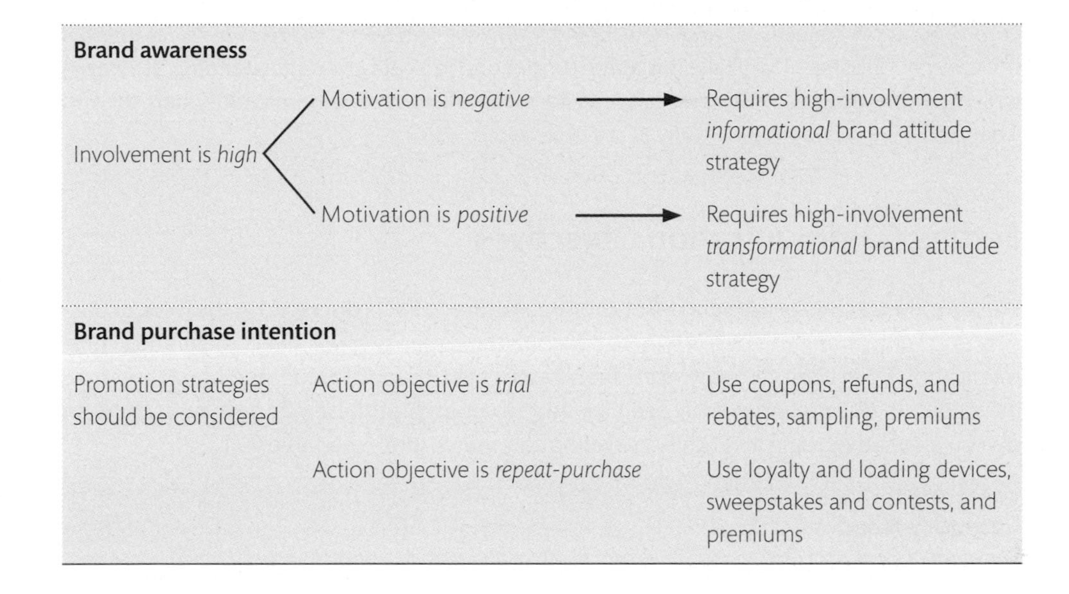

Brand awareness		
Involvement is *high*	Motivation is *negative* →	Requires high-involvement *informational* brand attitude strategy
	Motivation is *positive* →	Requires high-involvement *transformational* brand attitude strategy
Brand purchase intention		
Promotion strategies should be considered	Action objective is *trial*	Use coupons, refunds, and rebates, sampling, premiums
	Action objective is *repeat-purchase*	Use loyalty and loading devices, sweepstakes and contests, and premiums

Key concepts

1. Communication objectives are determined by which of four communication effects are needed: category need, brand awareness, brand attitude, and/or brand purchase intention.
2. While any of the four communication effects may be a communication objective depending upon the situation, brand awareness and brand attitude are *always* communication objectives.
3. Brand awareness strategy is determined by whether a brand at the point of purchase reminds the target audience of a need for purchase (recognition brand awareness) or whether the brand must come to mind when the need occurs (recall brand awareness).
4. Brand attitude strategy depends upon whether the level of perceived risk in a purchase is seen as low or high and whether the underlying motivation driving behaviour in the category is seen as negative or positive (the Rossiter–Percy grid).
5. Promotion strategy is considered when brand purchase intention is a communication objective, and specific incentive promotions are linked to trial versus repeat purchase action objectives.

We are now going to deal with communication strategy, and the first thing we must consider as we address this issue is the development of communication objectives. We have been through our initial planning stages—selecting a target audience, developing a model of consumer decision making, and positioning our brand. Now it is time to decide how to put together our message. Clearly, before we can create advertising or other marketing communication executions, we must have an overall communication strategy, and this begins with setting communication objectives.

In this chapter we will be looking at how to go about selecting communication objectives, with a special emphasis on brand awareness and brand attitude, which are *always* communication objectives, and how brand purchase intention triggers consideration of promotion. Chapter 11 will take this a step further and look at how understanding the way in which people process messages can lead to more effective communication, and then in Chapter 12 we will look specifically at creative tactics.

Setting Communication Objectives

We have already briefly introduced four communication effects discussed in the work of Rossiter and Percy, and it will be from these effects that the manager will select the brand's communication objectives: category need, brand awareness, brand attitude, and brand purchase intention.[1] In this section we will see how and when each of these effects may become an objective for advertising and other marketing communication (see Table 9.1).

Category Need

Category need refers to the target audience's feeling that it would like a particular product or service in order to satisfy a specific need. It is important to remember here that category need is a *perception*, and therefore it can be established by the advertiser. By successfully establishing a belief in the minds of the target audience that links the product category and a felt need, the advertiser can stimulate *primary demand* for the product category. Category need is the communication effect that causes primary demand. But note that category need, and the primary demand it can stimulate in the marketplace, applies to *all brands* in the category. To stimulate secondary or selective demand, the advertiser must also influence brand-level communication effects such as brand awareness, brand attitude, and brand purchase intention.

Because different consumers may be looking for different things in a product, category need can be seen differently, given the particular perceived needs of various segments of the target market. As an example, with the introduction of DVDs, people needed first to be informed about this new category, and interest in DVDs had to be stimulated. However, interest in DVDs can very easily be different among various consumer groups. One group may be interested because it is always interested in being first with anything new. A second group may be drawn to DVDs because of their better picture quality. A third may become interested

Table 9.1 Potential Communication Objectives

Category need	An objective only when it is necessary to remind the target of his or her need for the category or when you must sell the target audience the need
Brand awareness	Always an objective in order to enable the target audience to identify the brand in enough detail to purchase or use the brand
Brand attitude	Also always an objective because there must be some other reason to select one brand over another
Brand purchase intention	Not often a specific objective for advertising except when brand attitude is positive and a 'reason to buy' now is required, but always an objective for promotion

later because it cannot find videos any more. Category need in each case will be stimulated by different perceptions, and hence can require different communication strategies.

How do you decide when category need should be a communication objective? Category need must be present at full strength before purchase of a brand within that category can occur. In other words, the potential consumer must be in the market for the product (category). Category need is not very often required as a communication objective, because most brands are marketed in categories in which the perceived need is well established. But when circumstances dictate it, it is absolutely essential. There are two cases when category need must be a communication objective: when it is necessary to remind the target audience of its need for products in the category, or when you must sell the target audience the need for the category.

Reminding the Consumer of the Category Need

The first situation in which category need becomes a communication objective is when you must remind the prospective consumer of a latent or forgotten (but previously established) category need. Campbell's soup in the US provides a perfect example of reminding prospective buyers of the category need. Since the 1980s, whenever sales have begun to soften, Campbell's has run a campaign built around the category benefit 'soup is good food'. By reminding the consumer of the category need, eating soup because it is good food, Campbell's is able to renew interest in serving soup. It is able to support such a campaign because it dominates the category. As interest in soup increases, so do sales of the Campbell's brand.

Usually, however, reminding the target audience of a category need applies to product categories that are infrequently purchased, such as pain remedies. It also applies to one-time-purchase products that are infrequently used, at least in the opinion of the advertiser. Traveller's cheques are another good case where it is important to remind people of the category need because of infrequent use. Category need reminder campaigns can generally be achieved without devoting a lot of copy specifically to the category need. The purpose is merely to re-establish a previously held need. There is plenty of opportunity to address the brand. This is in sharp contrast to when it is necessary to sell a category need.

With Advert 9.1 we have a good example of reminding the consumer of a category need. While it is an advert for Planitherm window glass, it is also reminding the consumer of the need to conserve energy. The headline 'Keep the energy in' and the copy that follows are reminding people that their current windows could be a source of energy loss (the category need) and that Planitherm provides 'the most energy efficient window glass' to satisfy that need.

Selling the Category Need

When a category need has not yet been established in the minds of the target audience, the advertising campaign, often with promotional support, must sell the need. Selling category need is a communication objective for all new products and also for established products aimed at new users. If the target audience has not bought within the category before, advertising must include selling the category need as a communication objective. While it is easy to see that new product categories obviously must be sold to the consumer, you should also see how it is important to sell the category to anyone who has not yet purchased products in the category. This is why advertising always relies upon category need as an *effect* in communication,

Advert 9.1 **In this advert for Planitherm we have a good example of where category need is part of the communication objective, using the headline 'Keep the energy in' to remind people that their current windows could be a source of energy loss (category need).**

Source: Reproduced with kind permission of Saint-Gobain Glass UK Limited.

but selling category need becomes an objective only when the target audience is made up of people who have no experience with the category.

In order to sell the category to someone new to it, the content of the advertising requires the selling of *category* benefits in addition to brand benefits. Selling the category involves creating, in the potential consumer's mind, *category communication effects*. As a result, just as we have brand communication effects, we will have category awareness, category attitude, and category purchase intention. When selling category need, these category-level communication effects must be addressed *in addition to* brand-level communication effects. This is not an easy job, and almost impossible within a single execution. It requires a campaign.

Category awareness, category attitude, and category purchase intention, which must be addressed when selling the category, are no different conceptually from their brand counterparts—brand awareness, brand attitude, and brand purchase intention. But they are separate communication objectives, which must be decided along with brand-level communication objectives.

Brand Awareness

Brand awareness is the target audience's ability to identify a brand within a category in sufficient detail to purchase or use it. There are at least two ways in which to identify a brand: you can either *recognize* the brand or you can *recall* it. As we shall see in this chapter, this is a very important distinction to understand when setting brand awareness objectives.

The reason why we say that the brand must be identified in sufficient detail is that brand awareness does *not* always require identification of the brand *name*. For the consumer, brand awareness may be stimulated by a familiar package or an even more general stimulus such as colour. For years in the UK, before tobacco advertising was banned, Silk Cut cigarette advertising did not use the brand name in its adverts. Rather, it always featured a piece of purple silk, with a cut somewhere. Of course, this was possible only because the association of the purple silk with a cut and the brand name was built over many years before the name was removed from its advertising (something we will be dealing with in Chapter 13 when we talk about consistency). Identifications such as these still enable brand response, even though no brand name is mentioned.

You may not even need to remember beforehand the brand name or be able to describe the package or colour. Instead, brand awareness may occur through simply recognizing it at the point of purchase. When a package is recognized in a supermarket (for example, the red stripe over a picture of the Yorkshire countryside on packages of Yorkshire Tea) or when a fast-food restaurant sign is recognized on a trip (for example, McDonald's golden arches), brand awareness does not require brand recall.

We have already seen that at the product category level consumers will not buy unless there is a perceived category need. At the brand level, consumers *cannot* buy unless they are first made aware of the brand. As a result, brand awareness must always be considered first, before any other communication effect.

Recognition or Recall: An Essential Difference

Brand awareness is widely misunderstood even by the most experienced people in advertising. The difficulty relates to the essential difference between recognition and recall, a difference that is fundamentally important to advertising and all other forms of marketing communication.[2] Brand recognition and brand recall are two fundamentally different types of brand awareness, as we have pointed out in earlier chapters. The difference depends upon which communication effect occurs first in the consumer's mind: the need for the product (that is, category need) or seeing the brand in the store (that is, brand awareness). *Recognition* brand awareness is when the awareness of the brand reminds you of the category need. *Recall* brand awareness is when the category need occurs and you must remember brands that will satisfy that need.

Brand Attitude

Just as with brand awareness, positive brand attitude must always be a communication objective. If there is no brand attitude present among the target audience, there is very little likelihood that they will want to purchase the product. Why? If you think about it, for most product categories, most people are aware of more than one brand. Unless we believe that brand choices are made randomly from among the brands people are aware of, there must be something about the brands that lead a person to purchase one rather than another. That something is a brand attitude.

The study of attitudes is really based in psychology, but those who work in the area of consumer behaviour have adapted various theories of attitude as to why people behave as they do. It is from this body of knowledge that we borrow our definition of attitude. We look at brand attitude as the understanding a person has in terms of how he or she evaluates a particular brand and its ability to satisfy what he or she is looking for in the product. Because of the importance of brand attitude to effective communication, we will explore it in more depth later in this chapter.

Brand Purchase Intention

Brand purchase intention is the communication response that relates to the target audience's *decision* to purchase a brand or use a service. It refers not to the actual behaviour of buying the brand or using the service, but only to the *intention*. The target audience, as a result of processing an advert or promotion, says to him or herself: 'I think I'll try that brand' or 'I want to pick that up again next time I shop.' Remember, in the communication response sequence, the final step *after* communication effect is actual behaviour. All that marketing communication can do, if correctly processed, is generate either a low-level curiosity to try (with low-involvement product decisions) or a definite intention to buy (for a high-involvement product decision).

We should also take note here of the potential ways in which brand purchase intention may be influenced by advertising. It may not always be the same person who both intends to buy as a result of the advertising and actually makes the purchase, as we saw when we discussed the roles that people play in the decision process. A common example of this would be advertising to children for such things as toys or breakfast cereals. The advertising may be aimed at children in their roles as initiator and influencer, stimulating a brand purchase intention for some child-oriented breakfast cereal, but the mother will actually buy the product. You can surely imagine other cases in which the intention to purchase is really only a recommendation or proposal to someone else who will actually make the purchase decision. Nevertheless, for our purposes, we will consider all of this under the communication objective of brand purchase intention.

In those situations in which the strategy is to build or reinforce an image for a brand and there is very little risk involved in the purchase decision, brand purchase intention will almost surely be delayed, and therefore should *not* be considered as a communication objective. This situation occurs with products such as beer and soft drinks, certain well-established food products, and other generally inexpensive, routinely purchased packaged-goods products.

Let us illustrate what we mean here. If you see an advertisement for ice cream or beer or soft drinks, it is unlikely that you will say to yourself that you are going to go out and immediately buy that brand. What is more likely is that after you have seen the advertising a few times you will begin to feel good about the brand and begin to identify with it. Then if you are passing the ice cream section of the store, or see the advertised brand of beer or soft drink when shopping, you will remember the feeling and then, at the *point of purchase*, decide to buy.

Contrast this with other advertising you are familiar with, where there is 'information' provided. Advertising for such things as cold remedies, for example, provides you with a 'reason to buy' right then if you are suffering from a cold or cough: 'relieves sore throat pain' or 'helps you sleep'. You learn the information and form a tentative decision to try the brand because of what you have learned about it. In cases like this, brand purchase intention can be a communication objective.

Brand purchase intention is not often a communication objective for advertising, but it is *always* the primary communication objective for promotion. In developing a brand's communication strategy, the manager will use promotion when it is necessary to accelerate brand purchase intention to immediate action. While a promotion does not necessarily require an incentive to encourage that action, most do.

Brand Awareness and Brand Attitude Strategy

How do you decide which awareness response and which aspect of brand attitude should form the basis for a brand's communication objectives? We have seen that both brand awareness and brand attitude are *always* communication objectives. But with brand awareness, should it be recognition or recall? How do we look at the various aspects of brand attitude in developing an optimum communication strategy? In this section we will look into these questions as we take a more in-depth look at brand awareness and brand attitude strategy.

Brand Awareness Strategy

There are three possible ways for brand awareness to be used as a communication objective. As we have seen, brand awareness may be executed as brand recognition or brand recall, or in certain cases both may be appropriate. As noted in our discussion of positioning, the link between the category need and the brand is what brand awareness is all about. In effect, this is how advertising and other marketing communication 'brand' the product. Unfortunately, failure to brand effectively in advertising is an all too common problem. As a result, it is critical to effective branding in marketing communication that the creative tactics used are appropriate to the type of brand awareness most likely to be involved in the brand choice decision. The Behavioural Sequence Model, because it identifies how, when, and where a brand choice is made, helps the manager to identify how the brand is used in the decision, whether *primarily* when seen at the time of purchase (for brand recognition awareness) or when linked to the need for the product when that need occurs (for brand recall). Specific creative tactics for recognition and recall brand awareness strategies will be discussed in Chapter 12.

There is an important point to understand here. When we refer to a brand recall objective for advertising, we do not mean recall of the actual advertising. The reason we point this out is that many advertisers try to test their advertising with day-after recall experiments in which people are called the day after a commercial has run on television and asked if they remember seeing it. Our concern is with *brand* recall, regardless of whether or not the consumer can remember the advertising.[3] And, importantly, recall of the brand in response to the need.

When we have decided that brand recall should be the communication objective, advertising should repeat the name as often as possible, linked with the category need. With television, the name should be not only heard often, but seen as well. In radio, of course, the name can only be heard, and in print adverts only seen. But the critical point is that the brand is always *linked to the need*, so that, when the need occurs in 'real life', our brand will come to mind.

Encoding Specificity

This reflects an important principle of memory first talked about by the psychologist Endell Tulving called *encoding specificity*.[4] What this suggests is that to retrieve something successfully from memory there must be a match between the information encoded at the time of learning and the information available when it is retrieved from memory. This means that, for a brand to be recalled when the appropriate need occurs, it must have been encoded in memory linked to that need—and *in that order*. Because the need occurs first, and we must search our memory for an appropriate brand, the presentation in advertising should be need first, satisfied by our brand.

The retrieval cue available when the purchase or usage decision is made is the need, so that is the order in which we will want the target audience to learn the association between the need and the brand. And because this is not easy, this category need–brand association should be repeated within the advertising. One way in which to facilitate learning this need–brand association is to personalize the association between the need and the brand, for example by using personal pronouns such as *me*, *you*, and *I*. This is very well illustrated in the promotion for Warner Breaks shown in Advert 9.2. When the need for a break occurs, *you* are personally invited by Warner Breaks to satisfy that need at one of its thirteen UK hotels and resorts. This personalization is reinforced throughout the copy.

The encoding specificity principle is also at work with brand recognition awareness. It is why advertising must present the brand as it will be confronted when purchased, within an easily recognized category need. By ensuring that the brand–category need link is learned *in that order* for brand recognition awareness, being confronted with the package or brand name at the time of purchase will act as a retrieval cue, reminding the buyer of the need for the product. This is illustrated in Table 9.2.

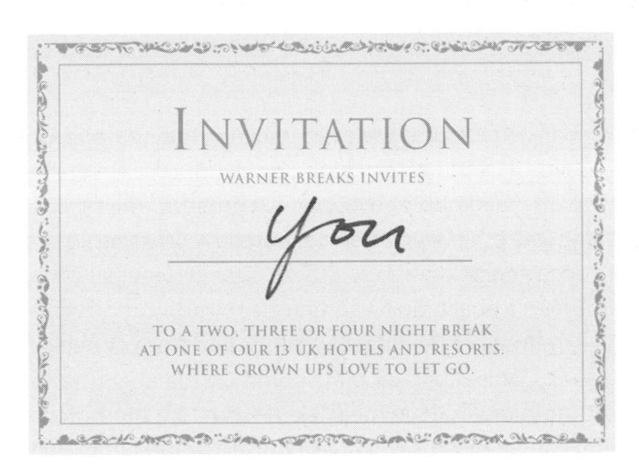

This is an invitation to 'why not?' and 'let's have another go'.
This is an invitation to laugh until it hurts.
This is an invitation to enjoy a bottle and not just a glass.
This is an invitation to show the real you.
This is an invitation to make friends with the Azaleas.
This is an invitation to surprise yourself.
This is an invitation to do nothing, but have fun.
This is an invitation to get lost in the music.
This is an invitation to have a fuss made of you.
This is an invitation to do exactly as you please.
This is an invitation to 'a nice bit of peace and quiet'.
This is an invitation to make new friends.
This is an invitation to just sit back and enjoy the show.
This is an invitation to a good ol' boogie.
This is an invitation to try something completely new.
This is an invitation to a world away from home.
This is an invitation to take the break you fully deserve.
This is an invitation to let yourself go.

Free prize draw: Closing date 30/04/2007. Available to those aged 21 or over. No purchase necessary to enter. Entry is restricted to one person per household.
For full terms and conditions please send a self addressed envelope to Susan, Warner Breaks, FREEPOST NAT4162, Hemel Hempstead, Hertfordshire HP2 4BR.

Advert 9.2 This promotion for Warner Breaks is a very good illustration of personalizing copy to facilitate learning.

Source: Reproduced with kind permission © Warner Leisure Hotels.

Brand Recognition and Brand Recall

Occasionally both brand recognition and brand recall should be considered as communication objectives. However, this is a very difficult objective to effect since it requires two different types of creative execution tactic, and may also require different media (since, for example, radio is unable to communicate visual recognition).

Table 9.2 Brand Awareness and Encoding Specificity

Brand recognition	Brand recall
Brand awareness → Category need	Category need → Brand awareness
Memory retrieved *at* the point of purchase	Memory retrieved *prior* to purchase

Nonetheless, there are two circumstances in which it may be appropriate to set a dual communication objective of brand recognition and recall. The first situation is when your target audience is generally made up of two major segments, one of which makes its brand choice prior to shopping, the other at the point of purchase. We should understand, however, that this is a very rare occurrence.

The second case in which a dual brand awareness communication objective may be called for is when the average member of the target audience finds him or herself frequently in both decision-making situations. This case is far more common than the first, but it too is not likely to occur often. An example of what we mean here would be the brand choice for alcohol. Frequently the potential buyer of gin, say, will recognize a brand name such as Gordon's at the store when shopping and be reminded of a need to buy, a situation calling for a brand recognition communication objective. When this same consumer is in a bar or restaurant and orders a martini, if the waiter asks whether any particular gin is preferred, it will be necessary to remember the brand name—a situation calling for a brand recall communication objective.

Brand Attitude Strategy

Again, brand attitude will always be a communication objective. There are several possible specific communication objectives related to brand attitude. Depending upon what beliefs the target audience holds for a brand, the brand attitude options are to create, increase, maintain, modify, or change its brand attitude. We can see that, without a prior knowledge of the target audience's brand attitude, the manager will not know which option will be best for the brand. So the first step is *always* to understand fully the attitudes of the target audience towards both the category in general and the specific brands that the target audience feels compete in that category.[5]

We need to *create* a brand attitude for new category users or when introducing a new brand. It is hard to imagine any other case in which someone in the market has no attitude at all towards a brand, always assuming that he or she is aware of it. When we find that our target audience has a moderately favourable brand attitude, the brand attitude communication objective will be to *increase* the already favourable brand attitude. Almost anyone who at least occasionally buys a brand will hold at least a moderately favourable attitude towards it. Even new category users may have formed some tentatively positive or negative attitudes about a brand. For example, young mothers have probably begun to form brand attitudes for baby food some time before actually having their babies. In such cases, if we find our target audience has at least some positive brand attitude, we will want to try to increase it.

If we find that the majority of the target audience already has a strong positive attitude towards a brand, the brand attitude communication objective will be to *maintain* that already favourable attitude. This is often the case in more mature markets, in which a large proportion of a brand's users tend to be relatively loyal.

The alert reader may wonder here how this idea squares with that part of our brand attitude definition which points out that brand attitude is *relative*. In a sense it is true that one is probably always trying to increase brand attitude. But in a case in which the competitive environment is stable and your brand has a generally loyal customer base and a dominant share, maintaining that strong brand attitude is a proper objective. However, the advertiser must always be alert to positive shifts in competitive brand attitude that could signal a shift in the brand attitude objective for its brand.

What we mean by *modifying* a brand attitude is basically repositioning a brand. In a sense, what you are trying to do is increase the potential target market by appealing to a different motivation or reason for seeking certain benefits in the brand. A good recent example of this is the way in which many diet control products have been repositioned from strictly 'diet-oriented' products to products that are good for 'watching' your weight, and then repositioned again as products that are 'healthier' for you. This type of change in brand attitude was recognized when Findus introduced Lean Cuisine, and positioned it as a product for watching weight rather than dieting to lose weight.

While almost any target audience could potentially be seen as appropriate for a modified brand attitude if the advertiser sees changes in the marketplace that demand this sort of action, modifying brand attitude can also be useful as a communication objective when it does not appear feasible to increase brand attitude. Examples here are the way in which Arm & Hammer baking soda modified brand attitude in suggesting to consumers that they should use a box of Arm & Hammer in the refrigerator to absorb odours, and how Vaseline Care extended its usage through repositioning as a lip balm.

It is necessary to *change* brand attitude when a significant proportion of your target audience holds a negative attitude towards the brand. Regardless of the number of positive beliefs a consumer may hold towards a brand, if there is a significant negative belief, it will, in almost all cases, 'overrule' the positive beliefs. Choosing to change brand attitude as a communication objective involves removing the negative link between the brand and the reason why a consumer purchases the product. If this link is not removed, regardless of what your advertising may say about a brand, the consumer will still be likely to think: 'Yes, that may be true, but . . .' It is essential to remove the reasons for this 'but'.

Look at Advert 9.3 for the Volkswagen Polo L. In the mid-1990s Volkswagen significantly reduced its prices in the UK, yet the image of Volkswagen as unaffordable persisted. People felt that Volkswagen made quality cars (positive belief), but also felt that they were expensive (negative belief). The creative challenge was to change the negative aspect of brand attitude while retaining the positive. This is always a tricky job when you are dealing with a price–quality interaction, but it is well handled in this advert, which ran in London Underground stations as part of a larger campaign. The obvious humour in the association with Underground 'danger' warnings helps to attract and hold attention as the eye is visually drawn to the price and then on to the tag line, 'Surprisingly ordinary prices'. The advert deals with the negative belief in a humorous way, stimulating generally positive feelings, without challenging or jeopardizing the quality image.

We cannot minimize the potential danger to a message if negative attitudes remain with the target audience, nor can we minimize the difficulty in changing a negative brand attitude.

motivations to watch their weight require different appeals. Women are driven by the positive motive of 'looking good' (sensory gratification or social approval), while men are driven by the negative motive of problem avoidance.

The Rossiter–Percy Grid

Given the importance of involvement and motivation in understanding how and why purchase decisions are made, Rossiter and Percy have suggested integrating these two dimensions into a strategic grid.[11] It is a logical extension of the important implications derived from the psychology literature in learning and persuasion on the role of involvement and motivation in the processing of messages and how people behave.

To begin with, as we have already seen in our discussion of involvement, there is a critical difference in what is required successfully to process a message dealing with a low- versus a high-involvement purchase decision. With low-involvement decisions, to initiate a positive brand attitude, the target audience needs only to pay attention to the message and learn something positive about the brand. That should be enough to form an intention to try, and with trial, to build brand attitude. On the other hand, with high-involvement decisions, the target audience must not only pay attention and learn something from the message; it must also accept or believe what is said in order to begin to build a positive brand attitude that will lead to purchase. Understanding the level of involvement is critical to building positive brand attitude because it affects the processing requirements for the advertising's message.

With motivation, we have seen how important it is to understand what motivates purchase and usage decisions for effective benefit selection and focus in positioning; and hence for building brand attitude (the link between the brand and the benefit). Also, motivation is linked to emotion, which plays a very important role in the processing of a message (as we will discuss in Chapter 11). To address positive versus negative motivations properly requires significantly different creative tactics.

Basically, when you are dealing with positive motives, you are creating a mood, and when you are dealing with negative motives, you are providing information to help to address a perceived (or potential) problem. In their model, Rossiter and Percy refer to brand attitude strategies when motives are positive as *transformational* (transforming your mood) and when motives are negative as *informational*.

Others in the past have attempted to deal with criteria that they feel are important to communication strategy by proposing various grids to help to identify types of marketing communication. Perhaps the best-known example is the so-called FCB grid introduced back in the 1960s.[12] Unfortunately, while many texts and even some practitioners continue to refer to it, the FCB grid has a number of problems.[13] Among other concerns, it does not distinguish between product-category choice and brand choice. Also, its 'think–feel' dimension is rather superficially conceptualized, making the mistake of many in assuming only positive emotions or feelings when *negative* feelings must also be accounted for.

The Rossiter–Percy grid begins with the distinction between recall and recognition awareness, reminding the manager that, whatever the brand attitude strategy, it must be associated with the correct brand awareness strategy. But the real strength of the Rossiter–Percy grid in planning is that it helps to focus the manager's thinking about a product or service in terms of

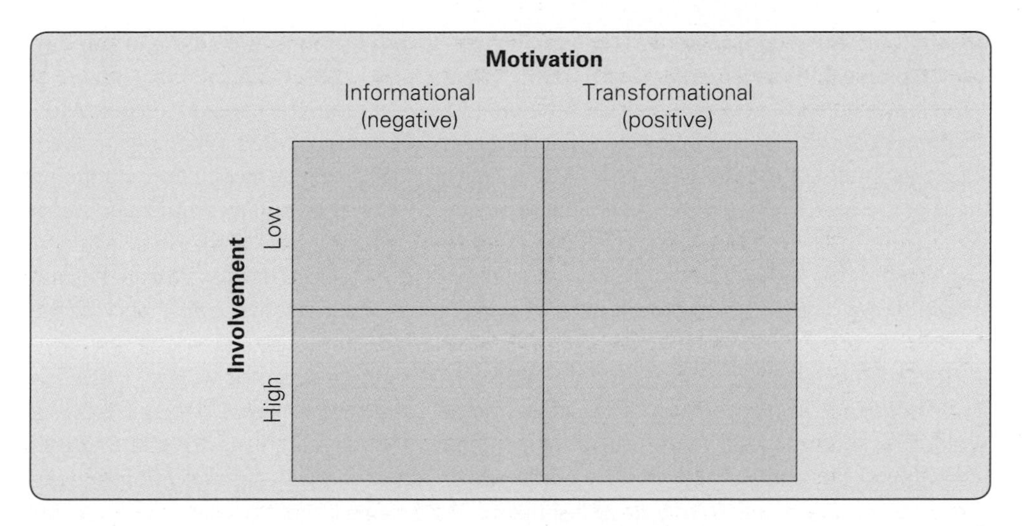

Figure 9.1 Brand Attitude Strategy Quadrants from the Rossiter–Percy Grid

the *target audience's* involvement with the choice decision and the motivation that drives its behaviour. This in turn alerts the manager to specific *tactical* requirements for creative execution (see Fig. 9.1).

Implementing a Low-Involvement Informational Brand Attitude Strategy

Low-involvement informational brand attitude strategies deal with low-risk purchase decisions driven by negative motivations. Because the motivation is to solve or avoid a problem in some way, we must supply information about the brand, in terms of the benefit, which will resolve the problem and provide 'relief' through the brand. In order to implement this, the message should be concerned with benefit claim support and how it is resolved. The obvious format to accomplish this is to present the problem first, 'solved' by the brand. This is virtually every Procter & Gamble advert you have ever seen: 'How did those clothes get so dirty!' (the problem); 'Tide cleans even the dirtiest clothes' (the brand solves the problem).

An effective creative tactic to use with low-involvement informational advertising is to present the benefit claim in the extreme. This is possible because there is little or no risk involved in the purchase, so you do not need to actually believe that the claim is true, only that it might be true. Look at the advert for Priorin shown in Plate V. Here is a great example of a low-involvement informational strategy in which the benefit of 'strength for your hair' is presented visually in a simple, yet extreme, way. Strength is clearly implied by the flexed 'muscle', which is easily recognized as hair. Additionally, for the recognition brand awareness objective, the package is clearly presented to facilitate recognition in the store.

Interestingly, it is not necessary to 'like' low-involvement informational advertising. The important thing is that the benefit is clearly communicated, even in the extreme. In one of the most successful campaigns ever, Procter & Gamble's Charmin toilet tissue for years featured an obnoxious store clerk named 'Mr Whipple'. He was always lurking around corners, while shoppers tried to avoid him so that they could 'squeeze the Charmin' because it was so soft (the benefit). But every time they tried, he would stick his head around the aisle and call out: 'Ladies, please don't squeeze the Charmin.'[14]

Everyone hated the commercials, but the brand soon became the category leader. Why? The benefit of 'softness' was being clearly and dramatically demonstrated. When people were shopping in the toilet tissue aisle and saw the Charmin package (the recognition reminding them of the need), they did not think: 'Oh, Charmin. It has that awful TV commercial, so I'm not buying that!' No, they were wondering if it really was that soft. Because it is a low-involvement decision, one with little or no risk, they gave it a try. This does not mean that you should go out of your way to produce advertising that people do not like, only that liking the advertising, at least when dealing with negative motivations, is not required.[15]

The Charmin example, in fact, illustrates each of the important considerations involved in implementing low-involvement informational brand attitude strategies. First of all, it uses a problem–solution format. The problem here is *implied*: toilet tissue that is not soft. Charmin is the solution: it is 'squeezably soft'. Secondly, you do not need to like the execution, and the target audience did not. Thirdly, keep it simple, using a single benefit or a group of benefits that reinforce each other. For Charmin, the benefit is clear: softness. And, finally, the benefit claim is stated in the extreme.

Implementing a Low-Involvement Transformational Brand Attitude Strategy

With low-involvement transformational brand attitude strategies, we are again dealing with a low-risk purchase decision, but the motivation is positive, based upon a 'reward' for using the product. Unlike when dealing with informational strategies, here the key is in the emotional portrayal of the benefit in order to arouse the correct emotional response; not in providing information. The advertising must 'ring true'. Beyond anything else, low-involvement transformational advertising must suggest *emotional authenticity*. The target audience must simply look at it and see it as 'real'. We put this in quotation marks because we do not mean that it must be literally real. What must happen is that the target audience must see itself emotionally in the role of using the products: 'That ice cream bar looks so good, I want one right now!' You can just *feel* how good it tastes by looking at the execution.

A really good example of what we are talking about here may be seen in Advert 9.4 for Nescafé Gold Blend. As you look at this advert, you can almost smell the 'golden aroma' rising from the jar. The enticing visual strongly links Nescafé Gold Blend with a rich, good-tasting coffee, providing a truly satisfying, almost sensual, experience. It will be the memory of this experience that will be remembered at the store when the shopper sees the package.

In effect, the benefit is *in the execution*. For this reason, when dealing with positively motivated behaviour, the target audience must like the advertising, because it is the execution itself that elicits the emotion, not the information in the message. This is often difficult for advertisers to accept. There is a strong temptation to include a more tangible benefit when advertising a low-involvement product purchased from positive motives, a kind of benefit that would be more appropriate when dealing with negative motivations.

An example of what we are talking about is illustrated in a test conducted in Sweden of two Toblerone commercials using Åke Wissing & Co.'s Ad Box technique, a procedure for pre-testing advertising. Toblerone is a chocolate bar, a perfect example of a low-involvement product where you need to address a positive purchase motive, sensory gratification. A good

Advert 9.4 This advert for Nescafé Gold Blend coffee illustrates a positive experience with the brand and provides a strong brand identification.

Source: NESCAFÉ, GOLD BLEND, the JAR shape and the SCOOP OF COFFEE BEANS scenery are all protected through intellectual property rights by Société des Produits Nestlé SA, Trade Mark Owners.

Advert 9.5 The same commercial, but with two different endings, (*a*) reflecting a positive emotional experience, and (*b*) a specific product attribute. The first version significantly outperformed the second, as we would expect for a low-involvement product where purchase is driven by positive motives.

Source: Åke Wissing & Co., Clear Channel Outdoor, and Mejerrerna. TOBLERONE is a registered trademark of Kraft foods.

commercial was produced creating a positive emotional experience, but there was some question as to whether the good feeling created by the commercial would be enough to drive purchase intent. A second version of the commercial was produced, identical to the first except for the ending, where an incentive was added: 'You can now buy Toblerone for the normal price, but you get 10 per cent more chocolate.' In other words, the original advertisement was turned into a *promotion* using a loading device (a bigger bar for the same money).

Frames from the two commercials are shown in Advert 9.5 illustrating the different endings. Results of the test showed that the original advertising version consistently outperformed the promotion version, including buying interest—65 per cent versus 55 per cent (see Fig. 9.2). This brings up another important issue: a promotion, while it must be consistent with the brand's advertising, must be created in its own right. Too often managers think all that is needed for a promotion is to add an incentive of some kind (frequently a coupon or price-off announcement) to an existing advert or commercial. As this example shows, one message may interfere with the other. This is all too likely when dealing with positive motives in advertising because a promotion incentive will almost always be addressing a negative motive unless carefully positioned.

While all advertising executions should be unique to the brand, it is doubly critical for transformationally driven strategies. An advert may provide an effective and authentic emotional portrayal, but if it is not firmly linked to the brand, it goes for naught. For this reason, a strong visual device, unique to the brand, can be effective when it is used consistently over time (something we deal with later on in Chapter 13). The visual component of the advertising

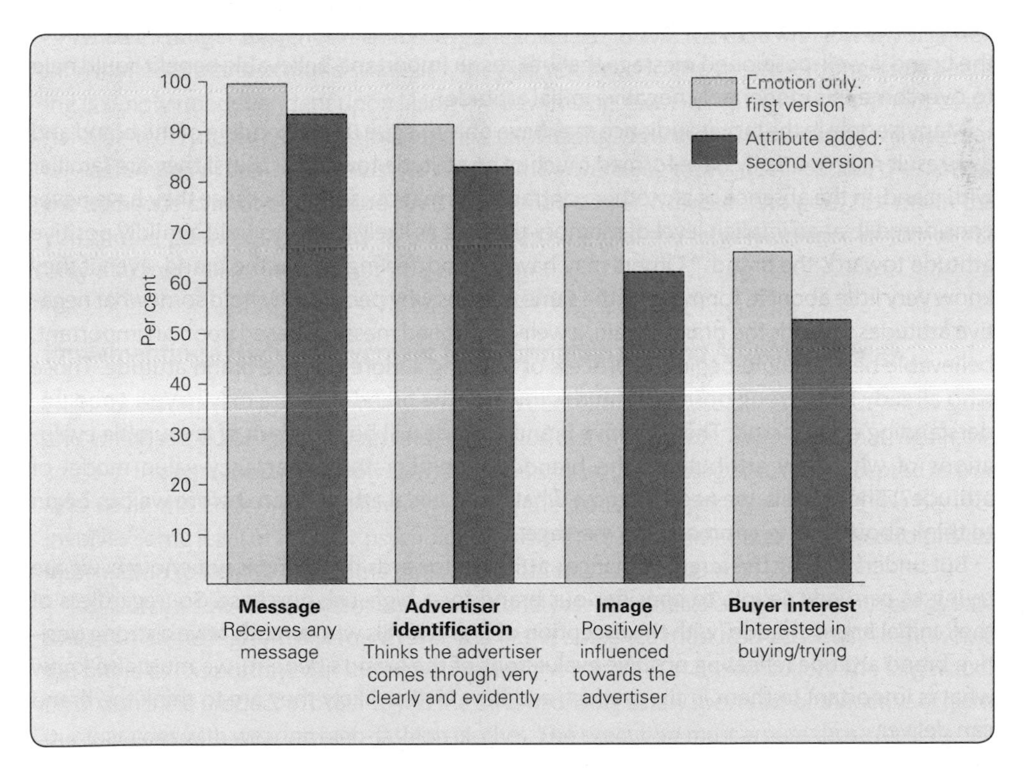

Figure 9.2 Communication Pre-Test Results from the Two Versions of the Toblerone Commercial

Source: Åke Wissing & Co.

Because of this, the target audience must 'like' the advertising. But that liking must go beyond simply liking the execution itself. The liking must be *product and brand* based. Because it is a high-involvement decision, in processing the message, the target audience must really believe that the brand, as portrayed in the advertising, is the one that will satisfy the sensory gratification or social approval motivation underlying its need. The brand must be portrayed in such a way that it elicits from non-declarative emotional memory the correct emotions, the *feelings* that the target audience wants to experience in using the product. (How this happens will be discussed in Chapter 11.)

The advert for Peugeot shown in Plate VI provides a good example of what we are talking about here. While simple in execution, the advert nevertheless does an excellent job in creating a strong emotional association with the RCZ, helping the target to 'feel' the excitement of driving one.

Reviewing Brand Awareness and Brand Attitude Strategy

A good way in which to appreciate what goes into the effective implementation of brand awareness and brand attitude strategy is to compare good executions of adverts for each of the four quadrants of the Rossiter–Percy grid. Such examples may be seen in Plates VII–X. First, look at the advert for Surf detergent in Plate VII. It provides an excellent execution of low-involvement informational advertising. The benefit is presented in the extreme, and in a humorous way. Are clothes cleaned with Surf detergent really so 'irresistibly clean' that people will snatch them right off you? Hardly, but the point is made. And when the brand is seen in the shop (and note the strong package presentation, facilitating recognition brand awareness), you are likely to remember the advert *and* importantly the benefit of irresistibly clean clothes. Could it really be that good? Since this is a low-involvement decision with little risk, why not give it a try? This is a well-done advert.

Contrast this with the advert for Bonne Maman in Plate VIII. The difference is immediately felt. Here, we have an enticing look at a warm scene in a country kitchen, with children and a cat, stimulating positive associations in memory, which are reinforced with the message 'Moments to cherish'. The emotional authenticity is real, communicating a sense of pleasure and contentment that will be associated in memory with the brand. Adding to this is the bottle of milk and the whisk, suggesting the wholesome ingredients of the product. The package is well presented for easy recognition at the point of purchase, so that, when seen in the store, it will trigger the good feeling and desire that you felt when you saw the advert, leading to purchase.

Looking at the high-involvement quadrants from the grid, the Panasonic advert in Plate IX provides a really good example of high-involvement informational brand attitude, and recall brand awareness, strategy. In terms of brand attitude strategy, the visual is strong and vivid, consistent with the benefit, and most importantly, believable. It implies the intensity and clarity to be found in the Viera HD plasma television. The image attracts your attention and draws you into the copy, which reinforces the benefit. While always difficult to accomplish in print, the recognition brand recall strategy is well executed. The 'need' for a better television experience is presented first via the visual, then linked to the brand. This link is then repeated in the copy, again in the correct need–brand sequence, with 'Enjoy wildlife as nature intended' (the need) followed by 'thanks to Panasonic' (the brand). When in the market for a new HD television to enjoy a more vivid picture, because this need has been linked to Panasonic, in the need–brand order, it should come immediately to mind as the way in which to 'solve' that problem.

Finally, the Gravetye Manor advert in Plate X offers a good example of a high-involvement transformational advert. The visual images are likely to elicit a strong positive emotional response from anyone interested in a possible country break. He or she will immediately identify with the images and the 'feeling', thinking: 'Wouldn't it be great to be there?' When the time comes to consider a break, Gravetye Manor will come to mind. That positive feeling generated from the advert is the benefit, and will encourage looking into a stay.

Corporate Image Advertising

This is a good point at which to consider corporate image advertising. Like all advertising, both brand awareness and brand attitude must be communication objectives (the brand here, of course, is the company). Obviously, corporations want their names to be *recognized*, hence recognition brand awareness strategies are called for. In terms of brand attitude, the primary objective is to build and sustain overall positive attitude towards the company. In effect, companies want people to 'like' them.

What brand attitude strategy, then, should be used? In almost all cases, corporate image advertising should follow a *transformational* brand attitude strategy.

Consider this for a minute. We know that transformational brand attitude strategies are needed when dealing with positive motives. What motive is involved here? There is obviously no *direct* purchase or usage decision involved, but in a sense there is a decision to consider the company. If someone pays attention to the advertising, is it to solve a problem? In the absence of any immediate concrete action being considered by the target audience, the answer is 'no'. Rather, if people pay attention to the advertising, it is probably because they wish to *learn* something about the company, and what they learn will inform their attitude towards the company. Learning in order simply to acquire knowledge is almost always positively motivated, and this indicates a transformational brand attitude strategy.

The difficult question is whether we are dealing with a low- or high-involvement decision. What is the 'risk' of making a bad decision about the company based upon what is learned from the corporate image advertising? This will depend a lot upon the specific target audience, and how or if people eventually act upon their feelings associated with the company. If the objective is to foster 'goodwill', building or maintaining a positive attitude towards the company, then a low-involvement transformational strategy will be all that is needed. Often after bad publicity, a company may wish to restore positive feelings among the population at large or among specific target groups. If the effect of the negative publicity was slight, again a low-involvement transformational strategy should work.

But what if the damage done to the company's image is serious? If that occurs, attitudes towards the company may have been seriously affected and as a result, for corporate image advertising to be effective, the target audience will need to be *convinced* by the message. This means a high-involvement transformational strategy. There are many other situations in which a high-involvement transformational brand attitude strategy would be needed. As an investor, you may 'like' a company, but you will also want to understand more about it; you need to feel convinced that it might be a good company in which to invest. We are not talking about the actual investment decision here, which would involve negative motivations, but the 'feeling' that an investor has about a company prior to seriously considering it as an investment.

Suppose the target audience comprises people working in government, in regulatory agencies. From the corporation's perspective, it will want them to have the strongest possible positive attitudes towards the company, and not just a general 'liking', because if it does become involved in any actions with a regulatory agency, it will want to be starting from a positive association in memory, not an indifferent or even moderately positive association—and certainly not from a negative one.

Corporate image advertising will almost always utilize a transformational brand attitude strategy, and usually a high-involvement transformational strategy, because, in the long term, the target audience must *accept* the message that this is a 'good' company. Corporate *image* advertising is not aimed at specific decisions on the part of a target audience. Of course, corporations also advertise in order to influence particular decisions: for example, to specifically influence investors to buy or analysts to recommend a stock or bond issue; or to specifically get a government agency to look favourably on something the company wishes to do. In such cases, the appropriate brand attitude strategy will be the one that reflects the risk and motivation involved in the particular decision being addressed, just as with any other brand advertising.

Promotion Strategy

Promotion must be considered as part of the communication strategy when brand purchase intention is a communication objective. While brand purchase intention may be a communication objective for advertising, as we have seen, that is rarely the case. In those situations in which it is necessary to accelerate purchase intention to immediate action, promotion becomes a part of the communication strategy. This may be a part of the initial strategic planning process; however, the need for a promotion may also occur during a campaign for tactical reasons. For example, a competitor may be about to introduce a new version of its product and you might want to encourage accelerated purchase of your brand to remove your favourable brand-switchers from the market just prior to the introduction, or you may find sales weak because of some unforeseen circumstance in the market. In either event, the execution of the promotion, its visual imagery and message, must be consistent with the brand's advertising.

We have defined promotion generally as that part of a brand's marketing communication strategy dealing with the more short-term tactical goal of immediate action. While this is certainly a useful definition, there is more to consider. For example, one important consideration is time. When consumer decision-making models were introduced in Chapter 7, we saw how important it is to understand the timing of various stages in the decision process. Just as with advertising, one needs to integrate the use of promotion techniques in relation to the target audience's decision process. Some promotions may be more helpful early in the decision process, prior to purchase or use of a service, others more appropriate at the point of purchase, still others after purchase or even during usage. When considering traditional promotion tactics, they must be considered as part of the overall marketing communication effort.

Table 9.4 Strengths of the Six Basic Consumer Sales Promotion Techniques in Terms of Trial and Repeat Purchase

Trial strength	Repeat purchase strength
Coupons	Loyalty and loading devices
Refunds and rebates	Sweepstakes, games, and contests
Sampling	Premiums
Premiums	

Promotion is used when you want to speed up the decision process, but should never be considered in isolation. As pointed out earlier, most promotions involve an incentive, and are known as sales promotion.

Sales promotions may be broadly classified as either *immediate* or *delayed*.[20] This idea of immediate versus delayed promotions is closely associated with the two target audience action objectives of trial and repeat purchase, which we introduced when we were discussing target audience buyer groups in Chapter 6.

Almost any promotion should help to generate trial or encourage repeat purchase. For example, while loyalty programmes are clearly designed to encourage and promote repeat purchase of and loyalty to a brand, if the loyalty programme is seen by non-users as particularly attractive, it could also encourage trial. Equally, while coupons are effective in attracting trial, they also encourage repeat purchase by existing customers by effectively reducing the price.

When we speak of a type of promotion being more oriented towards trial or repeat purchase, what we are talking about are general strengths (Table 9.4). If we look at the six basic types of consumer sales promotion, for example, coupons, sampling, and refunds are strong candidates for trial, while sweepstakes and loyalty promotions are best suited to repeat purchase. Premiums are a little more difficult to place because they can really be effective for either objective. An appropriately chosen premium could have a strong appeal to other-brand-switchers, providing just the incentive to get them to try our brand along with the others that they use. Say someone switches among two or three brands of condiments, but not your brand: offering a recipe booklet as a premium with the purchase of any of your condiments could provide the necessary incentive to give your brand a try. On the other hand, especially for more durable products with longer purchase cycles, a well-targeted premium could indeed get previous buyers to purchase again now. This would be particularly appropriate for those in the target audience just beginning to think about replacing, say, an appliance that is showing some age. There is no real need yet, but they are thinking about it. An attractive premium could very well get them to act now.

Strategically, repeat purchase sales promotion techniques are used for more targeted, short-term objectives. Unlike trial promotions, which are designed to attract new customers to the brand, repeat purchase premiums are used to affect the *timing* of purchases by brand users. You want your customers either to buy now, effectively removing them from the market in the short term to avoid switching, or to buy continually with little or no switching.

Table 10.2 Considerations in Matching Media with Communication Objectives

Visual content	Critical for recognition brand awareness and transformational brand attitude
Time to process message	Important for high-involvement informational brand attitude
Frequency	Higher frequency is needed for recall brand awareness and low-involvement transformational brand attitude

points for the manager to consider: visual content, the time available to process the message, and the frequency potential (see Table 10.2). Visual content is essential for recognition brand awareness, because you must be able to present the brand as it will be seen at the point of purchase. It is also important for transformational brand attitude strategies because of the need to facilitate emotional authenticity.

The time available to process a message is important for high-involvement informational brand attitude strategies because of the need for acceptance of the message. This is the case for most consumer durable products (televisions, home computers) and many business purchase decisions, for which the target audience will need time to process the message in order to learn enough about the brand. In other cases, such as with most fmcg products, only a brief exposure time is necessary. When more processing time is necessary, broadcast media such as television and radio will not do, but they will be very appropriate when only a short time is needed for processing.

The ability to deliver high frequency is important for recall brand awareness as well as for low-involvement transformational brand attitude strategies. Here there is a need for several exposures in order to build the link in memory between the category need and brand for recall brand awareness, and to build the emotional association with the brand for low-involvement transformational brand attitude strategies. Some marketing communication options, such as broadcasting and newspapers, offer the potential of high frequency. Think of how many commercials for a particular brand you see during the broadcast of a football match. Other media options, such as direct mail or monthly magazines, are much more restricted in terms of frequency. True, a brand could have multiple insertions in a single magazine, but, because of the narrow reach of magazines compared to something like television, this will not usually be a very efficient way of obtaining higher frequency. When the brand awareness objective is recall, higher frequency is required than when it is recognition. When the brand attitude objective involves a low-involvement, transformational strategy, we also need more frequency. Table 10.3 details how a number of primary media rate on these characteristics.

Primary Media

Media that satisfy these three criteria in terms of the appropriate communication objectives are called *primary* media. These are the options the manager looks to first in putting together a media strategy. Primary media must be capable of delivering the appropriate brand awareness *and* brand attitude communication objectives, as well as category need and brand purchase intention, if appropriate. Primary media for *recognition* brand awareness and brand attitude must first of all be able to present the brand as it will be confronted at the point of purchase, and then satisfy the processing requirements of the brand attitude strategy involved (see Table 10.4). Since most media will work for recall brand awareness, as long as a few possible cautions are taken into account with print media (especially with magazines), the primary media selected will be mediated only by brand attitude strategy communications (see Table 10.5).

Table 10.3 Media Ratings on Essential Media Selection Characteristics

	Visual content	Time to process message	Frequency
Television	Yes	Short	High
Radio	No	Short	High
Newspapers	Limitations	Long	High
Magazines	Yes	Long	Limitations
Posters	Yes	Long	Limitations
Internet	Yes	Long	High
Direct mail	Yes	Long	Low

Source: Adapted from J.R. Rossiter and L. Percy, *Advertising Communication and Promotion Management* (New York: McGraw-Hill, 1997).

Table 10.4 Primary Media for Recognition Brand Awareness and Appropriate Brand Attitude Strategy

Low-involvement, informational	• Television • Print • Internet • Posters
Low-involvement, transformational	• Television • Newspapers (if four-colour available) • Magazines (with attention to frequency) • Internet • Posters
High-involvement, informational	• Television (using 60-second or longer commercials, e.g. on cable) • Print • Websites
High-involvement, transformational	• Television • Newspapers (if four-colour available) • Magazines (with attention to frequency) • Posters

Table 10.5 Primary Media for Recall Brand Awareness and Appropriate Brand Attitude Strategy

Low-involvement, informational	• Television • Radio • Newspapers • Magazines (with attention to frequency) • Internet • Posters
Low-involvement, transformational	• Television • Newspapers (if four-colour available) • Magazines (with attention to frequency) • Internet • Posters
High-involvement, informational	• Television (using 60-second or longer commercials, e.g. on cable) • Newspapers • Magazines (with attention to frequency) • Posters
High-involvement, transformational	• Television • Newspapers (if four-colour available) • Magazines (with attention to frequency) • Posters

Just because a particular medium should not be considered as a primary medium does not necessarily mean that it should not be used at all. Often, it makes sense to use a medium because it helps to enhance the delivery of a communication objective, even if it is not appropriate for all of the core communication objectives. In these cases, the additional medium could be used to help to boost a particular objective. This is especially true for brand awareness. There may also be certain situations in which the manager may need to use a less-than-ideal medium because it reaches a part of the target audience that is not effectively covered, in terms of either reach or frequency, by the primary media.

The primary media presented in Tables 10.4 and 10.5 reflect what is necessary to achieve the two primary communication objectives effectively for most large audience advertisers. But, when dealing with certain types of advertising, there may be specific concerns that suggest that particular media are more or less appropriate. To illustrate, we will consider the cases of retail, business-to-business, and corporate image advertising.

Retail Advertising

In the case of retail advertising, it is almost always *local* regardless of the number of stores a chain may have, because any one store is only likely to draw customers from around its location. Additionally, most retail advertising must concern itself not only with promoting the image of the store, but also with the products it carries. This can make for a rather complex mix of communication problems. In the end, local media are what one should consider, with the type consistent with the requirements of the core communication objectives of brand awareness and brand attitude as well as, in all cases, brand purchase intention. Local television, newspapers, outdoor, direct mail, possibly the Internet or social media, and where appropriate, local radio could be considered.

Business-to-Business Advertising

Media options for business-to-business advertising are generally a function of the target audience's size and the roles that people in the target audience are playing in the decision process. When target audiences are small, when there are really only a limited number of decision makers, general advertising does not really make sense. Here, most marketing communication will be handled via sales calls, and the only media involved will be collateral (brochures and catalogues) and possibly direct mail. With a somewhat larger target audience, when it begins to make sense to use print media, trade publications and direct mail are appropriate, and in some cases targeted use of the Internet. The key here is to be certain to identify the different roles played by different segments of the target audience. With somewhat larger target audiences, it is likely that there will be both important, but lower-level, decision makers, as well as senior management, to consider. With larger target audiences, trade publications and more general business magazines with broader reach are appropriate, as well as the tactical use of direct mail and the Internet.

Corporate Image Advertising

You will remember from Chapter 9 that corporate image advertising almost always involves a transformational brand attitude strategy. A manager must keep this in mind when considering media for corporate image advertising. And, just as with business-to-business advertising, the size of the company will dictate media options to consider. With many small companies, image advertising as such may not make any sense. However, local sponsorships would be appropriate, and any product-related advertising could include a certain degree of corporate image messaging as part of the brand attitude strategy.

Larger companies should utilize the primary media associated with recognition brand awareness and transformational brand attitude strategies as appropriate. In addition, event marketing and sponsorships (which are compatible with the image sought) could also work. But if the target audience is small or specialized—for example, when directly addressing financial analysts—special interest publications, direct mail, or the Internet might be considered. It should also not be overlooked that, regardless of the size of a company, effective public relations should be *integrated* with any corporate image advertising—and the annual report is always a part of corporate image advertising.

We will now look at some of the implications of this for media selection decisions associated with brand awareness and brand attitude strategies in a bit more detail.

Brand Awareness Strategies

The difference between brand recognition and brand recall has important implications for media selection. Brand recognition requires an emphasis on the visual representation of the pack or logo, while brand recall puts the emphasis on frequency to build an association between the brand name and category need. This difference of emphasis, for example, would lead to the conclusion that radio is unsuitable for brand recognition, but offers cost-efficient, high-frequency repetition.

Brand Recognition

When brand recognition is our communication objective, we are looking for good visual content, not much time should be required for processing, and low frequency will do. If we look back at Table 10.3, we see that television, magazines, posters, the Internet, and direct mail could be considered. Radio is out because you cannot see the package, and, while newspapers might be a possibility, we must be sure that good colour reproduction can be counted on.

Brand Recall

If brand recall is our communication objective, our biggest concern is with frequency. Good repetition of the linkage of category need and brand name is necessary, and this requires high frequency. Looking again at Table 10.3, we see that television, radio, newspapers, and the Internet offer the potential for high frequency. Magazines and direct mail have obvious frequency limitations. Posters have a potential frequency limitation because they are stationary media (unless, of course, they are on a bus or train, which will have their own frequency limitations).

Brand Attitude Strategies

The correct matching of media to communication objective is important for brand attitude strategy. Here we will be looking at which media make sense for specific brand attitude communication objectives as defined by the Rossiter–Percy grid.

Low-Involvement, Informational Strategy

Brand attitude communication objectives that reflect a low-involvement brand decision coupled with negative motivation can be addressed by almost any medium. It is perhaps the easiest communication objective to deal with in terms of media selection. There is no strong visual requirement, only a brief processing time is needed, and high frequency is not necessary because the benefits used in adverts following this type of brand attitude strategy must be learned in one or two exposures if it is to be effective. This is why almost any medium can be selected. A possible exception would be if the benefit must be *demonstrated*, in which case the medium selected must be capable of presenting the demonstration.

Low-Involvement, Transformational Strategy

With a brand attitude strategy for a low-involvement brand decision when the underlying motivation is positive, *good visual content* is critical. Although only a brief processing time is required, a relatively high frequency is necessary because of a generally slower brand attitude development.

Here television is the ideal medium. All of the other primary media, with the exception of the Internet, are a potential problem because of processing time or frequency limitations. The exception here is radio, but it must be excluded because it lacks visual content. We should point out, however, that highly creative radio can sometimes overcome this problem if it can really make you 'see' the product.

High-Involvement, Informational Strategy

Because brand attitude strategies that involve high-involvement brand decisions and negative motives require a longer processing time for the more extensive information content necessary to convince the target audience, media selection emphasis is likely to be on print-oriented media. And since frequency is not an issue, again because the benefits must be accepted in one or two exposures, almost any print medium will do (including the Internet).

High-Involvement, Transformational Strategy

As with low-involvement strategies associated with positive motivations, visual content is critical. The key difference here is that there is no need for high frequency. You may think this strange, since we pointed out that brand attitude builds slowly in the low-involvement choice situation. The reason for this seeming contradiction is that most low-involvement/transformational brand attitude strategies involve fmcgs with a relatively *short purchase cycle*. This means that there is not a lot of time for the advertising to work. With high-involvement brand decisions, we are usually dealing with brand decisions for products with much longer purchase cycles. This is what permits a relatively lower rate of frequency. Of the primary media we have been considering, television and most print media could be selected. Newspapers have the potential colour limitation that we discussed earlier. Radio would not be appropriate.

A caveat should be noted here. Even though we are dealing with positive motives, because the brand decision is high involvement, eventually it might be necessary to provide a certain amount of detailed information. When that is the case, processing time will need to be considered in your media selection.

Brand Awareness and Brand Attitude Strategies

Taking all of these considerations into account, we can classify particular media as appropriate or not for the core communication objectives, in some cases subject to potential limitations. These options are summarized in Table 10.6.

An important point to remember in media selection is that an attempt must be made to accommodate *all* of your communication objectives. This means that, at the very least, the media selected must meet *both* brand awareness *and* brand attitude strategies. When recognition is the brand awareness communication objective, because all of the primary media are acceptable, selection will be driven solely on the basis of the brand attitude strategy. But when brand recall is the communication objective, you must be careful to consider the requirements for both brand recall and the brand attitude strategy in your media selection. The only medium that works regardless of the strategy is the Internet. In every other case you must check for compatibility between the two communication objectives involved, and look carefully at potential limitations.

Table 10.6 Media Selection Options to Satisfy Brand Awareness and Brand Attitude Communication Objectives

	Brand awareness recognition	Brand awareness recall	Low involvement		High involvement	
			Informational	Transformational	Informational	Transformational
Television	Yes	Yes	Yes	Yes	No	Yes
Radio	No	Yes	Yes	No	No	No
Newspapers	Limitations	Yes	Yes	Limitations	Yes	Limitations
Magazines	Yes	Limitations	Yes	Limitations	Yes	Yes
Posters	Yes	Limitations	Yes	Limitations	Limitations	Yes
Internet	Yes	Yes	Yes	Yes	Yes	Yes
Direct mail	Yes	Limitations	Yes	Limitations	Yes	Yes

Source: Adapted from J.R. Rossiter and L. Percy, *Advertising Communication and Promotion Management* (New York: McGraw-Hill, 1997).

Even if a medium cannot achieve total compatibility between these two objectives, it might still be worth using—but it should not be the *primary* media selection. For example, television is a perfect medium for driving up awareness of any kind. Even though it is not really suitable for high-involvement brand decisions when the motivation is negative, it could certainly be used to generate recall brand awareness, as long as another, more appropriate, medium carries the primary informational message with sufficient time for processing.

Demographic versus Direct Matching

Up to this point we have been talking about media types. Now we need to consider how to select specific media vehicles within types—for example, a particular television programme or magazine. Despite the many shortcomings of this method, media vehicles are often selected by 'matching' demographics. Demographic matching is the practice of defining a target audience in terms of specific demographic characteristics, then 'matching' that demographic profile with the demographic profile of a media vehicle's audience. This method is popular with media planners because data on the demographics (and other variables such as 'lifestyle') of audiences for television and radio programmes, and readers of newspapers and magazines, are readily available, and there are computer programs for putting together media schedules based upon optimizing these demographic 'matches'.

But there is a fundamental flaw in all of this, and that is why we have placed the word 'match' in quotation marks. Suppose usage for our brand is 10 per cent in the overall population. This means that the likelihood of finding a user randomly would be one in ten. Now suppose you select a target audience of women, 18–49 years of age, with incomes over €15,000 a year, because this group has a significantly higher concentration of brand users (if we have a repeat purchase target audience action objective) or potential triers (if a trial target audience objective) than the general population.

Obviously, the odds of locating a user will be much greater if we can find media that reach this group. But it is not that simple. There is no reason to believe that brand usage is evenly distributed among all media that have this profile. Some women in this demographic group may read *Elle* because they are interested in high fashion; others may read *Country Life*. If we are marketing country-casual clothes, what is the likelihood that our brand users read *Elle*?

If we really want to increase the odds of finding a brand user, why not find media that brand users read or watch? This is *direct matching*. It may require directly surveying your market to measure its media habits, but in most cases it will be worth the effort to identify directly the media habits of those who are attitudinally and behaviourally consistent with your target audience. As we have already pointed out in our discussion of target audience selection in Chapter 6, while demographic profiles provide useful diagnostic information, they should not be the basis of target audience selection.

Scheduling Media

One of the more vexing questions in developing effective media strategies is how to schedule media. Earlier we defined three basic types of scheduling: flighting, bursts, and continuity. While these basic types do indeed define the *structure* of most media scheduled, the actual scheduling itself is a much more difficult issue. There is seemingly an almost infinite number of circumstances that could have an effect upon how to optimize your media schedule. What is the purchase cycle for the category? Are sales seasonal? If so, do we want to break the pattern? How do competitors schedule their advertising? What creative units are to be used (for example, 15-second versus 30-second versus 60-second commercials, or half-page versus full-page versus two-page spreads in magazines)? How many different creative executions are being used? How difficult is it to reach the target audience? Is the target audience segmented? If so, how? You should be getting the idea.

There are, of course, many models available to help the media planner to put together a good media schedule. But most media models, by their very nature, make general assumptions and tend to average. It is virtually impossible for any one model to take into account all of the many variables involved. This has led to a number of rules of thumb among media planners. But again, because every brand's situation is different, and often changes from campaign to campaign, following well-known formulas may not lead to the most effective schedule.

Does this mean that the task of developing an effective media schedule is all but hopeless? Not at all. What it means is that each schedule must be carefully assessed, and assessed for *each* media plan developed. How to go about this task is quite beyond the scope of this book, but there are a number of good books that deal with scheduling in depth. One book in particular offers a great deal of insight into this problem: Simon Broadbent's *When to Advertise*.[6] Broadbent has had a significant influence on media issues, especially in the UK. What we like about his approach is that he defines a *process* to determine when to advertise.

He suggests that to schedule media effectively you must look at what you need to pay for the media, when you most want it to have an effect, and how you think the advertising will work. You can see how these points address the kind of issues raised by the many questions associated with trying to optimize a media schedule. There is nothing at all easy about how you go about implementing this process, but he offers a framework for addressing the problem. The important point is that he acknowledges the fact that effective media scheduling depends upon the 'particular circumstances; there is no single solution'.[7]

Target Audience Factors and Brand Ecology

In Chapter 6 we discussed at length the issues of target audience selection and suggested that brand loyalty segmentation based on attitude is the most effective method for developing communication strategy. While the customer's relationship with the brand is an essential element in communication planning and usually has to be based on primary market research, a relatively new approach to media selection also uses the customer's relationship with the media as an input into media selection. Syndicated audience research services provide a wealth of quantitative data about media use. The Target Group Index (TGI) in the UK also provides usage data on 4,000 brands in 500 product categories, cross-referenced to usage of print media and TV. In addition, it provides some basic attitudinal data, as well as standard demographics. Major media also supply extensive syndicated audience data. In the UK the Broadcasters' Audience Research Board (BARB) provides TV viewing behaviour on a continuous basis, showing audience figures per programme on the major terrestrial and satellite channels. Rich data on over 250 newspaper and magazine titles in the UK are provided by the National Readership Survey (NRS), and similar data are provided for radio by Radio Joint Audience Research (RAJAR). Similar services are available in other countries. These syndicated audience data sources are the basis of all of the major media planning systems, and are also utilized within the most sophisticated proprietary media systems such as Zenith Media's ZOOM Excalibur, which models effective frequency levels against marketing and media factors.

However, the fragmentation of the media landscape has led to the emergence of a new active media consumer, who can choose from a huge portfolio of media to construct a 'personal media network' using an increasing array of technology and information actively to edit his or her own media environment.[8] The opportunity in this fragmentation of audiences is that it offers the possibility of going beyond simple demographics to understand the relationship that smaller audiences have with their chosen media, and to develop an understanding of consumer 'brand ecology'.

Brand ecology considers not only the attitudinal, emotional, and behavioural aspects of brand consumption, but also explores how this brand-related behaviour integrates with wider social and cultural experience in the lifeworld of the active consumer. As we pointed out in Chapter 6, demographics and lifestyle analyses are not stable predictors of consumer behaviour across categories, and, as media choice explodes, multi-TV households become the norm, and technological aids such as the electronic programme guide (EPG) and catch-up TV proliferate, the media are responding with ever more focused offerings that can be built into a consumer's personal media schedule, all of which is highlighted by social media.

The close relationship between consumers and their personal media architecture is at least as important as any brand-consumer relationship, because it is from our trusted media that we construct our view of the world, and gain enjoyment, entertainment, stimulation, and information. A deep understanding of the consumer-media relationship can also be the prompt for great creative work, as it informs the creative brief with a three-dimensional picture of the target audience. As Henny has put it: 'Find out what makes them laugh. What makes them cry. What they think about current affairs, what books they read, what music they prefer, and if there are any other cultural things they are into because then I can rip those off for the creative execution.'[9]

Understanding Brand-Consumer-Media Relationships

The starting point for exploring media aspects of brand ecology is the wealth of industry audience data described above. Interrogating these data can set out the parameters of media usage, related to attitudinal and lifestyle dimensions. But for developing really effective media strategy, we require information on the emotional aspects of media consumption, its social and cultural context, and the meaning that it carries in consumers' lives. In an era of money-rich, but time-poor, people working ever-longer hours, media consumption often involves active choice behaviour between competing alternatives, and this choice behaviour is itself driven by attitudes and emotions to the various media and how its consumption integrates with other individual and social activity.

Consumers have media imperatives, such as a 'must-view' appointment with an episode of a soap opera, or a 'must-read' appointment with a heavyweight Sunday newspaper. Increasingly, the same consumer can consume a paradoxical range of media, often in a different mindset at different times of the day or week. One TV consumer may switch from low-involvement consumption of US comedies to high-involvement consumption of a high-brow arts programme, to high-involvement consumption of a football match, all on the same evening.

In order to match our brand attitude strategy with media consumption, we need to know how and why people are consuming the media, not only that they are in the same room as the TV. The *who* question of media consumption has a very complex answer once we recognize the variety of consumption modes within the same person's media architecture. Some media are often consumed alone—print media and 'new media', for example—while some depend on company for satisfying experience—for example, TV comedies. But consuming media in a social setting may itself vary greatly depending on the composition of the group, and the social rules and expectations that apply. The relationship with a medium may involve high levels of trust, respect, affection, and personal and family history. Alternatively, it may involve distrust, lack of respect, an absence of any emotional connection, and little history.

We need to be able to profile the members of our target audience on these and other emotional, social, and cultural factors, and be able to relate them to their brand relationships in order to maximize our ability to make appropriate media choices. This investment in researching our target group's media consumption is a vital step towards developing effective media strategy, because 'traditional data is simply too broad and too shallow to yield the detailed insights which can inspire imaginative media solutions'.[10]

Evaluating the Efficiency of Media Strategy

The demand for greater media accountability continues to grow,[11] and we now consider briefly some important approaches to evaluating the efficiency of media strategy. As will be discussed in Chapter 13, continuous tracking studies make a major contribution to evaluating the effectiveness of creative strategies, and they also have an important role to play in assessing media strategy in combination with creative content against communication objectives. However, the method of choice for evaluating media efficiency is 'media auditing'. A major media auditing operator is the Media Audits Group, which operates in sixty countries and provides media audit services for over 300 clients on US$3 billion adspend. Media auditing operates by comparing a specific advertiser's media expenditure with that of a very large data pool containing actual prices paid for media supplied by clients and then advising on buying efficiency. This comparison of price paid for media against the pool average gives powerful information to advertisers and allows them to put pressure on their media-buying agencies to lower costs. Using econometric models, a number of media auditors offer advice on such issues as media weighting, frequency rates, weighting between media, and regional effects.

New Media

Up to this point we have been talking broadly about what goes into media planning and strategy. In this section we will be looking more closely at what has become known as 'new media'. At several points in the book we have emphasized that in terms of how messages are processed new media are much like any other, and in terms of media strategy, they must be considered like any traditional medium in terms of communication objectives. Still, new media have offered both new opportunities as well as challenges to marketers, and new 'social media' have given the manager even more to consider. And, as you read this section, keep in mind that what we are talking about may have been overtaken by yet newer advents in new media technology and application.

One consequence of the rapidly changing media environment is the challenge it poses for media planning and placement agencies. Many now have dedicated staff whose job it is to follow the changes occurring and work on adapting their research methods to deal with how consumers are using the new media alternatives. Additionally, there are new 'digital specialists' whose job it is to be aware of everything going on in the digital world. Another change has been occasioned by the rapid diversification of many large media companies which now offer a wide range of outlets. These can include everything from traditional media vehicles to websites, podcasts, and mobile platforms.[12]

Google's CEO pointed out at the 2009 Association of National Advertisers conference in the United States that more information is now generated in two days than was generated from the beginning of time up to 2003.[13] Much of this, of course, is Internet based, and a Nielson survey of 27,000 consumers across fifty-two countries found that some 85 per cent of Internet users want content to remain free.[14] This also seems to be true for Apple's iPad. In a 2010 survey of iPad owners in the United States, 86 per cent said they would be likely to 'watch' adverts in order to have free content such as television shows, magazines, and newspaper articles. But even though they are willing to accept advertising on their iPads in exchange for free content, some 78 per cent say that advertising 'takes away from their enjoyment of their iPad'.[15] Nevertheless, this suggests that advertising will inevitably play an important role in new media.

In fact, an interesting new service offered to Internet advertisers enables interested users to store and revisit adverts. By including a small button in the shape of a 'K' in the corner of an advert, when users move the mouse over it, they are told that they can 'keep the ad' if they click on it and save it to a separate advert-collecting webpage, and continue browsing. Whether or not people will use this is an open question, but a number of major international advertisers such as Kraft Foods and Unilever have adopted it.[16]

Internet

In 2010, approximately 14 per cent of the total global spending on advertising of US$449.7 billion, some US$63 billion, was spent on the web. This is over three times the 2005 level of US$18 billion. Internet advertising is expected to rise to 18 per cent of the total in 2013, fuelled by video and social marketing, and is expected to overtake newspapers as the world's second-largest advertising medium, behind TV, in 2013. Nevertheless, at over 40 per cent of all advertising spending, TV remains the dominant global medium.[17]

Something that may challenge this growth is an EU law that took effect in July 2003 requiring *non*-EU companies to collect value added tax (VAT) on fees paid for Internet services, as well as products downloaded by customers over the Internet (for example, music, videos, and software).[18] As a result, for example, Europeans using eBay will have to pay VAT, and EU sellers will have to pay VAT on the fee they pay eBay to list their products. This is obviously an administrative nightmare for larger companies, but could be a deterrent to smaller business.

Even though the Internet is incredibly widely based, the top fifty websites account for almost all of the money spent on Internet advertising, with most of it concentrated with AOL, Google, and Yahoo. This is because these are the most visited sites and, as with all media, cost is a function of audience size. In 2010, December visits alone ranged from 180 million at AOL to 183.5 million at Yahoo, to 197.7 million at Google.[19]

Still, even these very large websites had not proved immune from economic downturns. In late 2007 and early 2008, Internet advertising was found to be more vulnerable than expected to a general slowdown in the economy. Sites such as Google experienced a significant decline in advertising revenue.[20]

One of the positive values of Internet advertising, in addition to its ability to reach very specific target audiences, is the ability to assess its impact on a daily basis by measuring the number of times someone clicks on an advert, opens, or downloads it. This encourages enormous flexibility in execution because of the opportunity to test and make modifications on very short turnaround. More recently, Internet and online advertising companies are gaining better tools for targeting display adverts to specific groups of users. Yahoo and Microsoft, for example, use web users' search habits and pages visited to pick which adverts to show when those people visit their own or partner websites. A technique called 'behavioural targeting' observes and analyses online activities of Internet users, keeping tabs on every website visited.[21]

But while advertisers like the ability to better target messages, there are issues with how much, and the way in which, personal data is collected from Internet users. More and more the practice of installing tracking tools such as 'cookies' on computers without the knowledge of the user, and often without the knowledge of the website, is drawing criticism from users and regulatory scrutiny. Major websites want to curb the use of cookies and other tracking techniques by outside companies, but not necessarily out of concern over privacy issues. Rather, many want the profits from the trade in personal data for themselves.[22]

Generally, a number of different companies are involved in the placing and tracking of advertising on the Internet, and any or all of them may be installing tracking tools on the computers of people who use a site. Websites will hire a company to place adverts on the site, those companies engage advertising networks that buy advertising and tech companies that help them to bid for them, and these advert buyers use yet another company to track or measure the advertising and for access to targeting data.[23]

In response to raising concerns over privacy issues related to these tracking tools, governments around the world are considering new regulations. Prior to 2009, European law required websites to permit users to 'opt out' or decline 'cookies'. (But, as just noted above, websites often are not aware of 'cookies' that are installed on the computers of people using the sites.) Leading up to proposing a new law in 2009, the EU Parliament suggested that users must 'opt in' before 'cookies' are installed. But this was beaten back by the industry. In the end, a new law was passed, including this wording: using Internet cookies 'is only allowed on condition that the subscriber or user concerned has given his or her consent, having been provided with clear and comprehensive information'.[24]

However, no one can agree on the meaning of the law. As of this writing, most of the EU's twenty-seven counties are expected to interpret the law as meaning that a browser setting will be sufficient to indicate user consent. But this remains a volatile issue, with much at stake for the €14.7 billion Internet-advertising industry.[25]

Online Video

In 2007, online video became the fastest-growing category of Internet advertising spending.[26] This growth was spurred by user dislike of pop-up adverts[27] and preroles (in which the user is forced to watch the advertising before viewing the video clip).[28] While online video continues to grow, there is no real consensus on what works and what does not. Some marketers are using graphics that slide over the bottom of the screen without interrupting the video clip, variously known as 'overlays', 'bugs', or 'trackers', or using advertising graphics that surround the screen, called 'player skins'. The viewer can then click on the graphic to pause the clip and see more information from the advertiser.

Advertising is shown alongside user-generated videos on sites such as YouTube. They offer a semitransparent advert that appears on the bottom 20 per cent of the video, appearing 15 seconds after the start of the video and disappearing 10 seconds later if the viewer does not click on it. If the viewer chooses to watch the advert, the main video pauses until the commercial stops. In a test before introducing the system, it was found that 75 per cent of viewers watched the entire advert, a five-to-ten times greater click-through rate than standard display advertising on websites.[29]

While online marketing is growing rapidly, even the largest social media sites such as YouTube and Facebook have failed to meet their own advertising revenue forecasts. Part of the problem is thought to be a reliance on more static advertising options such as banner adverts or homepage video adverts. One way in which to get around this problem is exemplified by the introduction of Toyota's 2009 Corolla Sedan. Toyota worked with YouTube on a campaign that created a new site exclusively for Toyota called 'Best in Test' in which YouTube identified up-and-coming comedy videos to feature on the site.[30] We shall have more to say about social media later.

Widgets

Widgets are small computer programs that enable people to incorporate professional-looking content on their personal web pages. As of this writing, widgets are the only way in which an advertiser can get inside MySpace pages. Advertisers are beginning to use widget-based content as a way of reaching young people with their message, and encouraging them to visit their websites. Many marketers see this as the next generation of Internet marketing. Reebok created a widget that enabled users to display customized RBK shoes for others to evaluate.[31]

A study of 9–17-year-olds in the US found that while these young people do not like banner adverts, there was a willingness to accept bits of marketing messages on their personal web pages, if they were seen as useful or entertaining. While spending on social network websites is not much now, it is expected to grow significantly over the next few years.[32]

Other Applications

There are many other ways in which the Internet is being used to deliver online advertising and promotion. Advertising messages are included as a part of video games. Adverts on online radio enable listeners to click on a box at the station's website, which directs them to the brand's website. Advertisers are creating entertainment programming specifically for the Web that weaves a product endorsement into the storyline. And perhaps the ultimate in product placement gives the viewer of a video the ability to stop and click to purchase the clothing worn by the actors. Advertising campaigns that let people interact with posters at bus stops, train stations, airports, and ferries have been tested in New York and London.[33]

Cutting-edge streaming video is being used by some advertisers—in effect, mini-movies that feature the brand. At BMWfilms.com, which is separate from BMW's home page, the company offers short streamed films that have been produced by well-known directors, using well-known actors.[34]

Promotions too are delivered via the Internet. Specific sites exist solely to provide incentive promotions for brands. Fatwallet.com sends out early-morning emails alerting people of online specials. Sites such as GottaDeal.com feature information about mail-in rebates, and sites such as CouponMountain.com and CouponCraze.com enable users to print coupons for both store and online retailers.

Apart from a relatively high cost relative to other media, an important implication of the Internet for developing media strategy is the question of control of brand messages, something about which we will have more to say in Chapter 13 when we discuss 'crowdsourcing'. Orthodox media strategy aims to control the different channels and methods through which the brand can target the consumer. However, with the rapid enabling of consumer networks of contacts and peers, brand messages are becoming increasingly uncontrollable, which means that official brand messages are becoming increasingly unimportant compared to the unsanctioned 'word of mouse' within a particular brand or anti-brand community.[35] The interactive and uncontrollable nature of the Internet raises serious issues for media strategy, and suggests that in the future we will have to engage consumers in dialogue rather than monologue format and attempt to invite customers to participate in 'conversations' rather than remain passive targets for messages. So once again we return to the need for in-depth understanding of consumer behaviour as the driver for all strategy, and in Chapter 11 we turn to examining how consumers process messages.

Social Media

There are many definitions of social media, but the most frequently cited is from Andrews and Haenlein.[36] They define it as: 'a group of Internet-based applications that build on the ideological and technological foundations of Web 2.0, and that allow the creation and exchange of User Generated Content.' As mentioned above, we shall have something to say about 'user-generated content' in Chapter 13 when we talk about creating advertising, but this does raise important questions.

As Drumwright and Murphy[37] have pointed out, compared with traditional media, social norms for new media, and especially for social media, have not yet been determined, and seemingly anything goes. A consequence is that social media users can not be sure when seeing an advert if it actually came from the brand. Another is how quickly a brand's image can be affected through social media. Many years ago well-known ad man Bill Bernbach is said to have remarked that a great advertising campaign would make a bad product fail faster. But in today's world of social media this can occur with lightening speed as someone's rage can be told in seconds to their 100 closest friends, which, by way of their social grid, or YouTube, or countless other ways, will reach millions.[38]

Perhaps a more important, or at least practical, issue concerning social media has been raised in an editorial by Rance Crain, editor of *Advertising Age*, the leading advertising trade publication in the US. He has said, 'it seems to me that the more prevalent social media becomes, the less we know about the power of persuasion,' and that 'advertisers don't even know what the primary purpose of social media is supposed to be'.[39] What does a Tweet influence a person to do, think, or believe, wondered *Advertising Age*'s editor at large? Is it anything more than a popularity contest? Burger King's extremely popular Subservient Chicken Internet promotion had very little effect upon sales.[40]

Don Schultz, one of the pioneers in integrated marketing communication, has gone even further. He agrees that social media may look like gold, but it really isn't. He sees it as possibly the equivalent of the 'marketing pyrite' of the twenty-first century (pyrite being a mineral often referred to as 'fool's gold'). Marketers seem to feel that they need to have 'new media' strategies, but few have a solid reason except for the 'boxcar number of participants or the fear of being left behind'.[41] He argues that social media were not created as advertising vehicles, but as personal media. Marketers must be invited into a social circle.

These new forms of media are negotiated, not persuasive, media forms. They are not channels for selling things, but rather ways in which people can maintain social contact in an increasingly impersonal world. Schultz feels that the problem is that 'in social media situations, marketers are interrupting, but for no reason other than they can'.[42] Consumers are not receiving anything in return.

Nevertheless, there is no denying the allure of the numbers. Social networks in 2010 accounted for 22 per cent of the total time consumers spent on the Internet, according to figures from most major markets around the world.[43] The average Facebook user in 2010 spent nearly five-and-a-half hours a day looking at profiles and photos, and playing games.[44] Even business-to-business companies are using social media. A 2010 survey of 230 business-to-business companies finds 24 per cent using things such as Facebook and Twitter, and another 36 per cent planning to use them in 2011. But in line with the concerns discussed above, they are having a hard time gaining followers, and an even harder time connecting with their target audience.[45]

Still, there are examples of how integrating social media with traditional media can lead to positive results. Owing to high unemployment and a poor job market, Monster.com, a job recruitment website, experienced a 33 per cent drop in sales for 2009. With marketing budgets cut as well, it initiated an ambitious programme using email to drive people to social media. With three Twitter and six Facebook accounts, it was using Tweets to provide career advice and help, with more in-depth conversations on Facebook. Social media components were added to all of its marketing communication to help to provide buzz. This included seeding messages ahead of time, teasing actual adverts, and exclusives with large online blogs. As a result, among other things, YouTube views of its 2010 SuperBowl were well over double what it had experienced the year before. Perhaps its success is because, as Kathy O'Reilly, then Monster.com's director of social media relations, put it: 'Social media does not exist within a silo here . . . our strategy really is right in line with PR and marketing. We are supporting what PR is doing as well as what our marketing team is doing.'[46]

In another case, a group calling itself Eepybird in 2006 began dropping Mentos mints into 2-litre bottles of Diet Coke, and watching them explode in a fountain of soda. The fountains were posted on YouTube and, in the four years since that first explosion, more than 500 million people have seen videos of the fountains. While Diet Coke was slow to pick up on using the idea in its marketing, Mentos was not. It was quick to develop a tie-in with Eepybird and the fountains, and this led to Mentos becoming heavily involved with social media.

Facebook followers by the end of 2010 had surpassed 500,000. This is a rather remarkably large number considering that the brand now relies almost totally on social media and Facebook display advertising. But traditional media may nonetheless be playing a part. It is quite likely that Mentos may, in fact, be benefiting from the US$13 million in traditional media advertising that Mentos chewing gum received during the first three-quarters of the year.[47] Regardless of the media, new or traditional, it is important to consider carry-over effects when evaluating effectiveness.

Mobile Marketing

The use of advertising on mobile phones began in the early 2000s in Scandinavian and Asian countries, but it was several years later before it entered Europe and the US, where there was a feeling that consumers would not like the idea. But by the mid-2000s major networks in the UK (e.g. Vodafone Group) and in the US (e.g. Sprint, Nextel, and Verizon) were offering advertising on their wireless networks.[48] Newer mobile phones have facilitated this, being much more like small computers.

While such mobile advertising is dominated by text messages, in 2007, some European carriers began offering video commercials. One of the UK's largest networks, 3, a unit of Hutchison Whampoa, was offering free information and entertainment video clips paid for by the advertising.[49]

The appeal of mobile advertising to marketers is the ability to tightly target messages to an audience that has given permission to receive it (at least in most cases). Additionally, they are

Advert 10.1 This is a good example of using mobile for a promotion, where Bluetooth and the Hard Rock Café have combined to make a specific offer.

Source: Reproduced with kind permission of Hard Rock Café.

better able to control the message environment, better able to time the exposure of the message, and better able to track exposure. It also provides a good opportunity for developing a database to better target messages, and to be available for more traditional direct marketing. A good database is essential for good mobile marketing because it must be driven by consumer data,[50] as with direct marketing. Advert 10.1 (actually a promotion) provides a good example of how this can be done. Mobile phones are the medium for a promotion, where Bluetooth and the Hard Rock Café have combined to make a specific offer.

In 2009 the casual game industry reported US$3 billion in mobile revenues. This encouraged advertisers to integrate their brands into mobile game content, and to merge online and offline experiences. In one very innovative application, Charles Chocolates, a small San Francisco brand, created a game in which users could opt to purchase real-life versions of the virtual chocolate that they created in the game.[51]

Coupons are being made available on mobile phones. Consumers may sign up online or by sending a text message to a mobile marketing company (e.g. Cellfine in the US) that provides coupons from client retailers. They collect personal information such as birth data and geographic area, which enables retailers to more tightly target to whom they send coupons.[52] In another unique application, outdoor posters and billboards have the ability to electronically beam messages to mobile phones.

Chapter summary

This chapter has introduced some of the concepts and terminology used in media planning and strategy. We began by pointing out some of the key issues of reach versus frequency. We then related media selection decisions to consideration of visual content, time to process, and frequency in relation to brand awareness and brand attitude communication objectives. We considered media scheduling decisions, and then went on to discuss the concept of brand ecology and the importance of understanding the consumer's emotional relationship with various media. Lastly, we discussed the new media, with special attention to the Internet and social media, and the implications for media strategy of the interactivity and uncontrollability factors related to brand messages.

Questions to consider

10.1 What must the manager consider in developing an effective media strategy?

10.2 How does the trade-off between reach and frequency influence media planning?

10.3 Why are visual content, time to process, and frequency of media important to consider in media selection?

10.4 What are primary media?

10.5 What are the media implications associated with brand awareness strategy?

10.6 What are the media implications associated with brand attitude strategy?

10.7 Why is direct matching better than demographic matching in selecting media?

10.8 Discuss the difficulties involved in building an effective media schedule.

10.9 What is meant by brand ecology, and how does it affect media strategy?

10.10 What are the advantages versus disadvantages of using 'new media'?

10.11 What problems are associated with the use of social media? What are its advantages?

10.12 In what way are new media likely to affect media planning and strategy in the future?

Case Study 10 **Domino's Pizza—Building a High Street Brand through a Change in Media Strategy**

Sponsoring *The Simpsons* on Sky One was the first attempt in trying to build a brand for Domino's. Using TGI's 'Specially Choose to Watch' analysis BLM identified *The Simpsons* as the ideal programme for our target audience. There were three further factors that were crucial to the selection of *The Simpsons*. First, it's the right time of day. Secondly, it's a great fit, and the attitude and personality of the show differentiate the brand. The final consideration was audience delivery. *The Simpsons* offered a large audience with →

→ remarkably little wastage for the task of reaching pizza eaters (67.6 per cent of those who 'specially choose to watch' *The Simpsons* 'like to eat take-away foods'; 44.3 per cent of Pizza Hut customers 'specially choose to watch' *The Simpsons*).

Over the first three years *The Simpsons* sponsorship created a competitive positioning for Domino's based on personality rather than product differentiation or innovation. In January 2001 Domino's stores used a major technological innovation called HeatWave that guaranteed your pizza was delivered 'oven hot' to your door. Our competitors didn't have the technology. Therefore we had the opportunity to attract two sets of new customers while adding to the service already provided to our existing customers. Qualitative research identified two new target audiences:

1. customers of competitor stores (specifically Pizza Hut);
2. lapsed/occasional pizza eaters who have (through experience) low expectations of home-delivered pizza.

The decision of focusing on sponsorship rather than advertising was justified. Sponsorship allowed Domino's to own a property and also allowed us to be on air every day of the year. On the other hand, the decision to commit the majority of the national advertising budget to broadcast sponsorship had its risks. First, it was a fairly new area in the media market. Secondly, with sponsorship, there were some pretty draconian laws around at that time about what you couldn't say in the credits; we could only make a reference to the programme and show the logo. However, the one thing that swung the decision for us was that we were going to get our brand on national TV every single day of the week at dinner time.

What Domino's managed to do was to use the new technology of interactive television and Internet ordering to take an existing relationship with a programme into new media and generate substantial returns through transactional channels. We have moved from what has been a highly successful niche marketing strategy to mainstream broadcast media.

The other motivation was that, by going into things such as interactive TV and the Internet, it rang all of the right bells with our target audience. Our core target audience is largely 18–24-year-olds, and the Internet, interactive TV, and new technology is their environment. Our first port of call was to get the deal with Sky Active; then within six months we had established an e-commerce platform with every single major interactive TV platform as well as having the online presence.

Source: This is an edited version of a case study submitted to the IPA Effectiveness Awards. The full case study can be found at ipa.co.uk or warc.com. © Copyright Institute of Practitioners in Advertising.

Edited by Elizabeth Mamali, PhD Researcher, Bath School of Management

Discussion questions

1. What are the benefits for the Domino's brand for selecting this media strategy?
2. Taking into account Domino's brand attitude strategy and target audience, evaluate the selection of media strategy.
3. What are the possible drawbacks of this media strategy in the long term?
4. Propose alternative media strategies for the coming years.

Further reading

Martin Bleck and Don Schultz, *Media Generations: Media Allocation in a Consumer-Controlled Marketplace* (Proper Business Development Corporation, 2009)

Andrew Green, *From Prime Time to My Time: Audience Measurement in the Digital Age* (London: Warc, 2009)

Two recent books provide new ways of looking at and measuring media. Bleck and Schultz, in using data from an annual BIG research study, argue for a new focus on the quality of media used, and how messages are received and acted upon. Green suggests that the media measurement focus moves from the media to the consumer of the media.

Jennings Bryant and Dolf Zillman (eds), *Media Effects: Advances in Theory and Research*, 2nd edn (Mahwah, NJ: Lawrence Erlbaum Associates, 2002)
An extensive examination of media effects from a theoretical standpoint.

R.E. Bucklin and C. Sismeiro, 'A Model of Website Browsing Behaviour Estimated on Clickstream Data', *Journal of Marketing Research*, 40/3 (2003), 249–67
Asserts that the attention paid to successive pages as one clicks onward from the home page falls significantly.

Sally McMillan, Jang-Sun Hwang, and Guiohk Lee, 'Effects of Structural and Perceptual Factors on Attitudes toward the Website', *Journal of Advertising Research* (Dec 2003), 400–9
Discusses the need to adjust to the specific demands of the Web, just as media planners did when there was a shift to broadcast media.

Notes

1. Perhaps still the best book available for anyone really interested in media strategy is John R. Rossiter and Peter J. Danaher, *Advanced Media Planning* (Norwell, MA: Kluwer Academic Publishers, 1998), which comes with its own disk containing all of the models discussed. Another good book is the latest edition of J. Sissors and L. Baumber, *Advertising Media Planning*, 5th edn (Lincolnwood, IL: NTC Business Books, 2002).
2. A. Tillery, 'The Strategic Importance of Media', in L. Butterfield (ed.), *Excellence in Advertising* (Oxford: Butterworth Heinemann, 1999).
3. A. Rutherford, 'Managing the Media', *Uniview Magazine* (1999).
4. *The Millward Brown Link Tests* (London: Millward Brown Ltd, 1997).
5. This issue of minimum effective frequency is discussed in some depth in J.R. Rossiter and L. Percy, *Advertising Communication and Promotion Management* (New York: McGraw-Hill, 1997).
6. Simon Broadbent, *When to Advertise* (Henley-on-Thames: Admap Publications, 1999). See also the books cited in n. 1.
7. Broadbent, *When to Advertise* (Henley-on-Thames: Admap Publications, 1999), 102.
8. See Tillery, 'The Strategic Importance of Media', in L. Butterfield (ed.), *Excellence in Advertising* (Oxford: Butterworth Heinemann, 1999).
9. G. Henny, 'Creative Briefing: The Creative Perspective', in Butterfield (ed.), *Excellence in Advertising* (Oxford: Butterworth Heinemann, 1999).
10. G. Michaelides, 'Street Wise', *Admap* (May 2000), 27.
11. J. Billet and I. Fermoi, 'The Agenda of Media Accountability', *Admap* (June 2000), 33–5.
12. See P. Andruss, 'Taming Media Overload', *The Wall Street Journal* (1 September 2007), 21.
13. See T. Iezza, *The Idea Writers* (New York: Palgrave MacMillan, 2010).
14. Neilsen, 'Changing Models: A Global Perspective on Paying for Content Online' (New York: The Neilsen Company, 2010), available online at http://blog.nielsen.com/nielsenwire/reports/paid-online-content.pdf
15. This is discussed in an article by Edmund Lee, 'iPad Users Prefer Advertising to Pay Model for Content', *Advertising Age* (17 January 2011), 21.
16. See Jessica E. Vascellaro, 'Banking on Surfers Saving Ads', *Wall Street Journal* (11 October 2010), B5.

17. These figures come from data reported by Bloomberg on 6 December 2010, in an article titled 'Internet Emerging Markets to Lead Worldwide Advertising Growth Next Year'.
18. This potential problem is discussed in the 20 October 2003 issue of *The Wall Street Journal* in an article by Matthew Newman , B5.
19. ComScore US panel data reported in *Advertising Age* (28 February 2011).
20. K.J. Delany, 'On the Web, Signs of a Click Recession', *The Wall Street Journal* (27 February 2008), B3.
21. These and other techniques for customizing adverts to particular targets are discussed in K.J. Delaney and E. Steel, 'Firm Mines Offline Data to Target Online Ads', *The Wall Street Journal* (17 October 2007), B1.
22. See Jessica E. Vascellaro, 'Websites Rein in Tracking Tools', *Wall Street Journal* (9 November 2010), B1-2.
23. See Jessica E. Vascellaro,'Websites Rein in Tracking Tools', *Wall Street Journal* (9 November 2010), B1-2.
24. See P. Sonne and J.W. Miller, 'EU Chews on Web Cookies', *Wall Street Journal* (22 November 2010), B1-2.
25. See P. Sonne and J.W. Miller, 'EU Chews on Web Cookies', *Wall Street Journal* (22 November 2010), B1-2.
26. E. Steel, 'Web's Niche TV Program with Sponsors', *The Wall Street Journal* (28 August 2007), B8.
27. K. Oser, 'Money, Mayhem to be First with Pop-Ups', *Advertising Age* (28 June 2004), 51.
28. K.J. Delaney and E. Steel, 'Are Skins, Bugs or Tickets the Holy Grail of Web Advertising?', *The Wall Street Journal* (13 August 2007), B1.
29. See E. Steel, 'YouTube to Start Selling Ads in Videos', *The Wall Street Journal* (22 August 2007), B3.
30. E. Steel, 'Toyota Makes Sharp Turn on the Web', *The Wall Street Journal* (7 March 2008), B3.
31. E. Steel, 'Web-Page Clocks and other "Widgets" Anchor New Internet Strategy', *The Wall Street Journal* (21 November 2006), B4.
32. E. Steel, 'Young Surfers Spurn Banner Ads, Embrace "Widgets"', *The Wall Street Journal* (2 July 2007), B3.
33. See S.E. Ante, 'Billboards Join Wired Age', *Wall Street Journal* (4 February 2011), B10.
34. A detailed discussion of the origin of BMWFilms.com may be found in Teressa Iezzi's *The Idea Writers* (New York: Palgrave MacMillan, 2010), 42-8.
35. Happy Dog website, http://www.happydog.co.uk
36. This definition is discussed in K. Andrews and M. Haenlein, 'Users of the World Unite! The Challenges and Opportunities of Social Media', *Business Horizon*, 53/1 (2010), 59-64.
37. Ethics in social media is discussed by M.E. Drumwright and P.E. Murphy in their article 'The Current State of Advertising Ethics: Industry and Academic Perspective', *Journal of Advertising*, 38/1 (2009), 83-108.
38. See T. Iezzi, *The Idea Writers* (New York: Palgrave MacMillan, 2010).
39. This editorial appeared as 'Just How Influential is Your Social-Media Program if it isn't Helping Sell Product?', *Advertising Age* (17 January 2011), 140.
40. The Subservient Chicken promotion has been described by Teressa Iezzi in *The Idea Writers* (New York: Palgrave MacMillan, 2010), 56, as marking a 'Watershed in the new era of interactive creativity. A weird watershed, but a watershed'. But, in a column in *Advertising Age* (10 January 2011), Al Ries reported that it had very little effect upon sales.
41. Don Schultz warns that there is no substantial evidence that brands should be using social media in his article 'The Pyrite Rush', *Marketing Ideas* (30 September 2010), 12.
42. See Don Schultz , 'The Pyrite Rush', *Marketing Ideas* (30 September 2010), 12.
43. These data are reported in the *Warc News* (18 June 2010).
44. See I. Sherr, 'LinkedIn Pushes Ad Tools', *Wall Street Journal* (26 January 2011), 39.

45. See S.E. Needleman. 'For B-to-B Companies, Finding Facebook Friends can be a Struggle', *Wall Street Journal* (21 October 2010), B8.
46. This case is discussed in an interview with Monster Worldwide marketing executives in *Marketing News* (15 November 2010), 22–4.
47. The Mentos case is described in J. Neff's article 'How Mentos is Still Making a Splash on Facebook', *Advertising Age* (3 January 2011), 4.
48. See L. Yuan and C. Buyan-Low, 'Coming Soon to Cell Phone Screens—More Ads than Ever', *The Wall Street Journal* (16 August 2006), B1.
49. A.O. Patrick, 'TV Ads Find Spot on Tiny Screen', *The Wall Street Journal* (5 July 2007), B4.
50. J.W. Peltier, J.A. Schibrowsky, and D. Schultz, 'Interactive Integrated Marketing Communication Combining the Power of IMC, New Media, and Database Marketing', *International Journal of Advertising*, 22 (2003), 93–115.
51. This and other interesting in-game examples may be found in the Irina Stutsky article, 'Nothing Casual about this Game Obsession', *Advertising Age* (10 January 2011), 2.
52. See S. King, 'Coupons Gain New Market on Cell Phones', *The Wall Street Journal* (11 September 2007), B8.

Visit the Online Resource Centre that accompanies this book for additional resources to support the text: **www.oxfordtextbooks.co.uk/orc/percy_elliott4e/**

Part 4

Making it Work

Processing the Message

Key concepts

1. There are four concerns in message processing: attention, learning, acceptance, and emotion. Attention and learning are necessary for all messages, and acceptance for high-involvement brand attitude strategies; emotion facilitates all message processing.
2. Attention may be either conscious or unconscious, and in advertising this distinction is often discussed in terms of reflexive versus selective attention.
3. Learning involves memory and, at a conscious level, this means declarative or explicit memory; and at an unconscious level, non-declarative or implicit memory. This distinction is tied to the idea of top-down (conscious) processing versus bottom-up (unconscious) processing.
4. The very nature of how memory 'works' can often lead to problems in processing or retrieving memories of an advertising message.
5. Unconscious, implicit learning from an advert is unlikely to have an effect upon brand attitude or brand behaviour.
6. Emotions associated with memories are stored in the amygdala and are activated when exposed to a message, framing how the message will be processed.

Processing a message is clearly critical to successful advertising communication, as we discussed in Chapter 4 when we introduced the idea of a communication response sequence. Processing is much more than an abstraction. While it does reflect what must go on in a person's head as he or she is exposed to advertising and other marketing communication, at the same time it also suggests what we must include in the execution if it is to be correctly processed. Once we understand what goes into processing, we will be in a better position to understand why and how various creative strategies and tactics are used in order to satisfy particular communication objectives.

What do we Mean by Processing?

For our purposes, we define 'processing' as that which goes on in a person's mind when he or she is exposed to an advert or any form of marketing communication in *response to it*. This would include all people's reactions when they are actively *or passively* looking at or listening to an advert, as well as after the exposure if they are still thinking about it. These reactions can quite literally be anything, as long as they are in response to the communication itself. For example, look at Advert 11.1, which appeared in a British women's magazine.

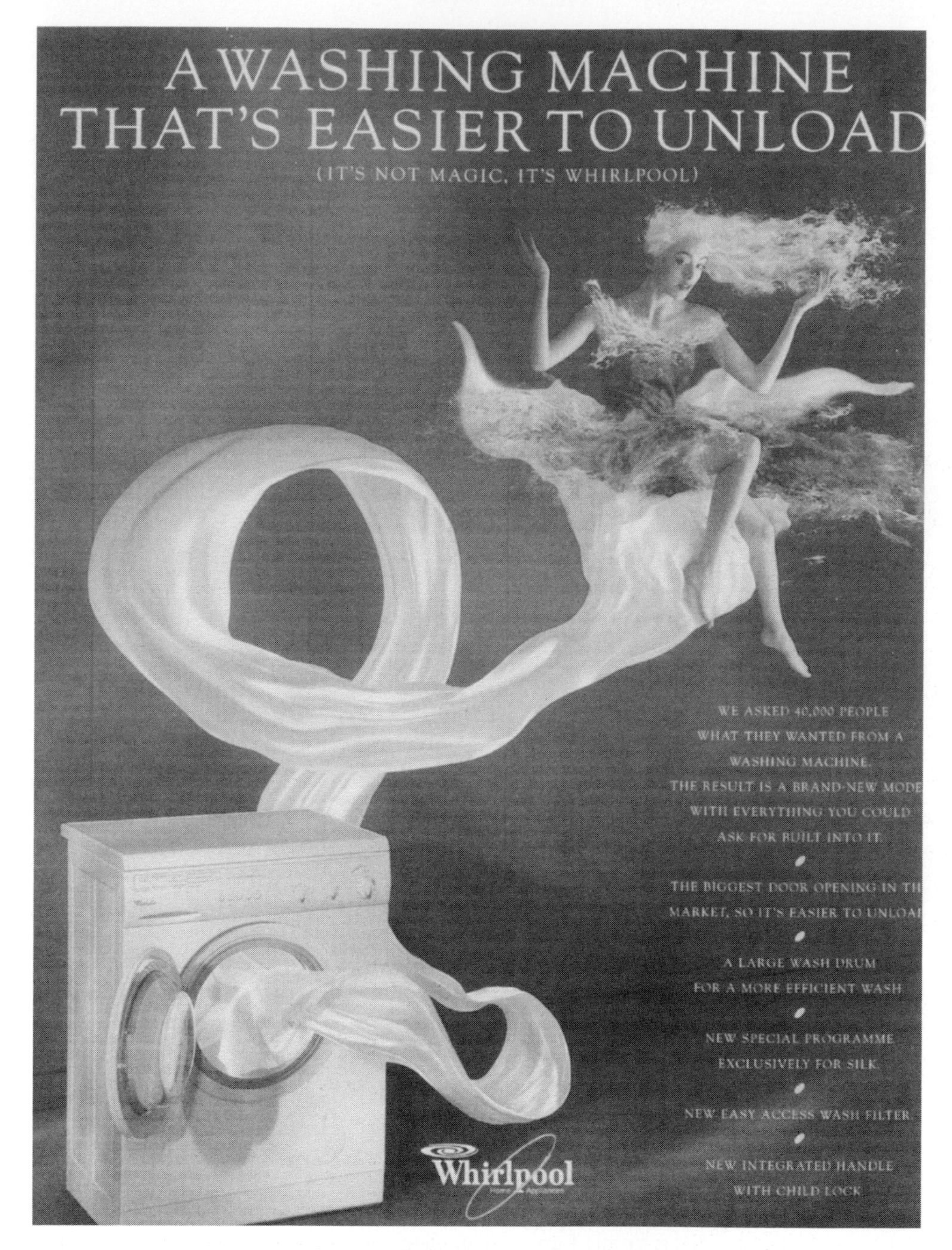

Advert 11.1 Whatever you are thinking about as you look at this advert reflects what and how you are processing the advert.

Source: Reproduced with kind permission © Whirlpool.

What are you now thinking about as you look at this advert? Whatever it may be, it reflects your processing of the advertising. You may be thinking: 'That looks interesting' or 'I wish I could float like that.' Perhaps you are thinking: 'I didn't think any washing machine was easy to unload.' You may even be thinking: 'I don't need a washing machine.' All of these responses represent processing the advertising.

There are four main processing responses that we are concerned with when people are exposed to advertising and other marketing communication:

- *attention* to the advertising itself;
- *learning* something from the advertising;
- *acceptance* of or belief in what the advertising says;
- *emotion* that is elicited by the advertising.

We shall briefly introduce each of these processing responses, and then delve much further into them.

Attention. Before anything else can occur, you must first pay attention to the advertising. In Chapter 4 when we introduced exposure, the first step in our communication response sequence, we pointed out that exposure was an opportunity to see the advertising. But until you pay attention to the advertising, you have not begun to process it. Exposure is necessary or you do not have the opportunity to process the message. Once you are aware of the advertising, you have paid attention to it and begun processing. This is true even if you go no further than to identify it as, say, an advert and not part of the programme you are watching, at which point you leave the room to get a snack.

Learning. Once you have paid attention to the advertising, you are in a position to learn something as a result of what is presented in the execution. In a sense, all that you are doing is acquainting yourself with the content of the advertising. Returning to the Whirlpool advert, assuming that you have looked at it in the magazine (and therefore paid attention to it), you probably learned that it is an advert for a washing machine. You may have even gone further and found that it also talks about how easy it is to unload.

The advert also says: 'It's not magic, it's Whirlpool'. If you read that, in terms of processing this would also be something that you learn. Yet an important point must be made here. You will have learned that the advert claims that the machine is easy to unload, but you may not necessarily believe it. Believing what the advertising says constitutes acceptance, and that is a separate processing response.

Acceptance. If you have learned something from advertising, you are then in a position to accept or reject it. The entire thrust of the various elements in advertising, both words and pictures, is to present the brand in the most positive way possible. Whirlpool quite literally wants you to believe that its machines are easy to unload. Interestingly, while the claim is made in the copy, the major impact comes from the visual. So, if your reaction when first seeing the advert was 'That looks easy', you have personally accepted the message as true. In terms of processing, you paid attention to the advert, learned from the pictures, copy, or both, and, from what you learned, accepted the fact that the machines must be easy to unload. In other words, if this was your reaction to this advert, this was how you processed the advertising.

When we discuss this in more detail below, we will see that it is not always necessary to accept the message for advertising to be effective.

Emotion. Beyond everything that we have just talked about, there is a fourth response to advertising that mediates both learning and acceptance. This is the emotional response that you have to advertising once you have paid attention. Emotional responses are something that just happen, actually a response of the autonomic nervous system. At its simplest level, you like something or you don't. For example, if your reaction to the Whirlpool advert was a positive sense of 'floating', or simply a pleasant response to the flowing illustration, you were reacting emotionally to the visual elements in the execution. These emotional responses will help to energize or stimulate learning and acceptance responses.

An important point to understand here is that, when we talk about processing advertising, we are not referring to some general or overall process. What in fact goes on is that each of the elements in the advertising has the ability to communicate, and therefore has the opportunity to be processed. Depending upon the medium, everything from the pictures to the spoken word, from the written word to music, can contribute to the overall communication of the message. Each of these components may be processed, and if they are successfully processed, they will follow the sequence described above: attention followed by learning and, if necessary, acceptance; and all of this will be facilitated by emotion.

If an advert is to be truly effective, the processing of each important component of the advert must be successful if the overall communication objective is to be reached. If recognition is the brand awareness communication objective, then the *package* must be processed, or, for verbal recognition awareness, the brand name. For recall awareness, the category need and brand name must be processed together, and in that order linked together in memory. In terms of awareness, whether recognition or recall, the brand name should be clearly communicated.

Brand attitude in many cases relies heavily upon visual components, and this is almost always the case in television adverts. While the copy can and does contribute to brand attitude, the real communication potential is more often conveyed by the visual representations. An interesting test of this for television commercials is to view them with the sound off and see what the visuals alone communicate. But it should go without saying that the visual and verbal components should reinforce each other in what they communicate.

Now that we have a feeling for what we mean by processing in advertising, it is time to take a closer look at each of the four main processing responses and how they facilitate achieving our communication objectives. First, we will address attention, learning, and acceptance.

Attention

As we have already mentioned, attention is necessary before any other processing can occur. This should be obvious. If you have not paid any attention to something, how can you learn or accept what has been said? But what exactly *is* attention? The concept of attention implies that somehow we focus a 'mental spotlight' on some activity in our external environment or internally on a memory or something that we are thinking about. This 'spotlight' could be conscious—for example, when you scan your memory for a name—or it could be unconscious and you are not aware of it. After a rather uneven history in psychology, researchers in both cognitive science and neuroscience have returned to the position first introduced 100 years ago by William James: 'Everyone knows what attention is. It is the taking possession by the mind, in clear and vivid form, of one out of what seems several simultaneously possible objects or trains of thought.'[1]

Over the last fifty years a number of theories of attention have been offered, the strongest being Broadbent's filter theory.[2] In effect filter theory suggests that we have the ability to block or weaken any message coming to the brand from our sense organs, meaning that the content of working memory is filtered by attention. Attention is a complex process that enables us to better understand and manage what is going on around us, and to control how information is processed.[3]

Unconscious versus conscious attention is a function of automatic versus conscious processing. Psychologists understand that certain behaviour can be performed with little if any focused attention (for example, skimming through a magazine). Such behaviour is directed by *automatic processing*, processing of information that occurs without conscious awareness, and, importantly, without interfering with other activity going on at the same time. If you are riding your bicycle and someone steps out in front of you, you will 'automatically' apply the brakes. On the other hand, conscious processing does require focused attention. If you are riding your bicycle down a street and are looking for a particular address, you must consciously focus attention on the street numbers, looking for the address you have in memory.[4]

One explanation for why we consciously pay attention to some things and not others is offered by Kahneman.[5] He suggests that we have a limited capacity to perform mental activity, so that, at any one point in time, that capacity must be allocated among the many alternatives at hand to process. Since one aspect of attention is the amount of effort that will be required to 'pay attention', the effort directed at a particular task will reflect the level of attention required. If the task is routine, little attentional focus will be used. If you are looking for something, however, attention must be focused.

Reflexive Attention

When thinking about advertising, this distinction between unconscious versus conscious attention is often discussed in terms of reflexive versus selective attention—and sometimes mistakenly as low- versus high-involvement processing. Reflexive attention is initiated every time there is a change in your environment, and it is a wholly involuntary reaction. For example, when a commercial comes on TV, even if you were only half attending to the programme, the switch in programming from the show to the commercial will cause you to notice the commercial. If you then jump up to run to the kitchen in order to get something to eat because of the commercial break, it is because the change in the stimulus (in this case the TV programming) involuntarily attracts your attention. The same thing occurs each time you turn a page in a magazine. Even if you are only skimming the magazine, each time the page turns, your attention will involuntarily be drawn to the page. If there is an advert on the page, you will process it at least far enough to identify it as such, and in most cases choose not to spend time actually reading it. Unconscious attention is being paid to the things in your immediate environment, but it nevertheless results in some cognitive processing.

Unfortunately, this reflexive attention does not last very long. If the stimulus is visual, such as the beginning of a TV commercial or a page turned in a magazine, reflexive attention lasts only about one-tenth of a second,[6] and if the stimulus is a word that your eye fixates upon or which you hear spoken, the reflexive attention will be only about three-tenths of a second.[7] Only if something in that brief period of attention *holds* your attention will you actually spend time with the advert.

This might be a good place to answer a question that may have come to mind as you read this material on reflexive attention: the question of subliminal perception. We do not intend to spend a great deal of time on this issue because, quite frankly, it is not a significant consideration in either the execution or the processing of advertising. The popular perception of the subliminal effects (*sic*) of advertising dates back to the 1950s when the words 'Drink Coca-Cola' and 'Eat popcorn' were said to have been flashed subliminally on the screen of a movie theatre, stimulating a rush to the concession stand. In fact, it never happened. In the 1970s the man behind it all (James Vicarey) admitted that he made it all up in order to promote his consultancy business.[8]

Even if some advertisers were to include subliminal cues in their advertising (and there really is no evidence that they do), it would have little, if any, influence. In some studies conducted by Moore,[9] it was shown that even when such cues were purposely included in an advert, they had no significant effect on the advertising's ability to communicate or persuade.[10] An extensive search of the literature in this area in the early 1990s came up with over 200 studies that failed to find any subliminal effects upon behaviour.[11]

Subliminal messages do have the potential to create a feeling of familiarity with a product that has been seen before.[12] Basically this is what is known in psychology as a priming effect, but such priming has no effect upon consumer choice. It would work only if the choice were between two unfamiliar brands. In that case, the unconsciously 'primed' brand would seem more familiar and, as a result, more likely to be selected. We shall return to the subject of priming in our discussion of implicit memory later in this chapter.

Selective Attention

Selective attention, on the other hand, occurs when you voluntarily pay attention to advertising. This could occur, for example, if you were to see an advert for a laptop computer when you were actively thinking about buying one. This is top-down, conscious processing. You would first reflexively attend to the advertising and, assuming that there is enough there to link the advert to your category need for a new laptop, you would probably pay further attention to the advertising. This is no guarantee that you will read or listen to the entire advert, but you will certainly spend more than a fraction of a second with the advertising. In such cases, attention must be maintained with a good execution.

From this discussion you should now appreciate that we pay conscious attention to some things and unconscious attention to others. But why is it that we do not seem to pay attention to certain things, even very important things? How often has something been brought to your attention and you cannot imagine how you missed it? One explanation is that our visual system must be filtering out some information, even if it is neurologically retaining it at an unconscious level.

In a classic experiment on inattention, Simons and Chabris showed a group who volunteered for the study a film clip of people tossing a basketball back and forth to each other. The participants in the study were asked to count the number of passes. After about 45 seconds a person in the film wearing a gorilla suit walked directly across the display and exited on the other side 5 seconds later. This was not a brief exposure, yet, unbelievably, over 70 per cent of those participating in the study did not see the gorilla! When shown the film clip again and asked to look for the gorilla, they easily saw it.[13]

Neurologically, it seems that activity in the frontal-parietal network simply filters out some information when your attention is focused on something else. Things that would otherwise be obvious are suppressed. This has clear implications for advertising and other marketing communication. If the execution draws attention to one thing, it could very well be to the exclusion of other information. In effect, inattention to something is a necessary fallout from the focusing of attention on other specific information.

How do we Maintain Attention?

The key to maintaining attention to an advert lies in the elements used in the execution, as we shall see in Chapter 12. While these can vary, depending upon the communication effects involved, let us take a brief look at the manner in which they relate to our two primary communication effects: brand awareness and brand attitude. Remember that all advertising must achieve these two responses, and, in fact, they are always communication objectives.

Brand Awareness

As you might suspect, it does not require a great deal of processing to effect positive brand awareness. In fact, once we have achieved exposure to the advertising and at least reflexive attention, one strategy that can be used to continue stimulating reflexive attention is to utilize something a bit different either visually or verbally within the execution itself. Another way of maintaining reflexive interest is with unexpectedly positioned ads. For example, you could use the equivalent of a full-page advert in a magazine horizontally run as two consecutive half-page spaces. Because we are so used to seeing advertising as same-page executions, reflexive attention should be maintained here as the mind tries to figure out what is going on. The same principle is sometimes used with broadcast advertising when a commercial is continued after a station break or other commercials. Specific creative tactics to help to maintain awareness are discussed in Chapter 12.

Brand Attitude

In our discussion of brand attitude as a communication objective in Chapter 9, we learned that brand attitude must be associated with the motivation that drives target audience behaviour in the category. Since attention is the first, and necessary, step in processing an advertising message, it is especially important in initiating the desired brand attitude. However, this is much more complex than the attention response associated with brand awareness. What we find with attention and brand attitude is that target audiences will be likely to attend *selectively* to advertising *only* if the message in the advert relates to their *current* motivation in the category. Here are a few examples to help to clarify what we mean. At the extreme, if you are a man, there is probably very little likelihood that you will selectively attend to a cosmetic advert for a new eye shadow. You will have no motivation to respond in this category. On the other hand, women could be motivated to respond to an advert for men's cosmetics, because they may want to encourage a friend or spouse to purchase or use the product. At a more general level, if you do not have a baby, you are unlikely to attend selectively to advertising for baby food, or if you do not have a problem with athlete's foot, you will not attend to advertising for an athlete's foot remedy.

In each of these examples, you would pay reflexive attention, enough to let you know that you were not interested in the category, and hence have no interest in further processing the advert. However, if you were actively seeking information in this category, once reflexive attention has oriented you to the content of the advertising, your selective attention would be activated as you related the subject of the advertising to your current category motivation.

Advert 11.2 is a poster for BP's MACK brand of low-price, self-service garages in Sweden. In a research study measuring recognition of the advertising we find clear evidence of selective attention. Among people who buy from full-service garages, only 25 per cent remember seeing the advert, while 35 per cent of those who buy from self-service garages recognize the advert. Among those who buy low-price petrol, 60 per cent remember the advert; among current customers, 72 per cent.

The underlying motivation to respond here has a great deal of significance for how likely you are to attend selectively to the advertising. If the underlying motivation is *negative*, unless the problem involved is current or likely to recur, there really is not much likelihood that you will attend to the attitudinal content of the advertising. On the other hand, if the motivation is *positive*, there is a greater likelihood that you will. After all, who does not like to see a really sensuous dessert or a 'glamorous' image? It simply makes you feel good. Now this does not mean that you will necessarily respond positively to the advert's message, only that you will be more likely to attend selectively to the message because of its positive reinforcement.

Of course, a well-executed advert will have the ability not only to attract attention, but to hold it as well. What we want to happen is for *something* to be learned, even if only at a sub-cognitive level. Reflexive attention alone provides enough time at least to impress the brand name and a positive association with the brand *if* the execution embodies this in a clear fashion. Then, the more unique the execution, the greater the selective attention. Advertising cannot assume that the target audience will pay attention. We must assume that it probably will not, and so ensure that we communicate something, if only during the reflexive attention span.

Advert 11.2 This poster for Mack, a low-price, self-serve petrol brand in Sweden, illustrates the effect of selective attention. Recognition of the advertising ranged from 25 per cent among those who buy at full-serve petrol stations to 60 per cent among self-serve, low-price petrol buyers.

Source: Åke Wissing & Co. and Clear Channel Sverige AB.

You should now have a pretty clear understanding of what we mean by paying attention to advertising. It is the first step in the processing sequence, but in and of itself is not sufficient to effect the desired communication response. For advertising to be effective, it must also stimulate a learning response and, in the case of high-involvement purchase decisions, an acceptance as well. In the next two sections we will explore the processing responses of learning and acceptance.

Learning

The second processing response necessary for effective communication is *learning*. What exactly do we mean by learning? This may seem obvious, but it is important to understand just exactly what is involved in learning and memory. Fundamentally, when we are talking about learning, we are referring to rote learning. This is a passive repetition before new memories for the learned response are retained.[14] This is one of the reasons why consistency in message and execution is so important.

At its most basic level, learning, occurs at the level of neurons. Changing the strength of synaptic connections, how neurons 'talk' to each other, is the basis for learning. Figure 11.1 illustrates the basic parts of a neuron and its surrounding glia. Information moves from one end of a neuron to another electrically as a single dendritic spine is electrically excited. With repeated stimulation (for example, the input of new information from an advert), an action potential is triggered and flies down the axon. Restimulating that same spine after a period of time, even after several weeks, will cause a 'potentiated' electrical response known as long-term potentiation (LTP).[15]

It is this long-term potentiation that influences long-term memory and declarative (or explicit memory), but it does not influence short-term working memory or procedural memory. We will have more to say about memory shortly. We might imagine reading an advert and exciting an appropriate neuron, and later on seeing it again and initiating an LTP, adding the information from the advertising to our memory—a very simplistic analogy, but it does describe more or less what happens.

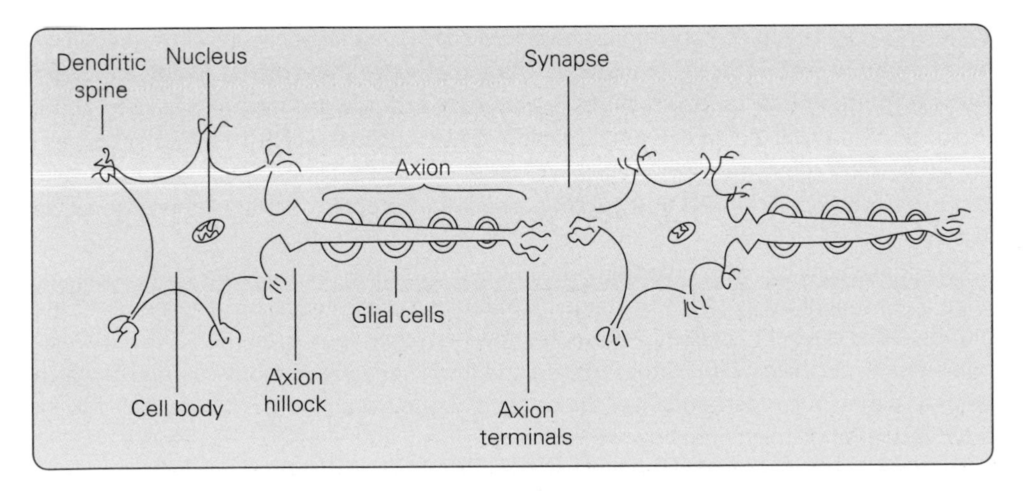

Figure 11.1 Basic Parts of a Neuron and the Surrounding Glia, and the Relationship between Neurons

Learning is the process of making certain neural pathways work more quickly than they did before. This is a relatively recent idea, although the foundation goes back over 100 years to Cajal's 'neuron doctrine'.[16] Earlier neurologists believed that when something new was learned, a new neuron or a synapse was formed. But we now understand that learning *strengthens* the functioning of pre-existing synapses, and only very occasionally is a new synapse developed.

You may be wondering why we are looking so closely at the neurology involved in learning and memory. It is because if we understand what is involved at the most basic level, we can begin to appreciate how we 'learn' from advertising—and how important our existing knowledge is in processing advertising. If we pay attention to an advert, and continue to process it, we will 'learn' something. But we will *not* necessarily be creating 'new' knowledge or memories. The information we are learning will be processed in terms of already existing knowledge in memory. We are not filling a 'hole' or adding a unique bit of information to memory. We will be tapping into existing synapses.

To be effective, advertising must be easily associated in memory with the appropriate neural configuration in order to ensure proper learning. To facilitate this, the execution should be unique to the brand. Otherwise, there is every possibility that it will be 'learned' in association with another brand for which an appropriate neural structure is already in place. The execution should also be consistent over time in terms of its 'look and feel' in order to reinforce learning (a subject we will be covering in depth later in Chapter 13).

How we learn as individuals is a function of the way in which layers of neurons overlap and form networks. We do not all necessarily 'learn' the same thing from the same advert. It all depends upon how our neural networks are 'wired', and this can differ from individual to individual. Neural networks are a series of neurons that form a network that interacts when it partially overlaps with another network. This is a complex process. Memory works by tapping into the neural network necessary to find the information you are trying to remember. We all 'know' different things because the overlapping projections of networks differ among individuals. Still, we have a lot more in common, in terms of a particular subject, than we differ—always assuming that we are 'learning' the same thing.[17]

To illustrate what is at work here, look at Fig. 11.2. Imagine that, among your memories from a course on nineteenth-century Impressionism, you have a number of neural networks reflecting what you learned. As the figure shows, you have knowledge about Monet, Renoir, and Sisley. Perhaps you attended a series of lectures, one on each artist. But you have also 'learned' about Impressionism as your neural networks overlapped. At the point at which the networks containing information about the artists overlap, we find our knowledge about Impressionism. Again, this is an oversimplification, but it suggests how we incorporate existing knowledge as we 'learn'.[18]

Consider an analogy with advertising and marketing. It would be fair to say that our knowledge of a product category will be made up of (among other things) our knowledge of the brands in that category. Figure 11.3 illustrates how that might 'look' in memory. We have neural networks associated with various brands, and they overlap in various ways, one of which helps to define our understanding of the category. Again, much more is obviously involved, but this does offer insight into how we learn.

Now that we have an understanding of what is involved with learning, we will take a look at how this facilitates brand awareness and brand attitude.

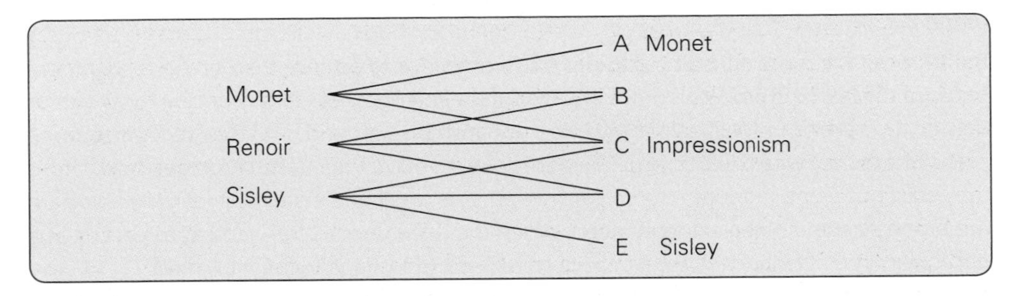

Figure 11.2 Learning through Neural Networks

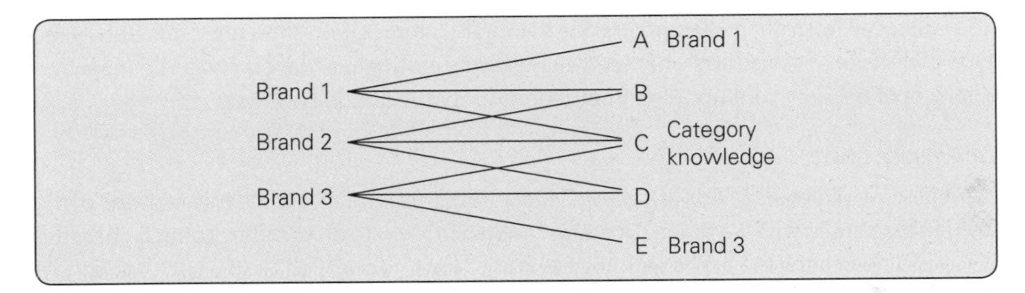

Figure 11.3 Brand Neural Networks Leading to Category Learning

Brand Awareness and Learning

If you stop to think of it, learning a brand name is very much like learning new words in a foreign language. Suppose you were studying German and were introduced to the word *schwarz*. Your attention is drawn to the word, and you form a verbal and visual image of the word in your mind. If this is all that you do, you should at least be able to recognize the word if you see or hear it again, and identify it as a German word. In this case you are associating the word with the category 'German words'. As we all know, this will not get you very far on a German test. You will also need to learn the meaning of the word.

In order to become aware of a brand such that you are able either to recognize it or to recall it when the time comes to make a decision to buy, you must learn the association between the category and the brand. You will remember that we spent a great deal of time on this point in Chapter 9. The category cue is critical, and will actually determine how likely it is that your brand will be chosen in various purchase situations.

Brand Recognition

When the brand awareness objective is recognition, what learning is required? From what we already know about brand recognition, when it is an objective, advertising should feature the package because it will be seen at the point of purchase. The target audience must learn what the package looks like so that they will recognize the package on the shelf; they should see a fast-food chain while driving, and think: 'I need that' or 'I'm hungry, so let's stop.' This is precisely what the learning response is for a brand recognition communication objective. You recognize the brand and associate it with the correct category need.

Brand Recall

Brand recall is a more difficult communication objective to achieve than brand recognition, because the learning process is more involved. If the members of a family decide to go out for dinner, they are not very likely simply to go out and drive around until they recognize some place where they would like to stop. They are going to make their destination decision before they start out. For a restaurant to be considered, the target audience must learn to associate the brand name with the category need. When the need does occur, wanting to eat out at a particular type of restaurant, we want the advertised restaurant to come to mind.

Brand Attitude and Learning

You will recall from our earlier discussions that brand attitude responses are a function of the type of decision involved and whether the underlying motive to behave is positive or negative. The type of decision has important implications for brand attitude learning.

Low Involvement

With low-involvement decisions, really all that is required is rather simple rote learning of the benefit associated with the brand. The target audience is aware of what the product is because it has just associated the brand with the category. Now the question is: so what? The benefit expressed in the advertising should answer that question. In effect what is going on here is that, while the target audience is processing the message, it will learn the connection between the brand and the benefit claimed for the brand, along with the *degree* of that connection.

High Involvement

This will not be the case with high-involvement decisions. The key to high-involvement decisions is *acceptance*, which we will be discussing next. But high-involvement learning is tied into acceptance. With low-involvement learning, you can be effective if the target audience only tentatively learns a positive benefit, but with high-involvement learning, there is usually more than one simple benefit involved.

Acceptance

Acceptance in processing is when the target audience *personally agrees* with something it has learned from one of the components in the advertising. Acceptance is required only for *high-involvement decisions*. With low-involvement decisions, learning is sufficient processing to generate purchase interest because there is little, if any, risk involved. But with high-involvement decisions, because of the need to be sure of your decision prior to purchase, the message (or at least a significant part of it) must be accepted as true.

Cognitive Responses in Processing

Now that we have a general idea of what we mean by learning and acceptance in the processing of advertising, we need to take a closer look at what is involved when the target audience is processing the message in an advert. The key to this explanation is something that psychologists call a *cognitive response*. In its simplest form, a cognitive response is the activity that occurs in your mind when you are confronted with something new. Think of what occurs to you when you are introduced to someone for the first time. Before that person says a word, your mind is already forming opinions. The way the person looks or is dressed provides visual impressions that you associate with various images. You may or may not like what you see, given previous experiences. If you are at a formal party, and this new person is dressed very casually, you may think: 'What a slob.' This would be a cognitive response that occurs because in your mind you expect people to dress according to circumstance, and those who do not, at least in your experience, leave something to be desired. Because of your existing beliefs, the contrast of what you expect and what you see generates negative images of this person. This is another example of top-down processing.

The same thing occurs when you look at advertising. You bring to the advertising a certain set of beliefs and expectations related to the product category or brand, as well as emotional associations, and you process the images and information in the advertising within that context. As you think about what you see or read, you will be generating a number of thoughts or feelings stimulated by the advertising, at least at the conscious level. To the extent that these thoughts or images, these cognitive responses, are generally positive, they will help to generate a positive brand attitude. If the cognitive responses tend to be more negative, a negative brand attitude will result.

Cognitive response theory assumes that you will generally try to make sense out of what is going on around you. As you are exposed to new information, from advertising or any other source, you will tend to compare it with what you already know and feel, utilizing what is known as declarative, or sometimes explicit, memory. Thinking specifically about advertising, this suggests that if you are really paying attention to the advertising and the advertising is for something you might be highly involved with, you are going to be very interested in what the advertising is saying. On the other hand, if the advertising is for something that does not require much consideration on your part during the purchase decision, you may or may not become actively involved with the message.

What this tells us is that, when you are *highly involved* with a purchase decision, for advertising to be effective, you *must generate* positive cognitive responses towards the brand and believe them. This is what leads to acceptance of the message. If your purchase decision is *low involvement*, active cognitive responses, while desirable, are *not necessary* except to the extent that they initiate a tentatively favourable response to the brand.

Learning and Memory

Since learning involves memory, it is important to have at least a basic understanding of the different forms of memory. You may be surprised to learn that our understanding of the different types of memory today is a relatively recent development. Psychologists long felt that there was a difference between what they thought of as 'short-term' versus 'long-term' memory. But today psychologists no longer regard short-term memory as a temporary holding state on the way to long-term memory as they did in the past. Rather, what was thought of as short-term memory is now understood to be how we store information while attending to it, or processing it. Baddeley and Hitch in the 1990s introduced the term *working memory* to emphasize this point.[19]

It was not until the 1980s that neuroscientists came to the realization that memory itself, what was thought of as long-term memory, comes in different forms: declarative memory and non-declarative memory. Basically, declarative memory deals with facts and events, and involves the hippocampus and medial temporal lobe. Non-declarative memory is normally inaccessible to the conscious mind, and is typically *reflexive* rather than *reflective*.[20] This includes what is known as procedural memory, the learning of skills and habits, and basic associative learning (as well as priming and non-associative learning), and involves the striatum, motor cortex, and cerebellum. Figure 11.4 provides an idea of where the areas involved in declarative and non-declarative memory are located in the brain. Playing the piano, typing, and riding a bicycle are examples of procedural memory. Emotion too is a part of non-declarative memory involving the amygdala, and we will be dealing with it in some depth later. Motor learning is a part of non-declarative memory, but of no interest in this discussion.

There are two fundamental features of declarative memory that we should understand. First, it is composed of a combination of 'event-based' memories known as *episodic memory* and of 'fact-based' memories known as *semantic memory*.[21] These two components combine to form declarative memory. We acquire declarative memory through everyday experiences. For example, experience with a specific brand will go into building episodic memory for the brand, and our ability to retain and recall it will be mediated by the hippocampus. But this experience with the brand will also be integrated with our general knowledge of the category and of products like those that have been acquired over time by linking experiences that 'share' information (recall our discussion of overlapping neural networks). This is our semantic memory, also mediated by the hippocampus. As we accumulate 'facts' about a brand by

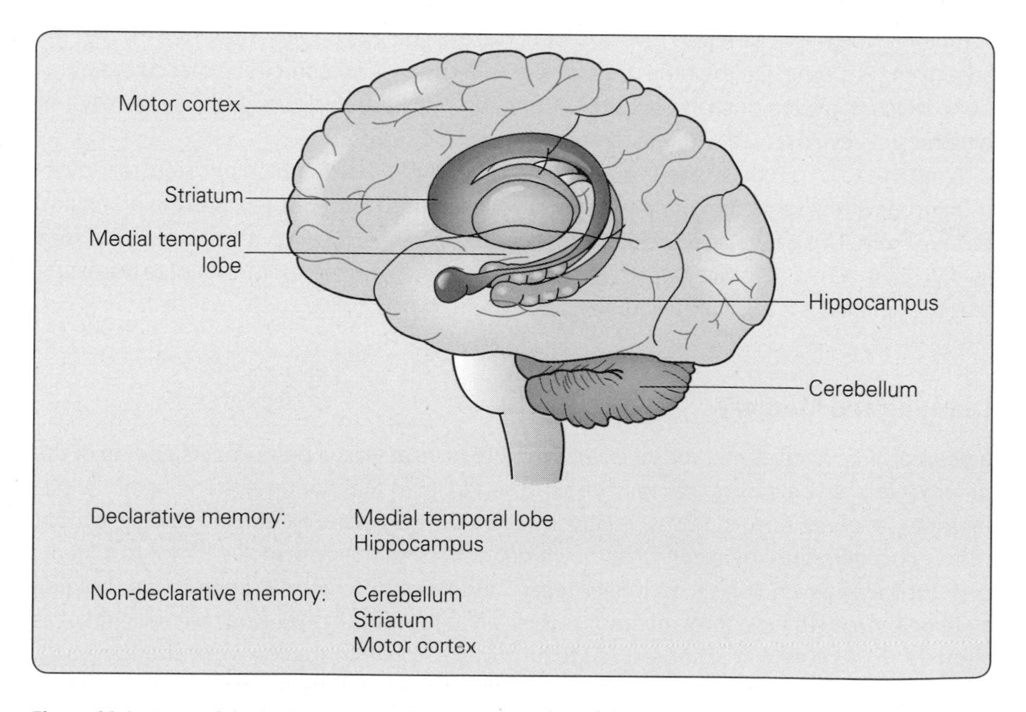

Figure 11.4 Areas of the Brain Associated with Declarative and Non-declarative Memory

integrating new information (for example, from advertising) with our existing general knowledge (basically how we learn, as we have seen), we will also be building episodic memories through actual experience with the brand. Together, these semantic and episodic memories combine to form declarative memory—what we know about the brand.

The second fundamental feature of declarative memory is that it is available to conscious recollection and we can talk about it. This means that declarative memories for both episodic and semantic information are special because a person can access and express these memories and use them to solve problems by making inferences from them. This is how we would make judgements about a new brand extension. We have access to appropriate memories of our relevant experiences and knowledge, and use these memories to help us to form our judgements about the new product.

Non-declarative memory, on the other hand, is acquired unconsciously and is not likely to be involved in the processing of advertising (at least not in any practical sense). It involves unconscious change in behaviour as a result of some previous experience. And because of the generally passive role of the encoding involved, voluntary recall of the memory is unlikely.[22] Figure 11.5 outlines some of the basic types of memory.

Another way of talking about this distinction between conscious and unconscious memory is in terms of *explicit and implicit* memory.[23] This terminology is more widely used outside of neuroscience, and reflects the types of test needed to measure the memory. Declarative, conscious memories are measured with explicit tests, asking questions such as: 'what brands of toothpaste can you recall?' Non-declarative, unconscious memories use indirect measures

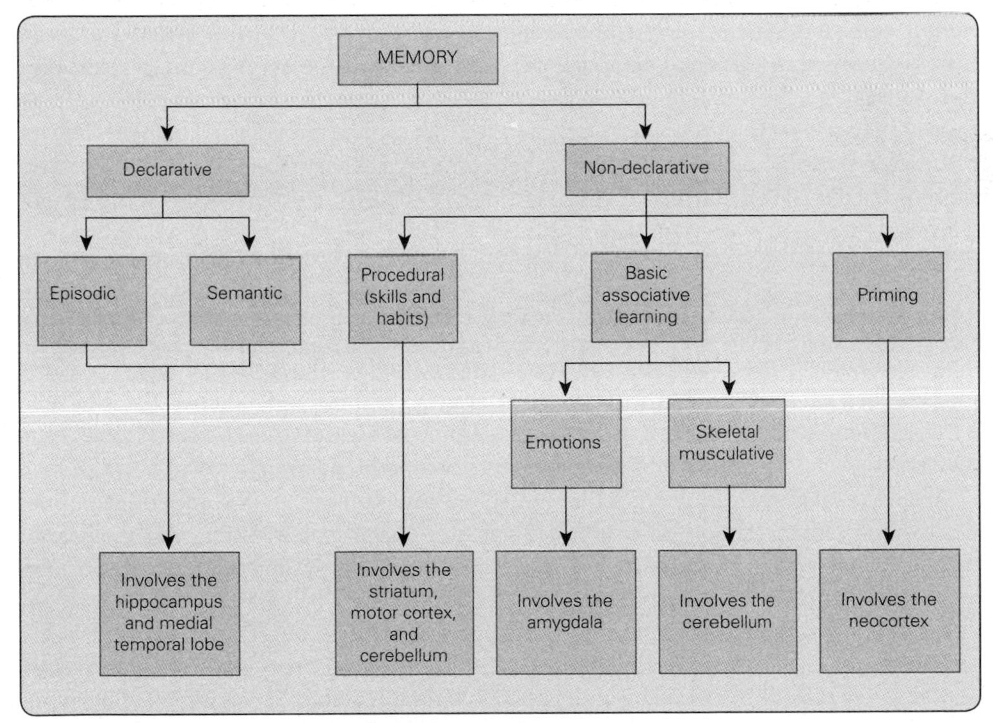

Figure 11.5 Types of Declarative and Non-declarative Memory

that do not require 'remembering' something. Implicit tests of memory include such things as the change in the speed of performance on a task (remember that motor learning is part of non-declarative memory) or bias in choice from priming.

Basically, priming is an unconscious memory function that results in an improvement in the ability to identify something after a recent exposure to it, but it is likely perceptual. A great deal of our understanding of priming comes from the work of Zajonc and his colleagues on something that they called the *mere exposure* effect.[24] In a series of studies they found that merely exposing people to words or pictures of faces leads to a slight preference for those faces later, even if they are not explicitly remembered.

Does this mean that we can 'prime' brand preference through advertising? Would not unconscious processing of an advert lead to a bias toward the advertised brand? In a word, no. The primary reason is that different neural circuits and brain structures are used for implicit and explicit learning. Most implicit memory functions (including priming) are associated with the neocortex and cerebellum, stimulating the basal ganglia independent of the temporal lobe and hippocampus where explicit memory is stored. [25]

As a result of implicit and explicit memories being operated on and housed in different neural structures, it would be difficult, if not impossible, for implicit memories to inform higher cognitive processes. Also, implicit memory is perceived in the same way as it is received, without any need for manipulation of the content at a higher, conscious cognitive level. Because of this passive role in encoding, it is very difficult to recall that memory. Even if advertising were to occasion implicit learning and memory, it would be very unlikely to have any effect upon either brand attitude or behaviour.[26]

On the other hand, because you play an active role in the processing of explicit information, all of the internal cues used in processing it may be used to activate recall of the information. If you see an advert and integrate it with existing knowledge of the brand, perhaps your belief that it is a high-quality product, when thinking of the category and cued with 'high quality', you will recall the brand. You should see that explicit memory will be necessary for recall awareness, because an association between the category need and the brand is required, and this will result from active processing of the links. It is also necessary for conscious learning that is used in decision making.

Knowledge and assumptions, our explicit, declarative memory, add a great deal to how we interpret what we see. Vision is not always directly related to the retinal image, which is why we often 'see' things that are not there. 'Seeing' an object involves general rules and knowledge about objects based upon previous experience, something known as top-down processing (see Fig. 11.6). In a wonderful painting by Degas of a woman and man sitting at a table in a cafe, we simply do not notice that the table does not have legs. We all know that tables have legs and do not float in the air, so we assume they are there.

When creating advertising and other marketing communication, it is important to keep this in mind. Not that anyone is likely to use an illustration of a table without legs, but it is not unusual to see adverts that rely upon visual puns. Unfortunately, unless the pun is obvious, there is every chance that the mind will 'correct' the image. If the message requires the receiver to understand the pun, but top-down processing corrects the error, the message will be lost. In fact, all visual images in advertising should be clearly understood. Anything too subtle runs the very real risk of not being understood in the way in which it was intended. Remember, in a very real sense, we see what we know.

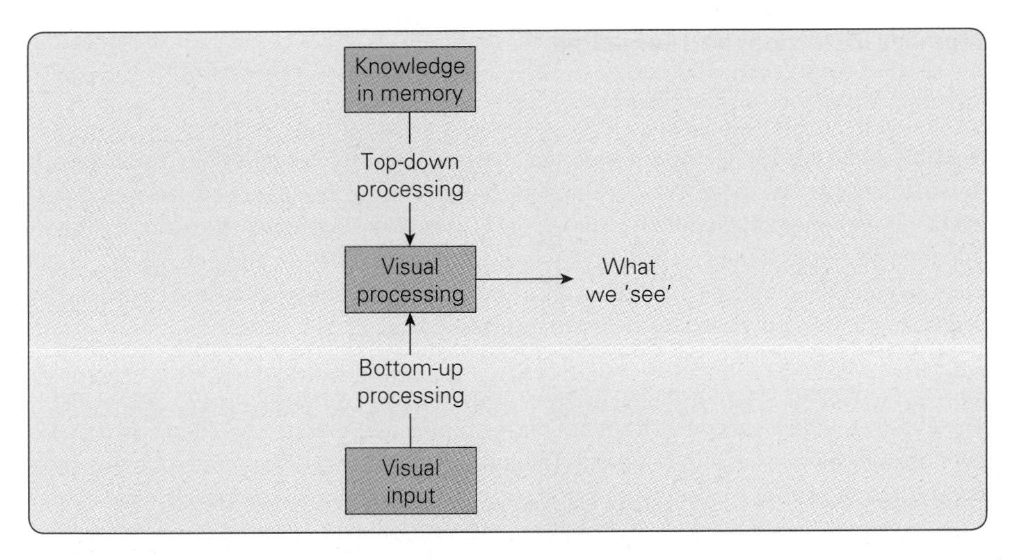

Figure 11.6 Top-Down versus Bottom-Up Processing in Visual Processing

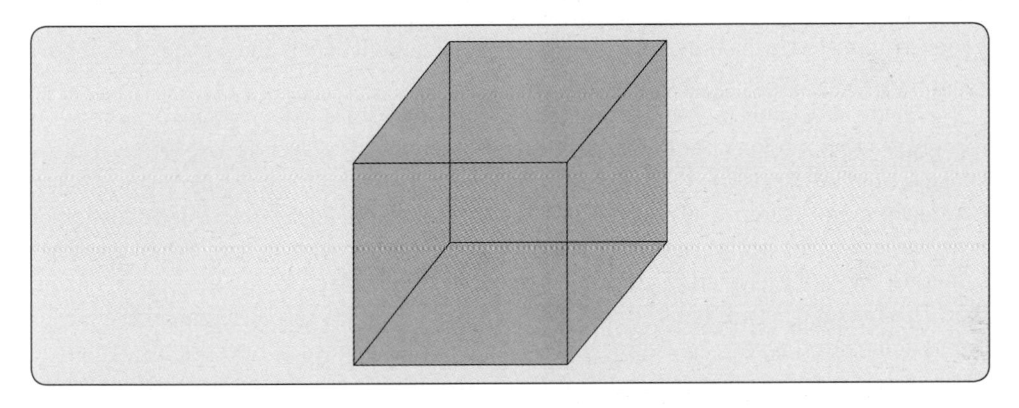

Figure 11.7 Necker's Cube, Discovered by the Swiss Crystallographer L.A. Necker in 1832

Perhaps one more point will help to underscore this idea. If you think about it, any retinal image could represent an infinite number of possibilities, yet we generally 'see' only one. Why? Because we have learned to associate that image with something specific, and that information is stored in memory. But there are exceptions, when we cannot make up our minds. Necker's cube (see Fig. 11.7) and other 'optical illusions' are examples of this ambiguity.[27] With no clear evidence, we entertain two roughly equal, but different, interpretations of the depth perspective. Does the cube recede or does it project outward? The image on the retina does not change (bottom-up processing), but we cannot decide upon what we 'see' because our experience tells us that either option is correct (top-down processing). What this tells us is that every act of perception, even something as simple as looking at the drawing of a cube, let alone something as complex as an advert, involves an act of judgement based upon our experience or prior knowledge.

Memory Distortions and Forgetting

Just because advertising has been processed and information stored in the memory does not mean that the memory actually reflects what was in the advertising, or that it will be readily available when needed. Things get distorted in memory, and we 'forget' things. This is a result of what Schacter has called memory 'imperfections', and he has identified seven potential problems with memory that he has intriguingly called 'The Seven Sins of Memory': absent-mindedness, misattribution, suggestibility, bias, blocking, transience, and persistence.[28] Each of these potential problems can impact on advertising effectiveness because each can distort processing or retrieval of an advertising message (see Table 11.1).

Most of these problems result from how we learn the information in advertising, how we encode or integrate the information from the advertising with what we already have in memory. Absent-mindedness comes from not paying proper attention to something, so that it is overlooked when we need to retrieve it. This is more likely to occur for more routine experiences, such as exposure to advertising, for which there is simply no compelling reason carefully to process the message. Misattribution and suggestibility occur when we remember something, but attribute it to the wrong source. In advertising, this can occur when the message does not bond in memory with the brand because it is too similar to information already in a memory associated with something else, or because we link it to a previous personal experience unrelated to the brand. Bias occurs when our current beliefs and feelings distort how we interpret what we see in advertising.

We all are very familiar with the problem of blocking. This is what is going on when you recognize someone, but cannot remember his or her name. The appropriate retrieval cue is in place, but the association is just not made. The problem stems from people's names being isolated in memory from any conceptual knowledge of them. Recall from our discussion of how we learn that neural networks are built upon existing knowledge. When we meet someone, we rarely have an appropriate neural network in place to link the person's name to it. This makes it very difficult to find it when we need it. This can be a real problem with brand names, and especially abstract brand names or the names of new brands, if there is not a strong association made in the brand's advertising with the appropriate category need.

Table 11.1 The Seven Sins of Memory

Absent-mindedness	Results from not paying proper attention to something
Misattribution	Remembering something, but attributing it to the wrong source
Suggestibility	Attributing something from an outside source to a personal experience
Bias	When current beliefs and feelings distort the processing of new information
Blocking	When appropriate retrieval cues are in place, but the association is just not made
Transience	Natural shift over time from specific recollection to more general descriptions
Persistence	Remembering something you would like to forget

In Chapter 12, we will talk about creative tactics that can help to minimize these potential problems with memory.

The remaining memory problems, transience and persistence, reflect simple forgetting or the persistent memory of something that you want to forget. Persistence is unlikely to be a problem with advertising. Not forgetting an advertising message will not be seen as a problem by the advertiser! But we certainly do not want people to forget something positive about a brand from its advertising. What seems to happen in memory is a natural shift from specific recollections of things to more general descriptions of what is learned. This is why in advertising recall studies people are likely to recall general ideas from advertising rather than specific details.

Emotion

Up to this point we have talked about processing in terms of its traditional role in information processing, as discussed in Chapter 4 in relation to the communication response sequence. Some element within an advert—the picture or illustration, headline, copy-points (ideally *all* of the elements working together)—must first of all be attended to and something must be learned from it. Then, unless you are dealing only with brand awareness or low-involvement brand attitude effects, if that learning is to communicate anything, it must be accepted as true. But the context within which this processing is occurring will also elicit a response: an *emotional* response. The advertising itself will trigger certain emotional responses and in certain cases this emotional response will mediate what is learned and whether or how a particular point is accepted.[29]

Look at the two images shown in Advert 11.3. What reaction do you have to these two images? Both are from adverts for a brand of washing powder. We know that emotional authenticity is not necessary for low-involvement informational advertising, but, regardless of the brand attitude strategy, we do want to elicit the correct emotional response. The benefit of 'soft' is reinforced in Advert 11.3*a* by a positive emotional response to the child. This does not occur with the image of a mother and child in Advert 11.3*b*.

Why is that? There is nothing warm or nurturing about this image, nothing to suggest a 'loving' mother, one who makes sure that her children enjoy the benefit of clean, soft clothes. There is nothing sincere in the mother's expression, and in fact she is not even looking directly at the child. As a result, there is nothing there to stimulate a positive emotional response. This is reflected in research on the two adverts, which found that the execution using the image in 11.3*a* generated a 55 per cent positive response to the advert versus 40 per cent for the advert using the image shown in 11.3*b*, and 50 per cent buying interest for 11.3*a* versus 30 per cent for 11.3*b*. These adverts were from the same campaign, for the same brand, but the emotional response to Advert 11.3*a* led to a much more positive processing of the message.[30]

What exactly is an 'emotion'? To begin with, it is not the same thing as a 'feeling', although in many ways our feelings are part of an emotion. Theorists in the field view emotion as having multiple components, and perhaps the most common view is the 'reaction triad'. This defines emotion in terms of physiological arousal, motor expression, and a subjective feeling. While we may not always be conscious of it, each of these components is at work when we have an emotional response to something. And we have emotional responses to just about everything that we experience, stored in our non-declarative emotional memory.

(a)

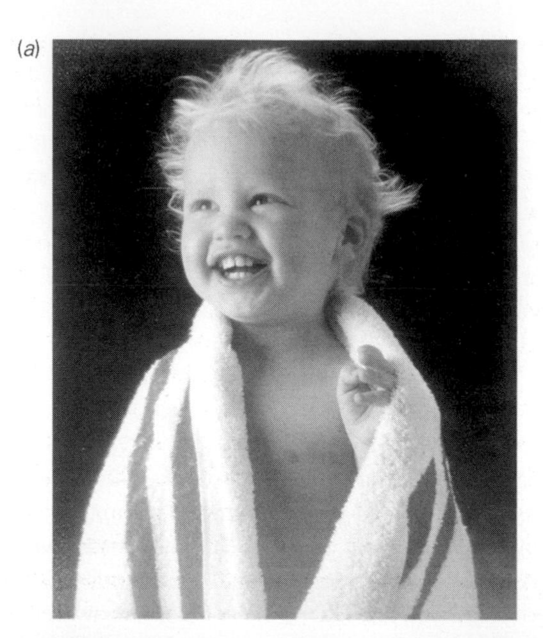

(b)

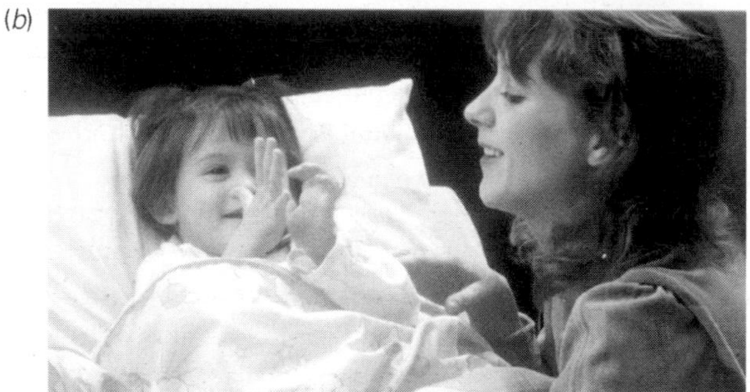

Advert 11.3 While both of these images show children, the image in *(a)* elicits a stronger emotional response than that in *(b)*.

Source: Courtesy Åke Wissing & Co.

To give you an idea of what this means, suppose you are walking home late on a dark night and decide to take a short cut down a dark alley. It is really dark in the alley and, about halfway down, you hear a loud noise. Even before you are consciously aware of that noise, you will have experienced an emotional response. Your heart rate will have risen and adrenaline will have been released into your system (physiological arousal), muscles will tense (motor expression), and you will 'feel' anxiety or fear (subjective feeling). All of this will occur *before* you are actually consciously aware of the noise. You are experiencing an innate emotional response to a potentially life-threatening situation. The body is being prepared for 'flight or fight' even before you rationally evaluate the situation. As you become consciously alert, you may notice a cat jumping down from a skip, and relax.

Most neuroscientists working with emotion identify six primary emotions: anger, fear, disgust, sadness, surprise, and joy. These primary emotions are universal. Other emotions such as guilt, pride, envy, etc. (referred to as secondary, or social, emotions) will be experienced by everyone, but how they are interpreted may differ from culture to culture. In Western cultures, for example, there is a strong connection between guilt and responsibility. Other cultures experience guilt, but lack this connection to responsibility. Damasio believes that these secondary emotions are acquired, and are triggered by things that people have come to associate with that emotion through experience.[31] Primary emotions are an innate part of the limbic system, part of the evolutionary systems in place to help us to survive as a species.

A perhaps subtle point, but one worth understanding, is that our *perception* of other people's emotions is processed in the right hemisphere, in the right temporal cortex area of the brain. This means that the dominant visual input will come from the left field of vision. While this is obviously not a 'rule', if the image of a specific emotion is important to the message, the individuals expressing that emotion in an advert should be on the left side of the page or screen to optimize visual processing through the left field of vision.

Russell has offered an interesting variation on Damasio's distinction between primary and secondary emotions, describing them as Type 1 and Type 2 emotions.[32] The important point is that Russell feels that Type 1 emotions do not require a person to consciously acknowledge experiencing the emotion, while one actually is thinking about Type 2 emotions as they occur. For example, one may be angry or happy without thinking 'I'm angry' or 'I'm happy'. But if you feel empathy with someone, you will be conscious of the fact. This could have important consequences in processing advertising and promotion messages, because if Type 1 emotions are associated in memory with a brand, they could automatically motivate approach or avoidance behaviour.[33] If you 'love' a brand, you will unconsciously be drawn to it and messages about it; if you 'hate' a brand, you will unconsciously avoid it and any messages about it. If this notion of Russell's is in fact true, it would act like an instinct.[34]

How we experience emotional responses is complex, but coordinated. They occur very rapidly after exposure to the stimulus that elicited the response, and their onset is typically involuntary; they unfold *without conscious direction*. This is very important in understanding how emotion works in mediating the way in which advertising is processed.

The area of the brain most strongly associated with emotion is the amygdala, which lies in the medial temporal lobe, in front of the hippocampus and surrounded by the parahippocampal cortical region.[35] As Winston and Dilan[36] describe it, 'the human amygdala is a crucial locus in associating stimuli with their appropriate emotional value'. Pathways through the amygdala provide the link between sensory inputs (visual, auditory, olfactory) and triggering emotional responses. This plasticity of non-declarative emotional memory is what enables it to support emotional memories in the absence of conscious recollection.

Even though our emotions, especially primary emotions, have limited involvement in actual cognitive processing controlling long-term action, they nonetheless will be strongly integrated into the cognitive processes leading to long-term planned action. In other words, emotional responses 'frame' our conscious cognitive processing. In advertising, if the emotional response elicited is consistent with experiences associated with using the product, any positive emotions activated on behalf of the brand by an advert should help to reinforce brand purchase intentions made as a result of that advertising.

How does this work? Damasio has pointed out that emotion is a cognitive *process* that actually leads to logical thinking.[37] He argues that the mechanisms of reasoning are significantly influenced by both conscious and unconscious signals from the neural networks associated with emotion. We all acquire emotional memories that are related to our experiences with

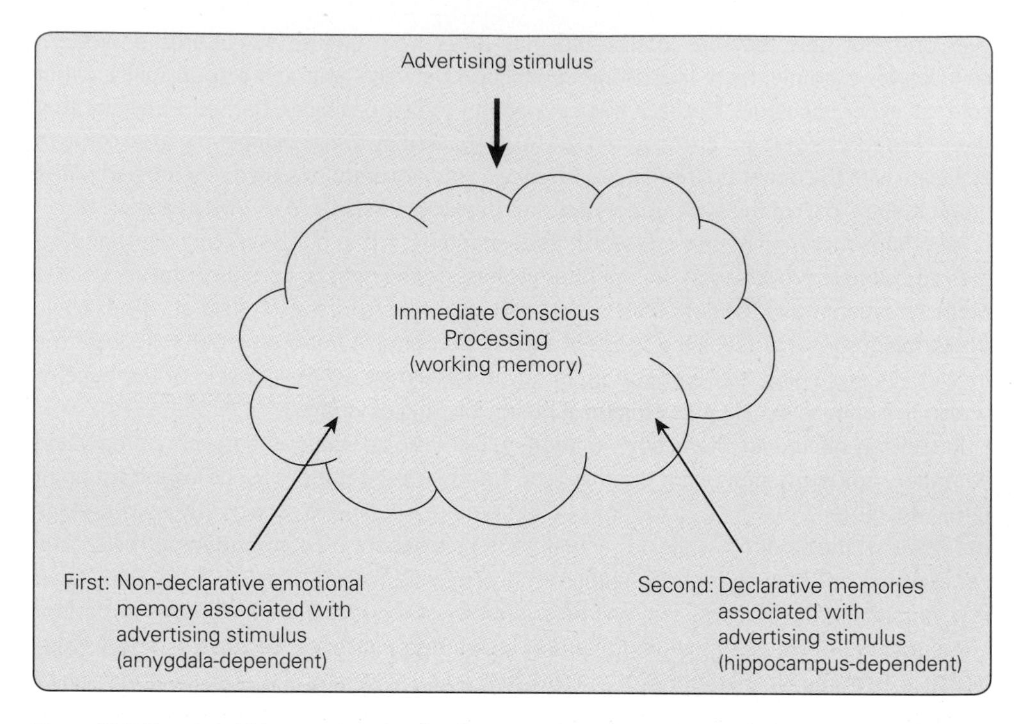

Figure 11.8 Emotional Memory Associated with Stimulus Precedes Declarative Memories into Working Memory for Processing

different things, and these feelings are unconscious and independent of any conscious, declarative memory that we might have of those same things. These emotional memories are stored in the amygdala. Emotional memory is the third element of what the neuroscientist Eichenbaum has referred to as the three major 'memory systems'.[38]

When someone is exposed to an advert, it will stimulate both conscious cognitive associations in memory (the top-down processing), as well as non-declarative emotional memories associated with various aspects of the execution. In fact, the emotional memories will actually precede the cognitively based hippocampal-dependent declarative memories into working memory for the processing of the message.

This means that if an advert activates memories, either of a positive experience with the brand or positive memories associated with the imagery in the advertising, the non-declarative emotional memory associated with these memories will immediately and unconsciously enter into our active processing of the advertising. We can see how this happens in Fig. 11.8. Emotion and cognition are intimately related, and are probably controlled by overlapping neural systems.[39] This is the only exception to the general understanding that explicit and implicit memory are not related neurologically, and do not interact. Emotion is the only non-declarative memory that does interact with conscious, declarative memories. The close relationship between the amygdala, where non-declarative emotional memories are stored, and the hippocampus, where conscious memory is thought to be centred, is shown in Fig. 11.9.

Eichenbaum relates a personal experience that perfectly illustrates what happens here. He had entered a lift alone on the ground floor, and when it reached the first floor it stopped and

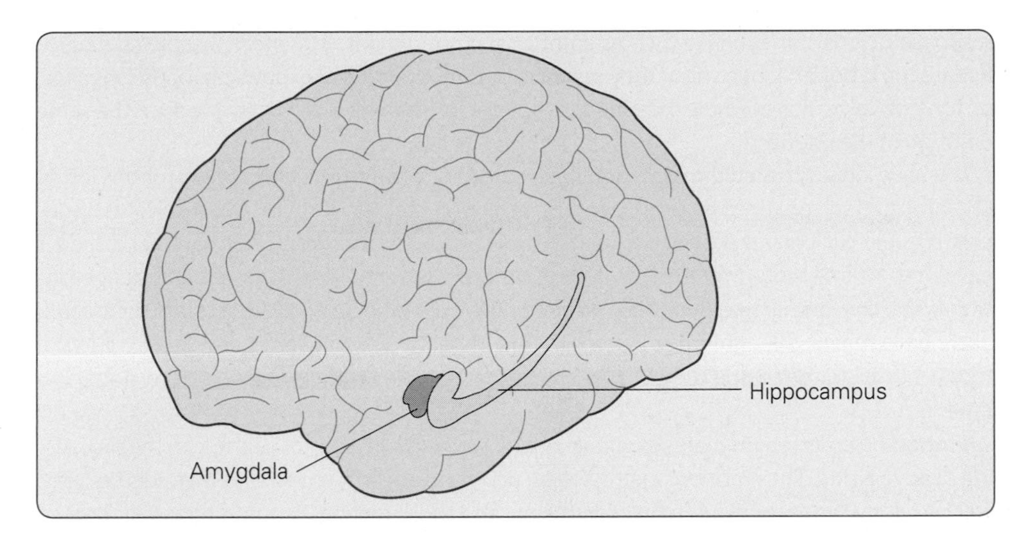

Figure 11.9 **The Close Relationship between the Amygdala and Hippocampus in the Brain**

a number of people stepped in. The first was a young woman who stood just in front of him. He immediately noticed that she was wearing perfume, and it was a vaguely familiar scent. Over the next few seconds he began experiencing a strong feeling of both familiarity and, as he described it, 'a sort of innocent sense of happiness'. He found himself emotionally transported back to the 'feeling' of high school. Within seconds he began to remember classmates he had not thought about in years. At last he fully recognized the scent, one that had been very popular among teenage girls in the early 1960s when he was at school—Shalimar.

The specific memories he had were, as he put it, 'run-of-the-mill declarative memories'. But that initial feeling of happiness and 'high-schoolness' was an example of emotional memory, one evoked by a past association, and here is the key point, 'even before the conscious recollection of the experience that provoked it'. The emotional memory framed his conscious memories. In the same way, non-declarative emotional memories elicited by advertising will help to frame conscious memories of the brand, and how we process the advertising.

Before we leave this, there is an important point to be made. While positive emotional memories can certainly initiate positive processing, they do not have the ability to override conscious considerations. If the brand or advertising imagery evokes positive memories, but there is something in the message that is not liked, the conscious, cognitive processing will take precedent. Recall our example of the noise in a dark alleyway. Once the association of the noise and the cat has been made, the original intense primary emotional response will no longer control your actions.

Embodied Emotions

An important way in which advertising elicits emotional response is through the posture, prosody, and facial expressions shown in adverts. Those exposed to the advertising use their perceptions of the emotional state of those shown in an advert to interpret and evaluate the emotional significance of what is going on in the advert, and this in turn will inform their own emotional response. This is something known as emotional embodiment.[40] In effect, people take on or initiate the emotional behaviour they perceive in someone's facial expression, body language, or tone of voice. For example, hearing a happy versus sad voice will likely produce the same emotion in the listener.[41]

We have already noted the evolutionary importance of emotion. One reason for this is that the information conveyed by other people's emotions can be critical for our survival as a species (e.g. fear will convey danger or threat; happiness, safety or comfort). In man's earliest days it was important to interpret the emotions of others in order to identify potentially dangerous situations, or whether positive social interaction would be possible. Getting this right could likely have meant the difference between life and death. We may not need this for survival today, but it still does operate because, being part of the limbic system, it does not know time.[42]

Embodied emotion mediates cognitive responses, and has a direct bearing on the processing of advertising. The emotions expressed by people in adverts, especially when seen as 'real', will be felt by those exposed to the advertising, and those feelings aroused by the embodied emotion will then inform cognitive responses to the advertising, just as we saw with emotional memories. Even when you think about the advert later, or about the brand as informed by the advertising, the original embodied emotions will be retrieved from non-declarative emotional memory and be a part of that thinking.

When an embodied emotion triggers a felt emotion, it biases cognitive processing toward a state consistent with that emotion. For example, if you see a smiling face, it will activate a smile in response, a tendency for approach behaviour, and positive valences leading to happiness and liking. Perceived, authentic smiles or happiness in adverts should lay a favorable foundation for processing the message.

In fact, while emotion is embodied from body language and tone of voice, the most important cue to someone's emotional state is facial expression, and it is the eyebrows that are the key to expressing negative emotion and the mouth positive emotion.[43] We mentioned earlier that primary emotions are universal, and this is also true of the emotions embodied from facial expression. When facial expressions are shown to people, regardless of where they live or their cultural backgrounds, all agree on the emotional meaning conveyed.[44]

This suggests that people shown smiling in an advert, for example, should elicit a feeling of happiness in those exposed to the advert. But this will only be true if the smile is 'real', one that is part of a true feeling of happiness on the part of the person smiling, and not forced. This is not easy to fake, even for experienced actors, because a truly felt positive emotion will occasion an involuntary response from specific facial muscles. A voluntary smile uses a different set of facial muscles, and will not be seen as 'real'. Real smiles, those occasioned by an emotional response, are known as 'Duchenne smiles' after the nineteenth-century anatomist who first wrote about this.[45] Getting all of this right, of course, is important for the emotional authenticity necessary for transformational brand attitude strategies.

Recently there has been some suggestion that the embodiment of emotion may utilize mirror neurons such as those that have been identified in motor response. While there is not enough evidence yet to confirm this, there have been studies that seem to support the idea. In one, it was found that people experiencing disgust showed brain activation in similar areas of the brain to those activated when seeing someone else experiencing disgust: the left interior insular and right anterior cortex (all part of the limbic system). The study concluded that this was a mirroring of the emotion involved and not a recreation of an observed goal or action.[46]

Processing Advertising in New Media

Back in Chapter 1 when we talked briefly about advertising and new media, we pointed out that basically it is processed like any other advert. Look at an example of a banner advert for homestore.com (Advert 11.4); everything we have been talking about in this chapter regarding how advertising is processed will apply to this advert.

First of all, someone must pay attention to the advert, then learn that gardening is made easy at homestore.com. Because this is a banner advert on the Internet, he or she does not really need to *accept* that gardening is made easy at homestore.com *to look further*. Clicking on the banner is a low-involvement decision, unlike actually visiting a garden centre. Finally, the copy headline will stimulate an emotional response that the advertiser hopes will facilitate the processing of the message. Specifically, the 'made easy' should stimulate curiosity or even excitement, encouraging the viewer to click on the banner.

But, because there is more to this advert's structure, there must be additional processing. Rossiter and Bellman have introduced the idea of a micro- and macro-structure of advertising.[47] They suggest that, while all advertising shares a common micro-structure, which they define as the links between content variables, the real difference between Internet adverts and other forms of advertising is caused by macro-structure if you click on the banner. They mean by this, roughly speaking, the association and link within the advertising's content between pages in the Internet advert. In other words, because of the macro-structure of Internet advertising, people must 'navigate through the Web ad' (in their words), and they are free to navigate in any way they choose. Their path will reflect what Rossiter and Bellman call a self-constructed Web ad schema, and this may *not* be the path that the advertiser would prefer they follow.

As Rossier and Bellman go on to point out, the macro-structure of a television or radio commercial is usually automatic, and it is obvious with collateral advertising such as brochures and direct response adverts. But with Internet advertising, the (advertiser's) preferred processing route is neither automatic nor evident. What this means is a potential loss of control for the advertiser. This is particularly true for the emotional responses associated with processing. Perhaps the most obvious example would be the result of any difficulty or frustration encountered in trying to navigate successfully through a site.

Advert 11.4 Everything we have discussed about how advertising is processed applies to Internet banner adverts like this one for homestore.com.

Source: Reproduced with kind permission © homestore.com.

Overall, what we have talked about in this chapter, as well as what we will discuss in Chapter 12, applies to advertising in new media, especially its micro-structure. What the manager must be concerned about, however, is facilitating and controlling (if possible) the processing of the macro-structure. This will be very difficult, because individual users of the Internet will be developing their own Web ad schema, or ways of navigating Internet adverts.

Chapter summary

In this chapter we have focused on the ways in which consumers process messages, and how knowledge about this can be used to develop creative strategy and tactics. We introduced the four basic processing responses of attention, learning, acceptance, and emotion, and then discussed in detail how each response can be used to facilitate the achievement of communication objectives. We explored the different levels of processing associated with different levels of involvement, the key role of acceptance in high-involvement decisions, and their links with cognitive responses with particular attention to learning and memory. Building upon this, we discussed the important distinction between declarative and non-declarative memory, and why, even if there is any implicit processing of an advert, it is unlikely to have any effect upon brand attitude or behaviour. We then considered the vital role of emotion in relation to advertising and how emotion mediates processing. Finally, we considered all of this processing in relation to the adverts in new media.

Questions to consider

11.1 Why is it important to understand how advertising is processed?

11.2 What are the different aspects of attention and how might they affect the way in which an advert is processed?

11.3 In what ways is memory involved in learning?

11.4 Does it matter if advertising is processed consciously or unconsciously?

11.5 What are the important differences between declarative and non-declarative memory, and how do these effect the processing of advertising?

11.6 How can memory interfere with the successful processing of advertising?

11.7 What role does emotion play in message processing?

11.8 Is the processing of adverts in new media different from the processing of adverts in more traditional media?

Case study 11 Growth by Innovation—How Lipton's New Story and Media Find Helped it to Stay Ahead

The marketing objectives highlighted for Lipton's thematic campaign were:

- hold value market share of Lipton Yellow Label in Arabia, Turkey, and UNECA;
- grow Lipton Yellow Label's value market share in Mashreq (the region of Arabic-speaking countries to the east of Egypt and north of the Arabian Peninsula) and Nigeria.

Our target group comprised of contemporary urbanites between the ages of 24 and 28, both male and female, LSM (living standards measure) 12+ (Arabia); LSM 7+ (Egypt, Turkey, Nigeria and UNECA). We opened the way for conversation and it didn't take us long to realize that our consumers live in a fast-paced modern world. Their success depends on their capacity to keep evolving, growing, and adapting. They are more health conscious and more demanding. Lipton Yellow Label's consumers are dynamic and ever-changing. And Lipton Yellow Label had to be the same.

Our consumers today have a very definite idea with regard to their thoughts and habits concerning tea. Tea has an important place in their lives; however, consumers don't realize or articulate the same. They think that tea makes them feel calm and clears their minds but they fail to make a spontaneous association with the benefit of this. They do drink tea as a habit, without really linking it to any end benefit. This is where our communication needs to step in and stand out from the competition.

Our purpose was to find a fit for our product in their lives. Lipton Yellow Label helps them to think clearly so that they can get the most out of their hectic day. Lipton Yellow Label can do this because it has natural theanine. Natural theanine is an amino acid found almost exclusively in tea. Combined with the goodness of tea, it clears one's mind and helps one to focus.

Television and radio capitalized on the famous Johnny Nash song 'I Can See Clearly Now', highlighting situations that need clear thinking. Four channels that stood out in terms of their effectiveness and innovation were as follows.

1. *Print*: We came up with a very imaginative use of the print medium. At first glance, the consumer sees the riddle. It's only when he turns the page upside down that he gets the answer to the riddle. And it's in this moment of 'clear thinking' that he also sees the brand message.
2. *Point of sale*: A gondola stand using the crossword as creatively and visually combines the communication message of 'clear thinking' with Lipton Yellow Label.
3. *Outdoor mupies*: A series of mupies people spend time (at bus stops, in malls) used the same device of riddles and puzzles to demonstrate the effect of 'clear thinking'.
4. *On-pack tea tags (new media)*: Riddles and illusions in both English and Arabic were created and printed on the tags. Each one required the drinker to spend some time solving the riddle or the puzzle while enjoying his or her cup of tea—an exercise that required a certain clarity of thought, which was exactly what the tea offered.

Source: This is an edited version of a case study submitted to the Warc Prize. The full case study can be found at warc.com. *© Copyright Warc.*

Edited by Elizabeth Mamali, PhD Researcher, Bath School of Management

Discussion questions

1. How did Lipton manage to maintain the attention of its target segments, taking into account processing responses discussed in the chapter?
2. How did Lipton manage memory interference with its campaign?
3. What would be a creative idea for a future Lipton campaign?
4. What alternative idea could you propose for the same product for a Western country?

Further reading

Marco Iacobori, *Mirroring People* (New York: Farran, Straus, and Girious, 2008)

Jacmomo Rizzolattimo Carrado Sinigaglia, *Mirrors in the Brain* (Oxford: Oxford University Press, 2008)

The notion of mirror neurons in processing is still an open question, but evidence is mounting—two books worth pursuing on the subject.

Stefano Putoni, Jonathan Sohettr, and Mark Rastin, 'Meaning Matters: Polysemy in Advertising', *Journal of Advertising*, 39/2 (2010), 51-64

Polysemy in advertising—the idea that there are at least two distinct ways of interpreting a message across audiences, or across time and situation.

J. David Sweatt, *Mechanisms of Memory* (Amsterdam: Elsevier, 2003)

A solid overview of the neurology involved in learning and memory.

Notes

1. It was the emergence of cognitive science that led to a re-evaluation of the behavioural view that such cognitive concepts as attention and consciousness were not necessary to explain behaviour, and a return to James's position from the late 1800s. See Bryan Kolb and Ian Q. Whishaw, *The Fundamentals of Human Neuropsychology*, 5th edn (New York: Worth Publishers, 2003), 577, 578, and the original work of William James, *The Principles of Psychology* (New York: Holt, 1890).
2. See D. Broadbent, *Perception and Communication* (London: Pergamon, 1958).
3. A good brief explanation of this may be found in R.L. Gregory's *The Oxford Companion to the Mind*, 2nd edn (Oxford: Oxford University Press, 2004).
4. This difference in conscious versus unconscious processing involves something known as top-down versus bottom-up processing. A good discussion of this may be found in Kolb and Whishaw, *The Fundamentals of Neuropsychology*, 5th edn (New York: Worth Publishers, 2003), 579, and, with special reference to visual processing, Richard L. Gregory, *Eye and Brain*, 5th edn (Princeton, NJ: Princeton University Press, 1997).
5. Our perceptual systems can overheat, creating what D. Kahneman has called a 'bottleneck' in processing: *Attention and Effort* (Englewood Cliffs, NJ: Prentice Hall, 1973).
6. See I. Bredeman, J.C. Rabinowitz, A.L. Glass, and EW. Stacy, 'On the Information Extracted from a Glance at a Scene', *Journal of Experimental Psychology*, 103 (1974), 597-600.
7. See G.R. Loftus, 'Tachistoscopic Simulations of Exposure Fixation on Pictures', *Journal of Experimental Psychology: Human Learning and Memory*, 7 (1981), 369-76.
8. This story and a very good discussion of subliminal advertising may be found in Max Sutherland's May 2007 online column at http://www.sutherlandsurvey.com
9. Although the idea of 'subliminal persuasion' has been widely sensationalized, especially by Wilson Key in his book *Subliminal Seduction* (Englewood Cliffs, NJ: Prentice Hall, 1974), Timothy Moore has convincingly demonstrated that, even if advertisers were to utilize subliminal cues in creative executions, they would not affect brand choice. See T.E. Moore, 'Subliminal Advertising: What You See is What You Get', *Journal of Marketing*, 46 (Spring 1982), 38-47.
10. For a review of how subliminal sexual imagery may in fact stimulate *sexual* arousal, see W.J. Roth and H.S. Mosatche, 'A Projective Assessment of the Effects of Freudian Sexual Symbolism in Liquor

Advertisements', *Psychological Report*, 56/1 (1985), 183–8. While Moore's work (see n. 9) shows that subliminal cues generally are not effective in advertising, what the Roth and Mosatche study suggests is that subliminal sexual imagery might have an effect in the specific case in which a purely emotion-laden benefit focus is appropriate.

11. See A. Pratkanis and E. Aronson, *Age of Propaganda* (New York: W.H. Freeman, 1991), 201.
12. More on this may be found in G.V. Johar, D. Maheswaran, and L.A. Peracchio, 'MAPping the Frontiers: Theoretical Advances in Consumer Research on Memory, Affect, and Persuasion', *Journal of Consumer Research*, 33 (2006), 139–49.
13. This experiment is reported in D.J. Simons and C.F. Chabris, 'Gorillas in our Midst: Sustained Inattentional Blindness for Dynamic Events', *Perception*, 28 (1999), 1059–74. A shortened version of this experiment may be downloaded from http://www.wjh.harvard.edu/~viscog/lab/demos.html
14. See E. Langer, A. Blank, and B. Chanowitz, 'The Mindlessness of Ostensibly Thoughtful Action: The Role of "Placebic" Information in Interpersonal Interaction', *Journal of Personality and Social Psychology*, 36/6 (1978), 635–42.
15. LTP is discussed at great length in Howard Eichenbaum, *The Cognitive Neuroscience of Memory* (Oxford: Oxford University Press, 2002), not only in terms of the cellular and molecular basis of learning for those interested in the neurobiology involved, but also, in an *understandable* way, in terms of memory.
16. Ramer y Cajal won the Nobel Prize for his observations that each nerve cell was contained within a membrane and was separate altogether in contact with other cells. For a review of his ideas, see Eichenbaum, *The Cognitive Neuroscience* (Oxford: Oxford University Press, 2002), 7–9.
17. See the chapters on memory in Kolb and Whishaw, *Fundamentals of Neuropsychology* 5th edn (New York: Worth Publishers, 2003), 447–52.
18. The work of Hubel Wiesel (discussed by James W. Kalat in his book *Biological Psychology*, 8th edn (Belmont, CA: Wadsworth/Thomson Learning, 2004)), provides this framework for understanding the pattern of activity in neural networks. It is also related to the idea of relational memory theory that suggests a memory space in which memories are connected by their common elements. For a discussion of this, see Eichenbaum, *The Cognitive Neuroscience* (Oxford: Oxford University Press, 2002), 127.
19. See A.D. Baddeley and G.J. Hitch, 'Developments in the Concept of Working Memory', *Neuropsychology*, 8 (1994), 485–93. This definition of working memory should not be confused with an earlier use of the term by David Olton, who was talking about the role of the hippocampus in learning and memory when the solution of a problem requires memory for a particular recent event.
20. A very readable and comprehensive book on memory is Larry R. Squire and Eric R. Kandel's *Memory, from Mind to Molecules* (New York: Scientific American Library, 1999). There is a particularly good discussion of declarative versus non-declarative memory.
21. This distinction between episodic and semantic memory was first introduced by Tulving in 1972. For a more recent discussion, see E. Tulving, 'Episodic Memory: From Mind to Brain', *Annual Review of Psychology*, 53 (2002), 1–25.
22. See B. Kolb and I.Q. Whishaw *Fundamentals of Human Neuropsychology*, 5th edn (New York: Worth Publishers, 2003).
23. See D.L. Schacter, 'Implicit Memory: History and Current Status', *Journal of Experimental Psychology: Learning, Memory, and Cognition*, 13 (1987), 501–18.
24. We should point out that the mere exposure effect is most likely to occur when exposure time is very brief, less than one second. This means that it is unlikely to be a factor for normal exposure to advertising, but only when someone is skimming a magazine or glancing at a poster, or when the radio

or television is on, but unattended. See R.B. Zajonc, 'Attitudinal Effects of Mere Exposure', *Journal of Personality and Social Psychology Monograph*, 9/2 (1968), 1–27.

25. See A. Pascual-Leone, J. Grafman, and M. Itallet, 'Modulation of Cortical Neural Output Ways during Development of Implicit and Explicit Knowledge', *Science*, 263 (1994), 1287–9.

26. A more detailed discussion of this issue is found in L. Percy's chapter 'Unconscious Processing of Advertising and its Effect upon Attitude and Behaviour', in S. Diehl and R. Terlutter (eds), *International Advertising and Communication* (Wiesbaden:Deutchen-Universtäts-Verlay, 2006), 110–21.

27. Necker's cube was discovered by a Swiss crystallographer, L.A. Necker, in 1832, while he was drawing rhomboid crystals seen with a microscope.

28. See Daniel L. Schacter, *The Seven Sins of Memory* (Boston, MA: Houghlin Mifflin Company, 2001).

29. Emotion in advertising is not only misunderstood, but often ignored. K. Fletcher, in *A Glittering Haze* (Henley-on-Thames: NTC, 1992), points out that when practitioners talk about advertising, they are more likely to talk in terms of information than any emotional contribution.

30. The research results are from a proprietary study conducted by Åke Wissing & Co.

31. See A.R. Damasio, *Descartes' Error: Emotion, Reason, and the Human Brain* (New York: Grosset/Putnam, 1994).

32. See J.A. Russell, 'Core Affect and the Psychological Construction of Emotion', *Psychological Review*, 110/1 (2003), 145–72.

33. See M. Chen and J.A. Bargh, 'Consequences of Automatic Evaluation: Immediate Behavioural Predispositions to Approach or Avoid the Stimulus', *Personality and Social Psychology Bulletin*, 25/2 (1999), 215–24.

34. John Rossiter and Steve Bellman offer a number of examples of how this idea of Type 1 and Type 2 emotions can be seen in the advertising of major companies: *Marketing Communication: Theory and Practice* (French Forest, NSW: Pearson Education Australia, 2005), 55–6.

35. The implications of this and emotion in general for advertising is discussed by L. Percy in 'Unconscious Processing of Advertising and its Effects upon Attitude and Behaviour', in S. Diehl and R. Terlutter (eds) *International Advertising and Communication* (Wiesbaden: Deutschen-Universitäts-Verlag, 2006), 110–21.

36. See J.S. Winston and R.J. Dilan, 'Feeling States in Emotion: Functional Imaging Evidence', in A.S.S. Manstead, N. Frijda, and A. Fisher (eds) *Feeling and Emotion* (Cambridge; Cambridge University Press, 2004), 216.

37. See Damasio, *Descartes' Error: Emotion, Reason, and the Human Brain* (New York: Grosset/Putnam, 1994).

38. See Eichenbaum, *The Cognitive Neuroscience of Memory* (Oxford: Oxford University Press, 2002), 200.

39. As Bryan Kolb and Ian Whishaw point out in *The Fundamentals of Neuropsychology*, 5th edn (New York: Worth Publishers, 2003), 542, this principle of a rational relation between emotion and cognition being controlled by overlapping neural systems is found in all major theories of emotion, especially Damasio's somatic marker hypothesis, Le Doux's cognitive-social interaction theory, and Gainotti's asymmetry theory.

40. A good discussion of this notion of embodiment may be found in P.M. Niedenthal, L.W. Barsalou, F. Riz, and S. Krauth-Gruber, 'Embodiment in the Acquisition and Use of Emotion Knowledge', in L.F. Barnett, P.M. Niedenthal, and P. Winkleman (eds), *Emotion and Consciousness* (New York: The Guilford Press, 2005), 21–50.

41. See R. Neuman and F. Strack, 'Mood Contagion: The Automatic Transfer of Mood between Persons'. *Journal of Personality and Social Psychology*, 79 (2000), 211–23.

42. The limbic system was first described by Paul MacLean in 1949. For a good discussion, see Eichenbaum, *The Cognitive Neuroscience of Memory* (Oxford: Oxford University Press, 2002), 264–5.

43. A number of studies related to how eyebrows and the mouth express emotion are reported in D. Linquist and A. Öhman, 'Caught by the Evil Eye: Nonconscious Information Processing, Emotion, and Attention to Facial Stimuli', in L.F. Barnett, P.M. Niedenthal, and P. Winkleman (eds) *Emotion and Consciousness* (New York: The Guilford Press, 2005), 97–122.

44. An excellent discussion of emotion and facial expression is offered by one of the foremost researchers in the field, Paul Ekman, in *Recognizing Faces and Feelings to Improve Communication and Emotional Life* (New York: Time Books, 2003).

45. The implications of this and emotion in general for advertising is discussed by L. Percy in 'Unconscious Processing of Advertising and its Effects upon Attitude and Behaviour', in S. Diehl and R. Terlutter (eds), *International Advertising and Communication* (Wiesbaden: Deutschen-Universitäts-Verlag, 2006), 110–21.

46. See B. Wicker, C. Keysus, J. Plailly, Jean-Pierre Royet, V. Gallese, and G. Rizzolatti, 'Both of Us in *My* Insula: The Common Neural Bias of Seeing and Feeling Disgust', *Neuron*, 4 (2003), 655–64.

47. John R. Rossiter and Steven Bellman, 'A Proposed Model for Explaining and Measuring Web Ad Effectiveness', *Journal of Current Issues and Research in Advertising*, 21/1 (1999), 13–31.

Visit the Online Resource Centre that accompanies this book for additional resources to support the text: **www.oxfordtextbooks.co.uk/orc/percy_elliott4e/**

Creative Tactics

Key concepts

1. There are a number of general creative tactics based upon how the mind processes words and pictures that will help to increase attention and learning.
2. There are also specific creative tactics that can be used to help to minimize the 'imperfections' of memory and help to increase memory for advertising messages.
3. Creative tactics for brand awareness strategies must take into account the differences between recognition and recall brand awareness objectives.
4. When dealing with informational brand attitude strategies the key creative tactic is how the benefit claim support is presented and the key creative tactic for transformational brand attitude strategies is the emotional portrayal.

Up to this point we have been concerned with communication strategy, and our focus has been on '*what* to say' in advertising and other forms of marketing communication. In this chapter we will turn our attention to '*how* to say it'. Creative tactics deal with the ways in which words and pictures are used in marketing communication to deliver the message. As we shall see, this is a much more involved issue than it might appear on the surface, because meaning in communication is dependent upon many things beyond the obvious content of the message. For example, the semantic and grammatical structure of copy can have a significant effect upon how well a message will be understood, as well as the way in which visual illustrations are presented.

The reason it is so important to understand this sort of thing is that the easier we make it for our target audience to process and understand our message, the more likely we are to achieve the desired communication effect. You will remember that in Chapter 4 we talked about a communication response sequence and McGuire's notion of compound probabilities. After exposure, the next step in the response sequence is *processing*. The more people who *correctly* process the message, the greater the number of people likely to make a positive response to the message. We talked more about processing in Chapter 11. After someone has paid attention to an advert or other marketing communication, it is then necessary for him or her to *learn* what we wish to communicate, and, when dealing with high-involvement decisions, to *accept* the message as well (what McGuire calls 'yielding').

In this chapter we will be discussing a number of general principles concerning how to use words and pictures to optimize attention and learning. It is important to remember as we discuss these principles that they are not immutable laws. They represent the results of research in the areas of psycholinguistics and visual imagery, and we know that, when they are followed, the likelihood of attention and learning increases. But this is not to say that they must be followed in all circumstances for advertising to be effective. Adverts are made up of a rich combination of words and pictures, and their creative use can sometimes produce interactions between and among the words and pictures that 'override' a particular principle.

The principles hold generally, and should always be a starting point, but they should not be used out-of-hand to dismiss a creative idea. However, when not following one of these principles, it is *essential* to test the creative in order to be sure it is effective even though it is not following a particular linguistic or imagery principle. After we have discussed these general principles, we will be looking more specifically at the creative tactics needed to effect the correct brand awareness and brand attitude communication objectives.

Tactics for Attention

When we consider what creative tactics can help to maximize attention, particularly *initial* attention, we must be concerned not only with how the advertising or other marketing communication is put together, but also the effect of the creative unit chosen. Creative units are such things as the size of a print advert (for example, full page, half page, two-page spread) or the length of a radio or television commercial (for example, 15, 30, or 60 seconds). In many ways the creative unit is important in media planning, but first and foremost it is a *tactical creative* decision. The creative unit must be considered in terms of the best way in which to deliver the message, not to satisfy a media plan.

In fact, long ago Rossiter showed that as much as half of the variation among print adverts, in terms of their ability to attract and hold attention, is accounted for by the advertising's *structure*. It is a print advert's length, size, and pattern layout, *not* its message content, that has the greatest effect upon attention.[1]

Creative Units and Attention

The most important factor in terms of creative units for generating attention in radio and television advertising is the length of the commercial. Attention to both radio and television commercials is directly related to length. Longer commercials stimulate greater attention than shorter ones, but the relationship is not proportional. On average, the typical 30-second television commercial (while admitting the difficulty in defining a 'typical' 30-second commercial) will attract the attention of about 65 per cent of the viewing audiences. But while a 60-second commercial will gain more attention than a 30-second commercial, the increase in attention is only about 20 per cent, not double, and while a 15-second commercial attracts less attention than a 30-second commercial, it will generate about 80 per cent of the attention of a 30-second commercial, not merely half.[2]

Maintaining interest in television commercials—that is, *holding* attention—requires a different presentation pattern for informational versus transformational executions. With informational commercials, we want to stimulate immediate interest in the 'problem' as presented, followed by a brief pause in the action as the brand's identity is established, then building to a peak again as the 'solution' via the brand is established. With transformational executions, we want the interest to build throughout the commercial, peaking at the end with strong brand identity. This follows the idea of human evaluative conditioning, which underlies how transformational advertising tends to work.[3]

Table 12.1 Advert Size and Attention

Advert size	Attention index	
	Consumer and business magazine adverts	Newspaper adverts
2 Pages	1.3	1.2
1 Page	1.0	1.0
1/2 Page	0.7	0.7
1/4 Page	–	0.5

Source: Adapted from J.R. Rossiter and L. Percy, *Advertising Communication and Promotion Management* (New York: McGraw-Hill, 1997).

This same rule of thumb also applies to print advertising. Larger ads tend to attract more attention than smaller ads, but not proportionately. Table 12.1 demonstrates this general rule for newspaper and magazine adverts.[4]

Word and Picture Influence on Attention

The key to attention in print-based marketing communication is the words chosen and the illustration; with broadcast communication, it is the initial audio (words or music); with television or the Internet, the visuals. The reality of advertising and most other marketing communication is that people simply are not inclined to pay attention. Why should they? It is the job of good advertising to draw attention to itself, and in so doing to communicate quickly at the very least a good positive brand attitude, and to *resonate* with the target audience. Good strategy helps to increase the likelihood of resonance, but the appropriate creative tactics help to ensure it. What we mean by 'resonance' is a recognition by the target audience that a particular advert is talking to it about something with which it is concerned. If you are not in the target audience, the advertising is unlikely to resonate, but it should leave a positive feeling for the brand. All of this must occur during the attentional response.

In order to maximize the likelihood of gaining attention, marketing communication must pay careful attention to the ways in which the words in a headline or subhead and in the initial audio of broadcast advertising are used, and how the visuals and video are presented. In this section we will review some of the things we know about how words and pictures can help to attract attention (see Table 12.2).

Attention and Words

In a very insightful analysis of words in advertising, Greg Myers has pointed out that 'when there are many ads competing for the audience's attention, there is an enormous pressure on finding patterns of language that are unusual or memorable'.[5] He goes on to suggest that one of the simplest ways in which to call attention to words in marketing communication, at least with the printed word, is to use unexpected letters. This can be accomplished, for example, by using infrequently encountered letters, such as *q*, *x*, or *z* (think of brands such as Exxon or Oxo), or by deliberately altering the spelling of words ('Smooooth!').

Table 12.2 How to Use Words and Pictures to Gain Attention

Words	• Use unexpected words or infrequently used letters such as Q, X, or Z • Vary emphasis or stress of certain words in headlines or audio content, or use them in unexpected ways • Keep headlines to fewer than 7–8 words
Pictures	• Use larger pictures • Use colour • Keep visual cuts in commercials to fewer than 20 per 30-second advert • Use pictures that hold attention for at least 2 seconds

You are no doubt familiar with the logo for French Connection UK. The FCUK logo attracts and holds attention because of the unexpectedness of what is first 'seen', and then the realization that it is not what the mind originally understood the word to be. While still somewhat controversial, it is a very good example of using something unexpected to gain attention.

Another good example is the advert for Newcastle Brown Ale shown in Plate XI. The headline 'Flavourrefreshment' provides a really good use of something unexpected in an execution in order to attract, and importantly, hold attention. Tying 'flavour' and 'refreshment' together engages the mind in initially wondering what the word means, then the satisfaction with figuring it out, and with that communicating the benefit. This is then linked to the brand via strong package identification.

Another way in which to draw attention to advertising is to vary the emphasis or stress of certain words in a headline or in the audio content of commercials, or to use them in unexpected ways. Our ear is accustomed to hearing things in a particular way and, when it confronts something unexpected, we pay attention. For example, in normal conversation, we are not likely to emphasize conjunctions such as *or* and *and*. But if the emphasis is placed on a conjunction, it is likely to attract your attention because you are not used to hearing this. Consider this line from a Baxters soup advert:

> What makes Baxters soup is what makes it

Now, suppose you heard the line as follows (or even saw it printed this way as a headline):

> What makes Baxters soup IS what makes it

The unexpected emphasis on *is* draws attention not only to the line, but also to the *relationship* between 'What makes Baxters soup' and its ingredients, 'what makes it'.

Headline Length

Another aspect of how words can influence attention to printed marketing communication is the *length* of the headline. Psychologists have found that when the number of words in a sentence or phrase is fewer than seven or eight, all that is required to understand what is there is simply exposure.[6] You do not really need to *read* the words to know what they say, only to *see* them. Look at this headline:

IF ONLY FINDING YOUR **DREAM** MAN WAS AS EASY
AS FINDING YOUR **DREAM** FOUNDATION

If you only glance at this headline, all that you really 'see' is a block of words, perhaps picking out one or two. Most people looking at this briefly will 'see' only the word 'dream' that because it is in bold type, and perhaps 'if only', 'man', and 'foundation' given their outside positions. To get any meaning from this headline you must *read* it. Now, look at this headline:

Let in the 'breze

Just glancing at this conveys the full content. It is not necessary to 'read' it to understand what it says. This is because the mind processes text not one word at a time, but in sets as you read.

This means that, when you turn the page of a newspaper or magazine, the reflexive attention that you automatically pay briefly to the new page to decide whether or not there is anything there worth paying particular attention to is sufficient to comprehend a headline if it is short enough. This is especially important for poster and outdoor adverts. To work, they must be able to communicate at a glance.

Attention and Pictures

As you might imagine, pictures play a more important role in gaining attention than do words. This is especially true of print advertising.[7] In fact, the average time spent looking at a magazine advert is about 1.65 seconds, and 70 per cent of that time is spent with the picture.[8] Without an effective picture to attract readers' attention and draw them to the text, it is unlikely that the advertising will work. The size of the picture and the use of colour can significantly affect the ability of a print advert to attract attention. In terms of picture size, the larger the image, the more effective it will be. There is an old rule of thumb in advertising that recognition of print adverts increases roughly with the square root of the size of the picture. In other words, if you increase the size of the picture in an advert four times, attention will double. While this holds for all print adverts, with high-involvement executions, in addition to one dominant focal point, there should be a short headline designed to engage the reader's attention and make him or her want to read the advert.

Regarding the use of colour, in both magazines and newspapers, full-colour draws more attention than two-colour, and two-colour more attention than black-and-white. While it is sometimes argued that using black-and-white adverts in a magazine in which all of the other advertising is in colour will attract more attention because it will stand out, there is no real proof that this is the case. Table 12.3 summarizes the probable difference in attention to an advert in both magazines and newspapers in terms of colour. For magazine adverts, attention to a black-and-white advert is likely to be about 30 per cent less than to a standard four-colour advert, and 20 per cent less than to a two-colour advert. With newspapers, the use of two colours tends to increase attention 50 per cent over a standard black-and-white advert; the use of four colours, 80 per cent. While these estimates may be somewhat overstated for full-colour, there is still no question that colour will be significantly more effective. Again, this argues against the notion of using a black-and-white advert to stand out in an otherwise full-colour newspaper format.

Table 12.3 Colour and Attention

Colour	Attention index	
	Consumer and business magazine adverts	Newspaper adverts
Four-colour	1.0	1.8
Two-colour	0.8	1.5
Black and white	0.7	1.0

Source: Adapted from J.R. Rossiter and L. Percy, *Advertising Communication and Promotion Management* (New York: McGraw-Hill, 1997).

Pictures, of course, dominate almost all television commercials. In terms of attention, an important consideration is the pacing of the scenes in the commercial. There has been a great deal of talk in recent years about the so-called MTV generation, and how young audiences are used to, and demand, rather frantic, fast-cut editing of visual content. Unfortunately, when the average scene time drops, so too does attention. In fact, at an 'MTV rate' of twenty or more cuts per 30-second commercial, the attention loss is about 17 per cent. And, even more interestingly, the loss of attention is an even *greater* 25 per cent among that very 18–34-year-old MTV generation.[9]

However, it should be pointed out that fast cuts can increase arousal during processing, which is helpful for transformational advertising. In our discussion of emotion in Chapter 11, we talked about how it facilitates attention, especially at high levels of arousal. Given the importance of emotional responses to transformational advertising, careful use of fast cuts might be considered. But this is *not* true for informational strategies because fast cuts make it difficult to process benefit claims if the structure of the commercial is changing at the same time.[10]

Before leaving the subject of pictures and attention, it is important to understand that it is not enough to look for pictures that will attract attention; pictures must *hold* attention. The advert for Cymex shown in Plate XII is a very good example of using a strong visual image to both attract and hold attention, and, importantly, an image that is linked to the product benefit. It will 'help kiss your cold sore goodbye.'

A number of psychological experiments have shown that pictures are recognized and remembered best if they can hold the reader's attention for at least two seconds.[11] This helps to explain why attention to television commercials drops when cuts in the visual come too rapidly. Remember too that attention is only the first step in the processing of marketing communication. Attention means very little in and of itself if it does not lead to fuller processing of the message *for the target audience*.

Attention and Music

Music is frequently a part of broadcast advertising, and in general, does seem to have a positive effect upon attention. But not just any music will do. One should be careful to ensure there is congruity between both the execution[12] and, if a radio commercial, the station's format. At the same time, popular songs should generally be avoided, unless the words to the song are not easily remembered. Otherwise, the target audience will be more likely to sing the words of the song to themselves rather than rehearse the brand name and key benefit.[13]

Music can also have a significant effect upon sales in a retail setting. There have been several studies that have shown that appropriate music will have a positive influence on sales. In one study, the tempo of the music played in a supermarket was varied between an 'easy listening' tempo of 60 beats per minute (bpm) and a 'rock' tempo of 120 bpm. Sales were 38 per cent higher with the 60 bpm tempo!.[14] One possible reason for this could be that 60 bpm is the resting heart rate of the average person. Another study has shown that the content of music, as well as tempo, can influence sales.[15]

Tactics for Learning

We know that, for any marketing communication to be successful, once someone has been exposed to it and has paid attention, he or she must fully process the message if the marketer is to achieve the desired communication effect. William J. McGuire, perhaps the foremost expert on attitude change theory, about whom we talked when we discussed the communication response sequence in Chapter 4, once remarked about communicating with advertising that it is not enough to lead a horse to water, you must push his head under to get him to drink.[16] Anything we can do to help to make it easier for our target audience to process our message makes it more likely that it will be correctly understood, and more likely that we will achieve the desired communication effect.

The words and pictures that we use obviously play the most important role in delivering the message, but *how* we use them can provide a real plus. A great deal of research has been done in this area, especially by psycholinguists and psychologists working in visual imagery, providing insight into the ways in which words and pictures can be used to facilitate learning. As we know, learning is essential for all marketing communication. In this section we will review a number of specific ways in which to use words and pictures to increase the likelihood that our target audience will learn what we want them to from our advertising or other marketing communication.

Words and Learning

It may seem almost too obvious to suggest that you must pay attention to what you say in advertising copy if it is to be understood. While this is certainly true, less obvious is the effect the way in which words are used may have on how they are understood. The often complex relationship between the linguistic construction of copy and the way in which the mind deals with it in processing the message is known as psycholinguistics.

We talked in a previous section about using words in unexpected ways to help to attract attention. While this will certainly help to gain attention, unfortunately the use of unfamiliar words in copy can get in the way of learning. There are literally dozens of studies that have shown that using familiar words in familiar ways helps learning.[17] This illustrates a problem McGuire identified long ago. Often the things that help to attract attention in communication are the very things that get in the way of comprehension or acceptance of the message.[18] What this means for us is that, while we may want to use an unfamiliar word or to use words in an unexpected way as part of a headline to gain attention, we do not want this in the subheads or copy, where learning is the objective.

Concrete, High-Imagery Words

One interesting concept in psycholinguistics that has a direct bearing upon copy in marketing communication, especially in advertising, is the notion of the 'concreteness' of the words used. Concrete words are generally described as those that refer to objects, persons, places, or things that can be experienced by the senses; those that do not are called abstract. Concrete words are more effective than abstract words in communicating ideas, and are better remembered.

The reason why concrete words help with learning is that they tend to arouse mental images quickly and easily.[19] While it is certainly not impossible, strictly speaking, for more abstract words to evoke visual images, it is a lot less likely. Consider the following headlines taken from adverts in a UK women's magazine:

Because it really matters
For skin this soft
Some days matter

Which of these headlines bring a visual image to mind? Most likely only 'For skin this soft'. This is concrete, while the others are more abstract. You can 'see' or imagine soft skin, but it is more difficult to focus upon a specific image for 'Because it really matters' or 'Some days matter'. Imagery value is important in facilitating easier communication and learning.[20]

Using Negatives

Overall, people are much more likely to make favourable rather than unfavourable judgements. As a result, in every language, for example, there are far more favourable than unfavourable adjectives. Additionally, a lot of research has shown that negative words or constructs are difficult to process, and should be avoided in communication. To understand the meaning of negative words or constructions requires a two-step process: you must recognize the negative for what it is, then 'reverse' the meaning. As a result, there is a chance that someone may misunderstand or overlook the negative while processing the message.

Consider this headline from a cruise line advert:

This is not a normal day

What the mind must do is consider first what is a 'normal day', then negate it—assuming that the eye picked up *not*, and didn't skim over it. You may be thinking to yourself that this is making a lot out of very little. After all, who is likely to misunderstand? Not many, we would hope, but some will. It depends upon the focus.

In an interesting study dealing with just this issue, it was found that, when two claims are made and one is stated in the negative, misunderstanding is greater when the negative claim is second.[21] People were asked to read one of the following headlines, and to decide whether taste or calories was the main emphasis (and to the advertiser, the answer was taste):

It's the taste that counts, not just the calories
It's not just the calories, it's the taste that counts

The number of people correctly saying 'taste' was only 77 per cent in the first example versus 85 per cent in the second. This is because the negative claim in the second example is not necessary to process the claim correctly, but it must be processed in the first example. Again, you may be thinking this is not much of a difference, but remember we need to ensure that the maximum number of people make it through the communication response sequence.

What do you make of this subhead from an advert for a skin cream for wrinkles around the eye?

> An innovation this big doesn't pass unnoticed

Here we have an example of two negatives in which one is *not* meant to negate the other. The intended meaning is that an innovation this big *will be noticed.* So why not say so directly? Why ask your target audience to go to the extra effort and time of dealing with the two steps needed to process negative constructions correctly? In fact, negative constructions are not often used in marketing communication, and for good reason.

Using Puns

Puns are a way of playing with meaning, and puns are often found in advertising. This is especially true of advertising in the UK, where both visual and verbal puns are often found in abundance. Look at these advert headlines from a single issue of a UK women's magazine:

> For a healthy diet—this Paper needs Fibre too!
> Anything less simply won't wash
> Have a shower with everything on
> Big cheeses on the board watch out
> When soap and water are out of reach

Without knowing the product being advertised, what do these headlines tell you? Even with the full advert in front of you, they require a lot of work, and that is the problem. Does it help you to know that these headlines advertise, respectively, the use of raw material in the paper industry, bathroom accessories, showers, cream cheese, and hand-cleaning gel? Perhaps a little, but not much.

Puns do require more work to process,[22] and, as we have said over and over in this chapter, our job is to make it *easier*, not harder, for the target audience to process our message. This is what facilitates learning. At the root of most puns are homonyms, words that have the same spelling or sound, but different meanings. (Did you know that the word 'taste' has some thirty-two meanings in *Webster's Unabridged Dictionary*?) Does this mean that we should never use puns? No, but if used, the meaning must be obvious and must reinforce the benefit. Ultra Chloraseptic's advert for its anaesthetic throat spray does get it right with the headline:

> Don't be a sucker . . . Spray

The word 'sucker' is appropriate both in its meaning of not being a 'fool' and not using throat medication that is like a boiled sweet.

Sentence Structure

The issue of how sentences are put together has a real impact upon how easy it will be to process marketing communication, and the likelihood that correct learning will occur. Unfortunately, it is beyond the scope of this book to go very deeply into this, because it is a very complex area. In fact, many of those who have studied it find it a very complicated subject with which to deal.[23]

It is important that we understand that there can be difficulties when sentence structure becomes more complicated, even with such a seemingly simple thing as where a clause is placed. To avoid potential problems, keep things *simple*. For example, we know that it is much easier to process and understand active than passive sentences. Researchers have found that passive sentences take longer to process correctly, and the likelihood of understanding passive sentences tends to be lower.

Let's look at this subhead:

> A fluoride supplement should be taken by children living in non-fluoride water areas

This is written in the passive voice. The grammatical subject is actually the psychological object. In effect, the passive construction has reversed the order in which words are usually encountered. We know that human memory is affected greatly by the order in which words are encountered. What if this were written in the active voice?

> Children living in non-fluoride water areas should take a fluoride supplement

While the meaning of both sentences is the same, the active construction will be easier to process. In addition, the main focus of the sentence, 'children living in non-fluoride water areas', is encountered first, and that will provide the desired cue in memory for fluoride supplements. If you were living in a non-fluoride water area and had children, which of these sentences would be most likely to catch your eye if you were flipping through a magazine containing this advert? You are much more likely to pay attention to something about your children than something about fluoride supplements, and that is how we want learning and memory to occur. We want the parent to learn 'my children need a fluoride supplement', *not* 'fluoride supplements are for my children'.

The form of a sentence itself can also aid message processing. Myers provides the example of the following Mars bar slogan:

> A Mars® a Day Helps You Work Rest and Play

He points out that this slogan will be memorable primarily because it draws attention to its *focus*. It establishes a rhythm, and it rhymes 'play' with 'day'. Also, of course, it echoes the old saying that 'An apple a day keeps the doctor away'.[24]

Another possible way in which sentences can help to facilitate processing of a message is by suggesting a personal, face-to-face interaction between the reader or viewer and the advertising. When you use such things as questions or strong declarative statements, you imply a certain sense of one person talking to another.[25] Look at the following headlines:

> Your love just gave you platinum
> Jet-lag? What jet-lag?

Feel Fabulous
Has the secret passed your lips?
Wake up your makeup

Each of these headlines engages you in an almost personal conversation because of its use of a personal question or declarative statement. This sense of personal address will help to facilitate processing (even though several of these headlines have more words in them than one would like).

Look at the advert for Tourism Australia in Plate XIII. We have seen how a strong emotional response is needed for high-involvement, transformational advertising, and one for which the target can personally identify. The visual here does a good job of creating that feeling, but it is reinforced by the headline, which talks *directly to you*.

Pictures and Learning

While the old adage of a picture being worth a thousand words may not be literally true, there is certainly a well-understood superiority of pictures over words in learning.[26] In fact, with most print advertising, some 70 per cent of the looking at the advert is directed to the picture. One of the reasons for this superiority of pictures over words is the way in which people interact with pictures. As we have just noted, one of the ways in which words can be used to help to facilitate learning is by using strong declarative sentences or questions, because this tends to engage the reader. Pictures automatically engage the reader or viewer, but in a different way.

When we read a sentence or listen to dialogue, our minds tend to provide an answer or response in words. Pictures, on the other hand, have the ability to provoke a much more elaborate response. Myers offers a good example of this. You would no doubt be very sceptical if you were to read or hear a claim that a particular brand of soap could make anyone beautiful. But if this same claim were *implied* by a picture of a beautiful woman holding the soap, you would be a lot less sceptical.[27] Additional support for the superiority of pictures over words comes from work by Bryce and Yalch.[28] They showed that information conveyed visually is significantly better learned than the same information content conveyed in the audio. As we look at any picture, a relationship is established between the viewer and the image. This goes for any visual image, from adverts to great works of art. There will be something about the picture that draws us to it. Depending upon the image itself, we will imagine ourselves as either *part* of what is shown in the picture, or *outside* observing what is there. The space between the viewer and the actual picture is something Shearman has called *liminal space*, and it becomes in many ways an extension of the picture itself.[29] Why should we be concerned with such a seemingly abstract notion as the space in front of a picture? Because in certain cases we will want our target audience to feel it is present and a part of the situation depicted in the advertising, while in other cases we will want it to feel it is outside the situation. The execution of the illustration or visuals in the advertising will dictate how the viewer will feel, and this applies not only to print advertising, but also to television.[30]

Look at the advert for Rotari's Talento sparkling wine in Plate XVII. It provides a really good example of the viewer being included in the message. The imagery is clearly inviting you to be a part of the experience of Italian Tolento, and elicits a strong positive emotional response.

Myers offers an interesting observation along these lines. He reminds us that pictures provide a point of view in much the same way as pronouns do in language. When there are people in advertising, their positions and where they are looking is important to how we respond. Pictures can also suggest prior or future action, as well as context for evaluation.[31] Getting all of this consistent with the message is critical to effective processing. Myers also makes an interesting point about the gaze of principal figures in advertising. He suggests that, more often, you will find women in advertising looking out at the reader or viewer, while male figures are more likely to 'keep to their own business'.[32] This observation may be anecdotal, but it is interestingly consistent with the pop-psychology idea that women are more concerned with bonding when communicating with people, while men are more concerned with establishing dominance.

Next, we will turn our attention to five areas in which we know there are direct relationships between the picture and learning: the size of the picture, the use of colour, showing the product with users or in use, high-imagery pictures, and word–picture interaction.

Picture Size

We have already talked about how larger pictures tend to attract more attention. It also seems that the larger the picture, the more visual images the mind will generate, and this, in turn, leads to better learning.[33] Research has shown that picture size has a positive impact on beliefs and brand attitude. In fact, it would seem that the larger the picture, the more favourable your attitude towards the advertised product.[34]

There is only one print advertising situation in which picture size is not important: direct-response advertising with long copy. With direct-response advertising, memory is not a significant factor, because the target audience is expected to respond immediately. Also, since a lot of direct-response advertising involves high-involvement product decisions, a great deal of information is needed to convince the reader to make a decision 'right now'. Consequently, there is a necessary trade-off between the space needed for a larger picture and that needed for more detailed copy. But, in all other cases, the larger the picture, the better.

Colour versus Black-and-White

Just as with picture size, we saw earlier that colour positively influences the gaining of attention. But colour also has a significant effect upon processing generally. Some years ago two psychologists in the research laboratories of Xerox Corporation demonstrated that the principal effect of colour in communication is motivation.[35] If all you need to do is communicate information, black-and-white pictures could be enough. This means that you should *never* use black-and-white pictures with advertising addressing positive motives. However, with informational advertising, black-and-white can be quite effective.

Product and User

People are more likely to learn something from advertising if they can make a familiar association with its content. This is known as *associative learning*, and is aided by pictures that show the product being used in some way rather than leaving it up to the reader or viewer to infer interaction between the product and the user or how the product is used.[36] The importance of interactive pictures or visuals is underscored when we consider the motivation underlying behaviour. People often buy status goods or other products because they suggest a particular image with which they wish to be associated, as we saw when we discussed positive motives and transformational advertising. On the other hand, when you are dealing with negative motives and informational advertising, a product or brand must be seen as suitable for solving or avoiding a problem. Showing users interacting with a product, or seeing a product in use, helps to connect the product with the motive to purchase or use.

While it is quite common to find these types of interaction in television advertising, they are much less common in print. Too often we see a picture of a user or endorser next to, but not using, the product, or the context for usage is discussed in the copy, but not shown visually. It is important in print adverts as well as in television to show the brand being used. Look at the Brittany Ferries advert shown in Plate XIV. It provides a very good example of not only the product in use, but also the user enjoying the benefit. You can easily imagine yourself on the deck of a Brittany Ferry, beginning a holiday.

High-Imagery Pictures

We saw earlier that concrete, high-imagery words help to facilitate learning. The same is true of concrete or high-imagery pictures. More concrete, higher-imagery pictures are those that tend to arouse *other* mental images quickly and easily. They are more realistic than abstract, low-imagery pictures. These realistic pictures are probably superior for learning for at least two reasons. First of all, people can relate more to concrete representations than to abstract ones. This in turn is probably a function of their *imagery* value, regardless of their specific content. Secondly, because of something psychologists call *dual coding*, people can more easily attach a verbal label to realistic visuals. Older children and adults automatically assign verbal labels to all but the most complex and novel pictures, and thus 'double-code' them in their minds as both picture *and* words.[37] For example, if you were to see a picture of an apple, you would encode not only the image of the apple in your mind, but also the label 'apple'.

Many television ads use animation, and often you see cartoons or drawings in print adverts. This can in fact be very realistic because of its simplified rendering of its subject. Using this technique can basically 'strip' its subject to its essential denotative characters, making them very concrete.[38]

Word–Picture Interaction

In a very interesting study it was found that learning is significantly increased if the eye confronts a *picture–word* rather than a *word–picture* sequence.[39] This may seem to imply that you should always place the headline in an advert towards the bottom of the page so that the picture will be easily seen first, but this is not necessary. The eye is generally drawn initially to an illustration, so an effective use of the picture relative to the headline will ensure that it is seen first, regardless of where the headline is placed. Look at the advert for Fairy non-biological detergent (shown in Plate XIX). There is no question that the eye goes first to the picture, then to the headline at the top of the page. Even though the headline is positioned first, its size relative to the picture means the eye is drawn first to the picture. What happens is that, when the picture is seen first, it tends to draw the reader into the advert to maximize communication,

Table 12.4 How to Use Words and Pictures to Help Learning

Words	• Use familiar words • Use concrete, high-imagery words • Avoid negatives • Be careful with puns • Keep sentences simple • Avoid passive sentences • Suggest a personal interaction with the advertising
Pictures	• Be certain picture is consistent with intention for viewer to be included or as observer • The larger the picture, the better • Use colour unless you only need to provide information • Show product being used or with user • Use high-imagery, concrete pictures or illustrations • Use pictures so that they are seen before words

and, as a result, facilitates learning. This same point also applies to television. Important spoken copy-points or printed 'supers' should either be *preceded* by an appropriate visual introduction or introduced simultaneously.

The advert for Colron Refined Danish Oil in Plate XVI offers a very good example of each of the points just discussed for using pictures to help to facilitate learning. In terms of Shearman's idea of liminal space, appropriately you are meant to be 'outside' of the action, observing the loveseat that was polished with the product. The picture is large, and dominates the page (without filling it); its unique imagery encourages visual elaboration to wood furniture of your own. The use of colour is especially well done, drawing attention to the wood. Even though this is an information-driven decision, the effective use of colour within the white space reinforces the benefit. The product is also shown 'in use', resulting in the 'beautiful wood sheen lustre' on the loveseat. As mentioned above, it uses a high-imagery picture, and the eye moves first to the picture, and then to the copy. This is an excellent example of how a strong and compelling visual image can be used to quickly and easily communicate a benefit, and link it to the brand.

Tables 12.2 and 12.4 summarize how words and pictures are used to maximize attention to, and the learning of, marketing communication.

Minimizing Problems with Memory

In Chapter 11 we spent a good deal of time talking about memory, and discussed a number of problems inherent in how memory works that can interfere with successful remembering. However, because we are aware of these problems, there are a number of creative tactics that can be utilized to help to minimize them.

Table 12.5 Creative Tactics for Minimizing Memory Problems

Minimizing misattribution	• Create a unique brand-benefit claim link
Minimizing absent-mindedness	• Establish links in memory to appropriate category need • Use distinctive cues not likely to be associated with other long-term memories • Ensure a consistent 'look and feel' over time to encourage familiarity
Minimizing blocking	• Make sure the link to category need is well integrated with *obvious* associations
Minimizing transience	• Ensure message is carefully integrated with how brand is understood • Encourage elaboration of points the target audience is interested in remembering
Minimizing bias	• Imply positive brand attitudes are of long standing • Use personal references, especially to positive memories

Perhaps the most important tactical consideration is to ensure there is a *unique* brand-benefit link established to avoid misattribution of the message to another brand. To help to get around absent-mindedness, use distinctive cues not likely to be associated with other long-term memories, and ensure a consistent 'look and feel' over time to encourage familiarity (a subject that we will cover in more detail in Chapter 13).

Also, to help to avoid problems with absent-mindedness, establish links in memory to the appropriate category need. Make sure that those links are well integrated with *obvious* associations to the category need to avoid blocking, as well as to tie the brand to appropriate emotions. Making sure that the message is carefully integrated with how the brand is understood will help avoid transience, as will encouraging elaboration by the target audience of points they are interested in remembering. Using personal references, especially to positive memories, and implying current positive brand attitudes are of long standing, are ways in which to help to capitalize upon memory bias.[40] These tactics are summarized in Table 12.5.

Brand Awareness and Brand Attitude Creative Tactics

Throughout this book we have discussed the importance of brand awareness and brand attitude as communication objectives for all marketing communication. In Chapter 11 we specifically addressed this issue. Because of the nature of recognition versus recall brand awareness and the differences in the four strategic brand attitude quadrants of the Rossiter–Percy grid, certain specific creative tactics are needed to ensure that you will achieve these communication objectives.

Brand Awareness Creative Tactics

The number one task of brand awareness is to associate the *brand* with category need in the target audience's mind. As we have seen, brand awareness as a communication objective is more than simply being aware of the brand. The brand must be linked to the appropriate need in the target audience's mind when that need occurs. But before that can happen, marketing communication, and advertising in particular, must first be seen as 'belonging' to your brand. This is the only way in which the message can be associated with the brand. This may seem almost childishly obvious, but how often have you thought about a particular advert, perhaps because it was entertaining or unique in some way, but been unable to remember the brand being advertised?

Only after you are sure that the message is firmly linked with the brand are you ready to address the issue of recognition versus recall brand awareness. You will remember from Chapter 11 that the appropriate brand awareness objective is dependent upon the *choice situation*. When and how the brand choice is made dictates a recognition or recall brand awareness strategy, and what is needed to implement each strategy differs, as we discussed.

Recognition Brand Awareness

When the brand choice is activated at the point of purchase, such as when shopping at a supermarket or pharmacy, recognizing the brand in the store will remind the shopper of a need. This means that in advertising the creative execution must show the package as it will be seen at the point of purchase, and the category need must be obvious. Some advertisers for fmcgs actually create an advert that quite literally looks like the package. Even though there is some brief copy, the overall impression is one of the package itself as it will be encountered at the point of purchase.

Recall Brand Awareness

When the target audience must think of the brand prior to the point of purchase, the brand awareness objective is recall. A need occurs, and you must think of brands that might possibly meet that need. This means that the creative execution must *clearly* link the need to the brand, *in that order*, and *repeat* the association. It also helps to personalize the association between the need and the brand. This is very easy to accomplish in radio and television advertising, but it is also needed in print when recall brand awareness is necessary.

These creative tactics for implementing brand awareness strategy are summarized in Table 12.6.

Brand Attitude Creative Tactics

The creative tactics needed for brand awareness help to link the brand to the need. The creative tactics for brand attitude help to *persuade* the target audience that your brand is the best alternative for satisfying the need.[41] In our discussions of brand attitude we referred to the expectancy-value model of attitude, in which attitude towards an object

Table 12.6 Brand Awareness Creative Tactics

Recognition	• Package must be shown as seen at the point of purchase • Category need must be obvious
Recall	• Category need must be clearly linked to the brand, and in that order • Repeat the association • Personalize the association between the need and the brand

Source: Adapted from J.R. Rossiter and L. Percy, *Advertising Communication and Promotion Management* (New York: McGraw-Hill, 1997).

(a brand in our case) is made up of what you believe about it weighted by the emotional importance attached to those beliefs, combined to form your overall attitude towards the brand. These same two considerations, beliefs and emotions, structure the creative tactics to be used to maximize brand attitude. Remember from our discussion in Chapter 9 of brand attitude strategy that, when dealing with informational brand attitude strategies, we must be primarily concerned with the information being provided; when dealing with transformational brand strategies, we must be primarily concerned with the emotion portrayed in the advertising.

Informational Brand Attitude

With informational brand attitude strategies, the key is how the *benefit claim support* is presented. When the decision is low involvement, you want to use a simple problem-solution presentation of one or possibly two benefits. Since the decision is low involvement, use *extreme* benefit claims, such as:

Automatically irresistible
Improvements are immediate

Why? Because the message does not need to be accepted as literally true. All that is necessary is what Maloney years ago called 'curious disbelie'.[42] There is little risk involved in the choice decision, so you can exaggerate the benefit in order to tempt the audience to purchase. It is not necessary that you really believe that a pain relief gel will literally work better than any other gel or that a moisturizer will really give you 'amazing' skin. You need feel only that the products *might* provide those benefits. If they do not meet your expectations, you simply do not repurchase.

The advert for Anthisan shown in Plate XV provides a really good example of this idea of 'curious disbelief'. Will Anthisan really take the sting out of insect bites? The strong visual certainly illustrates this in the extreme, and makes the point. Why not try it and see if it really does?

But when you are dealing with a high-involvement decision, you should *not* overclaim, but keep the claim at an acceptable upper level. The benefit claims must be believable because the message must be accepted. The following benefit claims appeared in an advert for a washing machine:

Load capacity that's 50% bigger than most
Extra large door and a tilted drum for easy loading
Specialized duvet cycle will cut out those trips to local dry cleaners

To be successful, the target audience must accept these claims as basically true. They are certainly pitched at an upper level of believability, especially the claim about cutting out trips to the cleaners. Because a washer is a high-risk purchase, for someone to consider this brand, he or she must believe the substance of these claims.

Really this means that, to ensure a *convincing* presentation of the benefit claims, it is essential to understand what the target audience's attitudes are towards the products in the category and the brands within the category. Following our example, does the target audience believe that it is possible for a washing machine to clean duvets? What about this brand? What is its reputation for reliability? For the benefit claims to be effective with high-involvement informational advertising, they must be within an acceptable range of believability among the target audience.

If you can actually deliver on a benefit, but the target audience finds it too far beyond its latitude of acceptance to believe, consider using a refutational strategy. With refutational advertising, the message begins by acknowledging that the target audience does not believe the benefit claim, but then goes on to provide evidence to 'refute' or counter its disbelief. By acknowledging that people do not accept your claim, you begin by having them agree with you rather than immediately reject the message. This then gives you an opportunity to build your case. Once it has been made, repeat the benefit claim firmly.[43]

In all cases, with informational brand attitude strategies, the creative presentation of the benefit should follow an $a \rightarrow c$ or $e^- \rightarrow c$ benefit focus (objective attribute supports a subjective claim for the brand, or a negative emotion associated with a problem is resolved by a subjective characteristic associated with the brand). Looking back at the Whirlpool advert in Chapter 11 (Advert 11.1), which reflects a high-involvement informational brand attitude strategy, we see an $a \rightarrow c$ benefit focus: 'The biggest door opening in the market' (a) is why it claims to be 'easier to unload' (c). The advert for Fairy laundry detergent (Plate XIX), which reflects a low-involvement informational brand attitude strategy, uses an $e^- \rightarrow c$ benefit focus: the negative feelings that are associated with 'prickly' clothes (e^-) are resolved by Fairy's 'soft' claim (c). In the low-involvement case only, a simple presentation of the benefit as a subjective characteristic of the product may also be considered as a benefit focus (c), as we see in the Anthisan advert (Plate XV): 'Take the sting our of insect bites and nettle rash'.

The benefit should be presented in such a way that it is instantly clear what the benefit is when it is a claim about a subjective characteristic of the brand (c), that the connection is easily understood when an attribute of the product is offered in support of a claim about a subjective characteristic ($a \rightarrow c$), or that a claim about a subjective characteristic of the product is easily seen as resolving a negative emotional state associated with the product category ($e^- \rightarrow c$).

The creative tactics for informational brand attitude strategies are summarized in Box 12.1.

Key is the benefit claim support

- Present the problem first, resolved by brand.
- Use only one or possibly two benefit claims for **low-involvement** decisions.
- Present benefit claims in the extreme for **low-involvement** decisions.
- Be careful not to overclaim for **high-involvement** decisions, staying within the target audience's acceptable level of attitude toward the category, product, and brand.
- Consider a refutational approach if the brand can deliver the benefit, but the target audience does not believe it.
- Ensure that the execution elicits an emotional sequence that first associates the problem with some level of fear or anxiety, and then delivers a sense of relief as the brand provides the solution.
- Utilize an **a** $\rightarrow$ **c** or **e**$^{-}$ $\rightarrow$ **c** benefit focus; or, for **low-involvement** decisions, a simple presentation as **c**, a subjective characteristic of the brand.

Box 12.1 Creative Tactics for Informational Brand Attitude Strategies

Transformational Brand Attitude

The key creative tactic for transformational brand attitude strategies is the emotional portrayal. With transformational strategies, the feelings evoked by the advertising are often the only brand benefit. As a result, it is absolutely essential that the creative execution be *unique* to the brand. Additionally, the target audience must like the advertising. Unlike advertising for informational strategies, in which it is not really necessary actually to like the advertising per se because the execution embodies the benefit, in transformational advertising, you must like the advertising to like the brand.[44]

Because this idea of a correct emotional portrayal is so important to transformational advertising, we will take a closer look at just what this means. When you look at a good advert for perfume or fashion, you want to *imagine yourself* as being similar to the person in the advert. If you can see yourself (or your imagined self) in the advertising, the emotional portrayal is authentic and that feeling you get becomes the benefit for the brand.

Emotional authenticity is required for both low- and high-involvement transformational brand attitude strategies. In the high-involvement case, the emotional authenticity should be tailored to the lifestyle group to which the target audience belongs or to which they aspire. This will help the target audience to *personally* identify with the emotional portrayal, a necessary condition because of the risk involved in the decisions. With high-involvement transformational strategies, because of the risk involved it may be necessary to provide some more tangible information to help to facilitate acceptance of the message, as we discussed back in Chapter 9 when considering strategies for implementing high-involvement transformational strategies. When doing this, it is often useful to overclaim a bit, but you must be careful not to go too far.

With transformational brand attitude strategies the creative presentation of the benefit should follow either a c $\rightarrow$ e^{+} or e^{+} brand benefit focus (subjective characteristic of the brand elicits positive emotion or purely a positive emotion). Looking back at the Nescafé Gold Blend coffee advert in Chapter 9 (Advert 9.4), which reflects a low-involvement transformational brand attitude strategy, there is a c $\rightarrow$ e^{+} focus on the benefit: the 'golden aroma' (c) will put

Key is the emotional portrayal

- Creative execution must be unique to the brand, employing a strong visual component.
- The target audience must like the advertising.
- The emotional portrayal must seem authentic, eliciting a strong positive emotional response consistent with the motivation involved.
- Some information may be needed for high-involvement decisions.
- Utilize a **c** $\rightarrow$ **e**$^+$ or **e**$^+$ benefit focus leading directly to the appropriate emotional response.

Box 12.2 Creative Tactics for Transformational Brand Attitude Strategies

you in a state of pure bliss (e$^+$). The advert for Heal's (Plate XVIII) is pure emotion (e$^+$): owning something from Heal's will quite literally make you feel 'Head over Heals' (e$^+$). Because transformational brand attitude strategies depend upon a positive emotional end state, the benefit focus in the creative execution must lead the target audience directly to the appropriate emotional response. These creative tactics for transformational brand attitude strategies are summarized in Box 12.2.

The advert for Heal's in many ways provides a good summary of what we have been talking about in this chapter. The creative tactics all work together, and facilitate both the processing and the acceptance of the message. The visual and verbal elements work together, reflecting the appropriate use of words and pictures which we talked about early in the chapter. Both the surprisingly inverted headlines, and the congruence between the brand, Heal's, and the visual imagery of a 'dog' at heel, helps to attract and hold attention. The advert illustrates the tactics needed for a successful high-involvement, transformational brand attitude strategy. It is emotionally authentic and the target audience can personally identify with the imagery. The 'attitude' portrayed is real. You can imagine yourself in the picture (if you see yourself as part of the target audience). Everything here works well towards building a positive brand attitude.

Brand Attitude Creative Tactics and Emotion

In Chapter 11 we learned that emotion helps to mediate the way in which advertising is processed. We discussed the important role that emotion, especially non-declarative emotional memory, plays in 'framing' how we think about a message. Another important aspect of the role of emotion is to ensure that the correct *sequence* of emotional response is elicited by advertising. For most situations in life we experience an ongoing series of emotional reactions, and good advertising executions will reflect this by eliciting a dynamic sequence of emotions that parallel what is experienced in using the advertised product.

In effect, advertising should elicit emotions that will not only encourage a positive affective response to the message, but also be consistent with the emotions that are associated with the underlying purchase motivation (see Table 12.7). Perhaps an example here will help to make the point. Why do people buy pain relievers or washing powder? They are negatively

Table 12.7 Relationships Linking Emotion to Motivation in Advertising

Informational brand attitude strategy	
Negative motive	*Emotional sequence*
Problem solution	Mild anxiety → Relief
Problem avoidance	Fear → Relaxation
Incomplete satisfaction	Disappointment → Hope
Transformational brand attitude strategy	
Positive motive	*Emotional sequence*
Sensory gratification	Dull (neutral) → Joy
Social approval	Apprehension → Flattered Ashamed → Proud

Source: Adapted from J.R. Rossiter and L. Percy, *Advertising Communication and Promotion Management* (New York: McGraw-Hill, 1997).

motivated to 'solve' the problem of a headache or dirty clothes. If you have a headache, you are probably feeling annoyed, and want to experience relief. This emotional sequence should be reflected in advertising for a pain reliever. The initial imagery in the execution should make you 'feel' the pain, reminding you of the problem; then you should experience the relief that comes with using the brand and eliminating the headache.

The theoretical basis for this comes from the work of Mower, who took a very simple dual position related to unlearned emotional states that motivate people: the fundamental relationship between pleasure and pain.[45] For Mower, when we sense danger, fear is elicited, and, as the danger subsides, relief. If we are feeling safe, we experience hope, but if we lose that sense of safety, we are disappointed. This is related to motivation, in that fear and disappointment elicit what psychologists call avoidance behaviour, while relief and hope drive approach behaviours. Hammond built upon this work, suggesting that hope and fear lead to what he called 'excitatory' behaviour, while relief and disappointment are 'inhibitory'.[46] You should see how this fits with the distinction we have been making between positively and negatively motivated behaviour, and its relationship to brand attitude strategy.

All of this has a direct bearing upon creating advertising. Emotions are linked to motivations. With informational brand attitude strategies for negative motivations, the advertising should portray a negative emotion first to underscore the problem to be solved or avoided, then move to a more neutral or mildly positive emotion associated with the brand as solution. Insurance advertising, for example, which deals with a negative problem-avoidance motive, should first raise a sense of fear ('What will your family do if you should suddenly die?'), then resolve that fear, 'inhibit' it in Hammond's words, creating a feeling of relaxation as a result of purchasing a life insurance policy.[47]

Look again at Plate XIX, the advert for Fairy laundry detergent. This is a perfect example of what we are talking about. The execution reflects an informational brand attitude strategy addressing a problem-solution motivation:

> The problem is most Non-Bios can leave your baby's clothes feeling a bit scratchy

The imagery of the unhappy baby with the 'prickly' clothes elicits a feeling of mild anxiety. But, with Fairy, you solve that problem and sense the relief. Note too the correct $e^- \rightarrow c$ benefit focus: the problem is resolved by the 'soft' brand.

With transformational brand attitude strategies for positive motivations, the emotional emphasis is on the positive end state that results from using the brand. In transformational advertising, the 'before' emotion is often assumed rather than shown or described, but could proceed from a mildly negative or neutral state. This is likely to be the case when dealing with social approval ('Think how your friends will feel when you serve them our reserve cognac'). But the important point when dealing with transformational brand attitude strategies is that the advertising leaves the reader or viewer with a strong positive emotional response.

The advert for Indian Ocean outdoor furniture shown in Plate XX offers a very good example of how this works. What really makes this advert effective in shifting your emotional state from neutral or even 'dull' to a strong positive emotional response is personalizing the headline, which is then reinforced by the visual. As you imagine yourself in the picture along with the furniture, you experience a positive emotion. Another subtle, yet effective, point is that when you 'put yourself in the picture', you are looking out at the horizon over water. This reflects something that Jay Appleton has talked about as Prospect and Refuge theory (see Chapter 3). In this theory, the horizon represents opportunity, and this is felt unconsciously at the limbic level where emotional memories are thought to be stored. This adds to the positive emotional response to the advert.

Notice how this idea of an emotional shift in the execution is consistent with the benefit focus when emotion is used as a benefit. With informational brand attitude strategies, when emotion is part of the benefit, the benefit focus is $e^- \rightarrow c$, when a negative emotion is resolved by the benefit associated with the brand. When using a transformational brand attitude strategy, emotion is always involved in the benefit, either $c \rightarrow e^+$ or simply e^+.

VisCAP

Psychologists have long studied what it is about a person who presents a message (whom they call a 'source') that influences how well it is received. For example, someone dressed in a white lab coat will be more convincing when talking about health problems than the same person dressed more casually. The first attempt to synthesize this work and apply it to advertising and other marketing communication was the VisCAP model of source effectiveness, introduced by Percy and Rossiter in 1980.[48] VisCAP is an acronym for visibility, credibility, attractiveness, and power, the main source characteristics in communication.

The source of a message in marketing communication can be anything from a person delivering a message, such as a friend, doctor, or salesperson (word-of-mouth marketing communication), to the medium through which the message is delivered. Think about an advert in a magazine. The type of magazine, the environment in which the reader finds the advert, can affect how you respond to the advertising. An advert for running shoes in *Runner's World* could be received very differently from the same advert in a general magazine. A source here is the magazine itself. The brand being advertised is itself a source of information, based upon the image it has in the mind of the target audience. But what we are concerned with here are the source effects communicated by people or characters that appear in advertising to present the benefit claim.

People or characters in advertising span a range from celebrity endorsers, to experts, to cartoon characters, to actors playing (or actual) ordinary people. What you must consider in the selection of the people or characters, to be used in advertising is how a particular person or character will affect the processing of the message. To facilitate processing, they should be selected in such a way that their personal characteristics are consistent with the communication objective. There are specific source characteristics that are best suited to specific communication objectives, and these are described by the VisCAP model.

The four components of the model are defined as follows.

- *Visibility* is how well known or recognizable the person or character is from public exposure.
- *Credibility* has two components: expertise, perceived knowledge of the source concerning what is being advertised; and objectivity, the perceived sincerity or trustworthiness in communicating what the source knows.
- *Attractiveness* also has two components: likeability of the source, and the perceived similarity of the source to the target audience.
- *Power* is the source's perceived ability to instil compliance on the part of the target audience.

The way in which these source characteristics match up with communication objectives is rather straightforward. *Visibility* helps to facilitate brand awareness, especially if a celebrity is used. But with a celebrity you must be very careful that attention to the celebrity does not overpower the brand. Awareness of the celebrity must be *transferred* to the brand. Also, when using a celebrity, you must remember that you are always subject to possible changes in his or her popularity. This is especially true for sports celebrities. Certain long-running characters or cartoons can achieve high levels of visibility, and this will continually be associated with the brand.

The source characteristic that helps to facilitate informational brand attitude communication objectives is *credibility*. You need to have perceived expertise in a source for both low- and high-involvement informational strategies, but objectivity in the source is needed only for high-involvement informational strategies. Why? Remember, you do not really need to accept a benefit claim as literally true with low-involvement informational advertising, but it must be believed and accepted as true with high-involvement informational advertising.

With transformational advertising, you want the source to be *attractive*. Here, *likeability* is the important source characteristic for low-involvement transformational advertising and *similarity* for high-involvement transformational advertising. Remember that one of the differences in creative tactics for low- versus high-involvement transformational advertising is the need for the target audience to identify personally with the high-involvement advertising. That is why perceived similarity to the source is important. This does not mean that the source must be seen as acting like members of the target audience, but it should be seen as similar to what they imagine or want themselves to be.

Power is not often a factor in advertising or marketing communication, because it is not easy to imagine how someone in an advert can reward or punish the target audience. One possible exception is with certain fear appeals. Another might be when '9 out of 10 doctors' recommend a certain behaviour for a particular problem. If you feel that you might have that problem and do not follow the recommendation of the advertising, you might feel that your doctor could 'punish' you if you must see him or her. To the extent that power might operate, it will help to facilitate the communication objective of brand purchase intention.

The VisCAP model is summarized in Table 12.8.

Chapter summary

This chapter first considered general principles of how to use words and pictures to optimize attention and message processing. It then went on to focus on specific creative tactics related to brand awareness and brand attitude communication objectives. We introduced the concept of the creative unit, and explained its use in generating and holding attention in various media. We considered various ways of using words and pictures to enhance processing, especially the role of high levels of imagery. We emphasized the different creative tactics required for informational versus transformational brand attitude strategies, and particularly the role of emotional authenticity in transformational strategies. Lastly, the VisCAP model was introduced, outlining the characteristics to look for in a source in order to optimize effectiveness.

Table 12.8 VisCAP Model of Characteristics to Look for in Matching People or Characters to Communication Objectives

Communication objective	Characteristic to look for	
Brand awareness	**Visibility**	How recognizable is the person or character?
Informational brand attitude	**Credibility**	
Low and high involvement	Expertise	Person or character's perceived knowledge of the product category
High involvement	Expertise and objectivity	Sincerity or trustworthiness of person or character in talking about the product category
Transformational brand attitude	**Attractiveness**	
Low involvement	Likeability	Person or character is seen as personable or attractive
High involvement	Similarity	Target audience sees person or character as similar to them
Brand purchase intention	**Power**	Perceived ability of the person or character to instil compliance with the message

Source: Adapted from J.R. Rossiter and L. Percy, *Advertising Communication and Promotion Management* (New York: McGraw-Hill, 1997).

Questions to consider

12.1 How can the insights gained from the fields of psycholinguistics and visual imagery help to create more effective advertising?

12.2 What can be done to minimize the effects of memory malfunctions on processing advertising?

12.3 What is the fundamental difference in the creative tactics for recognition versus recall brand awareness strategies?

12.4 What are the key differences between the creative tactics for informational versus transformational brand attitude strategies?

12.5 In what way can creative tactics be used to elicit specific emotions?

12.6 What is the relationship between motivation and emotion in advertising, and why is it important to understand?

12.7 In what way does the VisCAP model help creatives in the development of advertising?

Case study 12 **Oral-B—Power to the People**

Electric toothbrushes clean teeth and gums much better than a manual brush. In the ten years prior to 2008, Oral-B electric brush campaigns had taken a very rational approach and focused on this scientific truth. This approach had been effective and, by the middle of 2008, 23.4 per cent of the UK population had switched from a manual toothbrush to an electric one. However, this still left a tantalizing three-quarters of the population clinging to their manual toothbrush. Procter & Gamble wanted to challenge this inertia; it asked for a step-change in growth and also to persuade as many people as possible to change their habit of a lifetime. Toothbrushing habits are formed from a very early age, which made the task even more challenging. We knew that most people knew that electric was better, yet many people still hadn't changed their behaviour. Therefore we had to overlay something else on to the rational performance-superiority message.

Creative work focused on a notion of 'seizing power', and along the way positioned it as a 'revolution' in which millions of people are involved. Although we didn't realize it at the time of development, a campaign was created that put the power of social influence at its core. Unknowingly, we had created a very powerful campaign that reached out to an unexpected audience who were highly susceptible to a social-influence strategy. Whilst the notion of seizing power and taking control of their dental health affected the more disciplined, motivated parts of the brand target audience, the addition of the claim that millions of people were already using electric appeared to have driven sales beyond the established target audience.

The new audience we reached with this campaign were convinced that the status quo had changed. It shifted the anchor and the assumption that people make—that they, along with everybody else, used a manual toothbrush. Early adopters were motivated by the rational superiority claims. Previous campaigns had worked well to attract these people, without any need for a social influence message. However, to reach out beyond this audience, our evidence suggested that social influence messaging had a profound impact on later adopters. This suggested that social influence strategies may be most effectively deployed by products in the second stage of their life cycle, looking to jump the chasm between early adopters and the early majority.

The new campaign launched in September 2008. In order to achieve the desired step-change in growth, P&G had set ambitious targets. Specifically, the objectives were to increase the number of Oral-B electric toothbrushes sold by 35 per cent and to increase the value of total sales by 23 per cent. Both objectives were exceeded in the twelve months following the campaign launch. In the twelve months to September 2009, Oral-B volume increased by 58 per cent, which equated to additional sales of 382,800 units.

Source: This is an edited version of a case study submitted to the IPA Effectiveness Awards. The full case study can be found at ipa.co.uk or warc.com.

Edited by Esther K-Amoda, Doctoral Student, Bath School of Management

Discussion questions

1. How did the 'power to the people' campaign transform brand attitudes for Oral-B?
2. Discuss the impact of concrete, high-imagery words on the campaign.
3. How could the VisCap model be used to help the agency to develop and improve the effect of the campaign?
4. Discuss possible implications of using creative brand awareness tactics for Oral-B's traditional target groups.

Further reading

Christopher Chabris and Daniel Simons, *The Invisible Gorilla* (New York: Crown, 2010)

The cognitive psychologists who conducted the famous 'gorilla' study have a book that deals with this and other issues of attention and memory in a very understandable and often surprising way.

Rik Peters, Michel Wedel, and Rajeev Batra, 'The Stopping Power of Advertising: Measures and Effects of Visual Complexity', *Journal of Marketing*, 74/5 (2010), 48–60

The relationship between visual complexity and attention.

Kimberly Bissell and Amy Rask, 'Real Women on Real Beauty: Self-Discrepancy, Interrelation of the Thin Ideal, and Perceptions of Attractiveness and Thinness in Dove's Campaign for Real Beauty', *International Journal of Advertising*, 29/4 (2010), 643–68

How women see themselves in relationship to varying sizes and shapes of models in advertising (important for transformational strategy executors).

Shi Zhang, Frank Kardes, and Maria Cronley, 'Comparative Advertising: Effects of Structural Alignability on Target Brand Evaluations', *Journal of Consumer Psychology*, 12/4 (2002), 303–12

The issue of comparative advertising, and the specific case of the similarity of the benefit claims among competitive brands.

G.R. Frank, B.A. Huhmann, and D.L. Mothersbaugh, 'Information Content and Consumer Readership of Print Ads: A Comparison of Search and Experience Products', *Journal of the Academy of Marketing Science*, 32/1 (2004), 20–31

The importance of picture size for attention.

Peter Danaher and Guy Mullarkey, 'Factors Affecting Online Advertising Recall: A Study of Students', *Journal of Advertising Research*, 43/3 (2003), 252–67

A number of context factors such as text, complexity, and style for Web adverts are discussed.

Notes

1. This area was discussed for print adverts in John Rossiter's analysis of Starch scores in his paper 'Predicting Starch Scores', *Journal of Advertising Research*, 21/5 (1980), 63–8.
2. These attention estimates are suggested in J.R. Rossiter and L. Percy, *Advertising Communication and Promotion Management* (New York: McGraw-Hill, 1997). They are based upon a review of a number of empirical studies, including one conducted in South Africa utilizing 9,430 commercials, reported by E. DuPlessis in 'An Advertising Burst as Just a Lot of Drops', *Admap* (July/Aug 1996), 51–5.
3. The important difference between human evaluative conditioning and classical conditioning is discussed in J. DeHouwer, S. Thomas, and F. Baeyen, 'Associative Learnings of Likes and Dislikes: A Review of 25 Years of Research on Human Evaluative Conditioning', *Psychological Bulletin*, 127/6 (2001), 853–69.
4. Again, Rossiter and Percy, *Advertising Communication and Promotion Management* (New York: McGraw-Hill, 1997), summarizes a number of studies that support this rule for print adverts (see esp. ch. 10).
5. Greg Myers, *Words in Ads* (London: Arnold, 1994), 3.
6. See A.J. Wearing, 'The Recall of Sentences of Varying Length', *Australian Journal of Psychology*, 25 (1973), 155–61.
7. John Rossiter and his colleagues have offered a typology of visual elements for gaining attention in J.R. Rossiter, T. Langner, and L. Ang, 'Visual Creativity in Advertising: A Functional Typology', *ANZMAC Proceedings* (2003), 105–13.
8. See J.R. Rossiter, 'The Increase in Magazine Ad Readership', *Journal of Advertising Research*, 28/5 (1988), 35–9.
9. These results are reported in a rather extensive study of over 500 MTV-type commercials with more than twenty cuts versus 600 commercials with fewer than twenty cuts by J. MacLachlan and M. Logan, 'Commercial Shot Length in TV Commercials and their Memorability and Persuasiveness', *Journal of Advertising Research*, 33/2 (1993), 7–16.
10. In Rossiter and Bellman's *Marketing Communication: Theory and Application* (French's Forest, NSW: Pearson, 2005), an entire chapter is devoted to tactics for gaining attention, including a discussion of the effects of fast cuts.
11. This has been reported by, among others, B.E. Avons and W.A. Phillips, 'Visualization and Memorization as a Function of Display Time and Poststimulus Processing Time', *Journal of Experimental Psychology: Human Learning and Memory*, 6 (1980), 407–42.
12. See S. Oakes, 'Evaluating Empirical Research into Music in Advertising: A Congruity Perspective', *Journal of Advertising Research*, 47/1 (2007), 38–50.
13. Early research on this is reported in R.F. Yalch, 'Memory in a Jingle Jungle: Music as a Mnemonic Device in Communicating Advertising Slogans', *Journal of Applied Psychology*, 76/2 (1991), 268–75, and more recently in D. Allen, 'Effects of Pop Music in Advertising on Attention and Memory', *Journal of Advertising Research*, 46/4 (2006), 434–44.
14. This classic study is reported in R.E. Milliman, 'Using Background Music to Affect the Behaviour of Supermarket Shoppers', *Journal of Marketing*, 46/3 (1982), 86–91.
15. See A.C. North, D.J. Hargreaver, and J. McKendrick , 'The Influence of In-Store Music on Wine Selections', *Journal of Applied Psychology*, 88/2 (1999), 271–6.
16. Because of his work with attitude change, McGuire was frequently asked about the implications of his thinking for advertising. His seminal work is found in G. Lindsey and E. Aronson (eds), *Handbook of Social Psychology*, iii (Reading, MA: Addison-Wesley, 1969), 136–314.

17. A. Paivio, in his well-known book *Images and Verbal Processing* (New York: Holt, Rinehart and Winston, 1971), discusses research that found that more frequently used and more familiar words are heard, read, and repeated faster and with fewer errors. Lowenthal, in 'Semantic Features and Communicability of Words of Different Classes', *Psychonomic Science*, 17 (1969), 79–80, found that meaning is easier to grasp with more familiar words.
18. McGuire introduced something he called a two-factor analysis, in which low *or* high levels of arousal are less likely to lead to persuasion than some intermediate level. This so-called inverted U-shaped relationship is especially evident when fear appeals are used. A certain level of shock- or anxiety-causing copy or visuals will attract attention, but that very anxiety will inhibit processing of the message. See W.J. McGuire, 'Personality and Attitude Change: An Information-Processing Theory', in A.G. Greenwald *et al.* (eds), *Psychological Foundations of Attitudes* (New York: Academic Press, 1968), 171–96.
19. See M.P. Toglia and W.F. Battig, *Handbook of Semantic Word Norms* (Hillsdale, NJ: Lawrence E. Erlbaum and Associates, 1978).
20. C.C. Jorgensen and W. Kintsch, in 'The Role of Imagery in the Evaluation of Sentences', *Cognitive Psychology*, 4 (1973), 110–16, have shown that high-imagery sentences can be evaluated significantly faster as true or false than can low-imagery sentences. K. Holyoak, in 'The Role of Imagery in the Evaluation of Sentences: Imagery or Semantic Relatedness?', *Journal of Verbal Learning and Verbal Behaviour*, 13 (1974), 163–6, found that sentences rated high in imagery value are significantly easier to understand.
21. See L. Percy, 'Exploring Grammatical Structure and Non-Verbal Communication', in S. Hecker and D.W. Stewart (eds), *Nonverbal Communication in Advertising* (Lexington, MA: Lexington Books, 1988), 147–58.
22. See Myers, *Words in Ads* (London: Arnold, 1994).
23. See e.g. T. Lowrey, 'The Relation between Syntactic Complexity and Advertising Persuasiveness', in J. Sherry and B. Sternthal (eds), *Advances in Consumer Research*, xix (Provo, UT: Association for Consumer Research, 1991), 270–4.
24. See Myers, *Words in Ads* (London: Arnold, 1994), 30.
25. See Myers, *Words in Ads* (London: Arnold, 1994), 47–51.
26. See M.W. Eysenck, *Human Memory: Theory, Research and Individual Difference* (Oxford: Pergamon, 1977).
27. See Myers, *Words in Ads* (London: Arnold, 1994), 136.
28. W.J. Bryce and R.F. Yalch, 'Hearing versus Seeing: A Comparison of Learning of Spoken and Pictorial Information in Television Advertising', *Journal of Current Issues and Research in Advertising*, 15/1 (1993), 1–20. They make the point that, because of language differences, it obviously makes sense for commercials to be reasonably understandable from only the visual content.
29. John Shearman discusses this idea in a very interesting book, *Only Connect . . . Art and the Spectator in the Italian Renaissance* (Princeton, NJ: Princeton University Press, 1992). It may seem odd to be citing an art history book, but the art history literature can provide important insight into visual communication.
30. The implication of what this means, not only for marketing communication, but also for cross-cultural communication, is discussed in a paper by L. Percy, 'Moving beyond Culturally Dependent Responses to Visual Images', presented to the 2nd Conference on the Cultural Dimensions of International Marketing, Odense University, Denmark (1995).
31. See Myers, *Words in Ads* (London: Arnold, 1994), 146.
32. See Myers, *Words in Ads* (London: Arnold, 1994).
33. See S.M. Kosslyn, *Images and Mind* (Cambridge, MA: Harvard University Press, 1980).

34. Studies by both Rossiter and Percy, and Mitchell and Olson, have demonstrated the positive impact of larger picture size on evaluative responses and not just memory response. See J.R. Rossiter and L. Percy, 'Visual Communication in Advertising', in R.J. Harris (ed.), *Information Processing Research in Advertising* (Hillsdale, NJ: Lawrence Erlbaum Associates, 1983), 83–126, and A.A. Mitchell and J.C. Olson, 'Are Product Attribute Beliefs the Only Mediator of Advertising Effects on Brand Attitude?', *Journal of Marketing Research*, 18 (1981), 318–32.
35. See R.P. Dooley and L.E. Harkins, 'Functional and Attention-Getting Effects of Colour on Graphic Communications', *Perceptual and Motor Skills*, 31 (1970), 851–4.
36. See G.H. Bower, 'Imagery as a Relational Organizer in Associative Learning', *Journal of Verbal Learning and Verbal Behavior*, 4 (1970), 529–33.
37. This idea of double-coding was originally introduced by Paivio, and is well discussed in A. Paivio, 'A Dual Coding Approach to Perception and Cognition', in H.I. Pick and E. Saltzman (eds), *Modes of Perceiving and Processing Information* (Hillsdale, NJ: Lawrence Erlbaum Associates, 1978), 39–51.
38. See J.R. Rossiter, 'Visual Imagery: An Application to Advertising', in A. Mitchell (ed.), *Advances in Consumer Research*, ix (Provo, UT: Association for Consumer Research, 1981), 101–6.
39. See C.J. Brainerd, A. Desrochers, and M.L. Howe, 'Stages of Learning Analysis of Picture–Word Effects in Associative Memory', *Journal of Experimental Psychology: Human Learning and Memory*, 7 (1987), 1–14.
40. A detailed look at how the memory problems described by Schacter in his book *The Seven Sins of Memory* (Boston, MA: Houghton Mifflin Company, 2001) can influence how advertising is processed and what can be done creatively about it may be found in an article by Larry Percy, 'Advertising and the Seven Sins of Memory', *International Journal of Advertising*, forthcoming.
41. This idea is explored in more detail in Rossiter and Percy, *Advertising Communication and Promotion Management* (New York: McGraw Hill, 1997).
42. See J.C. Maloney, 'Curiosity versus Disbelief in Advertising', *Journal of Advertising Research*, 2/2 (1962), 2–8.
43. An interesting case one of the authors was involved with back in the 1970s illustrates how effective a refutational strategy can be. Potato consumption in the US had been declining for several years, and the National Potato Promotion Board (a potato farmer's cooperative) was obviously concerned. It had been running advertising that extolled the virtues of potatoes, especially their good taste. Unfortunately, while most people did like potatoes, there was a real concern that they were fattening. In effect, when people saw the advertising, they thought: 'Yes, potatoes do taste good, but . . .' The negative belief that potatoes were fattening overrode the positive taste. Fortunately, potatoes are not fattening, and are lower in calories than other popular carbohydrate side dishes such as rice or noodles. The problem was all of the things that people added to the potato. Advertising was created using a refutational approach that began with the headline 'You think potatoes are fattening'. But the advert then went on to refute the claim, pointing out all of the potatoes' healthy aspects, and finishing with the tag: 'The potato, something good that is good for you.' It worked. Per capita consumption of potatoes not only stopped falling; it increased almost 20 per cent over the three years the campaign ran.
44. This idea of 'liking' an advert can be troubling. On the one hand, there is research that shows the influence on brand preference from ad-liking is not strong: e.g. Jan Stapel, 'Viva Recall, Viva Persuasion', *European Research* (15 Nov 1987), 222–5. On the other hand, Gordon Brown, in 'Monitoring Advertising: Big Stable Brands and Ad Effects. Fresh Thoughts about Why: Perhaps Consistent Promotion Keeps them Big', *Admap*, 27 (1981), 32–7, has suggested that ad-liking has a long-term effect. You must look *carefully* at the adverts used in any research on attitude toward the advert. We should only expect a positive effect when dealing with advertising addressing positive motives. This important point has been underscored by Larry Percy in his paper 'Understanding the Mediating Effect of Motivation and Emotion in Advertising Measurement', in *Copy Research: The New Evidence*, Proceedings of the 8th Annual ARF Copy Research Workshop (1991).

45. Mower's theory was developed in two books: *Learning Theory and Behaviour* (New York: Wiley, 1960) and *Learning Theory and the Symbolic Process* (New York: Wiley, 1960).
46. Hammond's reconceptualization of Mower's work is outlined in 'Conditioned Emotional States', in P. Black (ed.), *Physiological Correlates of Emotion* (New York: Academic Press, 1970), 245–59.
47. See Larry Percy and John R. Rossiter, 'The Role of Emotion in Processing Advertising', in M. Lynn and J.M. Jackson (eds), *Proceedings of the Society for Consumer Psychology* (Madison, WI: Omnipress, 1991), 54–8.
48. Larry Percy and John R. Rossiter, *Advertising Strategy: A Communication Theory Approach* (New York: Praeger, 1980).

Visit the Online Resource Centre that accompanies this book for additional resources to support the text: **www.oxfordtextbooks.co.uk/orc/percy_elliott4e/**

Creative Execution

Key concepts

1. Traditional creative roles are in flux, as are the sources of creative ideas with such things as crowdsourcing.
2. Creative executions must be matched to the roles that the target audience play in the decision process.
3. It is essential that all aspects of a marketing communication campaign have a consistent look and feel that are maintained over time so that they eventually become immediately associated with the brand, facilitating brand awareness and a link with a positive brand benefit.
4. Social marketing communication goes beyond brand-driven marketing communication and the building of positive brand attitude, looking to *change* attitude and behaviour, taking into account social norms and values.
5. Strategy for a campaign must be clearly communicated to the creative team that develops the actual execution, and this is accomplished with a creative brief that summarizes the important elements of the strategy *as one page*. The creative brief must be agreed to by everyone involved with the campaign *before* work begins on the creative execution.
6. Once the creative executions are developed, it is important to pre-test them using a system that is based upon the communication objectives (and *never* with focus groups).

Many people are involved in the strategic planning and development of a marketing communication campaign, but when it comes to executing the strategy, producing the actual adverts and promotions, this is the job of the 'creatives'. For many, this is really what advertising is all about. But it is important to remember that even the most brilliant creative execution that is *not consistent with the strategy* cannot compete with even an average creative execution that is.

Everything we have been talking about so far in this book has dealt with the necessary tools for developing the right creative strategy for a brand. As we shall see in this chapter, all of this work is summarized in a single page, the creative brief. Once the creative idea has been formed and executed, the result will (or should) be tested to ensure that it is indeed consistent with the strategy.

Creating Advertising

Who is it that actually generates the creative executions used in marketing communications? Usually what comes to mind are the art directors and copywriters at advertising agencies—the 'creatives'. But we need to remember that a great deal of advertising is actually created by people who do not work for an advertising agency. Many large companies have in-house departments in which both the creation and media placement of advertising are handled by the advertiser on its own. Retail stores will frequently employ creative people to generate the many, many adverts they run in daily newspapers. Often small business advertising is created for the advertiser by the media that run it. For example, radio or television stations will develop advertising for a company, and the various 'yellow pages' have creative people who will develop small adverts for use in their books and online.

In today's advertising world, and especially in Europe, many advertisers no longer use their advertising agency for traditional media planning and buying functions (as we have already seen). Rather, they are turning more and more to specialized media institutes, using their agencies only for the development and execution of creative ideas. These media institutes are beginning to have a hand in overall strategic planning, and are even advising marketers on their creative product! It is almost as if the media institutes are beginning to 'morph' into traditional full-service advertising agencies. But, regardless of where the advertising is created, two basic functions will be involved: writing the copy and laying out a print advert or developing the visual content of a commercial.

With smaller advertisers, the entire creative function may rest with a single individual. At large advertising agencies there may be teams of copywriters and art directors working with production experts and directors to develop and execute a campaign. And, in today's digital world, these traditional functions are in flux, with the addition of new creative players and roles. Perhaps the biggest change in how creative departments work today may be summed up in two words: increased collaboration. While some version of the traditional art director/copywriter team is still the norm, that team is now expanding to include any number of other specialists. For example, now there are 'creative technologists' who provide expertise on what is creatively possible from a technical standpoint. Agency producers are increasingly part of the creative team as the lines between creation and production have blurred.[1]

Creative executions spring from a creative idea.[2] These creative ideas may come from a variety of sources, and manifest themselves in any number of ways. But, in the end, a creative idea *must be consistent* with the communication strategy and brand position. It is very important that creative thinking does not begin until a creative brief has been agreed upon. It is the creative brief, as we shall see shortly, that helps to guide the *direction* the creative execution must take in order to satisfy the strategy. With the creative brief in hand, the creative team assigned to the campaign can go to work.

Occasionally, however, special circumstances or events may trigger a creative idea outside of the original campaign. A good example of this was an update of Blackberry's corporate Twitter account on 4 May 2010. Why that date? It is National Star Wars Day, and the new Tweet read: 'May the 4th be with you.' Obviously tightly targeted, it nevertheless was one of the company's most effective, reaching 150,000 people and drawing a 15 per cent increase in followers. Perhaps one reason was the Church of Jediism, a 'denomination' that counts itself as the fourth largest church in the UK. Specialized knowledge like that can lead to taking advantage of situations as they come up in the creation of advertising. But it must still be consistent with the brand's overall creative strategy. In the case of Blackberry, the company happened to offer an app that turns the product into a faux light sabre.[3]

At its most basic level, a creative execution is simply made up of words and pictures brought together in a creative way to attract and hold the attention of a target audience, and to satisfy the communication objective. We spent a great deal of time discussing the tactics involved with this in Chapter 12. While occasionally you might find an advert with no words or one with no picture, all marketing communication will generally utilize both words and pictures (other than radio, where of course pictures are not possible). Obvious, of course. But this is also why it is so very important for creative teams to work closely together in the creation of marketing communication.

Creative teams, however, are not always completely free to execute an advert in any way they would like. Particularly with corporate or business-to-business advertising, companies may have guidelines in which particular requirements for the layout and execution of advertising are given, often as detailed as the type of font that is required. Creatives, with some justification, often feel constrained by such rules. While truly good creative people will always be able to work effectively regardless of the boundaries, these so-called 'style books' are much too restrictive and should not be used. The reasoning behind them is usually given as ensuring a consistent look to campaigns. But, as we shall see when we discuss this later in the chapter, this is not what ensures a consistent 'look and feel' to creative executions.

One of the areas that almost always falls under some advertiser restrictions, however, is the tagline, corporate signature, or logo. It is not unusual for advertisers to specify the size of the logo or tag. We do not endorse this, but at the same time you should never permit any creative licence with the tag or logo itself. Creative people should be involved in the original development of the tagline or logo, but, once established, it should remain consistent in all creative executions until it is changed.

Creative Execution and Decision Roles

This would be a good place to consider again the importance of thinking about creative executions in terms of the roles being played in the decision process.

Effective marketing communication matches a message with the role (or roles) that an individual plays. When we are trying to arouse interest in a product, we are talking to the consumer in his or her role as an initiator. We want him or her to initiate the process that will lead to purchase or usage of our product or service. This could be the same execution that is also used to address the consumer in his or her role as an influencer, but it need not be. For example, what if you were introducing a new product, especially a new product when there was no awareness of or experience with the category (think of when iPods were introduced)? All of your effort initially may be required simply to raise awareness of and stimulate curiosity in the new product (category need). Later, messages will begin to build more substantial understanding of the product, addressing consumers in their role as influencers and deciders.

We also need to keep in mind that influencers may exist well outside of the immediate circle of a consumer's family or acquaintances. Recall the discussion of a holiday trip. If you are advertising a holiday resort, you will want to make people aware of your great resort and spark an interest (initiating the decision process), as well as to begin to influence people positively to consider you as a holiday destination. But at the same time, you will also want to be talking with travel agents, encouraging them to influence their clients to consider your resort. This will surely be a different message from the one directed to consumers. Basically, no matter how many participants may be involved in a decision process, we want to be sure that initiators are aware of our product and positively inclined to suggest considering it (either to themselves or to others), and that influencers have reasons to recommend it (again either to themselves or to others).

In appealing to the consumer's role as decider, advertising and other marketing communication must stimulate a positive *intention* to buy or use the product. We have seen how consumers' perception of personal risk in buying or using a product is related to how they form intentions. For most low-involvement purchase decisions, the decider will be a single person. With high-involvement purchase decisions, the decider may be a single person; for large household purchases, a couple; or for certain major business decisions, a group. Once the decider makes the decision, the person in the role of purchaser actually buys the product or secures the services. It is important to remember that the decider and the purchaser may not be the same person. The significance of this means, especially for low-involvement purchases in which there is little or no risk involved, that there is a final opportunity to influence the actual purchase at the point of purchase with some form of marketing communication such as a special promotion or point-of-sale message.

The last role played in the decision process is that of user. If the product or service is never to be used again, or nothing else made or offered by that company likely to be bought, perhaps usage need not be considered when developing advertising executions. But, as we know, for most products or services a marketer is looking to encourage *repeat* purchase or usage. This means that in a real sense the user role is really the first step towards repeat purchase, and must be a part of the manager's thinking.

Roles and Message Objective

As we pointed out in our discussion of the behavioural sequence model (BSM) in Chapter 6, *what* you say in marketing communication is related to *whom* you say it, in terms of the roles that they play and not as individuals. Executions may need to accomplish different things depending upon where you are and what role you are playing in the decision process.

Under some circumstances, the same message may be appropriate regardless of role. This is especially true for low-involvement purchase decisions. For most fmcgs, communicating brand awareness and positive brand attitude will accommodate all five roles, whether played by a single consumer or by multiple individuals. The initiator, influencer, and decider must be aware of the brand, and have at least a tentatively favourable attitude towards it. This will in turn lead to at least an initial positive intention to try, which is required of the decider and the purchaser. Continued awareness and a favourable attitude maintain a positive intention to repurchase, which is the goal for a user. Because more people are likely to be involved in a high-involvement purchase decision, even though the role may require the same type of message, the *nature* of the role being played may require a different message. Consider the potential influencers in our earlier example of a holiday resort destination decision. The potential traveller and his or her friends, or others who may play a role as an initiator or influencer, will probably require a different message from travel agents in their role as initiators or influencers. The communication objective is the same: raise brand awareness and build a positive brand attitude for the resort. However, the specific messages directed to the consumer are likely to be different from those directed to the travel agent.

Beyond this difference, with high-involvement decisions, because there is risk, deciders must be *convinced* of their choice prior to a purchase. It is unlikely that a single advertisement for a high-involvement purchase will be able to build the brand awareness and positive brand attitude sufficient to satisfy the initiator and influencer, and also be able to ensure a positive intention to buy. You may see a great commercial for staying at a resort in the Alps and think that it might be a really great place for a holiday. But it is unlikely that you would pick up the phone and book without first learning a lot more about the resort. A specific message keyed to the person in the decider role is almost always required when dealing with high-involvement decisions.

A good example of this may be found when we consider the decision to buy a new car. Research into how people go about making a buying decision for a car suggests that it is at least a two-stage process.[4] In the first stage, potential buyers must *like* the car. They must see themselves behind the wheel, and feel that this particular vehicle reflects how they want to be seen by the world. This is the 'image' part of the decision, and reflects the positive motives associated with buying a car. Once this is satisfied and potential buyers are comfortable with the *idea* of owning a particular vehicle, in the second stage, they must satisfy themselves that the car meets their more *functional* criteria (mileage, service record, features, and so on), reflecting the negative motivations associated with buying a car. In our terms, one message is necessary to reach potential new car buyers first in their roles as initiator and influencer (and later as user); a very different, more fact-filled message (or messages) will be required for them in their roles as decider and purchaser.

Consistency in Creative Executions

One of the most important aspects of effective creative executions within a marketing communication programme and over time is *consistency*. Within a campaign, all executions must have a consistent look and feel. Whether adverts, promotions, collateral, or even packages, there should be a consistency about them that enables the target audience to recognize it immediately as coming from the brand.

Consistency and Brand Awareness

Consistency over creative executions in a campaign and over time is very important for brand awareness. You will remember from Chapter 8, when we discussed positioning, and Chapter 9, when we talked about brand awareness, the importance of establishing the appropriate link between category need and brand awareness. Consistency in creative executions enables the look and feel conveyed by the execution quickly to establish and reinforce this linkage. When a consistent look and feel to a brand's creative execution have been established, brand awareness will be triggered by the execution itself, without actual reference to the brand name. The brand name will only confirm what has been triggered by the look of the advertising.

A very good example of this was the long-running series of adverts for Silk Cut (a UK tobacco brand). For years its advertising featured little more than some combination of purple silk and a 'cut'. It finally reached the point at which it no longer even included the brand name. The consistent imagery of the purple silk and 'cut' automatically communicated the brand name. It was almost ironic to see a two-page advert in a magazine with nothing but a wave of purple silk and a pair of scissors . . . and a government health warning about the dangers of tobacco use. Tobacco advertising is now banned in the UK, and the last advert for Silk Cut featured a caricature of a large diva, arms wide and clearly in full voice, wearing a purple silk dress with a cut. It was a very clear reference to the old adage: 'It ain't over 'til the fat lady sings.' Well, the fat lady was singing, and advertising for Silk Cut was over.

Look at the adverts in Advert 13.1. They represent over a decade of advertising for H&M in Sweden. There is no doubt that the brand 'owns' this imagery, and that it is familiar to the target audience. This is an excellent example of a consistent look and feel over time. Consistently, well over half of the target market recognizes the advertising.[5] Over the years, other retailers in the market have copied this look, unsuccessfully. Why? As we learned in Chapter 11, when we talked about memory problems, the me-too adverts were misattributed to H&M.

With Jack Daniel's advertizing we have a long history of a consistent look and feel, one linked strongly to a heritage of Tennessee sipping whiskey. In Advert 13.2, the imagery and headline both convey the idea of 'relaxation' and old-time tradition in an emotionally realistic way. While any whiskey might use this imagery (and some have tried), because Jack Daniel's has so consistently used it over the years, it 'owns' it. If another brand were to adopt this imagery in its advertising, it would likely trigger associations with Jack Daniel's.

Actually, a consistent visual or pictorial feel in marketing communication has been found to be a faster trigger for brand identification than the actual brand name or company logo, because memory for visuals is superior to memory for encoded labels or words in general. Interestingly, over half of the brain's cortex is used for the processing of visual images.[6] What we are looking for is a general recognition on the part of the target audience that the pictorial or visual execution belongs to the brand. That is what permits variation in the executions. It is not necessary or even desirable for all of the creative executions to look the 'same', only that they reflect the same overall look and feel. In fact, if the executions in a campaign are seen as too similar, the campaign will tend to 'wear out' faster. Rather, you want enough variation in the executions so that they remain fresh, and can be extended over time.

Consistency and Brand Attitude

Just as with brand awareness, consistency in the look and feel of creative executions is important for brand attitude. We briefly mentioned above the dominance of visual elements in memory. Pictures may be thought of as 'quick shots' into memory. Studies of print adverts with eye-tracking cameras have consistently shown that on average some 70 per cent of the time spent looking at an advert is spent on the picture. As you might imagine, the visual element in advertising is critical to effective communication.

Building upon this understanding of the power of visual elements in effective marketing communication, it is desirable to find an image that the target audience readily associates with a brand's primary or key benefit. This is not as easy as it may seem at first glance. We are not looking for just any image that reflects the brand's benefit, but for one that is *unique* to the brand. We know from our discussion of positioning in Chapter 8 that we should seek a unique benefit for our brand, and, if that is not possible, at least execute the benefit claim uniquely. This last is absolutely essential.

Advert 13.1 These poster adverts for H&M in Sweden over the years provide an excellent example of consistency in the look and feel of a campaign.

Source: Åke Wissing & Co.

MADE AT A LEISURELY PACE.

TO BE ENJOYED AT A LEISURELY PACE.

JACK DANIEL'S OLD No7 BRAND TENNESSEE WHISKEY

Times change. Drinking responsibly doesn't.

for the facts **drinkaware.co.uk**

Advert 13.2 Jack Daniel's advertising has used this same imagery consistently for many years, and now 'owns' it, and if another brand were to try to use it (and some have), it would be associated with Jack Daniel's and not the other brand.

Source: Jack Daniel's © 2011. Reproduced with kind permission.

Because it is rather easy to identify 'ideal attributes', too often most brands in a category will focus upon the same basic benefit (or set of benefits). Advertisers are likely to fall back on clichés when dealing with a benefit. Truck manufacturers know that truck buyers want a 'tough truck', so they all tend to show their trucks travelling easily over the roughest terrain, or pulling or carrying incredible loads (or even both!). These clichés then become an image for the category, and do not help any individual 'name plate' (what automobile and truck companies call their brands) communicate that it is 'tougher' than any other.

In developing creative executions, you must be certain that the message and image are compatible with the target audience's schema. Images that are used must be chosen to be consistent with the brand's key benefit, and the linkage to the benefit must be easily made by the target audience. When trying to identify a visual image to correspond with a brand's key benefit, what on the surface may seem appropriate may not in fact be so. A company marketing a very high-involvement product to corporate executives wanted to associate a key benefit of relaxation with its brand. It felt that a picture showing a relaxed-looking executive, leaning against a door frame without his suit jacket, holding a newspaper and a cup of coffee, would embody this benefit. But the target audience did not see a man relaxing. What they saw was a man in the morning before work, contemplating the stress of the day to come. Obviously, this was not the imagery the advertiser wished to convey. It is always important to check how your target audience responds to your creative executions. We will be dealing with this in more detail later in the chapter.

An exceptionally good example of finding the right imagery and using it consistently over time to reinforce brand attitude was the long-running campaign in the UK for Oxo stock cubes. Although the campaign finally came to an end in late 1999, it ran for over sixteen years. Beginning in 1983, the advertising featured a family's day-to-day life experiences, centred around mealtimes. The campaign featured the same actors over the years, and the scenarios played out in the advertising were designed to tap into situations easily identified with the target audience's own family lives. In terms of execution, it was a perfect example of what we have described as the critical component of low-involvement, transformational advertising: it was 'real'. The look and feel evolved in keeping with the times as the actor family grew older, but it was always internally consistent and readily identifiable as Oxo advertising. There is ample evidence that this advertising made a significant contribution to the health and growth of the brand.[7]

In summary, every creative execution for a brand must contribute to a consistent look and feel for that brand. While individual messages and executions may (and should) vary, the underlying theme must remain consistent, and the key to this consistent look and feel should be a visual image that is associated in the target audience's mind with the brand's primary benefit. Consistency in creative execution facilitates brand awareness and, with the appropriate visual image, also facilitates brand attitude. Every exposure of a brand's marketing communication, when seen within the context of a consistent, positive image, helps to reinforce a favourable attitude towards the brand. This leads to a more receptive atmosphere for attending to the specific message content of the advertising.

Crowdsourcing

A real challenge to consistency in creative execution is the recent use of 'crowdsourcing'. The term 'crowdsourcing' first appeared in 2006 in an article in *Wired* that talked about how technical advances are breaking down the barriers that once separated amateurs from professionals:

'It's not outsourcing, it's crowdsourcing.'[8] One of the more successful examples of amateur crowdsourcing is the Doritos 'Crash the SuperBowl' programme instituted in 2007. It has resulted in several highly rated commercials produced by amateurs. In 2009, two brothers produced a commercial for a reported US$2,000, which ended up being ranked as the most popular advert on that year's SuperBowl. This earned the brothers a US$1 million prize from Frito-Lay for being among the top-three-rated adverts.[9] A point to be made about the crowdsourced Doritos SuperBowl adverts is that while they were all independently created, they nonetheless had a consistent humorous 'look and feel', and followed the creative tactics recommended for low-involvement transformational advertising.

But, more often than not, it is creative professionals and not amateurs who are involved in crowdsourcing. In 2009 Unilever took its Peperami brand from its long-time agency Lowe, and announced that it would crowdsource its creative. It posted a creative brief on a site called IdeaBounty.com, offering US$10,000 for the winning creative idea. In fact, Unilever admitted that it was counting on creative professionals, and not amateurs, to submit ideas. And that is what happened.[10] Crowdsourcing is now dominated by new agencies and creative services that specialize in it, many formed by creative directors from traditional advertising agencies.

Social Marketing Communication

Perhaps the key difference between marketing communication as we have been discussing it and social marketing communication is that, with social marketing communication, we are looking to do much more than build positive attitude. We must *change* attitude, a very difficult proposition (and why 'other-brand loyals' are seldom part of a brand's target audience), and we must also change behaviour. Part of the difficulty is that, in order to achieve the desired behavioural change, it is necessary to induce a motivation for the new behaviour that is at least as compelling as the motivation driving the socially undesirable or pathological behaviour. This is no easy task because we are dealing with deep-seated psychological drives or biochemical addiction (principally from dopamine).

Nevertheless, all of the principles we have been dealing with still hold, as does the framework provided by the strategic planning process. They hold because they reflect what is necessary to optimize the processing of a message—any message, whether commercial or social. However, as we shall see, social marketing communication will treat target audience selection differently, and a normative or social factor is added to the expectancy-value model in determining attitude toward social behaviour.

The most widely used Behavioural Sequence Model in social marketing is what has been called a 'stages of change' model, and perhaps the best-known example is the Transtheoretical Model of Behavioural Change offered by Prochaska and DiClemente.[11] This model proposes that one goes through five stages in changing socially relevant personal behaviour. The initial stage is *pre-contemplation*, during which a change in behaviour is not yet considered by those engaged in the undesirable behaviour. This is followed by the critically important *contemplation* stage, when the individual begins to actively evaluate and consider changing his or her behaviour. Next is *preparation*, when a decision is made to act and begin to try and put in place what will actually be needed to implement the change. This is followed by *action*, when the new

Table 13.1 The Transtheoretical Model of Behavioral Change

Pre-contemplation	Not thinking change in behaviour is appropriate at this time
Contemplation	Considering and evaluating change in behaviour
Preparation	Deciding to act and putting in place what is needed to implement change
Action	Engaging in new behaviour for first or first few times
Confirmation	Comitting to new behaviour with no intent and returning to old behaviour

Table 13.2 Andreason's Modifications of the Transtheoretical Model of Behaviour Change with Corresponding Communication Goals

Andreason's modified stages	Communication goal
Pre-contemplation	Raise awareness of the desired change and build interest in values associated with new behaviour
Contemplation	Persuade and motivate
Action	Help initiate new behaviour
Maintenance	Maintain new behaviour

behaviour begins, often shakily and tentatively. If successful, there follows a final stage, *confirmation*, when there is no longer any desire to return to the earlier behaviour (see Table 13.1).

These five stages were modified by Andreasen to four: pre-contemplation, contemplation, action, and maintenance.[12] If we consider Andreasen's four stages, the job of social marketing communication at the pre-contemplation stage will be to raise awareness of the desired change, and to begin building interest in the values associated with the new behaviour. At the contemplation stage, social marketing communication must persuade and motivate, arguably its most difficult task. For the action stage, it must help to initiate the behaviour, a stage at which some sort of incentive might be appropriate. Finally, at the maintenance stage, the communication is aimed at maintaining the new behaviour either positively by promising favourable consequence, or by negatively reminding the target of the negative consequence of slipping back into the old behaviour (see Table 13.2).

It should be clear from this that although social marketing is trying to change an individual's behaviour, moving him or her from the undesirable to acceptable behaviour, in effect that person becomes a different target audience at each stage, requiring a different social marketing communication message.

Target Audience

The social marketing literature looks at the population in terms of three groups: conformers, vacillators, and offenders. *Conformers* are those who are engaged in the desired behaviour and have not tried, or perhaps have merely 'sampled' the undesirable behaviour. *Vacillators* are those who may be contemplating taking up the undesirable behaviour, or who are engaged in it occasionally. *Offenders* are those who are engaged firmly and frequently in the undesirable behaviour. Conformers are at the maintenance stage of behavioural change, while vacillators and offenders would be somewhere among the other three, and each will require a message tailored to the stage at which they are.

It is possible to look at these three potential target groups in terms of the buyer groups we discussed in Chapter 6 'Target Audience Selection'. Those engaged in the undesirable behaviour, the offenders, correspond to Other-Brand Loyals—they are 'loyal' to the undesirable behaviour. Vacillators may be seen as Favourable Brand-Switchers (where 'favourable' relates to their being still engaged in the desired behaviour), who are either thinking about adopting the undesirable behaviour, or who are occasionally engaged in it. Conformers would be Brand Loyals because they are 'loyal' to the desired behaviour.

Just as we saw with the Buyer Groups, their *attitudes* are the key. As Rossiter and Belmann point out, there is a world of difference between someone who is not engaged in an undesirable behaviour and has a negative attitude toward it and someone who is not engaged in the behaviour, but is *favourably curious*, even if not actively considering it.[13] The same could be true of someone engaged in an undesirable behaviour, especially an addictive or compulsive behaviour (e.g. gambling); they may or may not prefer it. Recall the loyalty model discussed in Chapter 6 on target audience selection where we saw that just because someone appears to be 'loyal' to a brand because they buy it regularly, they may only buy it because they perceive too much risk in switching. With social marketing communication, just as with brand marketing communication, attitude is critical. Understanding the attitudes of the target audience toward the behaviour (acceptable and undesirable) and toward the social pressure and norms associated with it is essential to getting the message right.

Just as with brand marketing communication, it is important to conduct qualitative research and to develop a category-specific and target-audience-customized Behavioural Sequence Model. This BSM can build upon the 'stages of change' model discussed earlier, but must be more specialized. And while it is important to understand all who are involved and the roles that they play in the decision process for brands, it is *vital* for social marketing communication because of the impact of social influences on the behaviour.

Positioning

Positioning in social marketing communication follows the same general model of positioning discussed in Chapter 8. The answer to the 'what is it?' question must reflect how the target audience perceives the undesirable behaviour in relation to their needs (equivalent to category need for brands), and how they evaluate the perceived benefits associated with *both* the acceptable and undesirable behaviour, the answer to the question 'what does it offer'? Except for conformers, who are already engaged in the desired behaviour, in a sense you are almost always dealing with *repositioning*: either making the desirable behaviour more attractive or the undesirable behaviour less attractive, or both. Accomplishing this will require an understanding of the motivations and attitudes involved, as already pointed out. Failure to understand this, especially for vacillators, is probably the main reason why so many social marketing programmes fail.[14]

Communication Strategy

Perhaps even more so with social marketing communication, positioning and communication strategy are tightly linked. In business and consumer marketing communication, it is enough to link the brand to the category need and appropriate benefit for positioning or repositioning. Getting this correct ensures building brand awareness and positive brand attitude. But, this will not be enough when dealing with social marketing communication.

We have several times mentioned 'social norms' and values, and these must also be accounted for in the development of positioning and communication strategy for social marketing. The Fishbein-style expectancy-value model (introduced in Chapter 8) does a good job of dealing with attitude toward a behaviour, but something more is needed to explain (and predict) social change. It does not account for the influence of social values on behavioural intention (except perhaps in a rather general way if the social component is looked at simply as a 'belief' associated with the behaviour). Rather, in order to account for this, an extended expectancy-value model is called for, something that Fishbein and Ajzen called the 'Theory of Reasoned Action'.[15] According to them, this modified version of the expectancy-value theory has two major factors that together determine behavioural intention: a personal, or 'attitude', factor and a social, or 'normative', factor. This extended model is written as: $BI = A_b + SN_b$, where behavioural intention (BI) is a function of one's personal attitude toward the behaviour (A_b) plus a personally perceived social norm (SN_b) associated with the behaviour.

The first factor in this equation, A_b, is essentially the same as the expectancy-value model we are already familiar with; except that now the subscript 'b' refers to the behaviour rather than the brand:

$$A_b = \sum_{i=1}^{n} b_i e_i$$

where A_b = personal attitude toward the behaviour
b_i = the belief that performing the behaviour leads to consequence i
e_i = the person's evaluation of outcome i
n = the number of beliefs a person holds about engaging in the behaviour

The second factor dealing with social norms is similar in structure to the attitude component:

$$SN_b = \sum_{i=1}^{n} b_i m_i$$

where SN_b = the 'social norm' or influence of others on a person's behaviour
b_i = the person's belief that reference group or individual i think they should or should not engage in the behaviour
m_i = the felt motivation to comply with the reference group or individual i (which is unipolar)
n = the number of personally salient relevant reference groups or individuals

Any attempt to influence behavioural intentions will depend upon its effect upon these attitudinal and social norm factors. But the relative importance of the personal attitude toward the behaviour and the social norm will be dependent upon the individual and the type of behaviour. This, of course, underscores again the importance of understanding target audience attitude.

As Reisman pointed out many years ago, people differ significantly in terms of the values by which they guide their lives.[16] He talked about people as being either 'inner-directed' or 'other-directed'. Inner-directed individuals pay little attention to other people or groups, while other-directed pay close attention to what others expect of them. In terms of the model, inner-directed would be more driven by the A_b factor; other-directed, the SN_b factor.

Behaviour too differs in terms of type, for example varying in terms of whether the behaviour is socially visible or not and whether it involves others directly or indirectly. Private behaviour is likely to be less influenced by social norms, although some outcome goals may be. Note that drug-taking, for the most part, is not a socially conspicuous activity, although 'conformer' friends and family members, as well as voluntary support groups such as Narcotics Anonymous and Alcoholics Anonymous, play an important role in helping the addict to change to, and maintain, the desirable behaviour of abstinence. On the other hand, socially visible behaviour is more likely to be influenced by social norms. Traffic offences by drivers and pedestrians (e.g. excessive speeding and not crossing at marked crosswalks), smoking in public, and excessive drinking with peers are good examples of socially visible behaviours.

While the extended Theory of Reasoned Action model provides a very useful way of understanding how to influence behaviour change in social marketing, changing undesirable social behaviour, especially sociopathic behaviour or dopamine-reinforced physiologically addictive behaviour, remains a challenge. This is because individuals affected are likely to carry a genetic predisposition toward such behaviour. In fact, using the model for addictive behaviour has proven very difficult.[17] Additionally, Hornik has argued that social marketing communication has very little effect upon the personal attitude factor, but that over time it can have a cumulatively large effect upon the social norm factor.[18] An apparent example of this is the campaign over the years, with more recent government regulations, against the use of tobacco, which in many countries has made it socially unacceptable.

Adding to all of the difficulty in implementing social marketing communication is finding the right appeal. Too often a fear appeal is used, or shocking visual images (e.g. severely malnourished or disfigured children). More often than not these appeals will not work because of the very high level of anxiety they arouse, if attended to, among offenders. McGuire offered a two-factor analysis of anxiety, and it helps to explain the problem.[19] As a *drive* state, anxiety tends to increase the probability of attitude change, but as a *cue*, it will tend to elicit an avoidance response in the form of 'turning out' the message or increased counter-arguing by the frightened offenders.

What this means is that while strong anxiety arousal from social marketing communication would be likely to increase the likelihood of considering a behavioural change, that very same high level of anxiety will have minimized the likelihood that the target audience will pay attention to the message. What is needed is a message that stimulates some, but not too much, anxiety. This problem is illustrated in Fig. 13.1. You want to find yourself along the top of the inverted U-shape curve.

Additionally, not only must an appropriate level of fear arousal be used, but the message must also effectively *reduce* that fear. This follows from Hovland, Janis, and Kelley's original fear-driven model. [20] In this model drive reduction is the central causal mechanism: for social marketing communication, an adversive stimulus (the 'threat') is linked to the undesirable

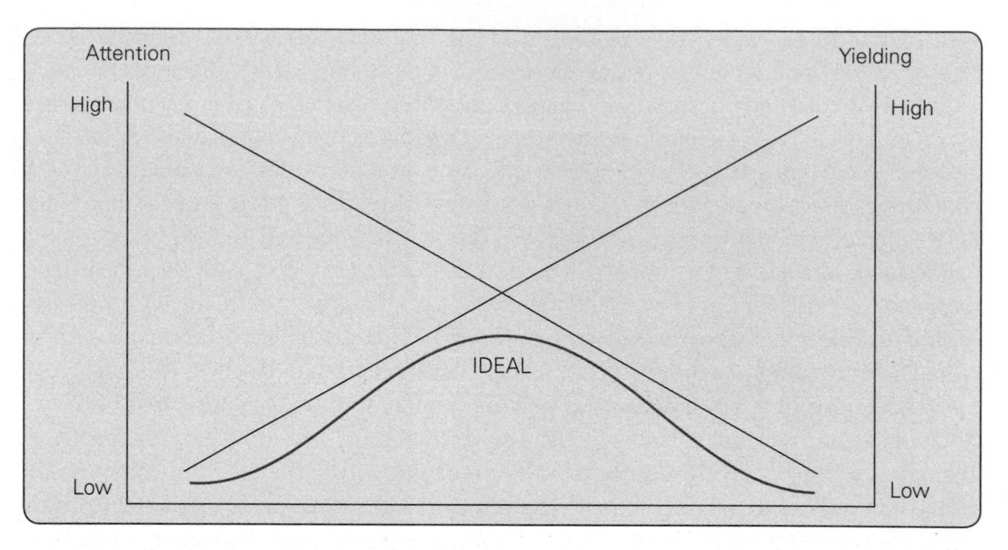

Figure 13.1 Non-Monotonic Response to Fear Appeal

behaviour, but then removed by showing that the desired behaviour will avoid it. [21] Without this resolution, when the desired behaviour is seen as removing the fear aroused by consequences following from the undesirable behaviour, social marketing communication will not be effective.

Look at an advert for fighting motor neurone disease in Advert 13.3. This is a very good example of finding the right balance between raising anxiety for others (in this case those suffering motor neurone disease), but not so dramatically as to put off people from attending to the message. The gran in the wheelchair and the child elicit sympathy and concern, but they are not offputting. And the anxiety aroused by the visual and initial headline 'Lucy will lose her gran to motor neurone disease' is nicely reduced by the final headline: 'Help her fight back.'

While not directly dealing with 'undesirable' behaviour as we have been discussing it, messages such as this that deal with such things as fighting, preventing disease, or animal welfare (for example) are part of social marketing communication. This is because of the importance of the social norm in soliciting help for a socially desirable cause.

Involvement and Motivation

By its very nature, social marketing communication requires a high-involvement informational communication strategy. One high-involvement informational creative strategy that is especially appropriate for social marketing communication is a refutational approach. Remember from Chapter 12 that a refutational strategy works well when dealing with a 'negative' target audience, one that does not accept the brand's primary benefit claim. In order to avoid the target audience immediately counter-arguing or rejecting the message, a refutational approach first acknowledges their objection, but then goes on to argue against it. This same idea in personal selling is known as the 'Yes . . . but' technique. Once the argument for the desirable behaviour is made, it is capped with the strongest benefit claim.

Advert 13.3 **This advert for helping to fight motor neurone disease is a very good example of finding the right balance between raising concern, but not so dramatically as to put people off attending to the message.**

Source: Reproduced with kind permission of the MND Association.

Ethical Considerations

One concern with social marketing communication is the widespread use of hyperbole exaggeration (a form of lying by commission rather than omission). Almost all social marketing campaigns exaggerate the undesirable behaviour and its consequences. How can this be justified? We argued in Chapter 1 that honesty must be at the heart of *all* marketing communication, yet most social marketing communication relies upon exaggeration to persuade: exaggerating negative consequences of the undesirable behaviour, and arousing fear for oneself or anxiety for others. In a word, much social marketing lies. You might argue from a teleological perspective that in such cases lying is to achieve a greater good, but we cannot accept any such argument. What constitutes a 'greater good'? Under what circumstance? Who is the judge? These are questions that philosophers over the millennium have failed to resolve, as we saw in Chapter 1.

Having said this, however, Rossiter and Belman raise an interesting point concerning this.[22] They argue that lying in social marketing communication could be ethically acceptable if telling the truth would cause definite harm. They also include lying by omission here if the truth would lead to harm. For example, they point out that if the truth were known about the extent of physician misdiagnosis, or about the disturbingly low actual cure rate of common medical treatments, many people would lose confidence in medicine and not seek *any* help or would turn to even more dangerous self-diagnosis and doubtful treatments. While perhaps this is just another way of looking at the exaggeration or lying as a greater good, we do think this is different.

Briefing the Creatives

Before turning our attention specifically to the creative briefing process, let us think about what O'Malley has called a contrasting style between those involved in strategy versus those in creative.[23] He remarks that successful advertising comes from two contrasting styles of problem solving, what psychologists have called convergent versus divergent thinking. In convergent thinking, you make deductions and draw logical conclusions from information. This is the type of thing we would expect from the strategist, and is inherent in most of what we have been talking about so far in this book. Divergent thinking is when you move outward from specific information to more broadly based generalization. This is the type of thinking we expect from creatives. Of course, both types of thinking will be found in each group. But, overall, in our planning we are looking for convergent thinking to uncover the 'hot button' most likely to influence consumer behaviour, and divergent thinking to drive creative executions that reflect this in an exciting or memorable way that will help to facilitate the effective processing of the message. What we discuss next is how we transfer the fruits of the strategists' convergent thinking to the creatives in order to stimulate their more divergent thinking.

In almost every case, before creatives are asked to begin developing creative ideas, there will be a briefing. This may run from a very loosely written statement of objectives to a rather detailed, formal description of all of the information that strategic people feel is important as background in understanding the nature of the consumer and advertised product.

While it is obviously quite important for those working on the creation of advertising to know as much as possible about a brand's market and the people who use the product, there is another, less tangible goal for the creative charge or brief. Creative people are always looking for the big idea, or at least some spark that will ignite the creative juices. The more a creative briefing includes unique and interesting facts about the product, brand, and consumer, the more likely the creatives will be to find that kernel of information that will spark the 'big idea' leading to effective execution. Really innovative briefings are considered so important by many advertising agencies, especially in the UK, that they make a point of spending a great deal of time on *how* they present the briefing. They are likely to go to great lengths in order to present the briefing to the creatives in interesting and exciting ways.

Areas that might be covered in a briefing include such things as:

- market characteristics;
- consumer characteristics;
- product characteristics;
- brand positioning;
- competitors' advertising;
- communication objectives;
- media considerations.

Market characteristics. This is usually a background section that discusses what is going on in the market at the time. How big is it? Is it growing? Is it changing? What are the brand shares? Are attitudes changing? It is important that creative people come away with a good feel for the market in which the advertised product is sold.

Consumer characteristics. We have already spent an entire chapter talking about who makes up the target audience for a brand. This part of the creative briefing will certainly not go into that much detail, but it will provide a vivid portrait of whom we see as the most likely customers for our brand. This description will include not only traditional descriptors such as age, family size, and income, but also more qualitative description such as how they feel about the product, how they go about making choices, the criteria that are important in choice, how they use the product, etc. For transformationally driven decisions, this will also include summaries of their dreams and desires—how the brand will 'transform' them.

Product characteristics. In this section the product itself will be described in detail. What can it do? How is it distributed? What are the specific attributes of the product? Are there real differences between brands? How is it packaged? How is it used?

Brand positioning. Here you are interested in how the market sees your brand as well as its competition. This is very important information, because the advertising created must be consistent with the brand's current image in the market (as we have just seen in the previous section)—unless, of course, the strategy is to change it. But to change the brand's image is a very serious decision, and a very difficult job to accomplish. Generally speaking, radical departures from a brand's current positioning create uncertainty in the market, and can erode the equity a brand has built over the years.

Competitors' advertising. It is very important to include a review of current and recent competitors' advertising in the charge to the creatives. This provides them with an idea of the general themes and executions that comprise the 'noise' or the environment within which the advertising they create will be seen. This review of competitors' advertising will also ensure that the new advertising that is created is different from their advertising in execution.

Communication objectives. As we learned in Chapter 9, creative work cannot begin until the communication objectives are set. It is the communication objectives that reflect where and how advertising and other forms of marketing communication will fit within the overall marketing plan.

Media considerations. While it is usually not necessary to restrict the creative department in terms of what media they should consider, often it is necessary to request specific media that they may not otherwise have considered. This is particularly true when your model of consumer decision making has identified points within the decision process at which such things as point-of-purchase collateral or direct mail might be effective, but also when something other than television or print is desired (for example, outdoor or even radio, which is not often considered).

Other areas may also be covered in the creative briefing, but this outline should provide a guide to some of the more typical kinds of information that will be included. In addition to the creative briefing, a summary document should be provided that acts as the 'blueprint' for the creative executions. This is the creative brief.

The Creative Brief

Most advertising agencies, and many marketers as well (especially of fmcgs), have a specific outline that they use for preparing a creative brief. There is no one 'correct' way of preparing a creative brief, but there are certain key areas that should be covered, as follows.

- What is the task at hand?
- What are the specific objectives and strategy?
- What, if anything, *must* the executions contain?

Figure 13.2 presents a general outline for a creative brief that addresses these questions. It is important to understand that, even though creative briefs are generally associated only with traditional advertising, they are equally necessary for promotion planning. In fact, a creative brief should be the basis for the development of all marketing communication. The outline that follows includes ten points, and, while specific creative briefs used by advertising agencies and marketers may not look exactly like this, in general these areas will be addressed in their briefs.

Task Definition

The first four areas covered in our outline for a creative brief help you to define the task at hand for the creatives. Here is where you are primarily concerned with important insights into the market and target audience. First, we want to identify a *key market observation*. What one point can be made about the market that will help those developing the creative

Brand
Task Definition
Key Market Observation
Source of Business
Consumer Barrier or Insight
Target Audience
Objectives and Strategy
Communication Objectives and Tasks
Brand Attitude Strategy
Benefit Claim and Support
Desired Consumer Response
Execution
Creative Guidelines
Requirements or Mandatory Content

Figure 13.2 Creative Brief

execution to understand and believe the brief? Next, what is the *source of business*? Where specifically does the brand expect to get business? This should not be general, but provide a quite specific definition. For example, a creative brief for a luxury sports car might see the source of business as current owners of competitors' luxury cars who are looking for something more exciting. You can see that for a creative brief you are trying to create *images* for the creatives. The third area seeks to provide a specific *consumer barrier or insight*. What one thing do you know about your target audience that would help to reach it? Or is there something about it that we may need to overcome in order to communicate successfully with it? Finally, you will want to provide a vivid description of the *target audience*. You should provide enough information here so that the creatives can form a true understanding of whom they are to address.

Objectives and Strategy

The next section of the brief contains four points that are primarily concerned with developing the creative execution. Here is where you are laying out the creative objectives and strategy, the positioning, and the key benefits and support, along with the *one benefit* that, if communicated, will achieve your desired objective. First, what are the specific *communication objectives and tasks*? Then, what specifically is the *brand attitude strategy*? Is the decision we are dealing with high or low involvement, positively or negatively motivated? Next, what is the *benefit claim and support*? This is by far the most difficult, and often contentious, area of the creative brief. Here is where the fruits of your positioning work are put into a few words that link the brand to the motivation. The benefit claim takes the benefit, what the consumer wants, and puts it in terms of the emotional response desired. This will be the heart of the creative execution. Finally, you address the *desired consumer response*. You want to provide a brief summary of what you expect to happen if the target audience successfully processes the message.

Execution

The previous two areas covered in our creative brief deal with specific executional factors. Here is where you provide any specific *creative guidelines* that you want to be certain are considered in the execution. For example, this is where the look and feel of the brand's advertising may be detailed. The final area covered in the creative brief contains any *requirements or mandatory content*. Often companies have specific requirements for their logos or other layout constraints (although constraining creative layout or production technique is rarely a good idea, as we have mentioned), and these would be detailed here, along with any legal requirements.

Figure 13.3 provides an example of a creative brief for a bank's Internet banking services that follows this outline. Perhaps the most important thing to notice about the brief is its size. It is complete on *one page*. In preparing a creative brief, there are really only two areas in which a lot of detail may be needed: the description of the target audience and the *support* for the benefit claim. Otherwise, keep the creative brief to the bare essentials. There will always be plenty of back-up available from the marketing plan and the communication strategy plan if the creatives want more. The key to an effective creative brief is that it is *brief*. This helps to ensure that the information provided has been carefully considered.

Creative Research

With the creative brief in hand, the job of developing the creative execution begins. More often than not, creatives will come up with ideas on their own, although there are a number of research techniques available that can aid this process. If any research is likely to be done at the creative development stage, it will be to explore or screen concepts. Again, there are a number of procedures available to help here as well.[24] The most important thing to remember if you do conduct creative-ideation or concept-screening research is to conduct the research among a sample of the brand's target audience. Once a concept has been agreed upon, one or more test executions will be developed. Actually, the more test executions created, the better, within reasonable constraints of time and cost.[25] While research may not have been involved in the development of the concept, it is *essential* that the test executions be pre-tested. A great deal of money will go into the production and media exposure of the final executions, and you will want to be as certain as possible that the creative execution satisfies the brief, meets the communication objective, and delivers the benefit claim in an understandable manner.

Many agencies and even marketers often do not feel it is necessary to pre-test their creative execution, feeling that they can rely upon their experience and knowledge of the brand

Product	Job	Date
Electronic banking		

Key Market Observations
Potential customers are probably going into branches or using the telephone to conduct business that could be done over the Internet

Source of Business
Current bank checking account/current account customers

Consumer Insight
They are comfortable using the Internet, and are heavy users of ATMs

Target Audience
Loyal and vulnerable, profiled as young and middle-income 'full nest' households with busy lives

Communication Objectives and Tasks
Brand attitude primary objective—to reinforce overall IMC convenience positioning

Brand Attitude Strategy
Low-involvement/informational brand attitude strategy driven by motivation of incomplete satisfaction

Benefit Claim and Support
Internet banking is more convenient. Support: pay bills almost any time, as well as transact basic banking business at any time

Desired Consumer Response
See that Internet banking really is more convenient than branch banking or using the mail

Creative Guidelines
Tie 'inconvenience' of banking to awareness of Internet banking (recall); consider exaggeration in execution

Requirements/Mandatory Content
Legal identifications

Figure 13.3 Creative Brief for an Internet Banking Service

and market to guide their decision. But, regardless of how experienced or knowledgeable someone is about a brand and market, it is foolish not to pre-test. In fact, one's very experience and knowledge can actually be a handicap in evaluating one's own creative executions. Because managers are so familiar with the brand and the creative execution, they 'see' and process it very differently from how the target audience possibly could. They naturally make connections between the brand and benefit claim *because* of their knowledge (recall our discussion of top-down processing), connections that may not be possible without that knowledge. It just makes sense to pre-test so that you are certain of how the target audience will respond to the creative execution.[26]

Manager Creative Evaluations

Having said this, however, if for whatever reason a decision is made to not pre-test new advertising, at the very least a disciplined evaluation of the rough executions should be made prior to final production. The creative brief should be used by the manager as a basis for the evaluation. In fact, even if there will be pre-testing of the advertising among the target audience, a manager evaluation makes sense because it helps the manager to focus upon how well the creative execution reflects the creative brief, and not only how well management 'likes' the executions (or been *sold* the creative by the creative team). Unfortunately, it is not at all unusual for an advertising execution to have strayed quite a bit from the original direction of the creative brief.

The manager should evaluate the rough executions in terms of how well they address the target audience and key communication objective, as detailed in the brief. Basically, this means answering the following questions.

- How likely is the execution to resonate with the target audience? Will they easily see that it is 'talking' to them?
- Is the brand awareness objective correctly executed?

  If *recognition*, is the package clearly shown as it will be seen at the point-of-purchase?

  If *recall*, is the need-brand link obvious, presented in that order, and repeated?
- Does the execution focus correctly on the key benefit?
- Are the creative tactics used consistent with the brand attitude objectives (as outlined in Boxes 12.1 and 12.2)?

Pre-Testing Creative Executions

The job of pre-testing creative executions requires original primary research among the target audience, custom-tailored to reflect the appropriate creative strategy. Relying solely on a standardized pre-testing procedure offered by a research institute or syndicated service may not be appropriate for the execution you are testing. Flexible procedures based on *the brand's advertising communication objectives* provide a much better fit and provide the manager with a better understanding of the execution's potential.[27]

The reason why you pre-test creative executions is to improve the chances that the advertising will work as planned when placed in the media. Whether or not it will work depends on three factors:

- the creative content of the executions;
- correct media placement and scheduling;
- competitive advertising activity.

Pre-testing deals only with the creative content of the execution. Tracking a campaign over time evaluates all three factors, and is addressed in Chapter 15. Pre-testing a creative execution ensures that it is consistent with strategy. It lets you know if the execution is likely to achieve the communication objectives set for the brand, and enables you to predict how it will 'work' in the market. A good pre-testing system also provides the manager with understanding that can be used to revise or improve the execution if necessary. In fact, in a summary of seventy-five top British advertising agencies, the reason given most often for pre-testing was for 'learning' and to improve future campaigns.[28]

Methods Unsuitable for Pre-Testing Creative Executions

Before we begin to examine the best ways of pre-testing creative executions, we want to discuss three methods often used in pre-testing that the manager should avoid: using focus groups to test executions, using advertising recall measures, and using physiological measures.

First, never use focus groups to pre-test creative executions. While focus groups are very helpful for formulating the communication strategy prior to the development of the execution, they are totally inappropriate for pre-testing executions. There are at least two compelling reasons for this. The first problem is that focus groups vastly overexpose the execution compared with how it will be seen in the market. In a group setting, they are thoroughly discussed, a far cry from the 30 seconds or so that a TV advert has to communicate in the real world or the 1–2 seconds that a print or outdoor advert has in which to gain the consumer's attention. The second concern is a validity problem. By their very nature, focus groups encourage group interactions that largely prevent individual reactions to the executions from occurring as they would normally. People process advertising as individuals, even if they are watching TV with others.

Secondly, advertising recall is *not* a valid predictor of communication effectiveness. The most that can be said about recall measures, especially day-after recall (DAR) testing, is that they may be a rough measure of attention to the advertising. But the fundamental flaw is that recall procedures are *advertising*-recall based, not *brand*-recall based. We are looking for *brand*-associated communication effects. *Brand* awareness and *brand* attitude are the fundamental communication objectives, not advertising awareness or attitudes towards the advertising. No *pre-test* measure based upon advertising recall that we are aware of has ever been shown to predict advertising effectiveness, and this is because the media vehicle (as in DAR) or the test situation (as in the case of most syndicated recall measures) is a cue that is irrelevant to the consumer's decision process.

Finally, physiological measures on their own are not particularly effective in pre-testing creative executions. Physiological measures generally measure only attention to an execution.

25. See Rossiter and Percy, *Advertising Communication and Promotion Management* (New York: McGraw-Hill, 1997).

26. An excellent review of the measures used to evaluate the effectiveness of advertising in the UK and Sweden may be found in two papers by Lars Bergkvist: 'Competing in Advertising Effectiveness: An Analysis of the 1996 British Advertising Effectiveness Award Case Histories', unpublished paper presented at the AEJMC annual convention, New Orleans, 4–7 August 1999; and 'Swedish Awards', unpublished paper presented at the 15th Nordic Conference on Business Studies, Helsinki, Finland, 19–21 August 1999.

27. See L. Percy, 'The Importance of Flexibility in Pre-Testing Advertising', *Admap*, 381 (1998), 29–31.

28. See M.P. Flandin, E. Martin, and L.P. Simkin, 'Advertising Effectiveness Research: A Survey of Agencies, Clients and Conflicts', *International Journal of Advertising*, 41 (1990), 203–14.

29. See L. Weinblatt, 'New Research Technology for Today and Tomorrow', in *Copy Research* (New York: Advertising Research Foundation, 1985), 180–92, and 'Eye Movement Testing', *Marketing News* (5 June 1987), 1.

30. See W. Kroeber-Riel, 'Effects of Emotional Pictorial Elements in Ads Analyzed by Means of Eye Movement Monitoring', in T. Kinneau (ed.), *Advances in Consumer Research*, xi (Ann Arbor, MI: Association for Consumer Research, 1984), 591–7, and B. von Keitz, 'Eye Movement Research: Do Consumers Use the Information They Are Offered?', *European Research*, 16 (1988), 217–24.

31. There are many references to this by-now-infamous Hoover promotion, including an editorial by K. Newman in the *International Journal of Advertising* 15/2 (1993), 94, and 'Hoover and its Publicity Start Dive', *Marketing* (UK) (8 April 1993), 18.

Visit the Online Resource Centre that accompanies this book for additional resources to support the text: **www.oxfordtextbooks.co.uk/orc/percy_elliott4e/**

Part 5

Integrating Advertising and Promotion

gear and apparel should be consistent with its rugged outdoor image. These are all part of the strategic considerations that go into effective advertising and promotion for a brand.

In this chapter we shall be discussing the major sales promotion techniques, and will provide an overview of a number of additional ways of delivering advertising and promotion from the broader communication mix.

Sales Promotion

In our discussion of promotion in earlier chapters we have been underscoring the *strategic* difference between advertising and promotion, and have seen that with promotion, in addition to brand awareness and brand attitude, brand purchase intention is always a communication objective. That is what promotion is all about: immediate action. We have also noted that an incentive is not an absolute requirement for a promotion. Nevertheless, most promotions do indeed include an incentive. They are generally referred to as *sales promotions*, and when defined in this way involve some direct purchasing incentive that is offered for making a specific purchase or taking a specific purchase-related action.[1]

In this section we will be departing somewhat from the strategic discussion of promotion, and will be introducing the specific sales promotion techniques that are used most often when promotion is a part of the communication plan. As we talk about the various sales promotion techniques, you should keep in mind that in reality they are just different ways of *delivering* the promotion, each with their own particular strategic advantages and disadvantages. And in fact, in some cases, a particular sales promotion technique will also be delivering an advertising-like message. For example, samples are a way of delivering a message about the brand as well as an opportunity for trial; coupons deliver a price-off message and, when well executed, the key benefit as well. While sales promotions may of course initially be delivered through any part of the communication mix, and this includes such things as personal selling, sponsorships, and other options that we will be discussing later in this chapter, and not just traditional media, after it is delivered the promotion itself may continue to be part of the communication mix. A sample's package continues to deliver an *advertising-like* message: the brand name and key benefit. A coupon that is clipped or saved continues to deliver a message every time it is referred to. It is important for the manager to think about the communication potential of sales promotions beyond their immediate objective of trial or repeat purchase.

Trade Promotion Techniques

There are three basic categories of trade promotion technique that we will consider: allowance promotions, display material promotions, and trade premiums and incentives. *Allowance promotions* provide the trade with a monetary allowance of some kind in return for buying or promoting a specific quantity of a brand, or for meeting specific purchase or performance requirements. *Display material promotions* usually involve the manufacturer in providing specific display material to be used in featuring the brand, often in conjunction with a trade allowance. *Trade incentives* are special gifts or opportunities to earn or win valuable trips or prizes in return for purchasing specified quantities of the brand or meeting specific sales quotas.

Allowance Promotions

The type of allowance offered to the trade can take many forms: everything from reduced prices across the board, to reduced prices according to purchase volume, to free goods. It is important to point out here that most governments keep a close eye on price allowances to the trade in order to ensure that they are equitably applied regardless of the size or type of distributor.

The potential weakness with trade allowances is that there is no real guarantee that they will have a positive effect on the customer base. You are hoping to secure a more positive position with the trade. Offering purchase allowances or free goods with certain order levels helps to build inventories, which is essential support for customer-based marketing programmes. Performance allowances, one hopes, will at least in part go to merchandising or retail advertising by the trade in support of the brand. Even though there is no guarantee that the trade will cooperate, at least to the extent one might wish, consumer, retail, and trade support *must* be integrated in order to maximize your efforts regardless of the cooperation given by the trade in response to the trade promotion.

One way in which to help to improve the likelihood of trade cooperation is to use trade coupons. Although trade coupons are offered to the trade, they are actually to be redeemed by consumers. The difference between a trade coupon and a retail coupon is that, with trade coupons, the marketer controls the conditions and value of the coupon, not the trade, which is generally the case with retail coupons. Trade coupons are a delayed promotion whereby the trade pays for distributing the coupons to its customers, and is then reimbursed by the marketer after the promotion. The brand's advertising and consumer promotions must be integrated with any trade coupons to ensure a seamless message to the target audience.

Display Material Promotions

Display promotions can be in the form of either a display allowance or actual merchandising material. Perhaps the primary use of display promotions is to help to reinforce consumer promotions, although they also play an important role in the introduction of new products and line extensions. Given that many purchase decisions are made at the point of purchase, especially with fmcg brands,[2] display promotions can be an important part of an integrated marketing communication programme. Good display material leads to better attention, especially important for brands driven by recognition awareness.

The use of display promotions has the advantage of generally being implemented quickly when needed, and the ability to support consumer promotion and advertising at the point of purchase. Good in-store merchandising material can also be a good way in which to effect cross-merchandising, whereby two different brands are promoted together. The disadvantage, as with all trade promotions, but especially here, is the need for trade cooperation. Unlike trade allowances or trade premiums and incentives, which we address next, in the case of display promotion, if it does not receive widespread trade support, it will not be effective.

Trade Incentives

This last area of trade promotion is more concerned with individual distribution sources such as wholesale or retail outlets, distributors, brokers, and trade personnel. Incentives can be offered to almost any level of trade, and tend to be very popular. They can be given for reaching specific sales goals, to individuals, departments, or stores. Awards or gifts might be offered to counter personnel for recommending or highlighting your brand, or to staff members who create new or innovative ways in which to promote the brand. Such incentive programmes can be a big help when introducing a new product or brand extension. They are also an effective way in which to help to move slow products off the shelf.

One of the advantages of trade promotions is that they are relatively inexpensive. Additionally, they can be implemented quickly and easily. However, a disadvantage is that segments of the trade, especially mass merchandisers, have policies against them or regulations that severely limit the type of incentive promotion they will accept.

Retail Promotion Techniques

We will be looking at three general areas of retail promotion techniques, but must remember that the trade promotions just reviewed are also used by retailers. Retail promotions are almost always price related. While they tend to be categorized in terms of specific *price-off* promotions, *point-of-purchase display* promotions, and *retail adverts*, the promotion itself almost always includes a price reduction.

Price-Off Promotions

There are many pricing strategies that retailers use in price-off promotions. They must consider concurrent or recent consumer price promotions, inventory balance, and competitive activity. Remember, a retailer is interested in *category* sales. Suppose L'Oréal Paris is running a major price-off promotion for Kerastase Aqua-Oleun in leading French women's magazines such as *Marie Claire* and *Biba*. The cosmetic manager of a major retailer may decide to offer a similar retail promotion for Jacques Dessange or other hair-styling products in order to drive business in the entire category.

Price-off promotions are almost always a part of retail adverts, and frequently a part of retail point-of-purchase displays. But there are also many other ways of implementing a price-off promotion: everything from in-store flyers to 'shelf-talkers', whereby the price reduction is highlighted at the shelf on a small poster. There is actually some evidence to suggest that different consumers pay attention to different means of presenting price-off promotions, so it is in the retailer's best interest to use several means of conveying a price-off promotion.[3]

Point-of-Purchase Display Promotions

In-store displays are a significant part of retail promotion. Retailers like point-of-purchase display promotions because they are effective. First of all, point-of-purchase displays draw attention to themselves. Shoppers are attracted by newly introduced contrasts or changes to their shopping environment, and will pay attention to discover what it is all about. This can be done with such things as store banners, end-aisle displays, or other stand-alone features. Secondly, point-of-purchase displays are perceived by consumers to be offering a price reduction on the featured product *even if it is not discounted.*[4]

Retail Advert Promotions

When you think of retail adverts, the first things that probably come to mind are newspaper, food, or pharmacy adverts. But, of course, almost any retailer can use retail adverts as promotion, and car dealers, mass merchandisers, shoe stores, and even banks frequently do. Retailers may carry out traditional advertising as well, and we must not confuse the two. Adverts are retail promotions when they feature products and prices, whether discounted or not. Advert 14.1 for PC World illustrates a typical retail advert promotion.

Consumer Sales Promotion Techniques

Consumers will not make a distinction between trade promotions delivered at retail outlets, retail promotions, and consumer promotions. If they see a special display in the store or have a coupon or see a price special, they are not concerned with whether it was the brand or the retailer that was responsible. But, from the brand's perspective, there is a world of difference. Consumer promotions are initiated by the brand, not the retailer, and the brand controls the content.

As it happens, consumers tend to have a pretty good idea about how often brands are promoted.[5] This is important to the brand, because it will affect consumer buying strategy for the brand in the light of the perception of the brand's availability on promotion. So, even if you do not have control over retail promotions that include your brand, it is essential that you have knowledge of them and include that knowledge in the promotion strategy. We introduced the six fundamental types of consumer sales promotion in Chapter 5: coupons, refunds and rebates, sampling, loyalty and loading devices, sweepstakes, and premiums (see Table 14.1). While there are many other possibilities—everything from the product itself to unique applications of distribution channels—generally speaking, we may think about consumer promotions in terms of these six basic techniques.

Coupons

Because of its relatively low cost, the coupon is the most common form of consumer promotion. It is widely used by both brands and retailers. However, not all countries permit their use. Such was the case in Denmark until a 2011 EU ruling required all EU countries to allow the use of coupons. There was strong feeling in the government and consumer council in Denmark against coupons, believing that they compromise the 'ideal of clear and comparable pricing', as they put it.[6]

The redemption rate for coupons can be expected to run between 2 and 5 per cent. The greater the value of the coupon and the longer the time available for redemption, the greater the redemption rate. It is absolutely essential that the expected redemption rate be carefully calculated. Remember that coupons represent a *budgeted* cost, and if the redemption rate is seriously underestimated, the overall cost of the promotion will exceed the budget. Some of the other cost considerations in budgeting a coupon promotion, beyond the face value of the discount, are such things as additional manufacturing and distribution costs, lost profit, and the resources needed to administer the programme.

Traditionally, coupons are distributed to consumers via print media or direct mail. In magazines or newspapers, coupons may be a part of an advert, as we see in Advert 14.2. This advert

Advert 14.1 A retail promotion advert featuring both price advertising and price promotion.

Source: Reproduced by kind permission © PC World.

Table 14.1 Six Basic Consumer Sales Promotions

Coupons	Are low cost, and the most common form of promotion
Refunds and rebates	Offer large price discounts, usually with more expensive products
Sampling	Provides an opportunity to try or use brand at little or no cost
Loyalty and loading devices	Encourage repeat purchase or use (loyalty) or change normal purchasing patterns (loading device)
Sweepstakes	Help to create excitement and reinforce brand image at a relatively low cost
Premiums	Help to facilitate purchase by offering a reward or bonus

for Weight Watchers from Heinz Fat Free Fromage Frais does a good job of integrating a 10p-off coupon within the execution without interfering with the advert's message. But most coupons, especially in newspapers, are delivered as FSIs, those often annoying 'free-standing inserts' of cards, single pages, or booklets, each with a coupon. Sometimes a coupon may be included in or on a package, good for future purchase either of that brand (often called a 'bounce-back coupon') or of a sister brand from the same manufacturer (called 'cross-couponing' or 'cross-ruff couponing').

Technology is providing innovative new ways in which to deliver coupons. With today's sophisticated scanner capabilities, companies (and retailers) have the ability to monitor customer behaviour, and offer coupons to consumers at the till. For example, people purchasing Flash antibacterial cleaner might be given a coupon for Domestos Germguard to be used the next time they are buying an antibacterial cleaner. Asda (acquired by WalMart in 1999) was one of the first grocery retailers in the UK to use this system. Research into redemption rates suggests a significant increase from the typical 2–5 per cent up to 6–8 per cent.[7] Additionally, this type of 'checkout' couponing offers the ability to target consumers much more tightly. Another application of technology for delivering coupons uses the Internet. Individual companies and services offering coupons from many companies provide online computer-generated coupons. Consumers need only to log on, select the coupons they want, and print them out. Unfortunately, this has also made coupon fraud easier. Hackers have found ways to capture online images of coupons. They have also found ways to use software to capture and manipulate barcodes that can be used to make more typical-looking coupons, as well as selling CDs with images of newspaper coupons that can be fitted with false barcodes.[8]

Groupon offers a new twist on the idea of online coupons and promotions. People subscribe to the site, and are then offered at least one promotion a day from a local business, museum, or performing arts group. But there is a difference. A certain predetermined number of people must respond to the promotion before it is activated. Once that 'tip' point is reached (as Groupon calls it), the coupon becomes valid for those who bought in. If enough people, say, were to agree to buy a €30 coupon for a €60 hair styling at a local salon, they would receive the deal and the merchant and Groupon would split the revenue 50/50.

The real upside for the business is that they are not paying to deliver the promotion message in more traditional media such as newspapers, radio, or even online new media; the promotion is free on Groupon. Also, unlike most other media in which there is not a lot of tight control

Advert 14.2 A coupon integrated within an advert without interfering with the advert's message.

Source: Reproduced by kind permission © H.J. Heinz Co. Ltd. (McCann Erickson).

over who receives the promotion, Groupon is able to target likely consumers. At the end of 2010, Groupon was in over 300 markets worldwide, and was looking to expand into China, India, and Korea.[9]

While coupons are largely used for fmcgs, there is no reason why a brand could not offer higher-value coupons for less frequently purchased products. However, directly discounting the price offers more control with higher-priced, less frequently purchased products.

Refunds and Rebates

The pendant to coupons for more expensive consumer durable products is refunds and rebates. The primary difference is that with refunds and rebates the price discount is not offered at the point of purchase, but after sending in some proof of purchase to the manufacturer. The face value of a refund or rebate can be either a specific amount or some proportion of the retail price. Again, as with coupons, the request for a refund or rebate will be directly related to its relative value, and must be carefully planned to estimate probable use.

Most refunds and rebates are paid directly to the consumer by the manufacturer, but with very high-ticket items, a manufacturer's rebate can be assigned to the retailer at the time of purchase. This is not unusual, for example, when car manufacturers offer rebates. Their dealers will apply the rebate directly to the purchase price.

Refunds and rebates are used most often as a temporary sales stimulus or sometimes as a defensive response to competitive activity. The primary strengths of refunds and rebates include the ability to generate interest in high-involvement products, especially those with high price points, and an ability to control price discounts *without* trade interference. The weakness of refunds and rebates is that the reward is delayed, and consumers may not think that the effort is worth the discount. To be effective, refunds and rebates must be seen as simple and easy to receive.

Sampling

Sampling provides the target audience with an opportunity actually to try or to use a brand at little or no cost. While most samples are free, specially sized samples are sometimes offered at a significantly reduced price to encourage purchase. The ideal candidates for sampling are products with low trial or products with a demonstrable difference (especially if the advantage is difficult to convey convincingly with advertising).

There are many ways of delivering samples to the target audience, and they come in a variety of forms. There are in-store use or taste tests, distribution of full-size packages of the product or specially sized smaller packages, and even in-house or in-business use of a product for a limited period of time (a good way in which to 'sample' high-priced, high-involvement products).

Passing out samples in specific locations or offering in-store sampling has the advantage of low distribution cost, but little control over who receives the sample. Direct mail offers more control, but there are obvious limits to what can be sampled (for example, not frozen or other perishable food items). Door-to-door distribution permits sampling of almost anything, but, while offering tight control, is inefficient and expensive. Certain products such as fragrances can be sampled with 'scratch and sniff' folds in magazines, and, as we see in Advert 14.3, it is

(*a*)

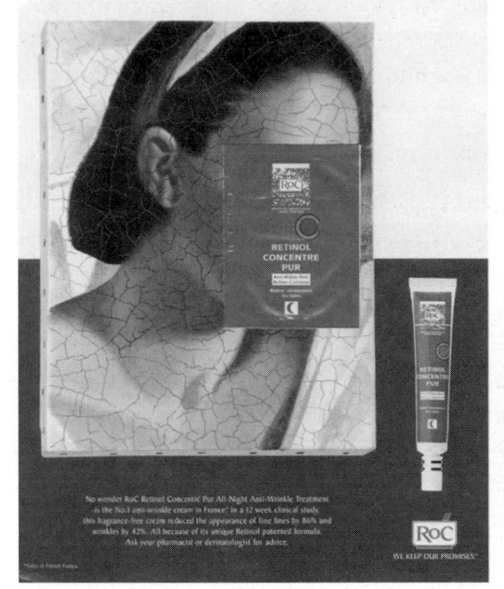

(*b*)

Advert 14.3 (*a*) A clever advert that includes a sample promotion. (*b*) Advert (*a*) after the sample has been removed, underscoring the benefit of using the brand.

Source: Reproduced with kind permission from © Retinol Concentré Pur.

even possible to offer small packs of cosmetics in magazines. This sampling promotion is part of a very clever advert that visually underscores the benefit of using Retinol Concentré Pur. In Advert 14.3*a*, we see the promotion as it appeared in women's magazines; in Advert 14.3*b*, we see the result when the sachet is lifted from the page—the benefit of smoother skin.

Loyalty and Loading Devices

As the name implies, loyalty promotions are designed to offer a reward to those consumers who are loyal to a brand. The goal is to energize repeat purchase of the brand, and has the advantage of providing an excellent opportunity for developing a strong database of a brand's best customers. The best loyalty promotions utilize *continuity programmes*, whereby the consumer is required to engage in a continuing behaviour (for example, saving stamps or accumulating some proof of purchase or use) over time in order to qualify for a reward. Perhaps the best-known loyalty promotions are airline frequent flyer programmes and hotel frequent 'stayer' programmes, through which customers earn points for staying at a particular hotel chain. This idea has been copied in recent years by a number of different retailers and marketers; it has been used in everything from shopping points for money spent at a retailer to reward programmes for using a specific credit card or telecommunications company. In addition, fmcg companies are increasingly using databases to identify heavy brand-users in order to offer them special programmes or rewards.

As technology advances, brands and retailers are finding more innovative ways of improving loyalty programmes. La Croissanterie, a French-style, Paris-based, fast-food chain with restaurants in France, Ireland, Belgium, Italy, and Portugal, is a case in point. In 2010 the company moved to strengthen its loyalty programme by integrating the latest radio frequency identification (RFID) technology and mobile loyalty capabilities. La Croissanterie's loyalty system was outdated, and importantly did not reward customers for everything they spent. They were rewarded only for purchases of a full meal rather than single items such as a beverage or sandwich.

The new loyalty programme enabled customers to receive relevant promotions using a store loyalty card, a mobile phone, or even a transit-pass. Cardholder purchase histories were tracked, permitting personalized discount offers via smart posts, Airtag Pad interactive displays, and NFC readers that are attached to existing store electronic point-of-sale equipment. At the store, customers can identify themselves in one of three ways: the barcode on their loyalty card, a smart-phone application, or an NFC-enabled public transit pass.

As the customer enters the restaurant, they sign in and are connected to an interactive touch screen that identifies the customer and immediately connects them to an online profile enabling highly targeted and relevant promotions. Because it is online, the customer can be offered immediate discounts based on previous purchases. And importantly, everything spent is now rewarded as part of the loyalty programme.[10]

Consumer loading devices differ from loyalty programmes in that they do not seek continuity, but rather seek to change a consumer's normal purchasing pattern. These promotions are designed to encourage customers to 'load up' on the brand by purchasing more than they normally do at one time. This is done by using special bonus packs, price packs, and price-offs. *Bonus packs* offer more of the product at the same price, either with a special larger size or an additional package bound to the original. *Price packs* are where a reduced price is printed on the package as part of the label, and *price-offs* are announced at the point of purchase. This can be a very effective and efficient way in which to encourage brand-switching and as a defensive tactic. For example, if you know that a competitor is about to introduce a 'new and improved' version of its brand, offering a loading promotion will in effect reduce the potential market for the competitor's initiative.

Of course, as always, there are strengths and weaknesses to loyalty and loading promotions. Bonus packs do create an immediate incentive to buy, but the trade does not like them, because they disrupt normal inventory stocking, and take up additional shelf space without necessarily providing additional profit for the retailer. Price packs and price-offs also offer an immediate inducement to buy, but, unless coupled with advertising or other marketing communications, tend to subsidize regular users more than attract new tryers or switchers. Continuity programmes certainly energize loyal usage of a brand, but require a long-term commitment by both the consumer and the brand. Because of the long-term nature of loyalty promotions, costs may end up being greater than expected.

Sweepstakes, Games, and Contests

Sweepstakes are a consumer promotion in which the winners are chosen by chance and proof of purchase is not required. On the other hand, with *games* and *contests*, there is some chance or skill involved, or a demonstration of knowledge, but almost always proof of purchase is required. With contests, someone may be asked to answer certain questions or to identify pictures related in some way to the brand. Not surprisingly, sweepstakes are more popular than games or contests, being much easier to enter, since no purchase is necessary. Soft-drink bottlers and fast-food chains frequently use games as a consumer promotion. You scratch off a square or a card given to you when you purchase food or you look under the cap of a soft drink bottle to see if you have won.

If you are not careful, things can go very wrong with these types of promotion. Smith relates the story of a disastrous game promotion sponsored by Pepsi in the Philippines in which the equivalent of £26,000 was offered to anyone finding a bottle top with a specific number.[11] Pepsi paid out £8 *million* before realizing that thousands of winning bottle tops had inadvertently been distributed, and then abruptly stopped paying. According to a report in the trade press, when Pepsi stopped paying, there were public demonstrations, its bottling plants were attacked with grenades, its lorries were burned, and its executives hired bodyguards before fleeing the country.[12]

The important thing to remember when using sweepstakes, games, or contests is that they must be *fully integrated* with the brand's other marketing communication, and consistent with the brand's image. A sweepstake in which the prize is a trip to an exotic island would be great for a brand such as Mars' Bounty chocolate bar, because Bounty has a history of using exotic island imagery in its marketing communication. It would not be appropriate for a ski-ware brand, for which a better prize would be a ski holiday.

Legal requirements are a real concern with sweepstakes, games, and contests. Unlike other consumer promotions, there are usually a number of legal restrictions concerning the wording, rules of compliance, and odds of winning; these can differ among countries. As one lawyer specializing in these promotions has put it, after you have set your objective and outlined the sweepstake, game, or contest, your next step should be to involve a legal expert. From a legal standpoint, it is the rules of the promotion that are most critical. Even if you have run the same promotion in the past, it is best to check, because even a seemingly insignificant change may mean that a new law applies. This is even more the case as the European Union adds a new level of regulation to the market.

Sweepstakes, games, and contests have the ability to help to create excitement about a brand, and this can help to reinforce the image of the brand, all at a relatively low cost. But the reward is limited to a small number of people and is delayed.

Premiums

There are many types of premium, as well as any number of ways of delivering them to the consumer. Using premiums as a consumer promotion helps to facilitate purchase, by offering the premium as a reward. Premiums may be free, or require a small payment from the consumer beyond the purchase price of the brand. When the consumer pays something, this is known as a self-liquidating premium because the price asked of the consumer is set to cover the cost of the premium to the brand. Because of the volume-buying power of the company offering the premium, coupled with potential discounts for joint merchandising (after all, the product offered as a premium is being promoted as well), the price to the consumer will be significantly less than he or she would otherwise be required to pay (usually 30–50 per cent of the retail price). The important thing, whether the premium is free or self-liquidating, is that the target audience perceives a real *value* in the offer. Premium promotions have the advantage of creating excitement for a brand, especially if the premium is available at the point of purchase. This, however, can be complicated by the need for more retail space to accommodate the premiums, with no direct return on that space to the retailer. Mail-in requests for premiums with proof of purchase have the advantage of rewarding customers without the need for extra retail space, but the reward is delayed. Regardless of the type of premium, it should be supported by advertising and in-store merchandising, as well as integrated into the brand's overall marketing communication.

Public Relations and Sponsorships

As with all marketing communications, public relations and sponsorships must be consistent with a brand's overall positioning. The link between the brand and need must be present and clear, and the key benefit must be communicated. In earlier chapters we have seen that the appropriate brand–need link is critical for establishing brand awareness, and this will only happen if an event or publicity clearly reinforces this link. For example Uncle Ben's wholegrain rice has used the dual-benefit claim 'deliciously healthy in half the time' in its advertising. It would make sense, if it were to wish to include sponsorships in its communication mix, to look for events or organizations promoting healthier eating; if using PR, it could create campaigns for better eating habits, reflecting its key benefit of 'deliciously healthy'.

With most PR and sponsorships it can be difficult to specifically present the key benefit. It must be communicated *indirectly* by the nature of the event or PR campaign,[13] as suggested in the example above. Not only would the link between Uncle Ben's wholegrain rice and the need for healthier eating be made, but sponsoring such events or placing stories, say about quick recipes for healthy meals with Uncle Ben's wholegrain rice, in newspapers or television shows that deal with healthier eating will be likely to associate the brand with both the 'healthy' and 'fast' benefits. The difficulty with such a PR campaign would be getting the brand name mentioned and not only recipes using wholegrain rice.

Public Relations

Most people think about public relations, or PR, as free publicity. There is, of course, nothing free about it. A good PR campaign can be very expensive. It has been estimated, for example, that worldwide some US $10 billion is spent annually on PR.[14] And while it is an important part of the overall communication mix for a brand, most PR practitioners prefer not to think of what they do as part of 'marketing'. They tend to look upon what they do as more concerned with enhancing the image and reputation of an organization. The Institute of Public Relations defines PR as 'the planned and sustained effort to establish and maintain goodwill and mutual understanding between an organization and its publics'. This definition may seem to distance PR from consumers and marketing with its emphasis upon the organization and its problems, but for most companies its most important 'public' is the consumer. While some PR activities are clearly outside the normal strategic planning process for marketing communication, those activities must nonetheless reflect the brand's overall marketing communication objectives.

Public Relations Strategy

Public relations strategy may be thought of as being either *proactive* or *reactive*. *Proactive* public relations involves planned activity that is designed to attract attention to a brand and to help to build positive brand attitude. *Reactive* public relations occurs when a company experiences negative publicity and must deal with 'damage control'. This is what happens when there are product recalls, for example. In social psychology this is known as impression management, whereby one is seeking to protect oneself by maximizing positive associations while minimizing negative associations.

Advantages and Disadvantages

There are both advantages and disadvantages to using public relations as part of a brand's marketing communication mix. Compared with traditional forms of marketing PR has the ability to reach highly segmented markets effectively. Because PR messages are not delivered as advertising or promotion, even when placed in traditional media, they avoid the clutter associated with advertising-like messages. And because they are not seen as advertising or promotion, the message is likely to be seen as more credible.

But, there are disadvantages in using public relations. Perhaps the greatest potential problem is the lack of control. It is almost impossible to ensure that a message will be exposed; and if it is, that it will be presented in the way the brand hoped. In addition, because the message is not seen as advertising, it is much more difficult for the target audience to make the desired link between the message and the brand.

Marketing Public Relations

We suggested earlier that many of those involved in public relations do not see their work as part of marketing. However, in the mid-1990s it was estimated that 70 per cent of PR activities were related to marketing.[15] In addressing this, Harris introduced the term 'marketing public relations' (MPR) to describe PR activities in support of marketing objectives. He specifically defined MPR as 'the process of planning, executing, and evaluating programmes that encourage purchase and consumer satisfaction through credible communicators of information and impressions that identify companies and their products with the needs, wants, concerns, and interests of consumers'.

This understanding of PR as *marketing* public relations is important for brands that use a source branding strategy. *Source branding* strategies are those in which the corporate brand is endorsing the quality of the product, in a sense acting as a guarantor. It is part of the brand name, but the product itself is the star. For example, when Kellogg puts its name on Special K or Frosties, it is alerting the consumer that these products are part of the Kellogg family. Any PR that helps to build and nurture Kellogg's image and reputation enhances the image of the Special K and Frosties brands.

Some of the ways in which MPR can contribute to achieving a brand's marketing communication objectives beyond simple publicity is through such activities as media relations, corporate communication, and sponsorships. Maintaining good *media relations* helps to ensure that publicity in the form of press releases and feature stories will be more likely to be used. This requires an ongoing nurturing of editors and journalists. *Corporate communication* includes not only corporate advertising and communications directed to specific target groups, but also things like internal communication and company newsletters. All of this must be informed by the marketing communication strategy. *Sponsorships* and *events* may be initiated as part of MPR, or independently as part of a brand's communication mix, as discussed below.

Buzz Marketing

In many ways one may think about word-of-mouth as a form of PR. Buzz marketing is the term given to a new trend in word-of-mouth communication for brands that emerged in the mid-2000s. It emerged from an effort to better reach younger consumers who are more and more difficult to reach with traditional media. The idea is to actively enlist the help of ordinary people to talk about specific brands. BZZAgent, a company in the US, recruits people over the Internet to talk with their friends and family about their client's brands. Those recruited are given free samples of the brand to try, along with an outline of some things they could talk about. In one case these 'bzzagents' (as they are called) were given a sample of a new perfume fragrance and asked to wear it, and then to talk with people about it. While they are encouraged to identify themselves as part of a marketing programme, the 'buzz' that results from talking about the new fragrance has more power than traditional advertising because it is generated among people who know each other.

Brands are also creating buzz by using their websites to encourage entertaining interactions that generate positive word-of-mouth about their brands. Some brands, such as BMW, are creating short films for the Internet featuring famous actors and directors, and relying on word-of-mouth to build buzz.[16]

Sponsorships and Event Marketing

Sponsorships can play an important role in a brand's overall marketing communication mix. A sponsorship involves a brand providing support for a particular event, organization, cause, or even a specific individual, using its brand name or logo in association with the sponsored activity or individual, and the ability to reference the sponsorship in its other brand marketing communication. This enables a brand to be presented in a favourable environment in which it has the potential of benefiting from an existing positive attitude toward the sponsored activity. It is important, however, to be certain that the sponsored activity or individual is indeed positively viewed by the brand's target audience.

The difference between a sponsorship and event marketing is that event marketing involves support for a single event rather than an ongoing relationship. For example, if a company were to support a concert to raise money for AIDS research, that would be event marketing. If it had an ongoing relationship with the Foundation for AIDS research, that would be a sponsorship. Sponsoring the Olympics is event marketing. In fact, the Olympic Games are one of the biggest examples of event marketing worldwide. But sponsoring an individual Olympic athlete over time would be considered a sponsorship. Worldwide, more sponsorships involve sports than anything else.[17]

While popular, there seems to be very little evidence that sponsorships and event marketing add directly to the bottom line, although they can certainly contribute to brand awareness and brand attitude. As mentioned, the Olympic Games are one of the most sponsored events in the world, yet a number of studies have shown that there is very little positive lift for sponsors.[18] While there may be some lift just prior to and during an event, this is very short-lived.[19]

The key to successful sponsorships and event marketing, assuming no bad publicity, is a reasonable fit between the brand and the sponsored event or individual.[20] There must be an association in memory that can trigger a link between the brand's position, especially its benefit, and what is being sponsored. Oktoberfest means beer and sausage, so a beer or sausage brand would be a good potential sponsor of an Oktoberfest event. The positive emotional benefit associated with the Oktoberfest should transfer to the sponsor. Tea or biscuits would make no sense. Hellmann's Extra Light Mayonnaise ('the lowest fat mayonnaise you can buy') should expect positive carry-over from sponsoring an organization involved in heart research; Häagen-Dazs would not.

The brand manager must look carefully at the fit between the brand and any potential candidate for sponsorship, just as the management of an organization or an event should ask if there is a good fit between them and the brand.[21]

Personal Selling and Trade Shows

Another important area of a brand's marketing communication mix involves personal selling and trade shows. Spending on direct, face-to-face selling in the US has been estimated at US$500 *billion* annually, a figure that is larger than the spending on all other marketing communication media *combined*. Too often people tend to forget that personal selling is more than direct selling to the trade. It is communication about the brand, and also involves sales to consumers at the retail level. At all levels, personal selling should be fully integrated with the overall marketing communication programme.

One reason why personal selling tends to be forgotten is that for many, if not most, fmcg companies sales and marketing are separate functions with separate budgets. Additionally, Dewshap and Jobber point out that for fmcg companies the retailer is the brand for the sales force, while the product is the brand for the marketing manager, further complicating things.[22] While it may not be practical to include personal selling as such in the strategic planning process when the functions are divided, the message that the sales force is to communicate should and must be consistent with the brand's overall marketing communication. This should go beyond sales support, such things as point-of-purchase merchandising material and sales kits. The sales force should be briefed on the brand's positioning and message in order to inform discussions with the trade.

We include trade shows and fairs with personal selling because they offer an excellent opportunity for personal interactions between business-to-business and industrial marketers and their customers. For these marketers, trade shows account for a significant part of their marketing communication budget, second only to advertising in business publications.

Personal Selling

Personal selling involves direct contact with consumers, or direct links to retailers or dealers in business-to-business and industrial marketing. The fundamental difference between personal selling and other components of the communication mix is that the messages go *directly* from the marketer to a specific member of the target audience, providing an opportunity for interaction and modification of the basic message to address specific concerns of that individual or company.

With business-to-business and industrial marketers, personal selling may be the primary or only form of marketing communication employed. In such cases the sales message must be developed in the same way as any other marketing communication, carefully positioning the brand and establishing optimum communication objectives, and it must be consistent with the overall positioning and communication objectives for the brand.

Rossiter and Bellman[23] have suggested that the management of personal selling depends upon the type of selling involved, and offer six basic types: regular retail selling, small business selling, trade selling, high-end retail selling, technical selling, and telemarketing. The first two are described as passive, in which the consumer controls the sales exchange. The remaining four are active in the sense that both the consumer and salesperson are involved in controlling the sales exchange. Only the four active types of personal selling are important to marketing communication.

Like all marketing communication, brand awareness and brand attitude are communication objectives for personal selling. Additionally, brand purchase intention will also almost always be an objective. The brand awareness objective will be recognition given that the salesperson will generally be calling on the customer rather than the other way around. In personal selling to retailers, and in business-to-business and industrial marketing, the purchase motive will almost always be negative (most likely problem solution or problem avoidance), requiring an informational brand attitude strategy, and the decision high involvement. This makes it essential that salespeople understand their target's *initial attitude* toward the brand because this understanding will be critical for framing message acceptance. The personal, interactive nature of personal selling permits a certain amount of probing to ensure a good understanding of how the target audience sees the brand.

An important consideration follows from this. Even if a brand can deliver its key benefit better than the target audience believes it can, a salesperson should not try to convince them it will. As long as the target is generally positive about the brand, the salesperson should present the benefit at the consumer's level of belief. If, when used, a product turns out to deliver a benefit better than anticipated, research has shown that overall brand attitude will increase.[24] This happens *because* there was a difference between anticipation and the actual delivery of the benefit.

Before leaving this, there is an important point that the manager must keep in mind when using personal selling to the trade. While an informational brand attitude is likely to be appropriate to 'close the sale', it would *not* be appropriate in talking about the *brand* and its benefit if the consumer brand choice decision involved positive motives. The transformational brand attitude used in the brand's marketing communication should be followed.

Trade Shows and Fairs

One might think of trade shows and fairs as falling somewhere between promotion and personal selling. It is not unusual for promotional incentives to be offered in order to encourage attendance at a trade show or fair stand; they are usually advertised in appropriate media and, like personal selling, there is direct contact with the target audience at the company's booth. Every industry has a trade show of some kind, and they can be especially important for small businesses unable to afford much (if any) other marketing communication. They play a significant role in the marketing of industrial products, where it has been estimated that trade shows and fairs account for 20–25 per cent of their marketing communication budget.[25]

The personal interactions that occur at trade shows and fair booths offer a number of opportunities.[26] For example, they provide a chance to identify and meet new customers, and an opportunity to nurture existing customers. They are an excellent forum for introducing new products, and for demonstrating products. The principle advantage of trade shows and fairs is that all of this can be accomplished within a relatively short period of time, and directly to members of the brand's target audience.

While trade shows and fairs offer a good opportunity for marketers and consumers to meet in a way where the marketer is offering information to interested consumers, there is some debate about their effectiveness. Some studies have shown that they generate awareness and interest leading to sales,[27] but other studies question the value of trade shows and fairs altogether.[28]

Effectiveness here has been defined by some in terms of leads that result in sales,[29] and this reflects how many managers who are heavily involved in trade shows and fairs measure their effectiveness.[30] Yet other researchers[31] have found that the non-selling aspects of trade shows and fairs are highly valued by managers. There do not seem to be fixed criteria for measuring success, and this complicates any attempt to calculate their cost effectiveness. Also complicating the issue of effectiveness is the tendency of managers to view trade shows and fairs on their own rather than as part of the brand's communication mix.

Product Placement

Including product placement as part of a brand's marketing communication mix has been on the increase for some time. It may be defined as the reference to a brand or its actual inclusion within some context in return for payment or other considerations. That context may be anything from movies and television programmes, to video games or even books. Although this is usually referred to as product placement, in reality we are talking about *brand* placement. Nonetheless, we shall follow convention and refer to it as product placement.

There are many people who consider the use of product placement to be unethical. Rossiter and Bellman have gone so far as to say that they regard it as 'ethically contemptible' because there is no guarantee that the audience will understand that an attempt is being made to persuade them.[32] They argue that even if the audience did understand, it is still unethical because the marketer *intends* to deceive. Sutherland complains that even while the use of product placements increase, less and less attention is paid to them by regulatory agencies.[33] He also makes the point that product placements distort the perception of what brands are popular (among other things), because people are not likely to make the connection between a brand appearing in, say, a movie or video game and the fact that it was put there by the marketer.

Product placement was not approved for use in the EU until the mid-2000s, and is only now being implemented (except in Denmark, where it is still forbidden). Each of the EU's twenty-seven countries is permitting the use of product placement under different conditions.[34] Long a controversial issue in the UK, that country remains one of the strictest in how it may be used. Although many US television shows are seen in the UK, product placement in such programming that is not permitted, such as alcohol or food that is high in fat or sugar, will be identified and pixelated (i.e. digitally blurred out).[35]

In addition to ethical concerns, there is the issue of whether or not product placement is effective. There are few empirical studies of product placement, and those that have been conducted do not tend to find them effective.[36] Despite this, there are many anecdotal stories about their effectiveness. One of the more well-known stories involves the 1986 movie *Top Gun* in which Tom Cruise is wearing Rayban Aviator sunglasses. Supposedly this led to a turn-around in the company's financial situation, which was in dire straits before the movie's release.[37]

If we assume that product placement can be effective, *how* the brand is placed will have an effect upon the likelihood that it will be noticed and impact brand attitude. If a brand is clearly seen being used by a celebrity or is talked about directly by brand name, the potential will obviously be better than if it is simply part of the background.[38] Perhaps the most likely effect from using product placements is raising brand awareness and salience. But to accomplish even this would require *conscious* attention to the placement, and this is problematic.

It is this need for conscious attention that minimizes the potential effectiveness of product placements in effecting brand attitude. While there may be implicit processing of the brand's placement, this will have *no effect* upon brand attitude or behaviour.[39] Again, it is likely only to be the small segment of viewers who actively identify with the celebrity or situation that are likely to attend to the brand. To be effective at a broader level, not only must there be conscious attention, but the placement must stimulate positive associations in memory with the celebrity or the situation within which the brand is shown, and this within the correct emotional context. If this happens, the placement has the potential to contribute to positive brand attitude by creating a sense of personal involvement with what is going on. But as suggested, this is a lot to ask of all but the most highly involved. However, there is an emerging belief among advertising practitioners that product placements will be more effective if accompanied by adverts for the product.[40]

The actual cost of product placement in absolute terms is generally less than other forms of marketing communication, but it is difficult to predict or measure whether or not any positive effect from the placement justifies even the relatively low cost. Regardless, if product placement is to be considered as part of a brand's communication mix, it must be used within a context consistent with the brand's positioning.

Packaging

Packaging is often overlooked as part of a brand's communication mix, yet it is a very important part of the brand's marketing communication. While some marketers do appreciate its importance,[41] too often it is underestimated by managers.[42] There are several key emotional and psychological benefits linked to packages.[43] They have the ability to attract attention, enhancing brand awareness, and they have the ability to express the brand's image, reinforcing brand attitude. Getting the package right is critical. In 2009, after PepsiCo redesigned its package for Tropicana Pure Premium orange juice, sales dropped 20 per cent in less than two months. This led to a fast return to the *old* package.

Look at Advert 14.4 for Nairn's. Here we see the package not only well integrated into an advert for recognition brand awareness, but that the package itself does a good job communicating the brand's benefit of 'oaty goodness'. The strong visual of the biscuits on the package, under the words 'oat biscuit' reinforces the advert's message. Every time you reach for a biscuit, the message is reinforced by the package.

Studies by the Point-of-Purchase Advertising Institute have shown that over 70 per cent of brand decisions in supermarkets are made in the store.[44] A well-designed package will attract attention at the point of purchase, which is critical for products where the purchase decision is triggered by brand recognition. If this recognition is linked to the appropriate need in the consumer's mind as a result of its other marketing communication (especially advertising), this aids purchase. The large number package facings in a store mean that the brand's package must be able to cut through competitive clutter, and this means that visual elements of the package must be different from competitors.

Additionally, the 'message' communicated by the package should be consistent with the brand's overall marketing communication strategy. This enables the package to reinforce the brand's image and key benefit. Many products, especially fmcg, are used directly from the package: everything from breakfast cereals to cold remedies, toothpaste to household cleaners. This means that every time the product is used, the package offers the brand an opportunity to reinforce its primary benefit, nurturing brand attitude. In a very real sense, a package can operate as post-purchase advertising. Rossiter and Bellman have put this nicely, describing packages as 'take-away or leave behind' communication vehicles.[45]

Channels Marketing

'Channels marketing' is a relatively recent term used to describe all levels of marketing communication to the retail trade. It came into being as a result of the increasing importance of trade promotion, coupled with the increasing power of retailers. Basically, it combines 'co-op advertising' with tactical marketing. Co-op advertising has existed for a very long time, and is essentially an agreement between a retailer and a brand to cooperate in part of the brand's marketing communication. The brand offers to produce advertising or promotions that include the retailer's name, and the retailer agrees to participate in funding the advertising or promotion along with the brand. Tactical marketing is a relatively new channel-oriented (that is, distribution) marketing communication system designed to return more control over promotion to the brand and to leverage incremental support for the trade, especially the retailer.

Traditional co-op advertising is generally broad in scope and *passive* in nature. Typically, it is open to a brand's entire retail base, conditioned on sales volume: the more of the brand sold, the more money available for co-op advertising. The adverts and other merchandising material are provided by the brand, but used by the retailer as it wishes. Then, on a periodic basis, the retailer is reimbursed for its expenditures according to the co-op agreement.

Advert 14.4 Here we see a package well integrated into an advert for good recognition awareness, and a package that also communicates the benefit on its own. Reproduced with kind permission © Nairn's Oatcakes Limited.

Source: Reproduced with kind permission © Nairn's Oatcakes Limited.

With their expanding power, many retailers were treating traditional co-op as a profit centre, diverting funds to offset operating costs. Retailers were also beginning to force brands, as a condition of stocking, to participate in retailer-initiated promotions that often were not consistent or integrated with the brand's overall marketing communication. *Tactical marketing* grew out of the desire on the part of brands to assume more control over the use of their co-op monies.

Tactical marketing, unlike traditional co-op, is always *proactive*. Programmes are designed for particular retailers, tailored to their specific needs. With the cooperation of the retailer, the brand funds the programme, in accordance with the retailer meeting specific sales goals, and *implements* the programme. The benefit for the brand is *control*. Tactical marketing offers the retailer complete coordination of the programme and production of the materials used, while maintaining control over the content and timing of the advertising and promotions. The pay-off for the retailer is the ability to go beyond the basic print orientation of most traditional co-op programmes (or at best very simple broadcast executions), and the ability to utilize the full marketing communication range of the brand within a plan optimized for each retailer.

Chapter summary

In this chapter we have looked at sales promotion techniques, and at a number of ways other than traditional media in which advertising and promotion may be delivered to a brand's target audience. We reviewed the basic sales promotion techniques associated with trade, retail, and consumer promotion, and discussed their strengths and weaknesses. An understanding of these strengths and weaknesses is what helps the manager to make strategic decisions as to which technique is most appropriate in given situations. Public relations was discussed, and the distinction between PR in general and marketing PR made. Also, where sponsorships, event marketing, personal selling, and trade shows fit within a brand's overall marketing communication programme was considered, as was the use of product placement and even packaging.

Questions to consider

14.1 In what ways do sales promotions provide a means of delivering a brand's key benefit? Find good examples of this.

14.2 What are the similarities and differences between trade and retail promotions and consumer sales promotions?

14.3 How can public relations contribute to a brand's overall marketing communication programmes?

14.4 What is the difference between public relations and marketing public relations?

14.5 Identify examples of sponsorships and event marketing, and discuss how they are contributing to the brand attitude.

14.6 Weigh the advantages and disadvantages of personal selling as part of a brand's marketing communication.

14.7 Discuss how trade shows and fairs contribute to a brand's communication objectives.

14.8 Why are product placements seen by some as unethical, and how do you see this issue?

14.9 Find examples of packages that do a good job of communicating the brand's key benefit.

14.10 How does channels marketing differ from co-op?

Case study 14 **Subway—On a Roll: How the Regional Trial of a Repositioned and Rebranded Existing Product for UK Sandwich Chain Subway Led to a Fully Integrated Global Communications Success Story**

The early to mid-2000s witnessed the beginning of a period of climactic change for the food industry. Seven out of ten consumers were confused as to what constituted a healthy diet. It was into this uncertain climate that Subway chose to launch itself into the UK as a serious contender. The brand was dogged by its American heritage from the off. Overtly American fast-food cues did not sit comfortably with the increasingly anti-American British public. McDonald's, Burger King, and KFC accounted for 92 per cent of QSR 2005 media spend. With Gregg's, M&S, Prêt, and more, the market was noisy. As well as the big players entering the 'sandwich' sector, research revealed that there was an additional barrier: other than the base of existing aficionados, consumers were often uncertain about Subway's offering.

Qualitative research into consumers' eating habits on the move revealed them to be promiscuous lunchers. Spoiled for choice, their expectations were high and loyalty low. These demanding consumers knew what they wanted, when they wanted it, and perhaps most importantly, how they wanted it. Herein lay the opportunity for Subway. Chameleon-like, it could be one consumer's healthy lunch option and another's Saturday morning hangover treat. Trial was key and we had to overcome the problem of intimidation about ordering.

Our solution? 'Sub of the Day®': a different, predefined, six-inch Sub every day of the week for only £1.99—the same offer in structure and product to the Daily Special, but rebranded and relaunched to embrace both franchisees and consumers. This would help to embed the word 'Sub' in the everyday vernacular and strengthen Subway's ownership of the product amongst the competition. And it would give new customers an 'easy order'. In terms of brand look, Subway had some really positive brand DNA—a contemporary logo, fresh colour palette, and the tagline 'Eat Fresh'.

Consumer research highlighted the importance of the in-store experience in addition to TV advertising (TV was the best way of achieving fame quickly and effectively). The new campaign was thus fully integrated through point-of-sale, staff uniforms, menus, flyers, and local PR support.

National results mirrored the success of the regional test—even during a seasonally more fallow period. Spontaneous brand awareness before the January campaign was 22 per cent; this increased to 31 per cent, on par with KFC, two months later. We were then briefed to create the first Subway brand campaign dedicated to the UK. Our strategy was to build empathy with the brand, whilst at the same time giving consumers rational reasons to try Subway by promoting the accessibility and value of Sub of the Day®. Our creative idea was to contrast things you don't want to witness with things you do—such as watching your sandwiches being freshly made. We used a TV mix of 30-second brand adverts and 10-second promotional ads with a full in-store campaign—leveraging brand appeal, whilst promoting the core competitive advantages and accessibility of Subway.

Source: This is an edited version of a case study submitted to the IPA Effectiveness Awards. The full case study can be found at ipa.co.uk or warc.com.

Edited by Elizabeth Mamali, PhD Researcher, Bath School of Management

➜

→ Discussion questions

1. In what ways did the 'Sub of the Day' offer help the Subway brand?
2. Discuss how an in-store offer informed a fully integrated promotional campaign.
3. Taking into account the increased importance of new media in advertising, suggest a new media creative idea for a future Subway campaign.
4. Suggest alternative in-store offers for Subway.

Further reading

R.V. Kozinels, K. deValck, A.C. Wojnicki, and S.J.S. Wilner, 'Networked Narratives: Understanding Word-of-Mouth Marketing in Online Communities', *Journal of Marketing*, 74/2 (2010), 71–89

Buzz and social media in terms of potential communication strategies.

Catharine Taylor, 'Pssst! How do you Measure Buzz?', *Adweek* (24 October 2005)

How to measure buzz.

Larry Yu, 'How Companies Turn Buzz into Sales', *MIT Sloan Management Review* (Winter 2005), 5–6

The effect of buzz on sales.

Rajesh Bagchi and Xingbo Li, 'Illusionary Progress in Loyalty Programs: Magnitudes, Reward Distances, and Step-Size Ambiguity', *Journal of Consumer Research*, 37/5 (2011), 888–901

How consumers deal with the magnitude of point accumulation and points required for redemption in loyalty programmes.

Y. Xi and H. Jeon, 'Effects of Loyalty Programs on Value Perception, Program Loyalty, and Brand Loyalty', *Journal of the Academy of Marketing Science*, 31/3 (2003), 229–48

The effects of loyalty programmes.

X. Dreze and D.R. Bell, 'Creating Win-Win Trade Promotions: Theory and Empirical Analysis of Scan-Back Trade Deals', *Market Sciences*, 23/1 (2003), 16–39

How to create effective trade promotions.

'So you Want to be an Olympic Sponsor', *Brandweek* (7 November 2005)

A good case history on sponsorship, it details the story of Visa's involvement in Olympics sponsorship.

Edith Smit, Eva van Reijmesdal, and Peter Neijens, 'Today's Practice of Brand Placement and the Industry behind It', *International Journal of Advertising*, 28/5 (2009), 761–82

Practitioner perceptions of product placement is integrated with a content analysis of brand placement.

Susan Chang, Jay Newell, and Charles Salmon, 'Product Placement in Entertainment Media: Proposing Business Process Models', *International Journal of Advertising*, 28/5 (2009), 783–806

Brand placement within entertainment media.

A.J. Dubinsky, 'A Factor Analytic Study of the Personal Selling Process', *Journal of Personal Selling & Sales Management*, 1/1 (1980), 26–33

The classic discussion of the stages involved in personal selling.

Notes

1. See L. Percy, *Strategies for Implementing Integrated Marketing Communication* (Lincolnwood, FL: NTC Business Books, 1997), 98.
2. In the US a 1995 study of consumer buying habits conducted by the P-O-P Advertising Institute found that more than 70 per cent of brand choices are made in the store.
3. See C.M. Henderson, 'Promotion Heterogeneity and Consumer Learning: Refining the Deal-Proneness Construct', in C.T. Allen and D. Roedder John (eds), *Advances in Consumer Research*, xxi (Provo, UT: Association for Consumer Research, 1994), 86–94.
4. This is a point made by Rossiter and Percy in a review of several studies dealing with the effect of displays without accompanying price reductions: see *Advertising Communication and Promotion Management* (New York: McGraw-Hill, 1997), 390.
5. See A. Krishna, F.S. Currin, and R.W. Shoemaker, 'Consumer Perceptions of Promotional Activity', *Journal of Marketing*, 55 (1991), 14–16.
6. This quote, along with more from an interview with Denmark's then head of the Office of Consumer Policy, may be found in an article by Mary Sandberg, 'Ready, Set, Clip: Coupons Coming Despite Objections', *The Copenhagen Post* (11–17 March 2011), 8.
7. See Chris Fill, *Marketing Communications: Frameworks, Theories, and Applications* (London: Prentice Hall, 1995), 376.
8. Jack Neff, 'Internet Enabling Coupon Fraud Biz', *Advertising Age* (20 October 2003), 3, reviews the economic impact of fake coupons generated on the Internet.
9. See B. Weiss, 'Groupon's $6 billion gamble', *Wall Street Journal* (15 December 2010), A15.
10. See M. Fielding, 'C'est De'licieux', *Marketing News* (15 September 2010), 6.
11. Paul Smith relates a number of stories of disastrous promotions in his book *Marketing Communications: An Integrated Approach*, 2nd edn (London: Kogan Page, 1998).
12. This story of the Pepsi Philippine subsidiary promotion was reported in *Precision Marketing* (26 May 1997).
13. See John Rossiter and Steve Bellman, *Marketing Communication: Theory and Application* (Frenchs Forest, NSW: Pearson Education Australia, 2005), 386.
14. See John Rossiter and Steve Bellman, *Marketing Communication: Theory and Application* (Frenchs Forest, NSW: Pearson Education Australia, 2005), 377.
15. The term 'marketing public relations' was introduced by T. Harris in *The Marketers Guide to PR: How Today's Companies are Using the New Public Relations to Gain a Competitive Edge* (New York: John Wiley and Sons, 1993).
16. The story behind BMWFilms.com is told in some detail in Teressa Iezzi's *The Idea Writers* (New York: Palgrave MacMillan, 2010), 37–45.
17. See T. Meehaghan, 'Current Developments and Future Directions in Sports Sponsorship', *International Journal of Advertising*, 17/1 (1998), 3–28.
18. There are a number of studies that have shown little lift resulting from sponsorships, including: A.D. Miyazaki and A.G. Morgan's 'Assessing Market Value of Event Sponsoring: Corporate Olympics Sponsorships', *Journal of Advertising Research*, 41/1 (2001), 9–15; J. Crimmins and M. Horn's 'Sponsorship: From Management Ego Trip to Marketing Success', *Journal of Advertising Research*, 36/4 (1996), 11–21; and L. Kinney and S.R. McDaniel's, 'Strategic Implications of Attitude-towards-the-Ad in Leveraging Event Sponsorships', *Journal of Sports Management*, 10 (1996), 250–60.

19. This was found in a large-scale study of sponsorship effect from the FIFA 2006 World Cup, and reported by Joe Acaoui in 'Brand Experience in the Pitch: How the Sponsors Fared in the World Cup', *Journal of Advertising Research*, 47/2 (2007), 147–57.
20. See D.T.Y. Poou and G. Prendergast, 'A New Framework for Evaluating Sponsorship Opportunities', *International Journal of Advertising*, 25/4 (2006), 471–88.
21. See K.P. Gwinner and J. Eaton, 'Building Brand Image through Event Sponsorship: The Role of Image Transfer', *Journal of Advertising*, 25/4 (1999), 47–57.
22. See B. Dewshap and D. Jobber, 'The Sales-Marketing Interface in Consumer Packaged-Goods Companies: A Conceptual Framework', *Journal of Personal Selling & Sales Management*, 20/2 (2000), 109–19.
23. See Rossiter and Bellman, *Marketing Communication: Theory and Application* (Frenchs Forest, NSW: Pearson Education Australia, 2005), 402.
24. This research is discussed in P.K. Kopalle and J.L. Assuncão, 'When to Indulge in "Puffing": The Role of Consumer Expectations and Brand Goodwill in Determining Advertised and Actual Product Quality', *Managerial Decision Economics*, 21/6 (2000).
25. See S. Gopalakrishna and J.D. Williams, 'Planning and Performance Assessment of Industrial Trade Shows: An Exploratory Study', *International Journal of Research and Marketing*, 9 (1992), 207–24.
26. See D. Shipley, C. Egan, and K.S. Wong, 'Dimensions of Trade Show Exhibiting Management', *Journal of Marketing Management*, 9/1 (1993), 55–64.
27. See n. 21.
28. This is discussed in C.M. Sashi and J. Perretty, 'Do Trade Shows Provide Value?', *Industrial Marketing Management*, 21 (1992), 249–53.
29. See A. Sharland and P. Balogh, 'The Value of Non-Selling Activities at International Trade Shows', *Industrial Marketing Management*, 25 (1996), 59–66.
30. See J. Blythe and T. Raymer, 'The Evaluation of Non-Selling Activities at British Trade Exhibitions: An Exploratory Study', *Marketing Intelligence and Planning*, 14/5 (1996).
31. See n. 22.
32. See Rossiter and Bellman, *Marketing Communication: Theory and Application* (Frenchs Forest, NSW: Pearson Education Australia, 2005), 352.
33. This is argued by Max Sutherland in 'Product Placement: Regulators Gone AWOL', *International Journal of Advertising*, 25 (2006), 107–10.
34. The variety of ways in which EU countries are dealing with product placement is discussed by James Morris in his article 'Product Placement Finally Arrives in Europe, but Local Caveats Make Crossover Complicated', *Advertising Age* (13 June 2011), 27.
35. See E. Hall, 'Product Placement Faces Wary Welcome in Britain', *Advertising Age* (8 January 2007), 27.
36. See L. Johnson and C.A. Dodd, 'Placements as Mediators of Brand Salience within UK Cinema Audiences', *Journal of Marketing Communications*, 6 (2000), 141–58.
37. This story is reported by B.R. Fischer in 'Making your Product the Star Attraction', *Promo* (July 1996), 58.
38. See J.R. Semenik, *Promotion & Integrated Marketing Communication* (Cincinnati, OH: South-Western College Publishing, 2002), 398.
39. This point is made by one of the book's authors, Larry Percy, in 'Are Product Placements Effective?', *International Journal of Advertising*, 25 (2006), 112–14.
40. This was reported in the *Wall Street Journal* (20 June 2005), B1.

41. See D. Walczyk, 'Packaging Should be a Critical Element in the Branding Schema', *Marketing News*, 35/23 (2001), 14–17.
42. See P. Southgate, *Total Branding by Design* (London: Kogan Page, 1994).
43. The psychological and emotional benefits associated with packaging are discussed by S. Charearlary in 'An Investigation of the Representation of Brand Image through Packaging', an MSC Marketing dissertation from Aston Business School, Aston University, Birmingham.
44. These studies are published by the Point of Purchase Advertising Institute in *An Integrated Look at Integrated Marketing: Uncovering P-O-P—Role as the Last Three Feet in the Marketing Mix* (Washington, DC: Point-of-Purchase Advertising Institute, 2000), 10.
45. See Rossiter and Bellman, *Marketing Communication: Theory and Application* (Frenchs Forest, NSW: Pearson Education Australia, 2005), 356.

Visit the Online Resource Centre that accompanies this book for additional resources to support the text: **www.oxfordtextbooks.co.uk/orc/percy_elliott4e/**

Putting it all Together

Key concepts

1. Integrated marketing communication (IMC) is the *planning* and execution of a marketing communication campaign, using a common set of communication objectives and a consistent look and feel to all aspects of the campaign.
2. Advertising and promotion each contribute unique strengths to a campaign. The primary strength of traditional advertising is building long-term, positive brand attitudes; that of traditional promotion is creating brand purchase intention for accomplishing short-term, tactical brand objectives.
3. If advertising and promotion are used together effectively, the interaction of the short- and long-term effects 'ratchet up' the overall effectiveness of the campaign.
4. Once the campaign is running, it is essential that the programme is monitored for both effectiveness and wearout.
5. Unfortunately, implementing truly effective IMC is very difficult because of organizational and, especially, compensation issues. Until a way is found to deal with these issues, it will be hard to convince managers in different areas of marketing communication to yield to others in order to deliver a more effective overall marketing communication programme.

Putting together a marketing communication programme requires a full understanding of the strengths and weaknesses of both traditional advertising and promotion. There are strengths and weaknesses to all aspects of marketing communication, which is why a truly integrated *planning* approach is so important to effective mass communication. What we want to look at now are the basic ways in which traditional advertising and promotion, as we have been discussing them in this book, differ in terms of their appropriateness in specific marketing and communication situations. Remember, when we are talking about *traditional* advertising and promotion, we are referring to their basic functions. Traditional advertising is marketing communication used primarily for long-term brand equity *delivered* via such media as print, broadcast, new media, direct mail, and packaging, as opposed to traditional promotion, which is marketing communication used primarily for short-term tactical goals, regardless of whether it is delivered via print, new media, direct mail, point-of-purchase collateral, or broadcast media.

Integrated Marketing Communication (IMC)

One of the most talked-about ideas in marketing during the 1990s was the notion of integrated marketing communication (IMC). And, while marketing managers (especially in the US[1]) still clearly feel that it is a valuable concept and one that will play an increasingly important role in their companies, there is unfortunately a great deal of evidence to suggest that *truly* integrated marketing communication is the exception rather than the rule.

There are a great many reasons for this, which we shall deal with at the end of this chapter. One problem is that too often IMC is thought to be nothing more than using several means of delivering a message. If a brand manager uses direct mail, television, and print advertising, along with some promotions and sponsorships, this is likely to be considered an IMC campaign. But simply using a variety of marketing communications does not necessarily mean an *integrated* marketing communication campaign.

Defining Integrated Marketing Communication

If using a variety of marketing communications does not define IMC, what does? You might briefly consider IMC as the *planning* and execution of all types of marketing communication needed for a brand, service, or company in order to satisfy a common set of communication objectives—or, put more simply, to support a single positioning. IMC means *planning*, and the ability to deliver a consistent message, all with a consistent look and feel. The importance of a consistent look and feel was stressed in Chapter 13.

Without planning, it is impossible to have IMC.[2] Centralized strategic planning is the very heart of IMC. The job of a marketing or advertising manager is to use whatever combination of marketing communication options is available to him or her in order to achieve the desired communication objective. But the use of these options must be *centrally planned and coordinated*, utilizing a systematic strategic planning process. In a very real sense this book has provided a detailed description and understanding of the tools involved in planning an effective IMC campaign. Chapters 6–10 laid out the necessary strategic planning process.

In our example above, if a brand manager uses a direct mail programme that is not tied into the advertising, that does not have the same 'look and feel', that is not developed from the same umbrella creative brief, it is not a part of an integrated campaign. If the promotions are not extensions of the advertising's message, they are not a part of an IMC campaign. If a sponsorship has little connection with the brand and its advertising, it is not part of an integrated campaign. In fact, it is quite possible to have an IMC campaign that utilizes *only* direct mail, or *only* advertising, or *only* some promotion, or *just* a sponsorship. How? If the manager went through a thorough strategic communications planning process and came to the decision that only one form of marketing communication was required to meet the brand's marketing communication objectives effectively, then the result is indeed an IMC campaign. Why? Again, because IMC is in the *planning*. All possible options were considered, even if only one was needed.

Traditional Advertising and Promotion in IMC

We must never forget that *all* forms of marketing communication may be considered in IMC planning: everything from product packaging to store signs, to more familiar forms of advertising and promotion, and, of course, the Internet and other new media. But, from a practical standpoint, it is easier to talk about marketing communication options in the traditional terms of advertising and promotion, our long-term strategic and short-term tactical marketing communication, as we have done throughout this book.

As we saw in Chapter 1, to understand the fundamental distinction between traditional forms of advertising and promotion, we need only look at the Latin roots of the two words. You will remember that the Latin root of advertising is *advertere*, which may be roughly translated as 'to turn towards', and the Latin root of promotion is *promovere*, which may be roughly translated as 'to move ahead'. This summarizes nicely the difference between the communication contribution of each: advertising contributes to long-term attitude, while promotion contributes to short-term action.

We have emphasized, and will continue to emphasize, that IMC is all about planning. The word 'integrate' comes from the Latin verb *integrare*, and is defined by the *Oxford Dictionary of Current English* as 'combine [parts] into a whole'. In IMC planning, we are looking at all of our available options in terms of their ability to satisfy the communication objectives of our brand. The parts that are 'combined' are various forms of traditional advertising and promotion, and the 'whole' is a consistent marketing communication programme.

You may be wondering why we have been using the adjective 'traditional' throughout this book in referring to advertising and promotion. This is to remind us of the *strategic* roles that each plays in planning marketing communication. But in today's world of marketing communication it is often not easy to tell an advertising execution from a promotion execution. Television commercials include direct response toll-free numbers or ask consumers to look for coupons in newspapers or magazines, and actually show the coupon. FSIs (those 'free-standing inserts' that clutter up Sunday newspapers and other print media), which are traditional promotion vehicles for delivering coupons, are often very like adverts in their appearance.

In the past there was a rather clear-cut difference between advertising and promotion media. Advertising was delivered via 'measured media' in such things as television, radio, newspaper, magazines, and outdoor. Today, however, it is not unusual to find advertising messages being delivered through direct marketing and channels marketing (trade-oriented marketing programmes similar to 'co-op' in which the marketer and the retailer cooperate on marketing communication programmes, and discussed in Chapter 14), which in the past were used only for promotional messages. In addressing this issue of traditional advertising versus promotion, Rossiter and Percy[3] have made two important points. Talking about the increase in the marketing monies going into promotion relative to advertising in recent years, they point out that, in spite of this swing, there has nevertheless been an *increase*, not a decrease, in the use of general advertising media because of an increase in the number of media options available for advertising (as we mentioned above). They also note that most of this growth in promotion spending, apart from all-but-required promotions to the trade, has been *additional* spending, and most of this increase has gone into promotions that look more like adverts.

A second point they make is very important. Familiar forms of promotion (things like sweepstakes, coupons, and samples) are not growing. What is growing is the use of promotion-oriented messages that are very much like advertising. As they point out, the fastest-growing forms of marketing communication are direct mail and telemarketing, which have traditionally been thought of as 'promotion' rather than 'advertising'. But both direct mail and telemarketing are as much 'advertising', in the traditional sense of 'turning towards' (for example, in terms of building brand awareness and brand equity), as they are 'promotion', in the traditional sense of 'moving ahead' some short-term action objective such as sales. As we have already discussed, even FSIs, which are by far the most widely used way of delivering coupons, are more and more like adverts in how they are being used to help to build awareness and brand equity at the same time as they offer a coupon.

As the old distinction between advertising and promotion becomes more blurred, thinking in terms of IMC is all the more important. What have in the past been thought of as traditional 'advertising skills' now play a critical role across the board with IMC. Planning an effective marketing communication programme with IMC requires a manager to address the creative and media questions that have always been addressed with traditional advertising. These same principles are simply being applied to a wider range of options.

Optimizing the Communication Objectives

One of the fundamental decisions a manager will be charged with is how to use traditional advertising and promotion in order to meet specific communication objectives in planning an IMC programme. Depending upon the communication effect, advertising and promotion will have different strengths. For marketing communication to be effective, it is important to understand the relative strengths and weaknesses of traditional advertising and promotion in contributing to the four basic communication effects. These relative strengths and weaknesses are discussed below.[4]

Category need. Neither advertising nor promotion is especially strong in stimulating category need. Category need generally springs from some felt need, the result of a particular consumer motivation. Advertising would have a hard time trying to *create* a motivation. Its strength would be in positioning a category so that it is seen as satisfying an existing motivation. Promotions have the ability to *accelerate* category need, but again are not likely actually to generate category need. As a result, neither advertising nor promotion is likely to have a major impact upon creating category need. (In fact, this is a case in which publicity can make an important contribution.)

Brand awareness. Brand awareness is a traditional strength of both advertising and promotion. However, the manager must remember to consider what type of awareness is involved. While advertising can deal effectively with both recognition and recall brand awareness, promotions are likely to be more effective for recognition brand awareness.

Brand attitude. Here we have the traditional strength of advertising. By its very nature it offers the message flexibility that is so very well suited for brand attitude objectives. But good promotions should also work on brand attitude, as we saw in Chapter 14. If proper attention is paid to how a promotion is executed (especially in terms of the words and images in the message), it will be able to contribute something to brand attitude. Nevertheless, advertising is still the strongest contributor to brand attitude communication effects.

Brand purchase intention. This is the traditional strength of promotion. Because of their generally short-term, tactical nature, promotions are geared to immediate action on the part of the consumer. Advertising can contribute to brand purchase intention, but if it is truly an advertisement and not a hybrid advertising message that includes a promotion, it is unlikely to make as strong a contribution.

The relative strengths of traditional advertising versus promotion are summarized in Fig. 15.1.

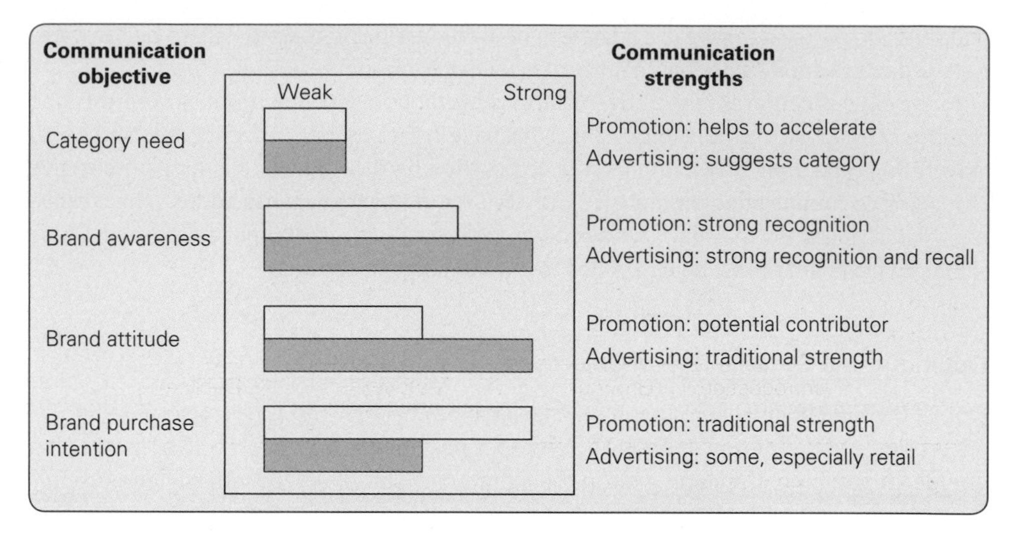

Figure 15.1 Relative Communication Strengths of Advertising and Promotion

Marketing Considerations Affecting Advertising or Promotion Emphasis

As we can see, the relative strengths of advertising and promotion are directly related to communication effects. But, apart from this, perhaps the next most important guide to the relative emphasis placed upon the use of traditional advertising versus promotion in marketing a product is where the product falls in the product life cycle.[5]

Product Life Cycle Influence upon Relative Emphasis

The product life cycle is generally presented in four parts, as shown in Fig. 15.2. There is an introductory phase, followed by a period of growth. After a certain point the product reaches maturity, and in the long run most products will decline. One of the key determinants of the shape of this curve is the effectiveness of the overall marketing effort. Ideally, a company would like to accelerate the early stages of the cycle, quickly introducing the brand and growing to a position of strength in the market. At this point it is possible to scale back marketing expenditures, while at the same time experiencing manufacturing efficiencies. This is the period of greatest profit from the brand, and every effort is made to prolong this period before the forces of the ever-changing market eventually push the brand into decline.[6]

Where do advertising and promotion fit in relation to the various stages that a brand experiences over its life? If you were to ask yourself when you would probably need to spend the most marketing monies over the life of a product, the obvious answer is during its introductory phase. This is the time when you must make potential consumers aware of the new brand, and teach them something about it in order to interest them in trying it. A very high level of spending is required here, for both advertising and promotion. The high advertising expenditure goes into helping to make people aware that the brand exists and just exactly what kind of product it is. The high expenditure for promotion is needed to help to make the target audience aware of the brand, and to induce them to try it. Both the advertising and

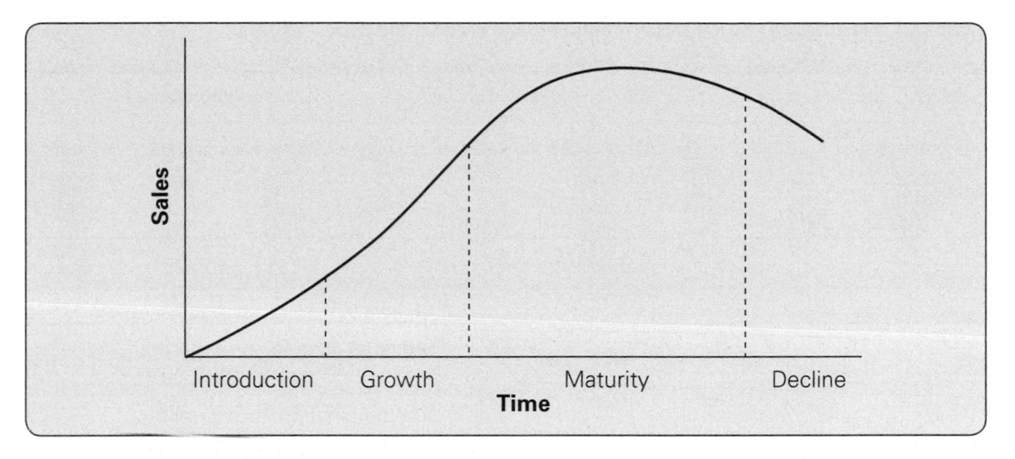

Figure 15.2 The Product Life Cycle

promotion efforts must be carefully integrated here in order to provide the consistent image we talked about in Chapter 14.

As the brand moves from the introductory stage into the growth stage, the proper distribution of advertising versus promotion expenditure will depend upon the nature of the product itself, or upon the marketing strategy undertaken for the brand. If the new product is a leader in the category or has a readily apparent difference that makes it more desirable than competitive brands, you will want to spend heavily on advertising. Why? Because, with advertising, you are able to underscore your competitive advantage and maintain high levels of awareness for the brand. Promotions really do not make a lot of sense here, since potential consumers should be interested in trying your brand because of the benefits associated with it, not because of some incentive.

On the other hand, if there is really not much to differentiate your brand from others in the category, you will probably spend less on advertising because you are counting on competitors' advertising to help to maintain interest in the category. But if you adopt this strategy, you must invest in promotional expenditures in order to entice consumers to try or switch to your brand once the category need has been established and maintained by the overall advertising expenditures in the category. However, you must be *very* careful not to overuse promotions to the point at which your target audience anticipates them, effectively lowering the brand's price point. In the growth stage of a product's life cycle, you can see that the relative roles of advertising and promotion will differ, depending upon the nature of the product. This same situation occurs when a product reaches maturity, only in this case the difference in expenditure will vary as a function of brand loyalty. If you enjoy a high degree of brand loyalty, it makes very little sense to spend much money on promotion, since all that you would be doing, in effect, is lowering the price of your product because most of your users would be buying the brand anyway. However, if there is very little brand loyalty in the category, with a great deal of switching among brands, you will spend less on advertising, but more on promotion. In this case advertising is primarily used to maintain awareness for the brand, while promotion is used to attract and hold customers.

Table 15.1 Relating Advertising and Promotion to the Product Life Cycle

Product life cycle stage	Utilizing advertising	Utilizing promotion
Introduction	Drive up awareness	Generate initial trial
Growth		
Differentiated brand	Underscore brand's advantage	Unnecessary
Undifferentiated brand	Rely upon category spending to maintain interest	Encourage switching to brand
Maturity		
High brand loyalty	Maintain loyalty	Avoid because it effectively lowers price point
Low brand loyalty	Maintain brand awareness	Use to attract and hold customers
Decline	Unnecessary	Maintain distribution until inventory is gone

Finally, once a product begins to decline, both advertising and promotion spending should drop too as the marketing manager begins to phase out support for the brand. Soon there will be no spending at all on advertising, and only minimal spending on promotion to the trade (not the consumer) in order to maintain distribution for the product until the company has used up its inventory of the brand. All of these relationships between the amount spent on advertising versus promotion during different stages of the product life cycle are summarized in Table 15.1.

Additional Marketing Considerations Affecting Relative Emphasis

In addition to the inherent strengths of advertising and promotion as they relate to communication effects, various characteristics in the market also suggest emphasizing either advertising or promotion. These market characteristics may be grouped into four categories, and are reviewed below (see Table 15.2).

Product Differentiation

Generally speaking, if a brand has a positively perceived difference over its competitors, there should be an emphasis on advertising in its marketing communication programme. Two potential differences to consider are quality and price. If you have a brand that consumers see as high quality, you will be likely to spend more on advertising in order to communicate its quality benefits and to support its 'quality image', reinforcing positive brand equity. If your brand is seen as lower quality, you will tend to spend more on promotion in order to persuade people to 'trade down'. Quality generally relates to price, so you will tend to find high-priced brands spending more on advertising in order to build and sustain a strong brand equity to justify their higher price. Lower-priced brands generally spend more on promotion, and usually price pro-

Table 15.2 Advertising versus Promotion Emphasis under Specific Market Considerations

Market consideration	Emphasis
Product differentiation	Advertising
Strong market position	Advertising
Poor market performance	Promotion
Competitive activity	Respond accordingly

motion, in order to appear to offer consumers a better value. Price promotion could certainly help tactically in the short term, but it will not help to justify a higher price in the long term.

If your brand is seen by consumers to have special benefits not found in other brands in the category, you will be more likely to spend money on advertising in order to inform your target audience about unique benefits associated with the brand. On the other hand, 'commodity' brands are thought of as similar and as a result tend to compete more on a promotion basis. Brands can be differentiated on the basis of obvious benefits, such as taste, but also on the basis of attributes that the consumer never really sees, such as special whitening ingredients in a detergent or the presence or absence of caffeine in colas. As long as a brand is perceived as different, advertising can have a greater effect than promotion.

Products that have a real risk associated with them, not just high-priced brands or ones with perceived psychological risk (that is, high involvement), tend to employ advertising to reassure consumers that they are making a safe choice. Such potentially high-risk products—for example, those needed for very serious health problems—are unlikely to use promotion.

Strong Market Position

If a brand has a strong market position, based upon either a high market share or frequent purchase, advertising should be emphasized over promotion. The key again is advertising's ability to help to build and reinforce a positive brand attitude, especially in a market in which there may be a lot of switching behaviour. Promotion, of course, can be used tactically, but to sustain a strong position in the market requires an advertising emphasis.

Poor Market Performance

If a brand is having problems in the market, promotion should be emphasized over advertising because of its more immediate impact. This emphasis makes sense at both the consumer and the trade levels when a brand is in need of a 'quick fix'. It is assumed, of course, that there is not an inherent product problem, or other serious marketing mix problem, because promotion will not provide a long-term cure.

Competitive Activity

A final and obvious factor in the relative expenditure of marketing monies for advertising versus promotion is the activity of your competitors. Suppose a direct competitor increases its advertising spending. If you are to maintain your relative position in the market, it will probably be necessary for you to increase your advertising spending. Likewise, if your major competitor turns to heavy use of promotion, it will probably be necessary for you to increase your promotion spending at least somewhat as well, in order to minimize the likelihood of people switching from your brand as a result of your competitor's promotions. Then again, this may not be in your brand's best interest. It is important to study each situation carefully and to respond accordingly.

As we shall see in the next section, one of the advantages of a good marketing communication programme that effectively utilizes the strengths of both advertising and promotion is that strong brand equity can help to minimize the effect of a competitor's promotions. And again we caution that you must guard against falling into the trap of regularly using promotions, effectively telling your target audience to make their choice on price. Another area to consider is the strength of private labels in your brand's category. If there is a strong private label presence in the market, it makes sense to emphasize advertising and not to try to compete on price with promotion.

It should be clear now that in marketing a brand you must make strategic use of both advertising and promotion. You should not think in terms of advertising versus promotion, but rather whether advertising *or* promotion is most likely to satisfy a communication objective, and whether or not certain market conditions suggest *emphasizing* either advertising or promotion. These are not unrelated. The market conditions discussed above will suggest the need for a particular communication effect, which will guide the selection of the communication objectives.

So we can see that, depending upon the desired communication effect (which could be a function of more than the market characteristics just discussed), there will be advantages to emphasizing either advertising or promotion. It is not enough to regard advertising and promotion as independent parts of the marketing communication mix. Rather, traditional advertising and promotion each have special characteristics that make them more or less appropriate to achieve particular marketing and communication ends. The decisions as to where you place your emphasis will be a function of specific circumstances in the market.

While it is certainly possible to use only advertising or only promotion, since both are able to produce each of the four basic communication effects, this is generally not desirable. The best course is an integrated marketing communication programme that builds upon the individual strengths of advertising and promotion, and the advantage of using them together, which is discussed next.

Advantages of Using Advertising and Promotion Together

There is no doubt that using advertising and promotion together offers real advantages over using advertising or promotion alone. Nevertheless, while a brand's marketing communication profits from using advertising and promotion together, for most brands, traditional advertising will almost always be more important. This stems primarily from advertising's brand attitude strength, and the fact that brand attitude should be the central communication effect for all brand marketing communication. This may seem surprising given the fact that traditional advertising receives only about one-third of all marketing communication spending. Unfortunately, too often brands get caught up in short-term competitive marketing and rely too heavily upon promotion.

What makes using advertising and promotion *together* so strong is the interaction between the long-term effects of brand attitude on building brand equity, and the tactical advantages of promotion. Without a strong brand attitude, promotion effectiveness suffers. When advertising has been effective in generating a strong brand attitude, all of the brand's uses of promotion become that much more effective. There are two principal reasons for this:

- when a strong positive brand attitude is developed through advertising, it means that, when a brand does use promotion, the target audience will see the promotion as better value;
- the strong positive brand attitude also means that, when a brand's competitors use promotion, the brand's target audience will be less likely to respond.

The logic here is straightforward. If consumers have a strong positive attitude towards a brand, they will be less likely to switch simply because of a competitor's promotion; when a brand consumers do like does offer a promotion of its own, they will be that much more pleased. Additionally, a promotion in that light will also tend to reinforce consumers' already-held positive brand attitude.[7]

There is another thing to consider here. What we have been discussing are the reasons why advertising and promotion work so well together in terms of communication effects. You might well be thinking that if advertising does such a great job building brand attitude and brand equity, and tends to immunize your target audience against competitive promotions, why promote at all? The reason is simple. Even with a positive brand attitude, most consumers will occasionally switch brands. If they were always loyal to your brand, there would be no need to promote. But most consumers tend to use more than one brand in a category, at least on occasion. That is why some promotion will almost always be needed for tactical support of the brand. We want to maintain as large a share of our customer's purchases as possible, and the effective use of promotion helps us to accomplish this task. While advertising is of critical importance to a brand, because without advertising it is very difficult to maintain strong brand equity, the overall strength of a brand is increased when it is used along with promotion. When advertising and promotion are used together, the overall communication effects are stronger.

The Ratchet Effect

A good explanation of how this mutual reinforcement between advertising and promotion works has been offered by Bill Moran, a marketing consultant. He calls his explanation a 'ratchet effect' and it reflects the discussion that we have been having.[8]

One of the behavioural consequences of most promotions is that they 'steal' purchases, either by moving forward a purchase by a consumer who would eventually be buying the brand anyway, or by taking a regular purchase away from a competitor. As just discussed, one of the reasons for a brand to promote, even when it enjoys a strong positive brand attitude, is to maximize the brand's purchase by the occasional brand-switcher. As a result, when a brand promotes, it should generate more sales than usual. But our objective is to increase sales not temporarily (except for an occasional short-term tactical reason), but *permanently*. Without advertising, after the promotional period, sales will drop below average levels for a while, then slowly return to normal as consumers return to their regular purchase patterns.

This is where advertising comes in. When advertising is used together with promotion, the effect of a promotion within or following a period of advertising is to stimulate the overall growth rate for the brand faster than with advertising alone. This is what is meant by a 'ratchet effect'. A well-conceived promotion, one that also addresses brand attitude, helps to reinforce the positive brand attitude of regular users. The occasional user of a brand who is attracted by the promotion will be more likely to stay with the brand, buying it more often after the promotion because of the effect of the advertising that ran along with or after the promotion, building upon the advertising-driven brand attitude that existed prior to the promotion. As this cycle continues, the regular base of consumers grows, 'ratcheting up' with each advertising-promotion cycle.

You can see how this happens by looking at the charts in Fig. 15.3. When only promotions are used, a brand experiences a short-term spike in sales, followed by a steady decline, until sales return to relative equilibrium and normal purchase cycles resume. Unless the promotion attracts new *loyal* users, the promotion will not have added incremental business. Over time,

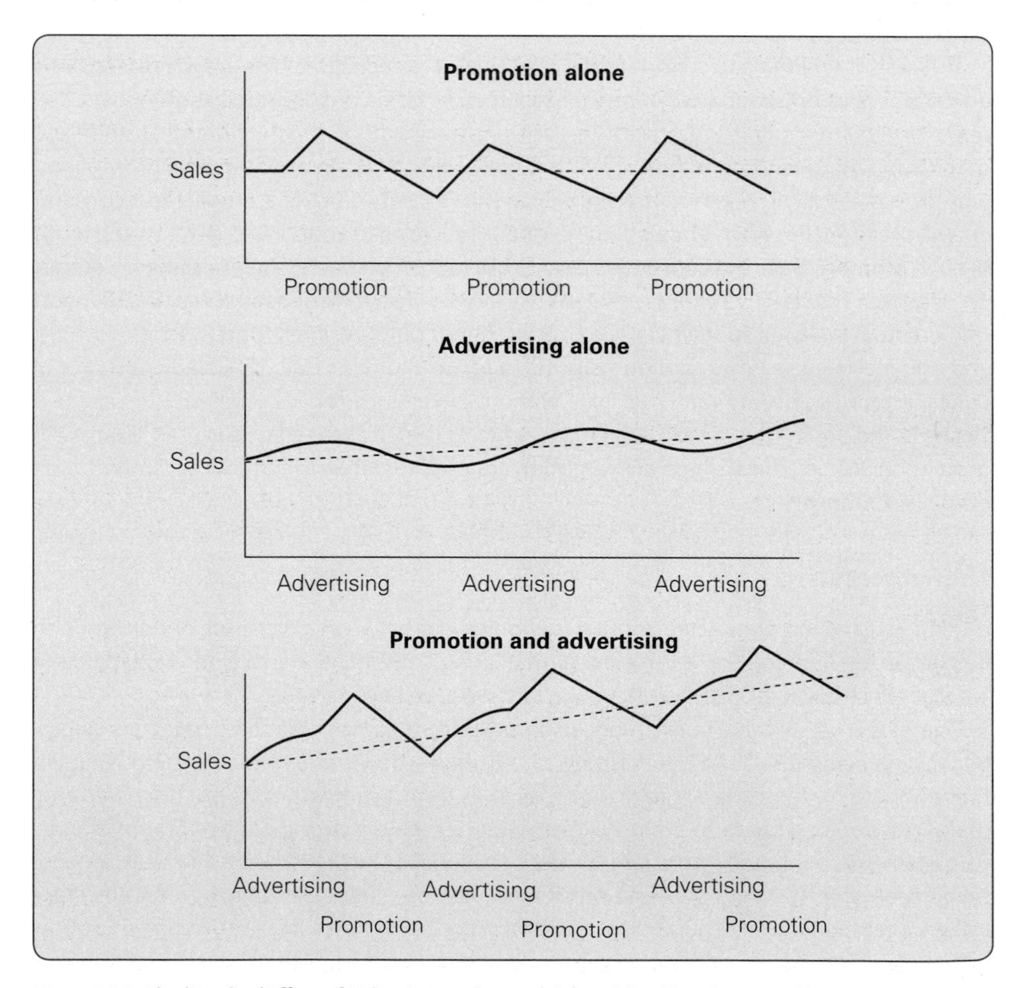

Figure 15.3 The 'Ratchet' Effect of Using Promotion and Advertising Together over Time

nothing has been gained. When only advertising is used, we see that sales generally build steadily, if not dramatically, over time as the effect of positive brand attitude develops more interest in the brand. But when advertising and promotion are used *together*, we experience Moran's ratchet effect. Promotion accelerates purchase, but ongoing advertising helps to sustain and build a customer base so that over time the overall effect on sales is greater than when advertising is used alone.[9]

Moran has suggested that this ratchet effect can be explained in terms of two kinds of demand elasticity: 'upside' and 'downside' elasticity. These are important considerations in communication planning, because they help to focus a manager's thinking on *how* the relationship between advertising and promotion that we have been talking about influences sales, and not simply on the overall price elasticity of a brand. These notions of upside and downside elasticity relate to a brand's pricing strategy as well as *competitor brand* pricing strategy. When prices are cut, either directly or via promotion (our interest here) and sales go up, we have upside elasticity; when sales decline as a result of a price increase, we have downside elasticity. It is important for the manager to remember that, when competitors aggressively promote, they in effect 'raise' the price of our brand.

As this discussion should make clear, the best defence against an aggressive promotion campaign by a brand's competitors is *not* necessarily to match their promotion spending, but to maintain a strong advertising presence to ensure a strong brand equity, while promoting *tactically* as necessary. Effective advertising stimulates high upside and low downside elasticity by building and maintaining strong brand equity through positive brand attitude.

Once again we are back to the importance of understanding communication effects and which communication effects are necessary for the effective marketing of our brand. And at the heart of this understanding is how to deal with the important and essential communication objective of brand attitude.

Monitoring the Campaign

The campaign is now ready to run, but the manager's job is not done. The ongoing advertising and other marketing communication must be monitored both for effectiveness and wearout.

Campaign Tracking

A carefully considered pre-test as discussed in Chapter 13 should help to ensure that the creative execution will deliver the desired message effectively, assuming that it has proper exposure among the target audience and proper attention is paid to the advertising. Whether or not the advertising works, however, is another question.[10]

Once the finished executions have been placed and are running in the market, to be certain that they are actually working requires *tracking*. Tracking a campaign is a good idea, even if every indicator you have suggests that the advertising is working well. Without tracking you can never be sure if it is the *advertising* that is causally responsible for sales or usage in the market, or whether other factors in the marketing mix, such as competitors' activity or even unusual market conditions, are mediating sales. Tracking can be expensive, but it is money well spent.

For tracking to be successful you must measure not only responses to your own advertising and other marketing communication (such as promotions or direct marketing activity), but responses to your competitors as well. Unlike pre-testing, when we are concerned only with specific executions, now we are concerned with how executions perform within the overall context of the market. This means that we must also measure not only our brand and competitors' brand advertising, but any marketing activity that might influence target audience behaviour. This includes such things as promotions, your brand and competitors' media spending, and even trade activity. For example, your advertising may be communicating very well, but if your competitor has just secured a special trade promotion for its brand, this could seriously affect overall market share.

There are basically four ways in which to track advertising campaigns. Some marketers simply monitor sales activity, correlating it with known advertising and promotion spending for their brand versus competitors. The problem here, of course, is that you are assuming that the advertising is *directly* responsible for any observed sales results. This can lead to serious misinterpretations because you simply cannot know what may be causing the activity observed in the market.

Another way of tracking advertising is to utilize a panel of consumers who are questioned about their purchases and recall of advertising. This does have the advantage of measuring causality at the individual level, but it has its own problems. Using a panel of consumers may sensitize those participating and influence their purchase behaviour over time. The most common way of tracking the effectiveness of a campaign is to take a series of measures over time, 'tracking' the results. With waves of interviews, a benchmark is established prior to a campaign and additional measures are taken at various points in time. These measures generally correspond to the end of major periods of advertising, providing a 'before–after' comparison. The biggest problem with taking periodic measures is that you do not know what is going on between the measurements.

Look at Fig. 15.4. If this were to represent what was actually going on in the market, periodic measures would significantly underestimate the effectiveness of the advertising campaign. What the graph suggests is that it takes a while for the advertising effect to build, and

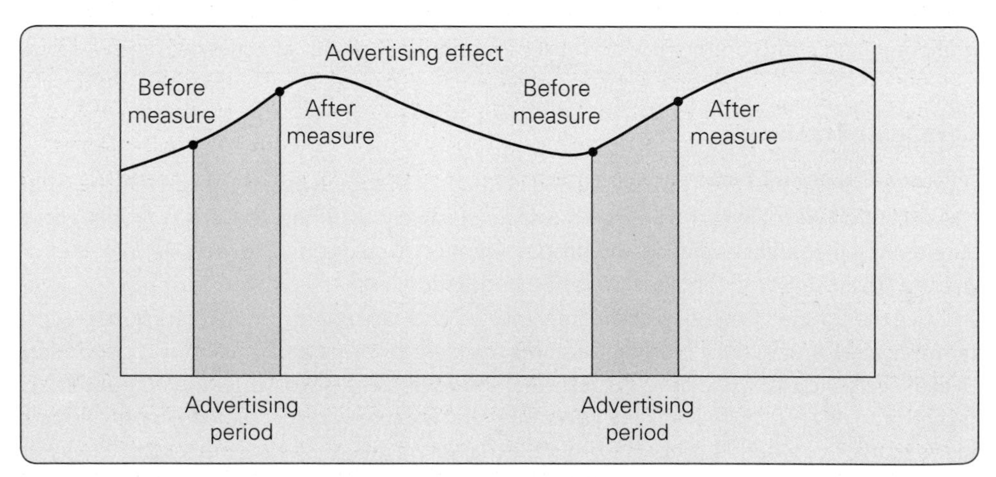

Figure 15.4 Potential Problem with Before–After Effectiveness Measures: Advertising Effects Continue to Build after the End of the Advertising Period

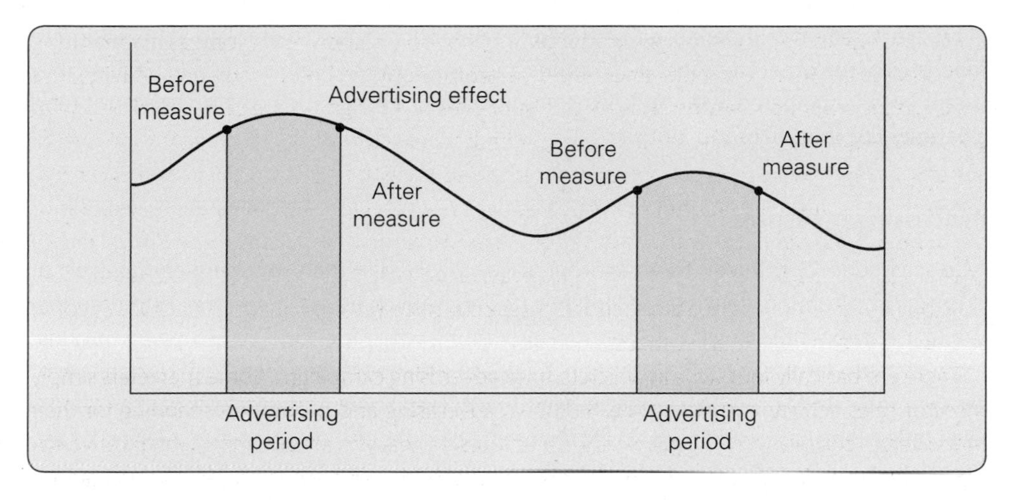

Figure 15.5 Potential Problem with Before–After Effectiveness Measures: Advertising Effects Peak before the End of the Advertising Period

that, by taking a measure at the end of the advertising flight, you are missing the true effect of the campaign. Figure 15.5 illustrates another possible scenario. By measuring the results at the end of the advertising flight, in this case you completely miss the advertising's effect, and in fact show no effect at all!

The best way in which to track advertising is with *continuous tracking*. Continuous tracking utilizes ongoing interviewing of small samples of consumers, 'rolling' the results, with moving averages for weekly, fortnightly, or four-weekly periods. This permits a relatively continuous measure of what is going on in the market, offering a sensitive measure of actual advertising effects. Because the measures are ongoing, it is possible to read the result for any period, at any time. This provides the manager with a powerful diagnostic tool, and avoids the danger inherent in other methods of misreading the effects of a campaign.

Of course, even with continuous tracking, the results will be only as good as your measures and analysis. The measures used in tracking a campaign reflect the four stages of the communication response sequence introduced in Chapter 4: exposure, processing, communication effects, and target audience action. In tracking a marketing communication campaign, the manager is not only interested in the 'results' (i.e. the target audience action), but also in each step that led to that result. It is only by looking at the entire sequence that one is able to *understand* the result, and to be in a position to correct any aspect of the campaign that is not working as planned.

Exposure Measures

Exposing the message is the job of media, so measures of exposure reflect the media plan, and may be measured in several ways. Perhaps the most frequently used measure is GRP (gross rating points), within the time period being addressed. This will include the audience figures for all of the media vehicles used during that period. A better measure would be some kind of estimate of the *minimum effective* reach, or the number of people exposed to the campaign during that period at the minimum level of frequency required for the advertising to be effective.

Measures of exposure are usually related to sales, but may also be looked at in relation to measures of the other steps in the communication response sequence. This can be especially useful when compared with specific communication effects such as increases in brand awareness or shifts in brand attitude.

Processing Measures

As discussed in Chapter 11, there are four stages involved in the processing of an advert or promotion: attention, learning, acceptance (for high-involvement decisions), and emotion. While it is impossible to actually measure processing when it occurs, in campaign tracking, indirect measures are used. For attention, this usually means some measure of recognition or recall of the campaign, which would suggest that at least some attention was paid and some level of learning achieved. If it is a high-involvement category, acceptance is inferred by appropriate measures of communication effects. If the campaign is remembered, it is possible to ask about any emotion associated with it.

Campaign recognition is generally measured by showing a member of the target audience the advertising or promotion from a campaign and asking if they remember seeing (or hearing it if radio). Recall of the campaign is measured by asking if they remembered seeing (or hearing) any advertising or promotion for the brand. If they do, they are asked to describe it. Only if the description matches the actual content of the executions is it considered an indication of processing.

A more rigorous variation of this, pioneered by Market Mind, is to prompt with the category, not the brand. A category cue asks for what advertising or promotion the target audience remembers seeing for the category, and to describe it. If the brand is not mentioned in the description, they are asked what brand it was for. This provides a very sensitive measure of how well the components of the campaign were processed, both in relation to category need as well as its link to the brand, and the salience of the outcome of the processing.[11]

Communication Effects

Basically, in measuring the communication effects of a campaign one uses the same measures as those used for communication effects in the pre-test. The only difference is in the order in which the questions are asked. You will recall that when we discussed pre-testing in Chapter 13 we made a point of how important the order of questioning is. While brand awareness measures are at the end or even delayed in a pre-test, they are measured first in tracking a campaign. This is because the brand must be either recognized or recalled first before it can be purchased.

Target Audience Action

In a tracking study, the measure of target audience action is asking what items were purchased during the tracking period, or what action was taken if the objective was something else such as going to a concert, calling an investment banker, visiting a trade fair, sending for 'more information', or, in social marketing, making the desired behavioural change. For fmcg products, marketers will also use retail scanner data.

Campaign Wearout

What we mean by 'wearout' is that the current campaign is not performing up to expectation, in the *absence* of external causes (such things as poor distribution or changes in market dynamics). If there were external factors that are adversely affecting the expected results of an advertising and promotion campaign, this would call for a careful review of both the marketing and advertising *strategy*. Otherwise, the manager must look to the campaign itself. This means either the media plan or the executions, reflecting the first two steps of the communication response sequence. Problems with the media plan would directly affect exposure and the opportunity to process the messages; problems with the execution would reduce the likelihood of successfully processing the message.

The first step is to check for problems with the media plan. The manager should determine if the plan is still delivering the necessary reach to be effective. This will require a careful examination of the specific vehicles being used, or specific programmes in broadcast, for target audience delivery. Tracking measures of advertising and promotion recognition and frequency can help to provide a check on whether the required minimum effective frequency is being obtained, the frequency level required for successful processing. If the media plan checks out, attention must then turn to the executions being used. Even though pre-tests of the executions indicated that they 'worked', over time there is the possibility of processing wearout. This may occur at any stage of processing: attention, learning, acceptance, or with the emotional responses associated with them.

A common cause of processing wearout occurs after an advert has been exposed several times, as a result of *diminished attention*.[12] This is especially true of print advertising where attention may be easily diverted. To help to prevent this, one can use a number of variations of the execution (always with the same consistent look and feel).

Processing wearout may also occur when learning is *interfered* with by better or increased numbers of executions for competitive brands. A change in competitive executional content or emphasis, or a change in media schedule, could interfere with the processing of a brand's message.[13] Interference can also result from a brand's own advertising, when new executions are introduced into a campaign. Carry-over from existing or previous advertising, especially when there is not a consistent look and feel, can interfere with the building of new associations in memory for weeks, or even months.

Overexposure, especially with broadcast, can lead to *attitudinal* wearout, which will affect the acceptance of a message. In fact, overexposure can even lead to a negative response to a brand's advertising, which can happen as counter-arguing increases with multiple exposures, leading to a rejection of the message.[14]

Problems in Implementing IMC

We mentioned earlier that, although most managers agree that IMC is the best way in which to approach their company's marketing communication needs, in reality true integrated planning for marketing communication is rare. Why should this be the case given such general acceptance of its value? Unfortunately, there are a number of potential roadblocks to the implementation of IMC.[15] Perhaps the single biggest problem involves the decision-making

Table 15.3 Problems in Implementing IMC

Decision-making structure	• Organizational structure too often is not conducive to sharing information • Too often marketing communication has a low priority and is peopled by specialists with a narrow focus • Organization character inhibits a common culture
Manager perceptions of IMC	• Resistance to change and politics associated with power inhibit sharing • Belief company already implements IMC • Niche- and micro-marketing are thought not to need common themes
Compensation	• Worries about position and salaries in a restructured IMC-oriented group • Compensation is based upon individual budgets, not contribution to total good

structure of most companies. The structure or organizational make-up of a company, and the way in which managers think or approach marketing questions, often create problems in trying to implement IMC programmes. While the decision-making structure is by far the biggest problem, there are at least two other areas that can cause problems: managers' perceptions of IMC and compensation considerations (see Table 15.3).

The Decision-Making Structure

IMC requires a central planning expertise in marketing communication. However, with widely dispersed resources, individual manager relationships with marketing communication agencies and vendors, and (critically) a lack of incentive to cooperate, it is no wonder there are problems when it comes to trying to develop and implement IMC.

A number of aspects of a company's decision-making structure contribute to these problems. Basically they reflect organizational structure and what we might call organizational character, or the way in which an organization 'thinks'.

Organizational Structure

We have noted that there is broad agreement among marketing managers over the need for IMC, but the very organizational structure of many companies stands in the way of effective implementation. At the heart of this problem is an organization's ability to manage the interrelationships among information and materials between the various agencies and vendors involved in developing and creating marketing communication. There are a number of specific structural factors that can make this difficult.

The Low Standing of Marketing Communication in an Organization

Unfortunately, for too many companies, marketing communication has a very low priority within the organization. For many in top management, spending money on marketing communication is seen as a luxury that can be afforded only when everything else is going well. One of the fastest ways for a company to send a lot of money to the bottom line is not to spend budgeted marketing communication money. When companies frequently employ this tactic, it is not surprising that those most responsible for marketing communication occupy lower-level positions within the organization.

Specialization

To manage IMC effectively, those in charge should ideally be marketing communication generalists. Unfortunately, there are very few people like this holding marketing communication positions. In fact, what you are most likely to find are people specializing in particular areas; and, even more problematically, these specialists rarely talk with each other. They have their own budgets and their own suppliers, and jealously guard the areas they control.

Given the narrow focus and understanding of such specialists, it is very difficult to bring them together in the first place, let alone to expect them to have the broad understanding and appreciation of the many marketing communication options necessary for effective IMC planning. But even if they had this understanding, getting them to give up control, especially when it is unlikely to be financially advantageous (which we shall discuss more specifically later), would be a lot to ask. Yet this is precisely what is necessary if IMC is to work.

How the Organization Thinks

In addition to the problems inherent in the way in which most marketing departments are structured, there are less tangible aspects of an organization's thinking and behaviour that also pose problems for implementing IMC. Because of the structural barriers we have just been talking about that can impede the flow of information, it is very difficult for an entire company to share a common understanding of its marketing communication.

But it is very important for everyone working at a company to understand and communicate the image being projected by the company's marketing communication. Anyone who has any contact with customers must reflect this image. This means store clerks, sales force, telephone operators, receptionists—all are a part of a company's marketing communication, and hence in many ways are IMC 'media'. Unfortunately, all too often only those directly involved with the marketing communication programme are familiar with it, and this can be a serious problem.

Manager Perceptions of IMC

How managers perceive IMC is something that can hinder its effective implementation. Managers with different backgrounds or different marketing communications specialities, either within the company organization or at marketing communication agencies or vendors, are likely to have different perceptions of what constitutes integrated marketing communication and what roles different people should play in its planning and implementation.

Resistance to Change

Different perceptions of IMC will certainly influence its effective implementation. But even more troubling is the natural resistance to change that the idea of IMC is likely to trigger, making it difficult if not impossible to implement even though IMC's benefits are generally accepted.

Perhaps the most serious problem associated with this is a fear that the manager responsible for IMC planning will not fully appreciate someone else's area of expertise. This is compounded when advertising takes the lead (which it should in most cases), because of long-held feelings that advertising managers simply do not understand or even consider other means of marketing communication (which, unfortunately, is all too often the case). This is aggravated by the conflict, for example, between the short-term tactical experience of those working in promotion and the longer-term thinking of advertising managers.

Politics and Power

Another way of looking at this tendency to resist change is in terms of both intra-organizational and inter-organizational politics. It does not matter if the motivation is individual self-interest or an actual belief by managers or employees in the superiority of their way of doing things: the result is the same. People, departments, and organizations want power and the rewards that go with it. Too often managers and their staff believe that they will be giving up too much personal responsibility if they are part of more broadly based IMC planning. Compensation (which is discussed next) is only one part of the problem. When lines of responsibility are blurred, it is easy for individuals to feel that their prestige and position, in many cases hard won, is threatened. This can be very difficult to overcome.

Already Implement IMC

When many managers are asked about IMC, they are likely to report that their company is indeed implementing it. But this is unlikely, at least in the way in which we have been discussing it. If a company is in fact implementing IMC in some limited way, or feels that it is, this makes it very difficult to get managers to think in different ways, or to acknowledge that they still have a way to go before they are effectively implementing IMC.

Not Needed for Micro-Marketing or Niches

Too often managers feel that micro-marketing segments or niches require their own distinct communication programmes. But if a single *brand* is involved, the most effective course is still likely to be one IMC programme. The *executions* will not necessarily be the same, but the overall look and feel must be if you are to maximize the impact of your communication expenditure. Even if it may be better to position a brand differently to different segments under certain circumstances, within each segment you should still be approaching the strategic development of the communications within the same IMC framework.

Compensation

While compensation issues are less of a direct problem with companies than with agencies and vendors working in marketing communication, they can still be a problem. When managers are worried about the importance of their positions in a realigned IMC-oriented marketing communication group, this leads quite naturally to worries about salaries and promotion, which lessens interest in IMC.

But the real concern about compensation is with agencies and vendors involved in the marketing communication needs of the company. Management at agencies working in the marketing communication field are traditionally rewarded on the basis of the total size of their business with companies. This means that they are very unlikely to suggest to their clients that they might be better off spending more of their money on some other form of marketing communication.

Somehow these managers must be compensated in terms of their contributions rather than of how much is spent on their particular speciality. Without such a scheme, effective IMC is impossible because those managing one type of marketing communication will be more concerned with 'selling' it, not with how their speciality will best contribute to an overall IMC programme.

Chapter summary

In this chapter we have seen how the notion of integrated marketing communication (IMC) defines how effective marketing communication programmes are developed. And importantly, we have seen that IMC is defined in terms of *planning*, the strategic planning process that is at the heart of this book. We then looked at the differences between traditional advertising and promotion, and how they can be integrated for optimal effect. Their relative strengths and weaknesses were outlined in relation to the four basic communication effects, and we discussed the way in which a product's position in the product life cycle can guide the relative emphasis placed on traditional advertising versus promotion. We examined the ratchet effect of combined advertising and promotion activity, but suggested that, although advertising and promotion used together offer real advantages over using only one or the other, the emphasis should almost always be on using advertising, because of its ability to build brand attitude strength. Then, we looked at the importance of tracking the campaign. Finally, we discussed barriers to the implementation of effective IMC.

Questions to consider

15.1 How would you define integrated marketing communication?

15.2 What are the roles of advertising and promotion in IMC?

15.3 In what way do advertising and promotion each contribute to an effective overall campaign?

15.4 Why is it important to track advertising over time?

15.5 Why is it so difficult to implement IMC successfully?

Case study 15 HSBC—How a Brand Idea Helped to Create the World's Strongest Financial Brand

In 1998 the hexagon logo and the HSBC name was introduced. This new identity provided a clear signal about belonging. However, in 2001, it was clear that there was room to continue the development of this young brand, and to use it to help to drive stronger organic growth. To be successful, the brand needed to be symbiotic with the business strategy it followed. HSBC has a view of the world that is not just a marketing view; it is about who it is as a company—a view based on a celebration of culture and humanity. So, while diversity for many global brands may seem a hurdle to be overcome, for HSBC, diversity would become its lifeblood. It was from this that the brand idea was born.

'The world's local bank' was created by Lowe in 2002. It was an idea that would define HSBC: a reflection of the business strategy and the brand's view of the world; a practical and emotional description of HSBC; literally, a large-scale global group, built from many 'locals'. This gives the scale and trust of a 'global' financial organization, allied with the intimacy of 'local', which customers and employees on the ground find reassuring. At a deeper level it taps into an attitude about the world. The arrival of this idea gave cohesion to the brand and its marketing, and was both representative of and helped to reinforce the business strategy.

The campaign went through different phases of meanings.

Never Underestimate the Importance of Local Knowledge

The 'Local Knowledge' strategy illuminated the differences in cultural and linguistic understanding across the world.

Different Points of View

In 2004 JWT developed a new expression of the idea that HSBC not only understood that people in different countries see things differently, but also that individuals can have very different points of view on the world around them.

Different Points of Value

'Different Points of Value' was based on the insight that people's values influence their financial decisions and the way in which they manage their money.

The campaign is in jet bridges in forty-nine airports in twenty-eight countries. Not just a creative message, but a terrific media moment to talk about being 'The world's local bank'. People are in the very act of experiencing the world. HSBC says goodbye at one end and hello at the other (complemented by TV advertising preceding the in-flight movies).

Between 1998 and 2002 HSBC existed as a logo, but without the brand idea. From 2002 to 2008, HSBC was a brand with a brand idea. With regards to customer effects, the brand idea creates a point of differentiation for the bank through scale, expertise, and its values of diversity and inclusion. This creates a brand that customers trust and have affinity with. Differentiation and affinity attract new customers and increase loyalty of existing customers, leading to revenue growth and profitability. Research has also shown that imagery perceptions of HSBC is significantly higher for being international, differentiated, and having brand momentum amongst those leisure and business travellers who have seen airport advertising.

Source: This is an edited version of a case study submitted to the IPA Effectiveness Awards. The full case study can be found at ipa.co.uk or warc.com.

Edited by Elizabeth Mamali, PhD Researcher, Bath School of Management

Discussion questions

1. What was in HSBC's case the key element for having a successful planning and implementation of IMC?
2. What are the elements that should be taken under consideration when deciding to implement IMC?
3. Discuss the relationship between the HSBC brand and the company's business strategy. How can companies achieve an equation between their brands and their strategies?
4. The HSBC campaign has already gone through three different phases of meanings. What could be a proposed future advertising campaign?

Further reading

Larry Percy, *Strategic Integrated Marketing Communication* (Oxford: Elsevier, 2008)
The principles discussed in this book are dealt with specifically in terms of IMC.

Gayle Kerr, Don Schultz, Charles Patti, and Ilchul Kim, 'An Inside-Out Approach to Integrated Marketing Communication: An International Analysis', *International Journal of Advertising*, 27/4 (2008), 511–48
A very interesting look at how IMC is being taught around the world versus established industry practice and key writers on the subject and published research.

S. Sayman, S.T. Hoch, and J.S. Raju, 'Positioning of Store Brands', *Marketing Science*, 21/4 (2002), 378–97
Store brands.

John R. Rossiter, *Measurement for the Social Sciences* (New York: Springer, 2011)
Measurement of advertising requires careful attention to the actual measures used; perhaps the best treatment of measurement issues.

Leslie Butterfield (ed.), *Advalue: Twenty Ways Advertising Works for Business* (Oxford: Butterworth-Heinemann, 2003)
An overall look at how advertising contributes to brand success may be found in this collection of twenty essays.

Notes

1. A number of US studies conducted in the early 1990s that researched marketing managers' opinions of integrated marketing communication suggested a positive response to the idea. A study reported by C.E. Caywood, D.E. Schultz, and P. Wang, *Integrated Marketing Communication: A Survey of National Consumer Goods* (Evanston, IL: Department of Integrated Advertising Marketing Communications, Northwestern University, 1991), found that senior marketing executives of major fmcg advertisers believed IMC to be a sound idea with real value to their company; and two-thirds said that they now practised IMC. In another study reported by T.R. Duncan and S.E. Everett, 'Client Perceptions of Integrated Marketing Communication', *Journal of Advertising Research* (May/June 1993), 30–9, communications and marketing managers overwhelmingly reported feeling that IMC was 'very valuable'.
2. A useful discussion of the need for planning in IMC can be found in L. Percy, *Strategic Integrated Marketing Communication* (Oxford: Elsevier, 2008), and J. Moore and E. Thorson, 'Strategic Planning for Integrated Marketing Communications Programmes: An Approach to Moving from Chaotic towards Systematic', in E. Thorson and J. Moore (eds), *Integrated Communication* (Mahwah, NJ: Lawrence Erlbaum Associates, 1966), 135–52.

3. J.R. Rossiter and L. Percy, *Advertising Communication and Promotion Management* (New York: McGraw-Hill, 1997).

4. When J.R. Rossiter and L. Percy first introduced their notion of communication effects in *Advertising and Promotion Management* (New York: McGraw-Hill, 1987), they also went into considerable detail discussing the relative strength of advertising and promotion in generating those effects.

5. See R.A. Strang, *The Practical Planning Process* (New York: Praeger, 1980).

6. Lodish and others have found that advertising elasticities are dynamic, and decrease during the product life cycle. See L.M. Lodish *et al.*, 'How Advertising Works: A Meta-Analysis of 389 Real World Split Cable TV Advertising Experiments', *Journal of Marketing Research*, 32 (May 1995), 125–39.

7. A number of case histories supporting the idea that effective advertising leads to better promotions are discussed by W.T. Moran in a paper presented to the Association of National Advertisers' research workshop in New York on 9 December 1981. This paper was summarized in 'Use Sales Promotion Yardstick ANA Told', *Advertising Age* (14 December 1981), 12.

8. See W.T. Moran, 'Insights from Pricing Research', in E.B. Bailey (ed.), *Pricing Practices and Strategies* (New York: The Conference Board, 1978), 7–13.

9. There is a great deal of empirical research that supports this notion. Lodish and his colleagues have found that short-term effects in marketing communication are necessary for long-term effects, as they point out in 'A Summary of Fifty-Five In-Market Experimental Estimates of the Long-Term Effects of Advertising', *Marketing Science*, 14 (1995), 6133–40. A more specific conclusion has been reached by John Philip Jones, who notes that short-term promotional effects are longer than advertising effects, and that short-term advertising effects diminish rapidly. See his 'Exposure Effects under a Microscope', *Admap*, 30 (February 1995), 28–31, and *When Ads Work* (New York: Lexington Books, 1995).

10. An excellent review of advertising effectiveness testing may be found in a paper by Flemming Hansen, 'Testing Communication Effects', in C. McDonald and P. Vangelder (eds) *The Esomar Handbook of Market and Opinion Research* (Amsterdam: ESOMAR, 1998), 653–724 . Also J.P. Jones (ed.), *How Advertising Works* (Thousand Oaks, CA: Sage, 1998), provides a number of informative chapters on research in advertising.

11. The Market Mind tracking system was developed by Max Sutherland, and his book with Alice Sylvester *Advertising and the Mind of the Consumer* (Sydney: Allen and Unwin, 2000) offers a good introduction to continuous tracking, along with extensive examples.

12. See C.S. Craig, B. Sternthal, and C. Leavill, 'Advertising Wearout: An Experimental Analysis', *Journal of Marketing Research*, 13/4 (1976), 365–72.

13. Dramatic interference effects were demonstrated in another early study by L.A. Lo Sciuto, L.H. Strassman, and W.D. Wells, 'Advertising Weight and the Reward Value of the Brand', *Journal of Advertising Research*, 7/2 (1976), 34–8.

14. With multiple exposures, counter-arguing can occur that leads to negative attitudes and rejection of the message. See B.J. Calder and B. Sternthal, 'Television Commercial Wearout: An Information Processing View', *Journal of Marketing Research*, 17/2 (1980), 173–86.

15. A more in-depth discussion of potential problems in implementing IMC may be found in two chapters in E. Thorson and J. Moore (eds), *Integrated Communication* (Mahwah, NJ: Lawrence Erlbaum Associates, 1996): D. Prensky, J.A. McCarty, and J. Lucas, 'Integrated Marketing Communication: An Organizational Perspective', 167–84; and L.A. Petrison and P. Wang, 'Integrated Marketing Communication: Examining, Planning, and Executional Considerations', 153–65.

Visit the Online Resource Centre that accompanies this book for additional resources to support the text: **www.oxfordtextbooks.co.uk/orc/percy_elliott4e/**

Glossary

acceptance believing a message; necessary to forming positive brand attitude when there is perceived risk in a purchase decision (high-involvement brand attitude strategies)

affect in cognitive psychology, this is the evaluative dimension of attitude (favourable or unfavourable)

affect programme theory the coordinated set of changes that constitute an emotional response, including physiological, behavioural, and subjective feelings

assimilation-contrast theory the idea advanced by Sherif and Hovland in the 1960s that a person's current position serves as a point of reference in relation to an attempt to persuade, assimilating positions close to his or her own and contrasting (or rejecting) positions discrepant from his or her own

attention partly an automatic process, and central to perception and consciousness, it is the first step in processing a message

attitude a relative concept, described by Fishbein and Ajzen as 'a learned predisposition to respond in a consistently favourable or unfavourable manner with respect to a given object'

attributes objective characteristics of something—for example, a brand

automatic processing what psychologists call processing of information that guides behaviour, but without conscious awareness, and without interfering with other conscious activity that may be going on at the same time—for example, driving slowly down a street (automatic processing) while looking for a specific address (conscious processing)

behavioural sequence model (BSM) a way of looking at how consumers make decisions in a product category, establishing first the stages they go through, then for each stage who are involved and the roles that they play, where that stage occurs, the timing, and how

benefit for a brand, the answer to the question 'What does it offer?', described in terms of attributes, subjective characteristics, or emotions

benefit focus how the benefit claim in a message is made, positioning a brand consistent with the underlying motivation driving behaviour in the category

bottom-up processing response to a stimulus directly in terms of what is seen or experienced

brand attitude a necessary communication objective reflecting the link between the brand and its benefit

brand attitude strategy one of four strategic directions reflecting the degree of perceived risk in the purchase decision (low versus high involvement) and the underlying motivation driving behaviour in the category (positive versus negative)

brand awareness a necessary communication objective reflecting the link in memory between the brand and the need it fulfils (category need)

brand awareness strategy how brand awareness is used by consumers in the actual purchase decision, either by recognizing the brand at the point of purchase, or recalling it when the need occurs

brand equity the perceived assets and liabilities associated with a brand, as reflected in people's attitude towards it, which add to or detract from its value in their minds

brand purchase intention a desirable communication effect, and a necessary communication objective for promotion, reflecting a positive disposition to purchase after processing a message

category need an essential communication effect that becomes a communication objective either when there is a diminished perceived need for a product, or when the need must be established—for example, with new product introductions

central positioning when a brand is seen as able to deliver all of the main benefits associated with the category, and in effect defines the category (usually a successful pioneer brand or the market leader)

cognitive in cognitive psychology this is the component of attitude that involves perceptual responses and beliefs about something (knowledge and assumption)

cognitive response theory relating existing knowledge and assumptions (cognitions) to new information—for example, when exposed to an advert, in order to generate message-relevant associations

communication effect one of four likely responses to a message: category need, brand awareness, brand attitude, or brand purchase intention

communication objective the desired communication effect, which must always include brand awareness and brand attitude for any marketing communication, and brand purchase intention for promotion

communication response sequence the sequence of steps necessary for the success of marketing communication: exposure to the message, processing of the message, achievement of the desired communication effect, and target audience action

communication strategy the selection of appropriate communication objectives, and the identification of the specific brand awareness and brand attitude strategy consistent with behaviour in the category

conative in cognitive psychology this is the component of attitude that involves actual behaviour

creative brief a one-page document that outlines the strategic direction for creative development, covering the specific task at hand, the communication objectives and strategy, and any elements that the executions must contain

cross-elasticity a way of defining markets in terms of price relationships between brands, when a change in price for one brand brings about a change in price for another brand

crowdsourcing the use of amateur or professional outsiders to provide creative input or executions for an advertising or other marketing communication campaign

decision roles whether a person is involved as an initiator, influencer, decider, purchaser, or user in the decision to buy or use a product or service

declarative memory what we 'know that we know' and can easily state in words

differentiated positioning a positioning based upon a benefit that gives a brand an advantage over other brands in the consumer's mind

direct marketing utilizing a database specifically to target consumers, bypassing traditional channels of distribution

Duchenne smile a smile in response to a true feeling of happiness with both the eye muscle and lips activated over the left temporal and anterior regions of the brain, areas not activated when a smile is fixed or posed

embodied emotion taking on or initiating the emotion perceived in someone else

emotional authenticity necessary for all advertising addressing positive motives (transformational brand attitude strategies), where the creative execution is seen as 'real' and not posed or artificial

encoding specificity an idea advanced by Endel Tulving suggesting that to retrieve something successfully from memory requires a match between how the information was originally encoded and the information available when trying to retrieve the memory

episodic memory memories of a single event, and part of declarative memory

ethos following Aristotle, persuasion based upon an appeal that concentrates upon the source of the message rather than the source itself

excitatory behaviour from classical conditioning, it is related to the underlying motivation that initiates an emotional sequence in the processing of a message

expectancy value perhaps the most widely used model of attitude (generally attributed to Martin Fishbein), it posits that one's attitude is a summary of everything believed about something weighted by the importance attached to those beliefs

explicit memory the conscious recall of information that is recognized as coming from memory

frequency the number of times that an individual in a target audience is exposed to a campaign in a specific time period

goals an objective (which is a broad aim or desired outcome) made specific in terms of time and degree—for example, increasing sales 20 per cent over the next year

gross rating point (GRP) the product of reach time frequency in a media schedule

hierarchal partitioning a way of looking at markets by determining the order in which consumers consider the characteristic of a product in the decisions they make

implicit memory the unconscious impact of recent experiences on behaviour

informational brand attitude strategy communication strategy for building positive brand attitude when the underlying motivation driving behaviour in the category is negative (for example, problem solution or problem avoidance)

information processing paradigm a model proposed by William J. McGuire to define the steps necessary for communication to change attitude: the message must be presented, attended to, comprehended, and yielded to, and that intention must be retained and acted upon

inhibitory behaviour from classical conditioning, it is related to the motivation and emotion associated with the end state in processing a message

innate releasing mechanism a natural response to such things as babyish features that elicit a nurturing behaviour in adults

integrated marketing communication (IMC) the planning and execution of all types of advertising and promotion (that is, any marketing communication) for a brand, service, or company in order to meet a common set of communication objectives in support of a single positioning

involvement the perceived risk associated with a purchase or usage decision, measured dichotomously as high (risk attached) or low (no risk attached)

learning an essential stage in the processing of all messages, it is the rote acquisition of some part of a message's content, and can occur without conscious effort

limbic system an area in the forebrain traditionally considered critical for emotion, and where innate responses required for survival as a species are thought to originate

logos following Aristotle, persuasion that uses an appeal to logical arguments that requires one to draw one's own conclusion based upon the argument presented

long-term potentiation (LTP) the neurological basis of learning, it is the process of stimulating a dendritic spine repeatedly, leaving it more responsive to new input of the same type

marketing plan a general term used to describe the overall plan for marketing a brand, which outlines goals and objectives for the brand, and how to reach them

memory studied by philosophers, writers, and scientists for hundreds of years, it is the reflection of an accumulation of all of our experiences, and is (as described by Howard Eichenbaum) 'who we are'

mere exposure described by Zajonc and his colleagues, it represents an example of unconscious affective memory, independent of declarative memory, in which a slight preference is expressed for familiar items even when they are not explicitly remembered

mirror neuron neurons that reflect motor responses observed in others, and perhaps other behaviour or emotion

motivation the innate or acquired drive that stimulates behaviour, and which may be negatively originated to solve or avoid a problem (for example) or positively originated for sensory gratification or social approval

negative motivation when a problem must be solved, avoided, or minimized

new media a general term covering non-traditional ways of delivering advertising or promotion messages, anything from text messaging to the Internet

non-declarative emotional memory centred in the amygdala, it is where emotional associations and experiences are stored out of consciousness, but nevertheless inform conscious processing

objective a broad or general description of a desired outcome

objective characteristic specific attributes or features of a brand or product, such as alcoholic content in beer or memory capacity in a computer

partitioning a way of looking at markets in terms of how consumers categorize products in relationship to perceived characteristics of the category

pathos following Aristotle, persuasion that uses appeals that involve feelings, values, or emotions

perceptions in both a colloquial and neuro-psychological sense, what your mind tells you something is

positioning in terms of marketing communication, locating a brand in the target audience's minds relative to competitors in terms of benefits

positive motivation when a personal or social desire is to be met

primary emotion following Damasio, universal emotions that are located in the limbic system and are triggered directly by sensory input without the mediation of higher brain centres: happiness, sadness, fear, anger, surprise, and disgust

primary media the key media in a campaign that provide the most effective media for achieving all of a brand's communication objectives

priming an unconscious exposure to a stimulus that results in an improvement in the ability to recognize or identify it after recent exposure

processing the immediate response to elements in an advert or promotion: attention, learning, emotion, and (for high-involvement purchase decisions) acceptance

product benefit-oriented positioning positioning a brand in marketing communication in which the product is the hero and is defined in terms of specific benefits, not the user

product life cycle traditional marketing understanding of the progress of a brand or product over time, moving through four stages: introduction, growth, maturity, and decline

psychographics term used to describe various target audience characteristics such as 'feelings' and other non-demographic variables

psycholinguistics the study of how verbal content of a message is processed, and what is needed for effective communication

ratchet effect following Bill Moran, the idea that using advertising and promotion together in an appropriate way enables promotions to 'ratchet up' the overall effect of advertising

reach the percentage of a target audience that has an opportunity for exposure to a campaign in a given time period

recall brand awareness when the category need stimulates the recall of a brand that will satisfy that need

recognition brand awareness when a brand is recognized at the point of purchase, and that recognition reminds the consumer of a need for the product

reflexive attention unconscious attention that occurs automatically, associated with bottom-up processing

refutational strategy when dealing with strong negative perceptions, begin by acknowledging the target does not believe the benefit claim, then provide evidence to 'refute' or counter the disbelief

schema following Bartlett, a way of organizing past experiences in memory so that when remembering one constructs or infers the likely parts of a memory and the order in which they occurred

secondary emotions following Damasio, emotions that are acquired such as embarrassment, jealousy, guilt, or pride, and which are triggered by things one has been sensitized to through experience

segmentation identifying niches or subgroups within a market, generally with the aim of more targeted communication

selective attention voluntary attention that occurs consciously, and associated with top-down processing

semantic memory everything one knows, not connected to any specific experience during which it was acquired (unlike episodic memory), and part of declarative memory

sequential planning a planning process in which the order in which the steps taken are critical to the result, such as the strategic planning process for advertising and other marketing communication

social marketing communication marketing communication aimed at changing socially undesirable behaviour or reinforcing socially desirable behaviour

social media a group of Internet-based applications that allow the creation and exchange of user-generated content

social norm the second factor of Fishbein's extended expectancy-value model, similar to the structure of the original attitude component, but reflecting the influence of others on a person's behaviour

strategic planning the specific process used to accomplish a task, such as the five steps necessary to develop an effective advertising campaign

strategy in the broadest sense, a specific way in which something is to be done

synapses the gap between two neurons, over which impulses lead to learning

tactic specific details or parts of a strategy, and how it can be implemented

target audience that portion of a market identified to receive messages in the form of advertising or promotion

theory of reasoned action Fishbein's two-factor model of attitude and behavioural change in which attitude toward a behaviour combines with a social norm

top-down processing the use of knowledge and assumptions in the processing of any stimulus, beyond simple sensory input (bottom-up processing)

transformational brand attitude strategy communication strategy for building positive brand attitude when the underlying motivation driving behaviour in the category is positive (for example, sensory gratification or social approval)

user-oriented positioning while utilizing brand benefits, the message is specifically addressing the user of the brand, not the product

visual imagery the images stimulated in the 'mind's eye' either by something concrete such as an advert or by a memory

working memory temporary storage of information while one is working with it or attending to it

Index

I

J

K

L

M

N

O

P

R